Teachers' Minds and Actions

Teachers' Minds and Actions:
Research on Teachers' Thinking and Practice

Edited by

Ingrid Carlgren, Gunnar Handal
and Sveinung Vaage

 The Falmer Press

(A member of the Taylor & Francis Group)
London • Washington, D.C.

UK The Falmer Press, 4 John Street, London WC1N 2ET
USA The Falmer Press, Taylor & Francis Inc., 1900 Frost Road, Suite 101, Bristol, PA 19007

First published in 1994

A catalogue record for this book is available from the British Library

Library of Congress Cataloging-in-Publication Data are available on request

ISBN 0 7507 0430 6 cased
ISBN 0 7507 0431 4 paper

Jacket design by Caroline Archer

Typeset in 9.5/11pt Bembo
Graphicraft Typesetters Ltd., Hong Kong.

Printed in Great Britain by Burgess Science Press, Basingstoke on paper which has a specified pH value on final paper manufacture of not less than 7.5 and is therefore 'acid free'.

Contents

Contents

List of Tables and Figures

Tables

Figures

Introduction

Ingrid Carlgren, Gunnar Handal and Sveinung Vaage

The International Study Association on Teacher Thinking — ISATT — celebrated its tenth anniversary at its sixth international conference in Gothenburg, Sweden, in August 1994. Although a decade is not an awe-inspiring age for an organization, ISATT derived some pride in this celebration. It means that the Association has been kept alive and thriving, well beyond the first enthusiastic founding years. It has arranged six international conferences attracting an increasing number of participants and contributions, and the research work accomplished by its members has been documented in six conference books — including this one — as well as in the international journal '*Teaching and Teacher Education*' with which ISATT has collaborated. At its last members meeting, ISATT even decided to launch a journal of its own, and *Teachers and Teaching — Theory and Practice* will be published from 1995 on, in cooperation with Carfax. These are external manifestations of some of the work of ISATT during the decade it has existed. Probably more important is the conceptual, theoretical, and empirical contributions that can be seen as fruits of its endeavours.

The Gothenburg conference was planned and carried through by a group of Scandinavian researchers.[1] In the programme committee we discussed the significance of a Scandinavian ISATT conference from two perspectives. First the perspective of broadening the interest for ISATT among Scandinavian researchers. In Scandinavia, there has been little research activity related to the teacher-education programmes; rather, there has been a tradition of locating teacher education outside of the university system.[2] This means that most educational research has been carried out outside teacher education and by people who are not teacher educators. However, as teacher educators are now becoming involved in research on a larger scale, ISATT offers one of the arenas of interest for many of them.

The second perspective was the influence of a 'Scandinavian perspective' on the organization of the ISATT conference. The Scandinavian countries can in a way be said to be 'in between' the European continental tradition and the Anglo-Saxon and North-American tradition in the way that, while there has been keen interest in empirical research, there has also been an inclination towards philosophical and theoretical questions. Therefore, the Scandinavian progamme committee wanted to introduce into the conference some keynote addresses presenting a more philosophical perspective on teacher thinking and action and on research in this field. This may be perceived as a sign of our more European roots. We felt that this philosophical and metatheoretical perspective had been rather under-articulated at previous conferences and that our research tradition might benefit from a selection of more 'external' perspectives on its work. In the book you will find that most keynote addresses — presented in part 1 of the book — introduce such perspectives. We hope that this may help strengthen the philosophical and self-reflective aspect of teacher-thinking research. You will also find that some of the chapters in part 2 — research issues — also raise ethical and metatheoretical aspects.

The title of the conference explicates another 'key idea' of the programme group: teacher thinking and action in varied contexts. We were interested in drawing the attention of the contributors to the role of the context for the way teachers think and act. Different lines of research have emphasized the importance of contextual factors. In Scandinavia there has been a strong tradition of looking at schools and the teaching–learning process through the perspective of the frame factors influencing it, thereby focusing on the importance of structural, material, economic and organizational factors for the characteristics and quality of the processes of education.

Parallel to this, we have seen within cognitively oriented research on learning and teaching that the idea of 'situated cognition' or context-bound learning has gained impetus. What we perceive, learn, think and draw upon as a basis for our actions, is closely related to the contexts or situations in which it takes place.

Thus — in naming the conference the way we did — we sent out signals to the research community to focus their papers in a way that highlighted the contextual frames for teachers' thinking and action. Even to claim that we were moderately successful in this would be an overestimate. Only a few of the papers at the conference actually fell within this preview. We draw the conclusion that so far this way of looking into teachers' thinking and action has not had a particularly strong influence on the research that ISATT members are engaged in.

Maybe this lack of interest in the context issue is a sign of what Maureen Pope (1993), in the latest ISATT book, called the hard-core assumptions of teacher-thinking research:

- the world is real, but individuals vary in their perception of it;
- an individual's conception of the real world has integrity for that individual;
- teachers use personally pre-existing theories to explain and plan their teaching;
- teachers test these theories for fruitfulness and modify them in the light of such testing. (Pope, 1993, p. 20)

These assumptions are seen as forming a different paradigm from what in the past has dominated educational research. The implication of 'hard core' is that the assumptions are not put to test but are kept intact. However, the assumptions are rather dualistic (the real world and the perception of it), personalistic (personal knowledge), mentalistic (teachers' theories) and rationalistic (theories are tested and modified). They clearly show the roots of teacher thinking in cognitive science and information processing. However, the last decade has been one where some theoretical and philosophical 'turns' (such as the linguistic, the pragmatic, and the reflective turn) have been noted also in 'applied' fields such as education. Within various research areas, e.g., theory of science, artificial intelligence, linguistics, learning theory, and philosophy, an awareness of the problems of dualistic thinking (for example mind and matter, thinking and acting, theory and practice and so on) is acknowledged and a shift of emphasis from 'mind' to 'practice', as in the following assumptions, can be discerned:[3]

- language is an expression of social interaction rather than representing 'inner thoughts' of individuals;
- language not only represents but also actually forms the world (or the objects of which it speaks);
- the prominence of social practice means that cognitions turn into socio-cognition and learning becomes 'situated'; and
- all knowledge is related to some practice as its invisible prerequisite.

In the light of these changes it is difficult to defend the 'hard core' assumptions of teacher-thinking research and hardly desirable to keep them intact in the continuing progress of this research tradition. The chapter on 'working knowledge in teaching' by Yinger and Handricks-Lee (1993) in the latest ISATT book shows, however, that this will not be the case. We may perhaps see a future development in different directions — one more person-orientated and one practice-orientated line of teacher-thinking research.

The shift of emphasis from mind to practice also makes the characterization of teacher-thinking research in terms of 'teacher perspective' problematic. However much the description of teachers' knowledge is adjusted to the way this knowledge is organized in 'reality', the very activities of describing do not belong to the teachers' tradition and are therefore expressions of someone else's perspective. Another implication is that 'teacher voice' is created in the interaction between researchers and teachers and is thus a social rather than an individual phenomenon.

During the work on this book it has struck us that rather than a teacher perspective it seems as if teacher-thinking research mainly expresses a teacher-education perspective. It is the perspective of teacher training — in-service as well as pre-service — that seems to form the kinds of questions and problems dealt with by teacher-thinking research. It offers knowledge about the character and organization of teachers' knowledge and how it can be developed, rather than knowledge about how to teach, select content, evaluate student learning, etc. The focal issues of teacher-thinking research are of importance for teacher educators rather than for teachers. Teachers' fundamental interest undoubtedly is teaching *per se*, including such questions as learning, ways of working, and selection of subject matter, whereas teacher educators' fundamental interest is teachers and their knowledge and work. This may look like an unnecessary distinction, especially with the emphasis on collaboration and mutual and negotiated constructions of knowledge within teacher-thinking research. It seems evident that teachers' interests are acknowledged just as much as the researchers themselves. This is beside our point, however. While teacher-thinking research often deals with what teachers think about and are concerned with, the content of this is not at the core of the researchers' interest. To explore teachers' knowledge is not the same as exploring what this knowledge is about. If for example teachers talk about lessons, the research object of teacher-thinking research is not the lesson *per se*, (which is probably the teachers' prime interest) but how teachers deal with lessons and their 'perception' of the lesson as a part thereof. While teachers are interested in different aspects of the lessons, teacher-thinking researchers are interested in teachers' perceptions of these aspects.

Members of ISATT have voted on a possible change of name of ISATT from 'teachers' thinking' to 'teachers and teaching'. While 'teachers' thinking' corresponds mainly to teacher educators' research interests, 'teachers and teaching' includes the interests of teachers as well as teacher educators. It is therefore interesting that while the ISATT meeting voted for 'teachers' thinking', the new journal starting in 1995 uses 'teachers and teaching'. Perhaps this inconsistency can be interpreted as expressing different lines of thought or knowledge interests within the organization?

One of the questions for the future of this organization is therefore whether or not teachers' focal issues are to be included as research objects. Regardless of whether teacher-thinking research will be research 'about' teachers' knowledge (which it is even if it is developed together with teachers), or also includes research on what this knowledge is about, there is a risk that knowledge 'about' teachers knowledge will be imposed on teachers as their knowledge, making teachers talk and think about their own thinking and its development rather than about the teaching that this thinking is about. Instead of teachers talking about children, teaching and learning, we will get a situation where teachers talk about how they reflect on these matters. A great deal of this century's educational research has been determined from the aspect of educational planning and administration and it is only recently that research for teachers rather than about them has started to grow (Doyle, 1990). However, even though this research is undertaken in collaboration with teachers, it may still concern issues that are not foremost in teachers' minds.

We are making this point not as criticism of the ongoing research efforts within the teacher-thinking research tradition; this research is valuable, interesting and important. The reason we are making this distinction is rather because we think it is important for clarification of both current and future research. It is probably impossible to predict the direction of future research in this field, nor do we think that ISATT in any way should make programme decisions about the course of research for its members. However, by trying — critically — to try out ideas of the possible — and possibly different — objects of teacher-thinking research, we hope to help clarify the field, so that selection of objects and purposes of future research can be made even more consciously and purposively.

The relation between research and practice has been a theme for teacher-thinking research as well as at the ISATT conferences. What has not been discussed, however, is: who are the researchers and who are the practitioners? It is often implied that the practitioners are the teachers. If we are right in thinking that teacher-thinking research concerns mainly teacher-education questions, then, consequently, the practitioners are teacher educators rather than teachers, which probably changes the discussion a trifle.

The use of the dichotomy of research and practice can be discussed — as even research is a kind of practice. The question is what kind of practice it is, can be and should be. Within teacher-thinking research it is quite often asserted that the highest form of research is when teachers and researchers together construct knowledge (Connelly and Clandinin, 1990). Since teachers and researchers belong to different 'speech communities' this may be an unattainable ambition. However, the idea of collaboration may be one way to resolve the distinction between research and practice, thereby creating a new form of practice where a new kind of knowledge may develop. But why, then, talk about research and practice?

The growth of the social sciences, which historically are linked with the humanitarian rhetoric of reform and progress, has involved a dividing of practices, by which experts and professionals have produced and promoted 'regimes of truth' (Foucault, 1980), thereby disempowering the 'un-knowing'. There has been a growing awareness concerning this within the social sciences and so also within the teacher-thinking research community, where the empowerment of teachers has been an important issue. Considerable effort has been made to get away from the neo-positivistic concept of science, including its technical-rational view of practice and progress. The irony seems to be that while we are striving to escape the consequences of distinguishing between science and non-scientific activities, made by the logical positivists early in the present century, we have got into a situation which on the one hand can be interpreted as the dissolving of Science with a capital S while on the other hand leading to a new discussion on demarcation. This time, however, the demarcation is not needed to distinguish between scientific and metaphysical assertions, but rather to distinguish scientific practices from other kinds of practices.

In planning the ISATT conference as well as in editing the book and writing an introduction to it, we have tried to combine a presentation of teacher-thinking research at its present state with some analytical and some alternative perspectives on it. We have introduced some philosophical perspectives on this field of research; we have suggested studying it in a more contextual perspective; we have tried to analyse its research objects and we have pondered over some dualisms embedded in the tradition. We have been doing this, not with the intention of critically characterizing the tradition or any of its researchers, but by adhering to the tradition's own highly esteemed critical self-reflection. Who are we? Where are we bound? What are our options? We do not have ready answers, but we think that by being unpredictable, the future is also exciting and interesting.

Notes

1   The conference programme committee: Ingrid Carlgren (Sweden), Taru Eskelinen (Finland), Gunnar Handal (Norway), Elisabeth Hesslefors-Arktoft (Sweden), Kirsten Reisby (Denmark), Sveinung Vaage (Norway).
2   The exception is Finland where faculties of education were established at eight universities in 1974 (Simola, 1993) and the number of professorships increased from around twenty in the beginning of the 1970s to over 100 in the early 1990s.
3   We are here using 'mind' in a rather narrow, mentalistic, meaning although we are well aware that in some traditions the concept of 'mind' is a much wider concept.

References

CONNELLY, F.M. and CLANDININ, D.J. (1990) 'Stories of experience and narrative inquiry', *Educational Researcher*, 19, 5, pp. 2–14.
DOYLE, W. (1990) 'Themes in Teacher education research', in HOUSTON, W.R. (Ed) *Handbook of Research on Teacher Education*, New York, London, Macmillan.

FOUCAULT, M. (1980) 'Power/knowledge', *Selected Interviews and Other Writings 1972–77*, GORDEN, C. (Ed), New York, Pantheon Books.

POPE, M. (1993) 'Anticipating teacher thinking', in DAY, C., CALDERHEAD, J. and DENICOLO, P. (Eds) *Research on Teacher Thinking: Understanding Professional Development*, London, Washington, DC, The Falmer Press.

SIMOLA, H. (1993) 'Educational science, the state, and teachers: Forming the corporate regulation of teacher education in Finland', in POPKEWITZ, T. (Ed) *Changing Patterns of Power: Social Regulation and Teacher Education Reform*, New York, State University of New York Press.

YINGER, R. and HENDRICKS-LEE, M. (1993) 'Working knowledge in teaching', in DAY, C., CALDERHEAD, J. and DENICOLO, P. (Eds) *Research on Teacher Thinking: Understanding Professional Development*, London, Washington, DC, The Falmer Press.

Part 1

General Theoretical and Philosophical Perspectives

In this part the invited keynote addresses are presented. They represent different perspectives emerging from different theoretical and philosophical traditions. In spite of their differences, they all, directly or indirectly, challenge assumptions underlying what we could call present 'mainstream' teacher-thinking research.

Kenneth M. Zeichner in his paper on different views on reflective practice in teaching and teacher education, points to different reasons why we in present research on teachers, teaching and teacher education focus so much on reflection. He analyses how different researchers analytically try to sort out dimensions according to which the use of the term 'reflection' varies and their ways of classifying positions held in the research community about this concept. He also presents his own contribution in the form of five different traditions of reflective practice in teaching and teacher education in the USA, and discusses these. Zeichner stresses that identification of traditions like these cannot be made with claims to universality but has to take into account the societal and cultural context in which the activity takes place. Zeichner strongly advocates a more partisan approach on the part of researchers in collaboration with teachers and in relation to i.a. politicians.

Ference Marton's approach is a phenomenological one. The key concept is intentionality and Marton refers to the principle of intentionality put forward by Franz Brentano over a century ago.

In his contribution, Marton questions the dualism between mind and world embedded in much of the research on teachers' thinking. He argues that thinking is something taking place between individuals and the world, it is not something that takes place only within a person or something that belongs to persons. Marton's suggestion is that research interest should instead be directed towards teachers' awareness and intentionality as well as concentrated on the content of this intentionality. Drawing on some studies done within the phenomenographic tradition, a Swedish methodological approach, he concludes that teachers' intentionality seldom includes the 'content' of schooling (see Alexanderssons contribution in Chapter 9).

Yrjö Engeström's chapter is written within the framework of culture-historical activity theory. He argues for a dialogic and discursive view of the mind, referring to authors like Vygotsky, Bakthin and Wittgenstein. He also points to today's cognitive science, where a parallel movement is going on under the label of distributed or shared cognition. On the background of these insights,

Engeström challenges what he calls the individualist and Cartesian bias in research on teacher thinking. His chapter is also analysing the process of collaborative thinking in an actual teacher team dealing with global education in California.

Hans Joas was invited because of his recent contribution within theory of action (Joas, 1992). Joas does not belong to the ISATT research community; the idea was to introduce some new perspectives into ISATT in order to challenge existing research and inspire future research. Joas combines traditions such as German critical theory and American pragmatism in his own approach. He argues that the topic of action has been crucial in many recent debates on social theory. He examines and discusses assumptions underlying what he calls the rationalist and the normativist approaches. Joas himself proposes a third position, which takes the creativity of human action seriously and tries to conceptualize creativity within a social theory of action.

Reference

Joas, H. (1992) *Die Kreativität des Handelns*, Frankfurt am Main, Suhrkamp Verlag.

Chapter 1

Research on Teacher Thinking and Different Views of Reflective Practice in Teaching and Teacher Education

Kenneth M. Zeichner

Introduction

In the last decade, the slogans of 'reflective teaching', 'action research', 'research-based' and 'inquiry-oriented' teacher education have been embraced by both teacher educators and educational researchers throughout the world.[1] On the one hand, teacher educators who represent a variety of conceptual and ideological orientations to schooling and teacher education, have, under the umbrella of reflective practice, tried to prepare teachers who are more thoughtful and analytic about their work in some fashion. On the other hand, educational researchers, including researchers identified with the research on teacher-thinking movement, have attempted to document and describe the processes of teacher reflection and associated actions, and the relationship between these processes and teacher development (e.g., La Boskey, 1990; Russell and Munby, 1991). Other researchers have focused on studying the social and individual conditions which influence the reflections of teachers (e.g., Ashcroft and Griffiths, 1989; Erickson and Mackinnon, 1991; Grimmett and Crehan, 1990; Wubbels and Korthagen, 1990; Richert, 1990).

Amid all of this activity by teacher educators and researchers, there has been a great deal of confusion about whether reflective practice is a distinct conceptual orientation or not (Feiman-Nemser, 1990; Valli, 1992) and about whether it is necessarily a good thing that should be promoted (e.g., Day, 1993; Zeichner, 1993b).

Although those who have embraced the slogan of reflective practice appear to share certain goals about the role of the teacher in school reform, that one cannot tell very much about an approach to teaching or teacher education from an expressed commitment to the idea of the teacher as a reflective practitioner alone. To say that we want to prepare teachers who are reflective, also does not translate directly into the content of a teacher education programme (Richardson, 1990). Underlying the apparent similarity among those who embrace the slogans of reflective practice are vast differences in perspectives about teaching, learning, schooling, and the social order. It has come to the point now where the whole range of beliefs about teaching, learning, schooling, and the social order have become incorporated into the discourse about reflective practice. Everyone, no matter what his or her ideological orientation, has jumped on the bandwagon at this point, and has committed his or her energies to furthering some version of reflective teaching practice.

I will do a few things in this chapter related to the idea of teachers as reflective practitioners. First, I'll discuss in a broad way the current reflective practice movement in teaching and teacher education, describing some of the reasons why I think it has come about, some of the goals shared by those who embrace it, and some of the attempts to identify different conceptions of reflective practice which underly these surface similarities in perspective. I will also share a conceptual framework that I have used to describe different traditions of reflective practice in teaching and teacher education in my own country, and present my own ideas about the conceptions of reflective practice that we ought to embrace in our practice and support through our research. I will argue for more partisan efforts in research on teacher thinking. Finally, although the concept of reflective practice has been associated with movements around the world to enhance the status and influence of teachers in school reform, I will argue that in practice, the reflective practice movement in teaching and teacher education has served to undermine and limit the status of teachers and their role in the process of educational reform.

The Reflective Practice Movement

On the surface, this international movement that has developed in teaching and teacher education under the banner of reflection can be seen as a reaction against a view of teachers as technicians who merely carry out what others, removed from the classroom, want them to do, a rejection of top–down forms of educational reform that involve teachers merely as passive participants. It involves a recognition that teachers should play active roles in formulating the purposes and end of their work, a recognition that teaching and educational reform need to be put into the hands of teachers.

Reflection also signifies a recognition that the generation of knowledge about good teaching is not the exclusive property of colleges, universities, and research and development centres, a recognition that teachers have theories too, that can contribute to a codified knowledge base for teaching. Even today with all of the talk about teacher empowerment, we still see a general lack of respect for the craft knowledge of good teachers in the educational research establishment which has attempted to define a so called 'knowledge base' for teaching minus the voices of teachers (Cochran-Smith and Lytle, 1992).

In addition to the invisibility of teacher-generated knowledge in what counts as educational research, many staff development and school-improvement programmes still ignore the knowledge and expertise of teachers and rely primarily on top–down models of school reform which try to get teachers to comply with some externally generated and allegedly research-based solution to school problems (Little, 1993).

The concept of the teacher as a reflective practitioner recognizes the wealth of expertise that resides in the practices of good teachers, what Schön (1983) has called knowledge-in-action. From the perspective of the individual teacher, it means that the process of understanding and improving one's own teaching must start from reflection upon ones's own experience and that the sort of wisdom derived entirely from the experience of others (even other teachers) is impoverished (Winter, 1989).

Reflection as a slogan for educational reform also signifies a recognition that the process of learning to teach continues throughout a teacher's entire career, a recognition that no matter what we do in our teacher-education programmes, and no matter how well we do them, at best, we can only prepare teachers to *begin* teaching. With the concept of reflective teaching, there is a commitment by teacher educators to helping prospective teachers internalize during their initial training, the disposition and skill to study their teaching and to become better at teaching over time, a commitment to take responsibility for their own professional development (Korthagen, 1993a).

This explosion of interest in the idea of teachers as reflective practitioners has come about for a variety of reasons in addition to those I've just mentioned. These include the growing popularity of cognitive as opposed to behavioural psychologies, the birth of the research on teacher-thinking movement and the formation of organizations like ISATT, the growing acceptance of diverse research methodologies and views of educational research in the educational-research community which have given us greater access to teachers' voices and perspectives on their work, and the growing democratization of the research process in which teachers have become less willing to submit to participation in research which seeks only to portray their behaviours. Most important of all, has been the growing recognition that top–down educational reform efforts that merely use teachers as passive implementors of ideas conceived elsewhere, are doomed to failure.

Attempts to Clarify Different Conceptions of Reflective Practice

Not surprisingly, the growth of reflective practice as a slogan for educational reform has stimulated many calls for greater clarification of the similarities and differences among attempts by teacher educators to implement and/or study reflective teacher education (Bartlett, 1989; Kremer-Hayon, 1990) and criticism of the lack of attention to the conceptual underpinnings of particular projects. Consequently, a research literature has emerged which has sought to clarify the conceptual distinctions among proposals for reflective teacher education (e.g., Calderhead, 1989; Grimmett, *et al.*, 1990; Tom, 1985; and Valli, 1990a).

Several important distinctions among different notions of reflection have been made in the teacher-education literature. In addition to those like Schön (1983, 1987), van Manen (1991) and Richert (1992) who have drawn attention to the distinction between reflecting before, during and after action, and those who have made the distinction between reflecting about teaching and reflecting about the social conditions which influence one's teaching (van Manen, 1991; Zeichner and Liston, 1987), another important distinction that has been made is between those programmes of work that emphasize reflection as a private activity to be pursued in isolation by individual teachers, and those which seek to promote reflection as a social practice and public activity involving communities of teachers. Despite an emphasis by some on reflection as an activity to be carried out privately by individual teachers, there has clearly been attention to reflection as a social practice, even in North America where an ethos of individualism has reigned supreme (e.g., Clandinin *et al.*, 1993; Lucas, 1988; Pugach and Johnson, 1990). Those who have stressed reflection as a social practice have argued that the lack of a social forum for the discussion of teachers' ideas inhibits the development of the teacher's personal beliefs because these only become real and clear to us when we can speak about them to others (e.g., Ross *et al.*, 1992; Solomon, 1987).

Another important distinction that has been noted in the literature is between reflective teaching as a detached rational and logical process and reflection as a process imbued with an ethic of care and passion. Maxine Greene (1986) and Nell Noddings (1987) are among those who have challenged the detached rationality that has dominated the literature in teacher education for a long time. Their critiques go well beyond Schön's (1983) criticisms of technical rationality, because the problems they identify, the lack of care, compassion, and passion in actions, can also be a problem in the epistemology of practice that Schön proposes as the new paradigm for conceptualizing reflective practice. Fred Korthagen's (1993b) recent criticisms, from a cognitive information processing perspective, of the exclusive attention to reflection as a left-brain activity and his call for more attention to the non-rational (right brain) elements of teaching in reflective teacher-education programmes is similar in many respects to the critiques of Greene and Noddings. Another important distinction that has been made in the literature is among different levels of reflection by teachers. In North America and Australia, the most well-known of these typologies is the distinction based on the work of Habermas and his theory of cognitive interests that have been made by both Carr and Kemmis (1986) and by van Manen (1977) among technical, practical, and critical reflection.

In technical reflection, the concern is with the efficiency and effectiveness of the means used to attain ends which are accepted as given. In practical reflection, the task is one of explicating and clarifying the assumptions and predispositions underlying teaching activity and assessing the adequacy of the educational goals toward which an action leads. Here every action is seen as linked to particular value commitments and the actor considers the worth of competing educational ends as well as how well the particular learning goals that he or she is working toward are achieved by students. Finally, critical reflection incorporates moral and ethical criteria into the discourse of practical action. Here the major questions are which educational goals, activities, and experiences lead toward forms of life which are more just, equitable and so on. For example, critical reflection would extend a concern with the worth of educational goals and how effectively they are being accomplished, to a consideration of such issues as who is benefiting from the successful accomplishment of those ends, all students or just some.

In Norway, Handal and Lauvas (1987) have developed a typology of levels of reflection that is similar to the one that has been popular in North America and Australia. Their distinction between reflection at the level of action, at the level of practical and theoretical reasons for action, and at the level of ethical justification for action closely resembles the levels of technical, practical and critical reflection and has been very influential throughout Europe.

A third typology of levels of reflection proposed by Griffiths and Tann (1992) of the UK is based on the depth and speed of the reflection and the degree of engagement of teachers' personal theories with public theories. Griffiths and Tann distinguish five levels of reflection:

1   rapid reflection — instinctive and immediate;
2   repair — habitual, pause for thought, fast, on the spot;

3   review — time out to reassess over hours and days;
4   research — systematic, sharply focused, over weeks or months; and
5   retheorizing and reformulating — abstract, rigorous, clearly formulated, over months or years.

Almost everyone who has developed or used one of these category systems for identifying qualitatively different levels of reflection has stressed the difficulty in helping teachers attain the 'higher' levels of reflection. For example, Handal (1991) found that Norwegian teachers were used to talking about their work and deciding what to do, when to do it, and how to do it, at what Handal refers to as the level of action, but that teacher reflection at the levels of reasons or justifications was rare.[2] Dan Liston and I (Zeichner and Liston, 1985) using the Habermassian distinction among technical, practical, and critical reflection (Habermas, 1974) found very little evidence of critical reflection among student teachers who were enrolled in a programme that stressed issues of equity and social justice. It is often argued that one of the main reasons that we find so little of the so-called 'higher' levels of reflection among teachers or why it is so hard to develop it, is because of the fact that most schools are hostile to critical inquiry. As Gary Sykes (1986) has argued:

> Despite variability in the organizational properties of schools, the tilt is toward conditions which do not favor inquiry. Rather, the physical structure of the school, the work patterns, the need to process clients in batches, the absence of time, and frequently the norms influencing interactions among teachers and administrators all work against any regular reliance on critical inquiry. (Sykes, 1986, p. 239)

It has become fashionable these days, in some of the most recent literature on reflective practice, to argue that teacher educators like myself who try to help teachers include ethical and political considerations about teaching and teaching contexts in their deliberations about their own work are wasting our time because of the limited time we have to work with prospective teachers and because prospective teachers are not up to the demands of this kind of reflection (e.g., Calderhead and Gates, 1993).

While I am sympathetic to the difficulties of promoting the so called 'higher' levels of reflection among teachers especially beginning teachers, my response to these criticisms of efforts to promote critical or ethical reflection among student teachers has been to reject the idea of levels of reflection. Although I fully agree with the arguments of those who have said that schools are not hospitable places for the idea of critical reflection, I do not accept the view, asserted or implied by some, that schools are totally oppressive environments with regard to critical reflection or that there is some state of developmental readiness that must be reached (e.g., five years of teaching experience) before teachers are ready to reflect about the social conditions of their practice and about the political implications of their practice, i.e., how what they do everyday in the classroom contributes toward or hinders the realization of a more humane and just society for all students.[3] The idea of levels of reflection implies that technical reflection at the level of action must somehow be transcended so that teachers can enter the nirvana of critical reflection. This position devalues technical skill and the everyday world of teachers which is of necessity dominated by reflection at the level of action.

I have come to refer to technical, practical, and critical reflection as domains rather than levels, and have taken the position, in agreement with Griffiths and Tann, that all of the domains of reflection are important and necessary. I have spent a lot of time recently trying to refute the argument that it is inappropriate or fantasy to try to help student teachers at the pre-service stage of their careers reflect about the ethical, political and moral aspects of their practice and the con-texts in which their practice is carried out.[4] My position has been that the critical is right there in front of student teachers in their classrooms (not just in articles and books written by professors and lecturers) and that the way to draw their attention to it is to start with student teachers' own definitions of their experience and facilitate an examination of different aspects of that experience, including how it is connected to issues of social continuity and change.[5] I have tried to feed externally generated literature into student teachers' deliberations when it becomes appropriate rather than starting with the analysis of others' experiences.[6]

McIntyre (1993), stressing the limited role of reflection on one's own practice in initial teacher education, appears to take the opposite stance of starting with the analysis of others' experiences and then moving at a later point to an analysis of one's own experience. Thus with regard to this important issue of different 'levels' of reflection, there are a number of issues which remain to be resolved. Are these qualitatively different kinds of reflection actually ordered in a hierarchical fashion corresponding to some developmental sequence of teacher learning or are they all relevant issues at each stage of a teaching career? Is critical reflection at the level of ethical justification beyond the capabilities of teachers and teacher educa-tors? If not, what is the best strategy for helping teachers attain it? There are a lot of issues here that I am obviously not going to try to resolve in this chapter. My purpose here is to try to illuminate some of the parameters of the debate.

Tradition of Reflective Practice in North America

There are many more distinctions among different forms of reflective practice in teaching and teacher education which have been made in the literature. I have tried to focus here on the ones that I think are the most interesting or that have had the most impact on the debates among researchers. In my opinion, one of the most notable limitations of this emerging literature on reflective practice is its ahistorical nature. Other than the efforts which have been made to situate individual projects in relation to the broader theories and world views from which they draw their support (e.g., critical theory), there have been few attempts either to discuss the emergence of the reflective-inquiry movement over time in particular countries or to locate individual projects in relation to the traditions of practice which have characterized the field. This historical amnesia with regard to reflective practice has contributed greatly to the lack of clarity about the theoretical and political commitments underlying specific proposals for reform.

Several efforts have been made in recent years to identify the major *traditions* of practice in teacher education either in particular countries or more generally. These include analyses by Kirk (1986) in Australia, by Hartnett and Naish (1980) in the UK and by Feiman-Nemser (1990) in the US. Drawing on these works and on the seminar contributions of my Wisconsin colleague Kliebard (1986) on the development of the public-school curriculum in the US during the twentieth century, Dan Liston and I (Liston and Zeichner, 1991) identified four major traditions of practice in US teacher education. This analysis was later extended by Bob Tabachnick and I (Zeichner and Tabachnick, 1991) to address the notion of traditions of reflective practice in teaching and teacher education. Four historically based traditions of practice were discussed in this extension of the original framework: academic, social efficiency, developmentalist, and social reconstructionist. Finally, in a more recent analysis (Zeichner, 1992), I have extended this framework again to include a fifth tradition of reflective practice, a generic tradition. These five traditions of reflective practice in US teaching and teacher education provide a way of situating proposals for reform in relation to the historical forces from which they emerged.

My purpose in briefly describing these traditions of reflective practice here is not to imply that these same traditions exist in other countries. The identification of traditions of reflective practice must, in the final analysis, be based on a study of the historical development of teaching and teacher education in particular countries. We need to be real careful about importing theories developed in one cultural context into another without sensitivity to the cultural conditions in both situations. My purpose in sharing this typology of traditions of reflective practice here is to try to stimulate similar work about reflective practice with a historical consciousness, in other countries. My brief discussion of these traditions in this chapter will stress contemporary examples of each tradition. I have written at length about the historical evolution of each tradition in the US elsewhere (Zeichner, 1993a; Liston and Zeichner, 1991).

Academic Tradition

The first tradition, the academic tradition of reflective practice, stresses reflection about subject matter and the representation and translation of that subject-matter knowledge to promote student understanding. Recently, Shulman (1986; 1987) and Buchmann (1984) among others, have advocated views of reflective practice which emphasize teachers' deliberations about the transformation of subject-matter content. Shulman and his colleagues (e.g., Wilson, Shulman and Richert, 1987) for example, have proposed a model of pedagogical reasoning which places the emphasis in teacher reflection on academic content. Shulman's (1987) discussion of representation as an element of pedagogical reasoning illustrates the emphasis within this tradition:

> Representation involves thinking through the key ideas in the text or lesson and identifying the alternative ways of representing them to students. What analogies, metaphors, examples, demonstrations, simulations, and the like can help build a bridge between the teacher's comprehension and that desired for students? (Shulman, 1987, p. 328)

While this conception of reflective practice does not ignore aspects of teaching expertise that are stressed in the other traditions (e.g., reflection about pedagogical knowledge derived from research on teaching and learning, students' understandings and developmental characteristics, and issues of social justice and equity, the standards for assessing the adequacy of the teaching evolve primarily from the academic disciplines.

The Social-efficiency Tradition

The second tradition, the social-efficiency tradition, has historically emphasized faith in the scientific study of teaching (by those other than teachers) to provide a basis for building a teacher-education curriculum. According to contemporary advocates of this view, research on teaching has, provided a 'knowledge base' that can form the foundation for the teacher-education curriculum (e.g., Good, 1990). According to the advocates of this tradition, teachers should focus their reflections on how well their practice matches what this research says they should be doing. Feiman-Nemser (1990) has identified two different strands within this tradition: (1) a technological strand in which there is an attempt to get teachers to closely follow what research says they should be doing; and (2) a deliberative strand in which the findings of research are used as one among many sources by teachers in solving teaching problems. Here the task for teacher educators is to foster teachers' capabilities to exercise their judgment about various teaching situations while taking advantage of research, experience, intuition and their own values (Zumwalt, 1982).[7]

While this conception of reflective practice does not necessarily ignore the social context of schooling, subject matter, students, and issues of equity and social justice, the emphasis is clearly on the application of knowledge produced by research conducted elsewhere.

The Developmentalist Tradition

The third tradition of reflective practice, the developmentalist tradition, prioritizes reflection about students, their thinking and understandings, their interests, and their developmental growth. The distinguishing characteristic of this tradition is the assumption that the natural development of the learner provides the basis for determining what should be taught to students and how it should be taught. Classroom practice is to be grounded in close observation and study of students either directly by the teacher, or from reflection on a literature based on such studies.

One contemporary example of reflective teaching practice within this tradition is the work of Eleanor Duckworth at Harvard University. Duckworth (1987) has elaborated a constructivist view of reflective teaching which emphasizes engaging learners with phenomena, instead of explaining things to students at the onset. According to Duckworth, teachers are both practitioners and researchers, and their research should be focused on their students. The teacher should then use this knowledge of their students' understandings to decide the appropriate next steps for their learning. The important thing according to Duckworth, is for the teacher to keep trying to find out what sense her students are making.

This developmental conception of reflective teaching has become increasingly popular in recent years with the growing influence of cognitive psychology in education (e.g., Wubbels, 1992). While it does not necessarily ignore issues related to subject mater, equity, and a 'knowledge base' produced through university-sponsored research, the emphasis is clearly on reflecting about one's own students.

The Social-reconstructionist Tradition

In the fourth tradition of reflective practice, the social-reconstructionist tradition, reflection is viewed as a political act which either contributes toward or hinders the realization of a more just and humane society. In a social-reconstructionist conception of reflective practice, the teacher's attention is focused both inwardly at his or her own practice and outwardly at the social conditions in which these practices are situated (Kemmis, 1985). The social reconstructionist tradition is the only one that does not adopt a benign view of the social conditions of schooling. A second characteristic of a social-reconstructionist conception of reflective practice is its democratic and emancipatory impulse and the focus of teachers' deliberations upon substantive issues which help them examine the social and political consequences of their teaching. For example, here teachers would consider such issues as gendered nature of schooling and teachers' work, and the racial and social-class issues embedded in everyday classroom actions (Liston and Zeichner, 1990). Contemporary examples of an emphasis on a social-reconstructionist conception of reflective practice include the increasing number of teacher-education programmes throughout the world which have incorporated feminist and anti-racist perspectives into their curricula (e.g., Gomez, 1991; Maher, 1991).

The Generic Tradition

In addition to these four traditions of reflective practice in US teaching and teacher education, there has recently been a great deal of advocacy for reflective teaching in general, without much comment about what it is the reflection should be focused on, the criteria that should be used to evaluate the quality of the reflection, or the degree to which teachers' reflections should involve the problematization of the social and institutional contexts in which they work. The implication here is that teachers' actions are necessarily better just because they are more deliberate or intentional. According to Linda Valli (1990b):

> How to get students to reflect can take on a life of its own, and can become *the* programmatic goal. *What* they reflect on can become immaterial. For example, racial tension as a school issue can become no more or less worthy of reflection than field trips or home work assignments. (Valli, 1990b, p. 9)

One of the clearest examples of this tendency to uncritically advocate reflection for the sake of reflection, can be found in the Ohio State University materials on reflective teaching which have been disseminated throughout the world. Drawing on the important distinction made by Dewey (1933) between reflective action and routine action, Cruickshank (1987) has argued that teachers need to become more reasoned actors, without at all addressing the issues of content, quality, and the context of reflection.

This position fails to consider the fact that all teachers are reflective in some sense. There is no such thing as an unreflective teacher. We need to move beyond the uncritical celebration of teacher reflection and making the tacit explicit, and become interested in more complex questions than whether teachers are reflective or not. We need to focus our attention on what kind of reflection teachers are engaging in, on what it is teachers are reflecting about, and on how they are going about it.[8] The analytic frameworks that I have alluded to in this chapter provide different answers to how we should think about these differences, but they all recognize that reflective teaching is not necessarily good teaching. All of the researchers who developed these lenses for viewing reflective practice, with the exception of the advocates of generic reflection, recognize that under some circumstances, more reflection may actually legitimate and strengthen practices which are harmful to students (Ellwood, 1992).

Also, although reflection has been touted as a vehicle for the further professionalization of teachers, it has in practice, actually served to limit the status of teachers and their role in the process of educational reform by doing such things as limiting the focus of teachers' reflections to thinking about the means to implement educational ends determined by others removed from the classroom. Teachers have also been encouraged for the most part, to focus their reflections inwardly at their own teaching and on their students to the neglect of any consideration of the social conditions of schooling that influence their work in the classroom. This individualist bias makes it less likely that teachers will be able to confront and transform those structural aspects of their work which hinder their accomplishment of their educational mission (see Zeichner, 1993b; 1993c).

My framework of traditions of reflective practice in US teacher education adds a historical perspective to the discourse aimed at clarifying the assumptions and commitments underlying particular projects of reflective practice in teaching and teacher education. The identification of each tradition in the contemporary debate is tied to long-standing controversies in the United States among interest groups which have competed for dominance of teaching and teacher education. As I said earlier though, I am not implying that these same traditions exist in other countries. Although I think traditions of practice need to be identified in particular cultural contexts, I would argue that in all countries, the identification of different approaches to the idea of reflective practice needs to contain historical and culturally specific dimensions. The effort by some to try to identify universal alternative approaches to reflective practice which exist without regard for different cultures, does not make much sense to me.

In identifying these five different approaches to reflective practice in teaching and teacher education in the US I am not suggesting that individual instances of teacher reflection or that individual teacher-education programmes can be viewed as pure examples of any of the orientations. On the contrary, all teacher-education programmes in the US reflect some pattern of resonance with all of the various orientations, emphasizing some and marginalizing others, and defining each one in a way that reflects the particular priorities in a situation. Similarly, certain emphases and absences can be detected in any set of programmes or in the reflective teacher-education movement in the US, in terms of these various orientations.

I have used this framework both to help clarify my own and my Wisconsin colleagues' commitments in our own teacher-education programme (Zeichner, 1993a) and to critique the commitments and assumptions embedded in other teacher-education programmes in the US (Zeichner, 1992). In doing so, I have spent a lot of time in the last few years trying to clarify to myself and others, what it is I mean when I use the term reflective teaching. In a recent paper (Zeichner, 1993a), I responded to those who have tried to label my perspective as only critical or radical (implying a lack of concern for the areas of teaching expertise emphasized in the other traditions) and tried to show how my teacher-education programme interprets each of the traditions of reflective practice. Although my perspective includes a lot of attention to reflection about issues of equity and social justice and the social and political consequences of teaching, it also includes a concern for teaching subject matter for understanding, teaching that starts with, and builds upon, the cultural resources and knowledge that students bring to the classroom, and for utilizing the knowledge generated by research conducted by academics and practitioners.

This does not mean that we need to try to be ideologically even-handed and work toward a grand synthesis of all perspectives. While all teacher-education programmes, whatever their priorities, reflect multiple commitments, they also have particular identities which come from the ideological and political commitments of the teacher educators who work in them. In my programme, the concern for fostering reflection that includes a focus on the social and political dimensions of teaching that are embedded in everyday classroom practice and on the social conditions which influence that practice colours our view of how we respond to the other traditions. The social reconstructionist impulse in our perspective causes us to raise certain questions about equity and social justice in relation to subject matter, students, research, and so on, which do not often get raised in programmes driven by other commitments. My point is that we need to be debating the kinds of reflective practice that we should be encouraging in our work both for teachers and ourselves, and not just describing reflective practice as it exits.

I want to close this chapter by discussing what I think the role is for research on teacher thinking in relation to different conceptions of reflective practice in teaching and teacher education.

Going Beyond Descriptions of Teachers' Reflections

It seems to me that much of the research that has been conducted under the label of research on teacher thinking has focused on merely describing, in a supposedly neutral way, teachers' reflections about their practice. Furthermore, much of this research, as Carlgren and Linblad (1991) have argued, has involved a reductionism that has isolated teachers from the social and historical contexts in which their teaching is embedded.

In recent years, we have seen a growing variety of lenses utilized in efforts to illuminate teacher thinking such as narrative and storytelling (Connelly and Clandinin, 1990), biography and autobiography (Butt, 1984) metaphor analysis (Bullough *et al.*, 1991), and descriptions of personal constructs (Ben Peretz, 1984). Some of this research has taken a developmental perspective and has illuminated how teacher thinking changes over time. And most importantly, a growing body of these studies have been conducted and reported by teachers themselves in their own voices (e.g., Branscombe, Goswami and Schwartz, 1992).

While we have gained a lot from this relatively recent field of research on teacher thinking, I want to take the position that we need to conduct less research that merely describes teacher thinking and actions and satisfies an intellectual curiosity, and do more research that adopts a partisan stance and attempts to further particular kinds of reflective thinking and action among teachers and to promote the creation of institutional environments supportive of the kinds of teacher reflection and action we want to encourage. I would also like to see less of a detached stance by university researchers studying teachers as 'the others', and more collaborative inquiry in which the practices of both teachers and teacher educators are jointly studied.

Acknowledging the Partisan Nature of Educational Research

A number of years ago, Clark (1986) criticized what he saw as a failure of moral courage in the research on teacher-thinking movement and challenged the ISATT membership to go beyond merely being curious about teachers' thoughts and actions, to become more concerned about 'doing good' with our research for students, teachers and communities.

My position on the role of research on teacher thinking in relation to different conceptions of reflective practice in teaching and teacher education is consistent with what Chris Clark had to say to ISATT in 1985. Rather than merely documenting and describing the actions and reflections and teachers in an allegedly neutral fashion, we need to recognize the inherently partisan nature of all educational research and openly use our research to tackle particular kinds of problems and to accomplish goals which reflect our passions and commitments as educators and as citizens (Lindblom and Cohen, 1979).

What this position means for research on teacher thinking is that whatever particular conceptions of reflective practice we are personally committed to, we should be working in our research to help achieve these partisan goals both at the level of persons and institutions. For example, I have spent a lot of my energy over the last fifteen years in trying to figure out ways in which I can help my students focus more attention on the social and political implications of their own teaching, on how what they are doing everyday is contributing to the life chances of their own pupils and to the realization of a more just and humane society. Others, reflecting the prioritization of other aspects of teaching expertise, have conducted research which focuses on ways to help student teachers become better able to understand and build upon what their pupils bring to the classroom or research which illuminates the process of transforming subject-matter knowledge for students. In all of these projects, researchers have recognized the inability of educational research to produce authoritative knowledge independent of partisan interests, have openly acknowledged their prejudices, and have tried to further the accomplishment of particular ends. This is as it should be.

I want to be clear that I am not advocating research which leads to prescriptions for teachers to follow with regard to the accomplishment of whatever goals the researcher wants them to achieve. This would be contrary to the idea of teachers as reflective practitioners as I see it. I am not interested in trying to force teachers to think in particular ways or to adopt certain views. I do think however, that we have a moral obligation to recognize the link between the generation of new knowledge and the moral task of stimulating the improvement of education (see Lowyck, 1990).

Clark (1986) charged that:

> None of the research on teacher thinking has directly addressed serious and difficult problems and crises in education . . . we have omitted attention to all of the more challenging problem areas in our educational systems including poverty, nationalism, cultural conflict, racism, sexism, discrimination, and a massive failure to learn in certain quarters of our educational systems. (Clark, 1986, p. 16)

It is time to see more research on teacher thinking which openly works towards the solution of these kinds of social problems and which goes beyond the mere assertion of trying to further teacher reflection. What kind of teacher reflection and action does our research encourage or discourage and for what purpose? Teacher empowerment for what ends and for whose benefit? As I argued earlier, just because teachers are able to make the tacit explicit, does not mean that they will necessarily be more capable of 'doing good'.

Establishing Collaborative Research Communities

It is not enough however, for research on teacher thinking to begin to focus more on its contribution to particular agendas for educational reform, if researchers only study the thinking and actions of others. A research programme on reflective practice in teaching and teacher education is a critical component of all teacher-education programmes that seek to develop the reflective capabilities of their students. As Arnstine (1990) has argued, the development of complex dispositions such as reflection requires an environment in the teacher-education programme that cultivates these dispositions. If prospective teachers are to become reflective about their practice in whatever sense one defines it, then they need to engage in activities during their pre-service preparation that fosters this reflectiveness. As part of this environment, they need to have models in their teacher educators of the dispositional qualities that are desired (Noddings, 1987). If the dispositional aim is reflection in some form, then not only do the teacher educators need to be examining their practice and the social conditions of that practice, they need to conduct this examination publicly so that their students are aware of it.

The research agenda that I support in teacher education is one that involves a continuing series of research efforts carried out publicly by teacher educators within their own programmes that focus on ways in which particular programme structures and activities, and their own actions, are implicated in the particular kinds of reflective practice evidenced by their students. As Richert (1990) has shown, different teacher-education programme structures encourage different kinds of reflection by student teachers. We need research that increases our understanding of the ways in which both individual and social factors affect teachers' reflections and actions so that we can continually adjust our actions in our programmes in response to these data. These accounts of the reflective practice of student teachers under particular programmatic conditions can also be used as reading material for teacher-education students to help them examine their own patterns of reflection.

None of what I've said here about the role of research on teacher thinking in relation to different conceptions of reflective practice has implied that we should fail to recognize the tremendous gains that we have made in the last fifteen years in this relatively new field of research. I am merely calling for more open acknowledgment of our own passions and commitments as educators and of the partisan interests served by our research efforts, and less of a detachment from the practices that we seek to understand through our research. All of this can be accomplished building upon the insights that we have gained from research on teacher thinking thus far.

Conclusion

In this chapter I have tried to describe some of the debates currently going on about different forms of reflective practice in teaching and teacher education. Although recognizing some of the assumptions shared by those who have embraced the slogan of reflective practice, I have rejected the idea of reflective teaching as a distinct conceptual orientation, have offered a variety of lenses for viewing the reflections and actions of teachers and have offered some of my own ideas about both how to think about different kinds of reflection and about the kind of reflective practice that we should be trying to promote both among ourselves and our students. I have also set forth a couple of proposals for the role of research on teacher thinking in relation to reflective-teaching practice, calling for a more open acknowledgment of the partisan nature of educational research and for more collaborative research conducted with prospective teachers and teachers about our own and their practices. I hope that these comments will contribute in some way to clarifying some of the debates that need to continue as we seek ways to develop further the idea of teachers as reflective practitioners.

Notes

1   One sign of the popularity of this slogan in the US has been the recent emergence of texts to be used in teacher-education programmes which focus on some version of the concept of reflective teaching. Some of these texts, such as Posner (1993) are among the best-selling teacher-education books in the US (see also Henderson, 1992; Ross, Bondy and Kyle, 1993). A similar emergence of reflective teaching texts for prospective teachers can be seen elsewhere as well (e.g., Pollard and Tann, 1987).
2   Handal (1991) and Handal and Lauvas (1987) do argue though that their method of counseling teachers can make these 'higher' levels of reflection more common.
3   See Zeichner and Teitelbaum (1982) for an elaboration of some of my arguments on this issue.
4   For example, see Zeichner (1993d) for a discussion of how I have attempted to help student teachers consider these aspects of their practice in an action research seminar.
5   See Zeichner (1993d); Zeichner (1994); Gore and Zeichner (1991) for specific examples of how we have tried to do this in our own teacher-education programme.
6   Also, despite the character and quality of teachers' work in many schools which makes reflection on action difficult, many teachers have managed to find ways, often outside of the offical staff-development system, to come together to think

about their practices. Teacher study groups and teacher researcher groups have become extremely popular in the US in recent years (e.g., Cochran-Smith and Lytle, 1992).

7   This distinction between the technical and deliberative strands of the social efficiency tradition reflects, according to Carr (1986), differences between an applied science (technical) and practical (deliberative) view of the relationship between theory and practice.

8   See the discussions in Ashcroft (1992) and Shulman (1988) criticizing the idea of reflection as deliberation without consideration to values which give direction to the deliberation. Shulman (1988) argues that our obligations as teacher educators are not fulfilled, until what is reasoned (by the reflecting teacher) is married to what is reasonable. What is reasonable must be determined by linking the teacher's reflections to standards provided by some ethical and moral framework. For example, Dan Liston and I (1991) have utilized Gutmann's (1987) ideas about democratic education to help us develop arguments about what is right and wrong action within societies which claim to be democratic.

References

ARNSTINE, B. (1990) 'Rational and caring teachers: Reconstructing teacher preparation', *Teachers College Record*, 92, 2, pp. 230–47.

ASHCROFT, K. (1992) 'Working together, developing reflective student teachers', in BIOTT, C. and NIAS, J. (Eds) *Working and learning together for change,* Buckingham, Open University Press, pp. 33–46.

ASHCROFT, K. and GRIFFITHS, M. (1989) 'Reflective teachers and reflective tutors: School experience in an initial teacher education course', *Journal of Education for Teaching*, 15, 1, pp. 35–52.

BARTLETT, L. (1989) 'Images of reflection: A look and a review', *Qualitative Studies in Education*, 2, 4, pp. 351–7.

BEN-PERETZ, M. (1984) 'Kelly's theory of personal constructs as a paradigm for investigating teacher thinking', in HALKES, R. and OLSON, J.K. (Eds) *Teacher Thinking: A New Perspective on Persistant Problems in Education*, Amsterdam, Swets and Zeitlinger, pp. 103–111.

BRANSCOMBE, N.A., GOSWAMI, D. and SCHWARTZ, J. (Eds) (1992) *Students Teaching, Teachers Learning*, Portsmouth, NH, Boynton Cook.

BUCHMANN, M. (1984) 'The priority of knowledge and understanding in teaching', in KATZ, L. and RATHS, J. (Eds) *Advances in teacher education*, Norwood, NJ, Ablex, pp. 29–50.

BULLOUGH, R., KNOWLES, G. and CROSS, N. (1991) *Emerging as a Teacher*, London, Routledge.

BUTT, R. (1984) 'Arguments for using biography in understanding teacher thinking', in HALKES, R. and OLSON, J.K. (Eds) *Teacher Thinking: A New Perspective on Persisting Problems in Education*, Amsterdam, Swets and Zeitlinger.

CALDERHEAD, J. (1989) 'Reflective teaching and teacher education', *Teaching and Teacher Education*, 5, 1, pp. 43–51.

CALDERHEAD, J. and GATES, P. (Eds) (1993) 'Introduction', in *Conceptualizing Reflection in Teacher Development*, London, The Falmer Press, pp. 1–10.

CARLGREN, I. and LINDBLAD, S. (1991) 'On teachers' practical reasoning and professional knowledge: Considering conceptions of context in teachers thinking', *Teaching & Teacher Education*, 7, 5/6, pp. 507–16.

CARR, W. (1986) 'Theories of theories and practice', *Journal of Philosophy of Education*, 20, 2, pp. 177–86.

CARR, W. and KEMMIS, S. (1986) *Becoming Critical: Education, Knowledge & Action Research*, London, The Falmer Press.

CLANDININ, D.J., DAVIES, A., HOGAN, P. and KENNARD, B. (Eds) (1993) *Learning to Teach: Teaching to Learn*, New York, Teachers College Press.

CLARK, C. (1986) 'Ten years of conceptual development in research on teacher thinking', in BEN-PERETZ, M., BROMME, R. and HALKES, R. (Eds) *Advances of Research on Teacher Thinking*, Amsterdam, Swets and Zeitlinger, pp. 7–20.

COCHRAN-SMITH, M. and LYTLE, S. (1992) 'Communities for teacher research: Fringe or forefront?', *American Journal of Education*, 100, 3, pp. 298–324.

COCHRAN-SMITH, M. and LYTLE, S. (1993) *Inside-out: Teacher Research and Knowledge*, New York, Teachers College Press.

CONNELLY, F.M. and CLANDININ, D.J. (1990) 'Stories of experience and narrative inquiry', *Educational Researcher*, 19, 5, pp. 2–14.

CRUICKSHANK, D. (1987) *Reflective Teaching*, Reston, VA, Association of Teacher Educators.

DAY, C. (1993) 'Reflection: A necessary but not sufficient condition for professional development', *British Educational Research Journal*, 19, 1, pp. 83–93.

DEWEY, J. (1933) *How We Think*, Chicago, Henry Regnery.

DUCKWORTH, E. (1987) *The Having of Wonderful Ideas*, New York, Teachers College Press.

ELLWOOD, C. (1992) *Teacher Research: For Whom?*, A paper presented at the annual meeting of the American Educational Research Association, San Francisco.

ERICKSON, G. and MACKINNON, A. (1991) 'Seeing classrooms in new ways: On becoming a science teacher', in SCHON, D. (Ed) *The Reflective Turn: Case Studies In and On Educational Practice*, New York, Teachers College Press, pp. 15–36.

FEIMAN-NEMSER, S. (1990) 'Teacher preparation: Structural and conceptual alternatives', in Houston, W.R. (Ed), *Handbook of Research on Teacher Education*, New York, Macmillan, pp. 212–33.

GOMEZ, M.L. (1991) 'Teaching a language of opportunity in a language arts methods class', in TABACHNICK, B.R. and ZEICHNER, K. (Eds) *Issues & Practices in Inquiry-Oriented Teacher Education*, London, The Falmer Press, pp. 91–112.

GOOD, T. (1990) 'Building the knowledge base of teaching', in DILL, D. (Ed) *What Teachers Need to Know*, San Francisco, Jossey Bass, pp. 17–75.

GORE, J. and ZEICHNER, K. (1991) 'Action research and reflective teaching in preservice teacher education: A case study from the US', *Teaching & Teacher Education*, 7, 2, pp. 119–36.

GREENE, M. (1986) 'Reflection and passion in teaching', *Journal of Curriculum & Supervision*, 2, 1, pp. 68–81.

GRIFFITHS, M. and TANN, S. (1992) 'Using reflective practice to link personal and public theories', *Journal of Education for Teaching*, 18, 1, pp. 69–84.

GRIMMET, P. and CREHAN, E.P. (1990) *Conditions Which Facilitate and Inhibit Teacher Reflection in Clinical Supervision: Collegiality Re-Examined*, Paper presented at the annual meeting of the American Educational Research Association, Boston.

GRIMMETT, P., MACKINNON, A., ERICKSON, G. and RIECKEN, T. (1990) 'Reflective practice in teacher education', in CLIFT, R., HOUSTON, W.R. and PUGACH, M. (Eds) *Encouraging Reflective Practice in Education*, New York, Teachers College Press, pp. 20–38.

GUTMANN, A. (1987) *Democratic Education*, Princeton, NJ, Princeton University Press.

HABERMAS, J. (1974) *Theory and Practice*, London, Heinemann.

HANDAL, G. (1991) 'Promoting the articulation of tacit knowledge through the counselling of practitioners', in LETICHE, H.K., VANDER WOLF, J.C. and PLOOIJ, F.X. *The Practitioners Power of Choice in Staff Development & Inservice Training*, Amsterdam, Swets and Zeitlinger, pp. 71–84.

HANDAL, G. and LAUVAS, P, (1987) *Promoting Reflective Teaching: Supervision in Action*, Milton Keynes, Open University Press.

HARTNETT, A. and NAISH, M. (1980) 'Technicians or social bandits? Some moral and political issues in the education of teachers', in WOODS, P. (Ed) *Teacher Strategies*, London, Croom Helm, pp. 254–74.

HENDERSON, J.G. (1992) *Reflective Teaching: Becoming an Inquiring Educator*, New York, Macmillan.

KEMMIS, S. (1985) 'Action research and the politics of reflection', in BOUD, D., KEOGH, R. and WALKER, D. (Eds) *Reflection: Turning Experience into Learning*, London, Croom Helm, pp. 139–64.

KIRK, D. (1986) 'Beyond the limits of theoretical discourse in teacher education: Towards a critical pedagogy', *Teaching and Teacher Education*, 2, pp. 155–67.

KLIEBARD, H. (1986) *The Struggle for the American Curriculum, 1893–1958*, Boston, Routledge and Kegan Paul.

KORTHAGEN, F. (1993a) 'The role of reflection in teachers' professional development', in KREMER-HAYON, L., VONK, H. and FESSLER, R. (Eds) *Teacher Professional Development: A Multiple Perspective Approach*, Amsterdam, Swets and Zeitlinger, pp. 133–45.

KORTHAGEN, F. (1993b) 'Two modes of reflection', *Teaching & Teacher Education*, 9, 3, pp. 317–26.

KREMER-HAYON, L. (1990) 'Reflection and professional knowledge: A conceptual framework', in DAY, C., POPE, M. and DENICOLO, P. (Eds) *Insight into Teachers' Thinking & Practice*, London, The Falmer Press, pp. 57–70.

LA BOSKEY, V.K. (1990) *Reflectivity in Preservice Teachers: Alert Novices vs. Common sense Thinkers*, Paper presented at the annual meeting of the American Educational Research Association, Boston.

LINDBLOM, C. and COHEN, D. (1979) *Usable Knowledge*, New Haven, CT, Yale University Press.

LISTON, D. and ZEICHNER, K. (1990) 'Teacher education and the social context of schooling: Issues for curriculum development', *American Educational Research Journal*, 27, 4, pp. 610–36.

LISTON, D. and ZEICHNER, K. (1991) *Teacher Education and the Social Conditions of Schooling*, New York, Routledge.

LITTLE, J.W. (1993) 'Teachers' professional development in a climate of educational reform', *Educational Evaluation & Policy Analysis*, 15, 2, pp. 129–51.

LOWYCK, J. (1990) 'Teacher thinking studies: Bridges between description, prescription, and application', in DAY, C., POPE, M. and DENICOLO, P. (Eds) *Insight into Teachers' Thinking and Practice*, London, The Falmer Press, pp. 85–104.

LUCAS, P. (1988) 'An approach to research-based teacher education through collaborative inquiry', *Journal of Education for Teaching*, 14, 1, pp. 55–73.

MAHER, F. (1991) 'Gender, reflexivity, and teacher education', in TABACHNICK, B.R. and ZEICHNER, K. (Eds) *Issues & Practices in Inquiry-Oriented Teacher Education*, London, The Falmer Press, pp. 22–34.

McINTYRE, D. (1993) 'Theory, theorizing & reflection in initial teacher education', in CALDERHEAD, K. and GATES, P. (Eds) *Conceptualizing Reflection in Teacher Development*, London, The Falmer Press, pp. 39–52.

NODDINGS, N. (1987) 'Fidelity in teaching, teacher education and research for teaching', in OKAZAWA-REY, M., ANDERSON, J. and TRAVER, R. (Eds) *Teachers, Teaching, and Teacher Education*, Cambridge, MA, Harvard Educational Review Reprint Series No. 19, pp. 384–400.

POLLARD, A. and TANN, S. (1987) *Reflective Teaching in the Primary School*, London, Cassell.

POSNER, G. (1993) *Field Experience: A Guide to Reflective Teaching*, New York, Longman.

PUGACH, M. and JOHNSON, L. (1990) 'Developing reflective practice', in CLIFT, R., HOUSTON, W.R. and PUGACH, M. (Eds) *Encouraging Reflective Practice in Education*, New York, Teachers College Press, pp. 186–207.

RICHARDSON, V. (1990) 'The evolution of reflective teaching and teacher education', in CLIFT, R., HOUSTON, W.R. and PUGACH, M. (Eds) *Encouraging Reflective Practice in Education*, New York, Teachers College Press, pp. 3–19.

RICHERT, A. (1990) 'Teaching teachers to reflect: A consideration of programme structure', *Journal of Curriculum Studies*, 22, 6, pp. 509–27.

RICHERT, A. (1992) 'Voice and power in teaching and learning to teach', in VALLI, L. (Ed) *Reflective Teacher Education: Cases & Critiques*, Albany, New York, SUNY Press, pp. 187–97.

ROSS, E.W. (1992) 'Teacher personal theorizing and reflective practice in teacher education', in ROSS, E.W., CORNETT, J. and MCCUTCHEON, G. (Eds) *Teachers Personal Theorizing*, Albany, New York, SUNY Press, pp. 179–90.

ROSS, D., BONDY, E. and KYLE, D. (1993) *Reflective Teaching for Student Empowerment*, New York, Macmillan.

RUSSELL, T. and MUNBY, H. (1991) 'Reframing: The role of experience in developing teachers' professional knowledge', in SCHÖN, D. (Ed) *The Reflective Turn: Case Studies In and On Educational Practice*, New York, Teachers College Press, pp. 164–88.

SCHÖN, D. (1983) *The Reflective Practitioner*, New York, Basic Books.

SCHÖN, D. (1987) *Educating the Reflective Practitioner*, San Francisco, Jossey Bass.

SCHWAB, J. (1971) 'The practical: Arts of eclectic', *School Review*, 79, pp. 493–543.

SHULMAN, L. (1986) 'Those who understand: Knowledge growth in teaching', *Educational Researcher*, 15, 2, pp. 4–14.

SHULMAN, L. (1987) 'Knowledge and teaching: Foundations of the new reform', *Harvard Educational Review*, 57, pp. 1–12.

SHULMAN, L. (1988) 'The dangers of dichotomous thinking in education', in GRIMMETT, P. and ERICKSON, G. (Eds) *Reflection in Teacher Education*, New York, Teachers College Press, pp. 19–30.

SOLOMON, J. (1987) 'New thoughts on teacher education', *Oxford Review of Education*, 13, 3, pp. 267–74.

SYKES, G. (1986) 'Teaching as reflective practice', in SIROTNIK, K. and OAKES, J. (Eds) *Critical Perspectives on the Organization and Improvement of Schooling*, Boston, Klower Nijhoff, pp. 229–45.

TOM, A. (1985) 'Inquiring into inquiry-oriented teacher education', *Journal of Teacher Education*, 36, 5, pp. 35–44.

VALLI, L. (1990a) 'Moral approaches to reflective practice', in CLIFT, R., HOUSTON, W.R. and PUGACH, M. (Eds) *Encouraging Reflective Practice in Education*, New York, Teachers College Press, pp. 39–56.

VALLI, L. (1990b) *The Question of Quality and Content in Reflective Teaching*, Paper presented at the annual meeting of the American Educational Research Association, Boston, MA.

VALLI, L. (1992) 'Introduction', in VALLI, L. (Ed) *Reflective Teacher Education: Cases and Critiques*, Albany, SUNY Press, pp. xi–xxv.

VAN MANEN, M. (1991) *The Tact of Teaching*, Albany, New York, SUNY Press.

VAN MANEN, M. (1977) 'Linking ways of knowing with ways of being practical', *Curriculum Inquiry*, 6, pp. 205–28.

WILSON, S., SHULMAN, L. and RICHERT, A. (1987) '150 different ways of knowing: Representations of knowledge in teaching', in CALDERHEAD, J. (Ed) *Exploring Teachers Thinking*, London, Cassell, pp. 104–24.

WINTER, R. (1989) *Learning From Experience: Principles & Practice in Action Research*, London, The Falmer Press.

WUBBELS, T. (1992) 'Taking account of student teachers' preconceptions', *Teaching & Teacher Education*, 8, 2, pp. 137–50.

WUBBELS, T. and KORTHAGEN, F. (1990) 'The effects of a preservice teacher education program for the preparation of reflective teachers', *Journal of Education for Teaching*, 16, 1, pp. 29–44.

ZEICHNER, K. (1987) 'Preparing reflective teachers', *International Journal of Educational Research*, 11, 5, pp. 565–75.

ZEICHNER, K. (1992) 'Conceptions of reflective teaching in contemporary US teacher education programs', in VALLI, L. (Ed) *Reflective Teacher Education: Cases and Critiques*, Albany, New York, SUNY Press, pp. 161–73.

ZEICHNER, K. (1993a) 'Traditions of practice in US preservice teacher education programs', *Teaching & Teacher Education*, 9, 1, pp. 1–13.

ZEICHNER, K. (1993b) 'Connecting genuine teacher development to the struggle for social justice', *Journal of Education for Teaching*, 19, 1, pp. 5–20.

ZEICHNER, K. (1993c) 'Action research: Personal renewal & social reconstruction', *Educational Action Research*, 1, 2, pp. 199–219.

ZEICHNER, K. (1993d) Reflections of a Teacher Educator Working for Social Change, Paper presented at the annual meeting of the American Educational Research Association, Atlanta, GA.

ZEICHNER, K. (1994) Action Research and Issues of Equity and Social Justice in Preservice Teacher Education Programs, A paper presented at the annual meeting of the American Educational Research Association, New Orleans.

ZEICHNER, K. and LISTON, D. (1985) 'Varieties of discourse in supervisory conferences', *Teaching & Teacher Education*, 1, pp. 155–74.

ZEICHNER, K. and LISTON, D. (1987) 'Teaching student teachers to reflect', *Harvard Educational Review*, 57, 1, pp. 1–22.

ZEICHNER, K. and TABACHNICK, B.R. (1991) 'Reflections on reflective teaching', in TABACHNICK, B.R. and ZEICHNER, K. (Eds) *Issues and Practices in Inquiry-Oriented Teacher Education*, London, The Falmer Press, pp. 1–21.

ZEICHNER, K. and TEITELBAUM, K. (1982) 'Personalized and inquiry oriented teacher education', *Journal of Education for Teaching*, 8, 2, pp. 95–117.

ZUMWALT, K. (1982) 'Research on teaching: Policy implications for teacher education', in LIEBERRMAN, A. and MCLAUGHLIN, M. (Eds) *Policy Making in Education*, Chicago, University of Chicago Press, pp. 215–48.

Chapter 2

On the Structure of Teachers' Awareness

Ference Marton

Introduction

My aim is, on the ground of certain doubts about the focus on teachers' thinking; to speak to an interest in the differing ways in which teachers experience, and are aware of, their professional world.[1] This I will do partly through a theoretical discourse and partly through illustrating — by bringing together some recent studies — the kinds of insights which a focus on teachers' awareness could yield. In passing, I also want to deal with the perplexing fact that two dynamic fields of research — teachers' pedagogical content-knowledge on the one hand, and students' understanding of the content on the other hand — are rarely connected. This I will do by pointing to a bridge between the two fields, in terms of the relatedness of the students' ways of being aware of some particular content to the teachers' ways of being aware of the same content.

As the present volume originates from a conference on teachers' thinking, and as I am going to talk about their awareness, I feel obliged to briefly juxtapose the two. Let us start with thinking.

The Idea of Thinking

As individuals and as a species we develop a common-sense knowledge of the world around us and of ourselves by progressively differentiating various kinds of entities and aspects and relating them to each other. Very early on, we learn to separate ourselves from the world: the little child separates himself or herself from what is 'not he or she'. People around him or her can be divided into critically important categories like 'mummy' and 'not mummies', later on 'people known' — with progressively differentiated members — versus 'people not known'. And then another classification crossing it, children versus adults, or boys versus girls, uncles versus aunts etc. Distinctions between and within sets such as objects, plants, animals etc., are arrived at.

Once the individual has separated — or distinguished — himself or herself from the rest of the world, the question of the relationship between the individual and the world arises. Without making things too complicated, we might say that there are two major links between the individual and the world — both being directional. Firstly, human beings are equipped with sense organs and obtain information about the world through them: sound, light, smell, etc. Secondly, human beings act in the world: talk, move, do things. These are visible links between the individual and the world. In order to make sense of what people actually do, we assume that there are hidden entities and processes behind what they are doing: they have knowledge, memory; they have thoughts (for instance, prior to talking), they have feelings; they have a will, motivation etc., they may solve problems, make decisions or remember things without actually showing any signs of what is going on. Where are these invisible entities located? Where are these invisible processes taking place? Well, it must be in people's heads, obviously. What we know; what we remember; what we think about, must be in our heads as well. Out of the information about the surrounding world which we receive through our sense organs, a model — or a representation of the world — is built. Thinking, making decisions, solving problems, means an inner 'doing something' in the model world. There are thus two worlds according to this view: a real world out there and a replica of that world in people's heads. This is a view, usually referred to as 'cognitivism', which rests on a dualistic ontology, separating subject and objects. This is surely not the only way of understanding things, but it is very common. And it has certainly been the dominating way of understanding in the research specialization called 'teacher thinking'. My interpretation is that the driving force behind it has been the idea that we can understand (and perhaps even predict), teachers' ways of acting if we find out their ways of thinking, making decisions, solving problems. There is causal flavour to this line of reasoning: teachers' acts are affected — if not caused, or controlled — by the thoughts they have arrived at, the decisions they have made, the solution to the problems they have found. 'Teacher behaviour is substantially influenced and even determined by teachers' thought processes', Clark and Peterson (1986) say in their well-known handbook chapter. Reasoning precedes action; thinking precedes speech. From this perspective, thinking appears to be seen as a kind of ongoing inner-speech, an ever-ongoing mumbling in the language of thought. In order to express thinking it has to be translated into words; words which belong to a specific language — English, for instance.

Being in the World

This does not seem to be an entirely accurate view of human functioning in general, or teachers' ways of functioning in particular. Usually we are fully engaged in the ongoing activity; be it hammering, speaking or teaching a class. Our acts, or our speech, is not preceded by internal events. We are in the world; we direct ourselves to people or things in our surroundings, to the real people, to the real things and not to their mental representations. We do withdraw from the ongoing flow of events — to contemplate the next step to take or the way in which we want to express something — occasionally. But this is the exception and not the rule. Taking their point of departure in Heidegger's philosophy, Winograd and Flores (1986) make a strong case for our ever-ongoing involvement with the places, situations, events, which we are in.

To the extent that thinking, in the above-mentioned sense, can be meaningfully referred to at all, it hardly represents the most interesting aspect of teachers' functioning. According to Carlgren and Lindblad (1991), the idea of the teacher as a rational decision-maker has been abandoned by now: teachers are seen as 'constructivists' and 'sense-makers', and teachers' actions are not seen so much as being caused by, but rather as reflecting, their thinking.

This transition from information processing to constructivist paradigm does not, however, make any difference in relation to the dualistic ontology, because the latter views the teacher as being locked into his or her own, more or less privately constructed, representational world.

The Idea of Awareness

I would like to advocate an alternative focus for our interest in teachers. In order to understand teachers better we have to understand the structure of their awareness. Such an alternative does not take subject and object as separate entities which we have to find a way of connecting. Instead, we take our point of departure in the relation between subject and object. The reason for doing so is that a subject without an object is inconceivable, just as an object without a subject is. What does that mean? Let us consider the first claim. Quite obviously we cannot imagine a human being (the subject) without a world in which he or she is situated. Nor can we imagine him or her without being in touch with his or her world. He or she is perceiving, and there cannot be perceiving without something being perceived; he or she is thinking and there cannot be any thinking without something thought about and so forth. This is the principle of intentionality put forward by Franz Brentano over 100 years ago. He tried to distinguish conceptually between psychological and non-psychological phenomena and came to the conclusion that all that is psychological points to something beyond itself:

> No hearing without something heard, no believing without something believed, no hoping without something hoped, no striving without something striven for, no joy without something we feel joyous about etc. (Brentano, quoted by Spiegelberg, 1982, p. 37)

One possible implication for research is that we may be interested in exploring the structure of intentionality; the person's directedness, what he or she is oriented towards and in which way.

Studies of Teachers' Awareness

Now I would like to draw on some investigations of teachers' awareness, carried out in our research group in Gothenburg, in order to point to an — in my understanding — highly significant aspect of their way of experiencing their professional world. Andersson and Lawenius (1983) aimed at exploring teachers' views of their work and of the context of their work in as much of an open-minded way as possible. First they carried out a pilot-study with thirty-six teachers from all levels in the Swedish compulsory school, (for Years 7–16), and then the main study with fifty-three teachers, (also from all levels: junior grades 1–3, intermediate grades 4–6 and upper grades 7–9). In the pilot-study, the teachers were

Table 2.1: Themes dealt with by teachers when commenting on their work

1 The aims and goals of teaching
   - what teaching is all about;
   - what teaching should be about;
   - the responsibility of the teacher.

2 Teachers teaching
   - Does the teacher make any differences?
   - What does it take to learn?

3 The frames of teaching
   - curriculum;
   - teaching aids;
   - colleagues;
   - parents.

4 School marks

5 Students with special needs
   - students lacking motivation;
   - students with learning difficulties.

6 The school of the future
   - what it is going to be like;
   - what it should be like.

Source: Andersson and Lawenius, 1983

asked during the course of individual interviews to read a short text from the National Board of Education, on the principles for the development of a new curriculum. To begin with, the teachers made comments on the text, to continue with whatever came to their mind concerning school, teaching, to be a teacher and so forth. The interviewer asked questions that sprung from the teachers' spontaneous comments, and dialogues lasting between forty-five minutes and two hours developed between the teachers and the interviewer. A content analysis of the interviews in the pilot-study yielded altogether six main domains with twenty-two subcategories. The six main domains that thus evolved and which can be seen as reflecting the teachers' more or less spontaneous way of structuring the scenario of their working life are shown in Table 2.1.

In the pilot-study, during about fifty hours of talking about teaching, the content of teaching was hardly ever mentioned. How the teachers deal with specific content, i.e., questions about methods of teaching, didactical questions in the content sense, or questions of how students deal with specific content and the way in which they should be able to deal with it, i.e., the questions of the goals of teaching in the most concrete sense, were not mentioned at all.

Let us assume that about 10,000 words are uttered during an hour's talk. Thirty-seven teachers talking for fifty hours altogether would then utter half a million words. This means that out of half a million words on teaching, uttered by teachers, not a single one concerned what may be seen as the heart of teaching: the teacher is doing something with some specific content in order to develop the students' capability of understanding that content, of knowing it, of using it in one way or in another.

In the main study, the interviews were semi-structured in accordance with the pattern of themes and questions that evolved on the collective level in the pilot-study, i.e., when the various problems dealt with by the individual teachers were pooled. Twenty-two themes, grouped into the above six categories, made up the point of departure for the individual interviews in the main study, in which fifty-three teachers from different levels in the compulsory school participated. This time each interview lasted for about one to one and a half hours. There was another sixty hours' teachers' talk about teaching or another 600,000 words uttered. And, again, no particular means-ends relations with the view of developing the mastery of some specific content were present. If we take the pilot-study and the main study together, we can conclude that out of over one million words uttered by teachers about teaching, not a single one was about the teachers' ways of dealing with some particular content in order to help students develop the mastery of that content.

Surprising as these results may seem, they appear less extraordinary in the context of other findings. Annerstedt (1991) carried out an interview study in which he, in individual interviews, asked fifteen student teachers (ST), fifteen teachers (T) and fifteen teacher educators (TE) (all in physical education) what their subject was all about.

A majority of the participants did not single out the skills and insights specific for physical education to be learned. They seemed to see physical education as instrumental to making the students feel good; being useful in relation to general educational goals or in relation to other subjects etc., as exemplified by the following excerpt from an interview with a student-teacher:

> **I:** . . . if you as a teacher would get the question at a parents' meeting 'Can you tell us briefly what you are doing in physical education, what is your subject all about?' how would you react . . .?
> **ST2:** It's difficult, but I believe . . . I think that physical education should be a form of recreation, the kids should have fun. This is what is most important . . . I don't think that there are certain things they have to do necessarily, that there are certain things they have to manage necessarily . . . (p. 184)

One third of the participants argued that the purpose of physical education is that the students should develop capabilities specific for physical education. They emphasized learning, the students should be expected to learn not only to jump higher or cast longer, but to realize *how* to do it, what has to be improved and why, as reflected in the following interview excerpt, for instance,

> **TE12:** . . . Well, if we then look at skills, I think if we give them opportunities for going on with . . . gymnastics and sports in a way so they experience that they manage, they will pick up quite a few skills which make . . . not only their self-confidence higher, because they feel that they are capable and they have mastered . . . but they also become physically better equipped, quite simply. There are no doubts, as I see it, that what one has succeeded with in school and become interested in and what one keeps doing . . . well the things we are enabling them to do in physical education, they will carry with them the physical prerequisites for, which they will, I believe, have use for. (p. 206)

The majority of those holding this view were — just as the participant quoted here — teacher-educators and, on the other hand, the majority of the teacher-educators expressed this view (nine out of fifteen).

Annerstedt (ibid.) also explored the way in which the participants viewed the competence of a teacher in physical education. The introduction to this theme in the interview was the question, 'I have a neighbour working at a bank who is active in a sports club in his leisure time (*idrottsledare*). He asked me one day, "What is it in actual fact you can do as a teacher in physical education which I cannot?" What would your answer have been?' This was followed up with several questions on the teachers' sense of professionalism. While a majority of the participants singled out capabilities such as being good at creating an enjoyable atmosphere in the class, managing the classroom or presenting something, ten of the forty-five participants emphasized the capability of bringing about learning of how to see what the students do wrong and what they should improve on in order to develop. This is often referred to as 'the experienced physical educator eye' (*det tränade idrottslärarögat*) and is a capability for analysis and reflection in the motor domain (p. 221). One of the teacher-educators expresses this in the following way:

> **I:** What do you think about teaching methods in relation to our professionalism? Is it important?
>
> **TE7:** Yes, I believe it is. The likelihood is great for you as a professional being good, better. You ought to be, because not only have you the physiological bit, but also the biomechanic bit. You have the capability of analysing the full-blown movement in order to find out all its possible aspects. It is a capability that an amateur hardly could have, in any case they don't have any educational prerequisites for this capability. And . . . if you can't analyse the full-blown movement well, you don't have a chance to develop a good method for developing it. You can, of course, find in the literature a method which some expert has written down, but then you are entirely bound to that person's method. It's not your method, but it is someone who is good at it, who is professional who has developed the method and you pick it up and buy it. But in order to develop a method yourself you have to be professional. This is a good example of, I believe, that one who is professional ought to be better.

Again the majority of those expressing this view are teacher-educators. Crossing the two dimensions mentioned, Annerstedt finds that only five out of forty-five participants (i.e., $^1/_9$) see the main purpose of physical education is to develop specific insights, knowledge and skills in the students *and* see the most important aspect of the competence of the teachers as being capable of bringing about such learning. From the tables we can conclude that at least four of these five participants are teacher-educators.

Johansson (1992) studied how lecturers in preschool education view their own subject. One of the themes he was interested in was how the lecturers felt about the aims of the subject in the sense of the competence they intended to develop in the student-teachers for dealing with children in the preschool. Few, if any, explicit statements were made on this issue. Johansson therefore searched

Table 2.2:   Relationship between conceptions of aim and origin of pre-school methods

Origin of subject	Examples of aims			
	No examples	Support development	Skills/ knowledge	Total
Preschool	22	1	—	23
Child psychology	3	3	—	6
Subject content	—	—	10	10
Early childhood education	—	—	1	1
Total	25	4	11	40

Source: Johansson, 1992, p. 268

through all the interviews for examples of something a preschool teacher was trying to teach or develop in children. Only in fifteen cases of forty-two were examples of this kind found. In several interviews, the children were not mentioned very much at all. The examples were of two kinds: giving support for the children's spontaneous *development* on the one hand, and actively developing their *understanding* of the world around them and their *skills* for dealing with it, on the other hand. This second kind of example can be illustrated by the following interview excerpt in which a lecturer is telling about an episode illuminating how the idea of measurement can be developed in children,

> But then she said (the teacher in 'nature orientation'): 'Well, then you can go out and measure how deep the snow is. And then you make a note, that this and this day the snow was 50 cm deep'. And then I felt, you can't do this with pre-school children. But then it should be something like this: 'Well, how do we do it with 3-year-olds?' And how do we do it with 5-year-olds? Well, for a 3-year old it boils down to looking, 'There is so much snow that it's higher than your shoes'. Or, 'There is so much snow that it goes up to your bottom'. While an 8-year-old can take a stick, put it down and we make a mark on the stick. 'So much snow did we have'. While for a 6-year-old, that's the question. You have still to use the stick, I believe . . . (p. 265)

Another question Johansson was studying was what the lecturers saw as the ground for their subject. Most of them referred to the preschool itself, others pointed to developmental psychology, others again saw their main task as teaching the students how to make use of other subjects within preschool teacher education such as mother-tongue, music, art, science, etc. One lecturer took her point of departure in research in early childhood education. The pattern that evolved when crossing the two dimensions was clear enough.

Partly using the empirically found correlation between the views of the aim of the subject implied and views of the ground of the subject expressed, and partly the lecturers' description of their own professional development, Johansson argued that there is a relation between the awareness of educational goals and the means through which they possibly can be reached, on the one hand, and the transcending of one's experiences as a preschool teacher, on the other hand.

In the three studies mentioned here, it was found, by using individual interviews, that student-teachers, teachers and teacher-educators are, to a very limited extent, focusing on what children are supposed to learn, what specific capabilities, if any, one would like to develop in them. Hence there were very few comments on means-ends relations, i.e., on the way different methods or technical solutions are used to achieve certain particular aims. Now does this suggest that teachers, (including student-teachers and teacher-educators) are not driven by the aim that the children should develop certain specific capabilities, (skills, knowledge, understanding)? Although the above results would suggest such a conclusion, we can entertain the alternative hypothesis that the specific learning goals and ways in which they are reached are self-evident; they are taken for granted and therefore not talked about. Partly in order to answer this question, Alexandersson (1994) carried out a very detailed investigation of the structure of teachers' awareness while teaching.

Twelve teachers, (working in grades 4–6) participated in the study. Each teacher and their class was video-taped during one working period, (approximately one hour). The subjects taught during these sessions varied widely. The video-tape was played back after each session and the teacher was asked to stop it every time when there was something worthwhile to comment on in relation to the questions what they were doing, what was happening and why they had chosen to work in the way they did. These reviews were followed up with individual in-depth interviews concerning questions such as why they had chosen to stop the tape at particular points, what was the main aim of the working session as a whole and how they would define their own working methods. There were 581 accounts (48,4 on the average) identified, each one expressing the directedness of the teacher's intentionality. Alexandersson found three qualitatively different ways of relating to teaching in all these cases. The structure of teachers' awareness differed insofar they were primarily oriented towards:

1 ongoing activities: 'The kids are talking, I am looking at them.'
2 aims of general nature: 'Well, I want to wake them up. What I mean with my words, here, is that we shall think about it: what is it like in actual fact.' Then I won't ever use my own body as a scene for afterthought.
3 the specific content to be learned about: 'I go there to make sure that everyone knows what it is, if that is the angle in the triangle. It may well be that they believe that the whole thing is angle for them . . .'

For seven of the teachers there was one or no accounts falling in the third category (i.e., focusing on the pupils' learning of specific content). In ten cases it was the least frequent category, only in one case was it the most frequent one. The twelve teachers in Alexandersson's study were experienced, well-qualified teachers, several of them had been involved in in-service training, one of them (the one whose most frequent incidents were content related, i.e., fell in the third category, was by the time of the investigation, conducting studies at the master's level in education.

The Erosion of Content

The general picture that the investigation yields is that learning goals in terms of the pupils' mastering of some specific content did not appear as a major driving force of the teachers' acts, at least not as reflected by the research approach adopted.

The impression we get from the studies referred to here is that the teachers participating in those were rarely oriented toward specific learning aims and hence were rarely focusing on means-ends relations. This lack of emphasis on learning may seem strange. Are not schools about learning after all? As a matter of fact, I have been focusing on three aspects of the results yielded by the studies discussed above. One is exactly the relative overall lack of emphasis on learning and on the content of learning just mentioned — this is reflected in all four studies, the second aspect appears in Annerstedt's study whereby teacher-educators seem to focus on goals specific for learning the subject to a greater extent than teachers and student-teachers do. The third aspect is reflected in Johansson's study whereby some teacher-educators focus on specific learning goals; others do not.

The discussion here is of a very general kind; for the sake of argument and, somewhat imprecisely, we will here disregard the obvious differences between the groups participating in the four investigations.

Let us consider the first of these three issues. In the history of education, child versus content constitutes a fundamental dimension of variation. From time to time one pole or the other has been emphasized, (see, for instance, Marton, 1980). Also at one specific point in time there is often a variation between different actors along this dimension. The so-called 'black papers' in Britain and the 'knowledge movement' in Sweden are surely to be considered as reactions against what has been seen as too much child-centredness in the curriculum and school practices and too little emphasis on content. And, indeed, we can easily see a number of potential factors that may have contributed to the *erosion of content* in schools. The fairly widespread critical scrutinization of the western capitalist society and its institutions, reaching a peak in 1968 and the years thereafter implied, among other things, a questioning of the societal function of the school. The taken-for-granted assumption that schools are for creating conditions for children to acquire knowledge and skills was seriously questioned. The primary function of schools is — the critics argued — that through the sorting, disciplining and socializing mechanism that schools reproduce the class structure of the capitalist society. Furthermore, there have been — and there are — pedagogically grounded arguments against teacher-centred didactic models of teaching. The learners' own activities are stressed. Focus on relevance; discovery-learning; problem-based learning; the view of the learners as the creators of their own knowledge advocated by the more and more influential constructivist theory; the argument for general thinking and learning skills against the background of the exponential growth of knowledge — all this might have contributed to the lessening of the likelihood of teachers being primarily oriented toward the teaching of specific contents, by using specific methods contemplated in advance.

Stevenson (1992) recently summarized a series of studies in which American children in grade 1 and grade 5 were compared with children in Japan, Taiwan and China with regard to learning outcomes in mathematics, (and in some other subjects as well). In accordance with another recent study carried out by Geary, Fan and Bow-Thomas (1992) Chinese children (just as Japanese and Taiwanese children) are by far superior to their American peers in grade 1. By grade 5 the difference is even more pronounced: the best school out of twenty in Chicago was found to be on the same level as the weakest one out of eleven schools in Beijing. As a possible explanation — or at least as a factor that can possibly contribute to an explanation — of this somewhat shocking difference between children from the greatest economic power in the world on the one hand, and children from a developing country on the other hand, Stevenson points to the lack of emphasis on learning (on what is learned and how it is learned) among American teachers. They are focusing on what the children need and not on what the children need to learn. In China, on the other hand, teachers use only 60 per cent of their working time for teaching. The main part of the rest of their time is used for discussions among the teachers about the children's difficulties with the content of teaching (and learning) and about the ways in which these difficulties could be possibly handled. Under such circumstances, the content as dealt with by children is much more focused and the teachers have a more central role.

If a primary orientation toward students and the subsequent neglect of the content is one pole of the relevant dimension of variation, the other pole is a primary orientation toward content and a neglect of students. Although such orientation can easily be found, for instance, among university teachers, (see Fensham and Marton, 1991) or academics who are not teachers (see Sundqvist, 1993), this is hardly what the Chinese teachers, referred to above, represent. After all, what they are focusing on — according to Stevenson — is not the content as such, but the content as dealt with by the students, i.e., their difficulties with it, and the content as dealt with by the teachers, with the aim of helping the students overcome their difficulties. Nor were the participants pointing to content, in the investigations referred to above, talking about content in itself. They were discussing or illustrating goals of learning and goals of teaching in a specific sense. Frequently, it was done in relation to more general educational goals. Content in these cases has to be understood as the kind of knowledge, skills and insights which the teachers aim at developing. Often this was linked to the way in which the teacher would try to contribute towards the students developing the knowledge, skills and insights deemed necessary.

In actual fact, one could argue that accepting the primacy of general goals such as learning to learn; becoming good at solving problems etc., in no way contradicts — but rather presupposes — a focus on the learner and understanding specific content.

There are arguments such as, 'What is really important is learning how to learn', or, 'What schools should aim for is to develop the students' general thinking and reasoning skills, empowering them to critically examine claims, propositions, conclusions', or, 'What employers are looking for is people who are good at dealing with novel problems in creative ways, people with powerful analytic skills and flexible frames of mind.' These arguments may seem convincing. Of course we want our students to be good in as a general sense as possible and we want to prepare them for all kind of situations which we could not possibly envisage, much less specify in advance, at the time when the teaching is taking place. If we accept claims like the above, and, in fact, it seems pretty difficult to do otherwise, does this imply that content is of a peripheral, secondary interest only?

The point I am driving at is that the tentative implication, just mentioned, would be completely wrong. Drawing on results from research on student-learning as well as on Nobel laureates' descriptions of scientific intuition (Marton, Fensham and Chaiklin, in press) we could characterize 'good learning' (i.e., learning that is likely to yield a better understanding of the phenomenon) roughly as follows.

Good Learning

Characteristics of 'good learning' is a clear focus on the phenomenon (the content) to be learned about (this is basically the idea of the 'deep approach'), an openness to the basic structure of the problem dealt with (see Ahlberg, 1992, on children's approaches to solving mathematical problems), delimiting the phenomenon and relating it to its context (or to various contexts), delimiting its parts and relating them to each other in as a holistic a way as possible, letting aspects of the phenomenon vary in experience, i.e., playing around with various ways of looking at the phenomenon, adopting different perspectives to it, following up lines of thought about it (see Marton, Asplund-Carlsson and Halász, 1992 on reflective variation and differences in understanding). Furthermore, learning in a deep sense — as revealed, for instance, by great scientific achievements — seems to originate in extensive and varied experience of the phenomenon. 'Good learning' in students, as well as in scientists, seems to spring from a combination of a highly-focused attention on the phenomenon in question and a sensitivity and openness towards it — a kind of readiness to seize 'the truth of the situation' (see Wertheimer, 1945). The somewhat paradoxical fact is that the most general and most powerful learning and thinking capability is to take the phenomenon studied, the situation dealt with, very seriously without locking yourself into a preconceived pattern of acting. The acting should originate instead from the sensitive experience of the phenomenon. Ideally, there is oneness between subject and object, between learner and learned (see Laurillard *et al.*, 1991, about how such 'oneness' can possibly be brought about in a computer-simulated environment).

The most general learning and thinking capability is thus the capability of experiencing fully, in as focussed and as open a way as possible, every phenomenon and every situation in question. Now, this capability can hardly be developed without giving the content of learning the most central role. In actual fact, the most generalisable capability is that of being able to as fully as possible immerse oneself in the specific phenomenon being dealt with. Such a potentially generalised frame of mind can only be developed by focusing on the particulars — even if there is the aim of developing what is general. Teaching thus always has to take its point of departure in its content, but the way of dealing with this content may have important implications on whether or not the development of more general capabilities (such as, for instance, being able to focus on the specific content) will be facilitated (support for this is provided, for instance, by Martin and Ramsden, 1987, and Pramling, 1990). As the philosopher, Ernst Cassirer (1953) declared:

> It is, as it were, the fundamental principle of cognition that the universal could be perceived only in the particular, while the particular can be thought only in reference to the universal. (Cassirer, 1953, p. 86)

Although it has not been a target of detailed scrutinization, I would like to argue that the participants in the above-mentioned investigations, who have been focusing on goals of learning and teaching, did it very much in this sense. Although they were referring to some specific content, they were doing so in terms of goals, of learning and teaching, in terms of capabilities that the students were supposed to develop. These specific goals were frequently seen in relation to more general goals, and also in relation to ways in which the teacher could possibly contribute to bringing about these goals. Dealing with goals of learning in a specific sense implies thus in these cases — explicitly or implicitly — dealing with relations. Relations between content and learner, relations between specific goals and general goals, relations between goals and means.

Analytic Awareness

To the extent it is the case, it throws light on the systematic differences between the participants in the four studies dealt with in relation to whether or not they focus on specific goals for learning (i.e., on specific content). Concerning the second and third aspects of the studies mentioned above (Annerstedt, ibid.) found in his study that teacher-educators, as compared with teachers and students, more frequently focused on specific learning-goals. Johansson (ibid.) whose investigation deals with teacher-educators (lecturers in preschool methods) argues that being able to discuss specific goals of learning in relation to general goals and/or in relation to methods for reaching those goals, is related to whether or not the lecturer has transcended his or her own personal experience of the preschool as his or her knowledge base. Johansson claims that the transition from the context of preschool to the context of preschool education drives the lecturers toward such a transition — to teach people how to work in the preschool is different from actually working in the preschool. One's own personal experiences do not suffice when it comes to preparing students for a wide range of future situations. There is thus a need to analytically discern comparatively abstract, generative aspects of concrete situations and relate them to each other. This is the way in which means-ends relations or relationships between what is specific and what is general, are established. As far as the differences between the teacher-educators are concerned, the above takes place, according to Johansson, when the lecturer finds a handle or frame of reference outside the concrete situation. It may be disciplinary knowledge, e.g., in psychology or in a content domain; it may be research in preschool education. Occasionally, one can transcend one's personal experience by making the pool of collective knowledge explicit. Possibly it is this function that is served by the Chinese teachers' discussions with each other about the students' difficulties with certain content and about ways of dealing with those difficulties. This transcendence of one's taken-for-granted experiential world as a teacher means the ascent of a kind of analytic awareness: a capability of abstracting aspects of concrete situations and seeing these aspects of concrete situations in relation to each other. It seems that it is exactly this analytic awareness, or rather the lack of it, that Lortie (1975) is talking about in his classical study of the culture of teaching. The point he is making is that teachers lack a shared technical culture; they lack an explicit and generalizable awareness of the relationships between means and ends in teaching.

The concept of 'analytic awareness' can be related to Whelan's work in clinical-problem solving. He identified three qualitatively different strategies used by medical students in clinical-problem solving. One, called 'exclusion', involved the selection of a clinical feature followed by a selection of diagnosis by association. A checklist of clinical features was then generated and a diagnosis was ruled out if any of the clinical features were missing (false negatives would usually be ignored). The second strategy, called 'pattern matching', involved the selection of a diagnosis which was associated with one or several clinical features. Additional information was not taken into consideration and alternative diagnoses were not advanced. Students using the third — and least frequent — strategy called 'diagnostic interpretation', moved from clinical features to diagnosis via pathophysiological explanations. They generated hypothesis — or conjectures — and tested them moving from clinical features to diagnosis and vice versa. Two cases were used in Whelan's investigation. In the first one, five medical students out of forty used the strategy 'diagnostic integration', in the second case four out of forty-three.

The reason for bringing in Whelan's investigation is that it — in my understanding — also deals with analytic awareness. The students using the strategy 'diagnostic interpretation' are actually discerning relevant aspects in the situation and relating them to each other in functional terms. The relations are, in this case, between clinical features and physiopathological patterns underlying the illness diagnosed. In the case of teachers, relations reflecting a reasonably high degree of analytic awareness are between the intended goals, and the way in which the students are expected to understand a particular content, on the one hand, and the means by which those goals can be reached, on the other hand. The similarity between the two cases should be seen in terms of the nature of the relationships employed. These are of an internal, functional kind, based on knowledge of how understanding is constituted in relation to a particular content in one case, and on knowledge of how the human body functions in a particular respect, in the other case. Such knowledge is theoretical knowledge in the sense that it is generalizable and generative, it is, or it can be, decontextualized and made explicit. Analytic awareness is thus a function of theoretical knowledge, the availability of theoretical knowledge. Maybe this is exactly why a transcendence of one's own personal experiences is a necessary condition for the development of analytic awareness, just as Johansson (ibid.) claims.

Forms of Analytic Awareness

Now, analytic awareness is not necessarily a homogenous entity, even in relation to a particular content. Teachers who are distinctively oriented towards the students mastering — or understanding — a particular content in a particular way may still differ widely on what this understanding should look like, (and hence also in relation to how this understanding should be achieved). First, the very content can be understood differently and hence taught differently by different teachers. Tullberg (1993) gives a very convincing illustration of the radically different ways in which chemistry teachers in secondary school, and even at university level, understand the mole in chemistry and how these differences are reflected in their teaching. Second, the very nature of the subject can be understood differently by different teachers. Kate Patrick (1992) shows how physics takes on different meanings for different teachers; they establish different curricula at the classroom level and teach accordingly. They may see physics being primarily about developing the students' understanding of the physical world around them, about enculturating the students into the scientific practices of physics — theory, observation, experiment etc., or about making the students capable of handling mathematical relationships and manipulating variables. She demonstrates how differences in the way in which physics is conceptualized are reflected in the way a particular content — in her case harmonic motion — is taught. Furthermore, there may be differences on an even more general level. Teachers do have different views of what teaching is all about and again these differences are frequently reflected on the level of the teaching of the specific content (see Prosser and Trigwell, in press).

There are thus various aspects of teaching, of aims of teaching, of the particular content, in relation to which teachers differ significantly. These aspects are different layers of the teachers' awareness, which are simultaneously present. In the concrete way of teaching a concrete content, all the increasingly general aspects of the teachers' awareness, (and surely not of their long-term memory) are inherent. Everything is there — admittedly not always clearly; not always explicitly — in every moment of the very teaching of the very content. Moreover, the meaning of what is taught is intersubjectively constituted by the teacher and by the students (although somewhat differing aspects may come to the fore in the individual awarenesses). The taught content reflects the teachers' understanding, but to an increasing extent the students' understanding as well. Tullberg (1993), Patrick (1992) for instance, demonstrate how the teachers' differing understandings on various levels of generality are reflected in their students' understandings. The content of teaching and learning is there, in this social space of the classroom, and it is there in the world to which the phenomenon belongs, it is shared, it is an object of awareness — or more correctly of awarenesses. And surely it is not a mentalistic thought object residing inside the solitary head of the solitary teacher.

Note

1   This chapter was presented for the first time as an invited address at the 6th Conference of the International Study Association on Teacher Thinking, August 10–15 1993, Gothenburg, Sweden. It was written with the financial support of the Swedish Council for Research in the humanities and social sciences, while I was a visiting research fellow at the Educational Research and Development Unit of the Royal Melbourne Institute of Technology.

References

AHLBERG, A. (1992) *Att möta matematiska problem*, Göteborg, Acta Universitatis Gothoburgensis. (Meeting mathematical problems)

ALEXANDERSSON, M. (1994) *Metod och medvetande*, Göteborg, Acta Universitatis Gothoburgensis. (Method and consciousness)

ANDERSSON, E. and LAWENIUS, M. (1983) *Lärares uppfattning av undervisning*, Göteborg, Acta Universitatis Gothoburgensis. (Teachers' conceptions of teaching)

ANNERSTEDT, C. (1991) *Idrottslärarna och idrottssämnet*, Göteborg, Acta Universitatis Gothoburgensis. (Physical education and teachers in physical education)

MARTON, F., BEATY, E. and DALL'ALBA, G. (1993) 'Conceptions of learning', *International Journal of Educational Research*, 19, pp. 277–300.

CARLGREN, I. and LINDBLAD, S. (1991) 'On teachers' practical reasoning and professional knowledge: Considering conceptions of context in teachers' thinking', *Journal of Curriculum Studies*, 7, pp. 507–16.

CASSIRER, E. (1953) *The Philosophy of Symbolic Forms* (Volume 1: Language) New Heaven, Yale University Press.

CLARK, C.M. and PETERSON, P.P. (1986) 'Teachers' thought processes', in WITTROCK, M.C. (Ed) *Handbook of Research on Teaching* (3rd edition), New York, MacMillan.

FENSHAM, P. and MARTON, F. (1991) 'High-school teachers' and university chemists' differing conceptualisations of the personal activity in constituting knowledge in chemistry,' *Department of Education and Educational Research,* University of Göteborg, no. 1.

GEARY, D.C., FAN, F. and BOW-THOMAS, C.C. (1992) 'Numerical cognition: Loci of ability differences comparing children from China and the United States,' *Psychological Science,* 3, pp. 180–5.

JOHANSSON, J.-E. (1992) *Metodikämnet i förskolärarutbildningen,* Göteborg, Acta Universitatis Gothoburgensis. (Pre-school methods in pre-school education)

LAURILLARD, D., LINDSTRÖM, B., MARTON, F. and OTTOSSON, T. (1991) 'The computer as a tool for developing intuitive and conceptual understanding,' *Department of Education and Educational Research,* University of Göteborg, no. 3.

LORTIE, D. (1975) *School Teacher. A Sociological Study,* Chicago, University of Chicago Press.

MARTIN, E. and RAMSDEN, P. (1987) 'Learning skills, or skill in learning', in RICHARDSSON, I.T.E., EYSENCK, M.W. and PIPER, D.W. (Eds) *Student Learning,* Milton Keynes, Open University Press.

MARTON, F. (1980) 'Innehållsrelaterad pedagogisk forskning — en programförklaring', *i Innehållsrelaterad pedagogisk forskning,* Stockholm, Skolöverstyrelsen. (Content-related educational research — a manifesto)

MARTON, F., ASPLUND-CARLSSON, M. and HALÁSZ, L. (1992) 'Differences in understanding and the use of reflective variation in reading', *British Journal of Educational Psychology,* 2, pp. 1–16.

McCABE, V. (1982) 'The direct perception of universals: A theory of knowledge acquisition', *Synthese,* 52, pp. 495–513.

PATRICK, K. (1992) 'Teachers and curriculum at year 12: Constructing an object of study', Paper presented at the 1992 joint conference of the Australian Association for Research in Education and the New Zealand Association for Research in Education, 22–26 November, Deaking University, Geelong, Victoria.

PRAMLING, I. (1990) *Learning to Learn,* New York, Springer Verlag.

PROSSER, M., TRIGWELL, K. and TAYLOR, P. (in press) 'A phenomenographic study of academics conceptions of science learning and teaching', *Learning and Instruction.*

SPIEGELBERG, M. (1982) *The Phenomenological Movement,* The Hague, Martinus Nijhoff.

STEVENSON, H.W. (1992) 'Learning from Asian schools,' *Scientific American,* 267, 6, pp. 32–8.

SUNDQVIST, R. (1993) *Didaktiskt tänkande: En studie om uppfattningar av undervisning,* Vasa, Finland, Åbo Akademi.

TULLBERG, A. (1993) 'Student's conceptions of 1 Mole and Educators conception of how they teach "the Mole"', *International Journal of Science Education,* 16, pp. 145–56.

WERTHEIMER, M. (1945) *Productive Thinking,* New York, Harper and Row.

WHELAN, G. (1988) 'Improving medical students' clinical problem solving', in RAMSDEN, P. (Ed) *Improving learning: New perspectives,* London, Kogan Page, pp. 199–214.

WINOGRAD, T. and FLORES, F. (1986) *Understanding Cognition and Computers,* Norwood, NJ, Ablex.

Chapter 3

Teachers as Collaborative Thinkers: Activity-theoretical Study of an Innovative Teacher Team[1]

Yrjö Engeström

Abstract

An individualist and Cartesian bias is noted in studies of teacher thinking. A more collaborative approach, based on cultural-historical activity theory, is suggested and elaborated. On this view, thinking is seen as embedded in practical collective activity, thus essentially as interactive, dialogic and argumentative. The activity-theoretical framework is applied in a study of a teacher team. The planning of a curriculum unit by the team is analyzed as a cycle of collaborative thinking. The planning discourse was characterized by a lack of pauses and conventional turn-taking, by a prevalence of conditional statements and strings, and by continuous circling back and repetition of issues. This open-ended, spiral-like mode of planning may be characterized as 'imagining together'. It was connected to the teacher team's rejection of pre-packaged materials and its almost exclusive reliance on oral means of thinking.

Introduction

After reading through a number of prominent reviews and overviews of research on teacher thinking from recent years (Clark, 1986; Clark and Peterson, 1986; Clark and Yinger, 1987; Calderhead, 1987; Elbaz, 1990), I had to conclude that in spite of the diversification of approaches used in the field, something quite crucial was missing. This missing something may be detected by glancing at a sample of key quotes from the reviews.

> *The* maturing professional *teacher* is one who has taken some steps toward making explicit his or her implicit theories and beliefs about learners, curriculum, subject matter, and the teacher's role. (Clark and Peterson, 1986, p. 292, my emphasis)

> Just as a doctor possesses formal knowledge of physiology and pathology, together with knowledge acquired from experience about patient behaviour (. . .), *the teacher* has acquired knowledge about the curriculum,

teaching methods, subject matter, and child behaviour together with a wealth of other particular information resulting from the experience of working with children in numerous contexts and with different materials. (Calderhead, 1987, p. 1, my emphasis)

One teacher's sense of her 'classroom as home', another teacher's view of her subject matter sometimes as a barrier 'to hide behind', other times as 'a window on what students are thinking', both provide us with immediate contact with *the teacher's* experience precisely as she sees fit to express it. (Elbaz, 1990, p. 21, my emphasis)

Regardless of the differences in their approaches, there is a common denominator in these quotes. All of them speak of the teacher as an individual thinker and actor. The idea of teachers as collaborative thinkers and actors is missing. I would call this the individualist and Cartesian bias in research on teacher thinking. I emphasize the word bias. I do not want to imply that research on teacher thinking is somehow systematically and deliberately based on Cartesian and individualist doctrines. Rather, I see it implicitly and partially reproducing certain crucial features of these doctrines (on Cartesian conceptions of cognition, see Markova, 1982).

As a possible explanation to the bias, one might point out the traditional image of the teacher as a lonely and autonomous practitioner in his or her self-contained classroom (e.g., Lortie, 1975; Hargreaves, 1993). Obviously individualist and Cartesian notions of thinking have been dominant in psychology and cognitive science for a long time. Research on teacher thinking is no exception. However, along with the dominant notions, important alternative ones exist. What surprised me was the absence of those alternatives in the reviews. In this chapter, I will try to elaborate an alternative approach that makes a case for studying teacher thinking as collaborative, distributed cognition and mediated action.

Foundations for an Alternative

The individualist and Cartesian bias is manifested in our common tendency to view thinking above all as a private, internal process. In psychology, it was Vygotsky who initiated the still ongoing revolution in this regard, maintaining that internal, private thought is derivative of external, practical and interindividual action (Vygotsky, 1978). On this view, thinking is no more seen as an autonomous process. Attention is called to the socially organized, historically evolving activities in which thinking is embedded. As V.V. Davydov (1991, p. 33) put it, thinking and other traditional cognitive processes 'are no more than specific components of general activity structure that help the realization of its other components'.

Being originally and primarily embedded in collective activities, thinking itself has an interactive, that is, dialogic and argumentative, character. Much due to the discovery of Mikhail Bakhtin's legacy (e.g., Bakhtin, 1982), and of the late works of Ludwig Wittgenstein (1953), many students of human cognition are today working toward a dialogic and discursive view of the mind (e.g., Engeström, 1992; Harré and Gillett, 1994; Markova and Foppa, 1990; Sampson, 1993; Wertsch, 1991). Billig crystallizes the thrust of this movement.

If witcraft is a basic form of thought, then we can expect private thinking to be modelled upon public argument. In consequence, it should possess a dialogic, rather than monologic, character. Thought, then, would not be seen as a process which is inevitably locked within the recesses of the brain and which is only dimly reflected in our words. Instead, the structure of the way we argue reveals the structure of our thoughts. To put the matter in a paradox, which should not be interpreted too literally: humans do not converse because they have inner thoughts to express, but they have thoughts because they are able to converse. (Billig, 1987, p. 111)

In today's cognitive science, a parallel movement is going on under the rubric of distributed or shared cognition (see Galegher, Kraut and Egido, 1990; Hutchins, in press; Resnick, Levine and Teasley, 1991; Salomon, 1993). Much of its motivation stems from a rather dramatic increase in demand for collaboration in core intellectual work processes such as research, design and management, brought about by both the increased complexity of tasks and the rapid development of computer networking capacities.

One of the most persistent methodological difficulties of studying thinking has to do with access to online data from thought processes. When thinking is defined as a private, individual phenomenon, only indirect data is accessible. Thinking embedded in collaborative practical activity must to a significant degree take the form of talk, gesture, use of artifacts, or some other publicly accessible mediational instrumentality; otherwise mutual formation of ideas would be rendered impossible. Collaborative thinking opens up access to direct data on thought processes.

Distributed Cognition in Activity Systems

I will analyse teacher thinking within the framework of cultural-historical activity theory (see Leont'ev, 1978; 1981; Wertsch, 1981; Engeström, 1987; 1990). In line with the basic tenets outlined above, this framework sees thinking as embedded in object-oriented and artifact-mediated collective activities which evolve and change over time. Teaching is a work activity undergoing historical transformation. The emergence of new forms of organizing teaching work, such as teacher teams, may radically change the nature of teacher thinking (Hargreaves, 1994).

Activity is here seen as a collective, systemic formation that has a complex mediational structure. Activities are not short-lived events or actions that have a temporally clear-cut beginning and end. They are systems that *produce* events and actions and evolve over lengthy periods of socio-historical time. I use the schematic diagram of Figure 3.1 to represent the mediational structure of an activity system.

The model reveals the decisive feature of multiple mediations in activity. The subject and the object, or the actor and the environment, are mediated by instruments, including symbols and representations of various kinds. The less visible social mediators of activity — rules, community, and division of labour — are depicted at the bottom of the model. Between the components of the system, there are continuous transformations. The activity system incessantly reconstructs itself.

Figure 3.1: The mediational structure of an activity system

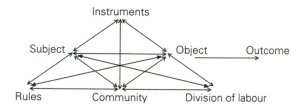

Source: Engeström, 1987, p. 78

Figure 3.2: A standard image of teaching depicted as an activity system

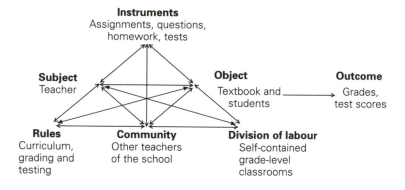

An activity system contains a variety of different viewpoints or 'voices', as well as layers of historically accumulated artifacts, rules and patterns of division of labour. This multivoiced and multilayered nature of activity systems is both a resource for collective achievement and a source of compartmentalization and conflict. A conceptual model of the activity system is particularly useful when one wants to make sense of systemic factors behind seemingly individual and accidental disturbances, deviations and innovations occurring in the daily practice of workplaces.

Thinking is not only distributed socially between participants of a collective, and instrumentally between humans and their artifacts. It is also distributed temporally, in time (Cole and Engeström, 1993). To understand processes of thinking embedded in activities, a longitudinal approach is needed. In work activities such as teaching, thinking, planning and problem-solving often proceed through a sequence of steps between which there may be considerably long periods of time.

In Figure 3.2, a standard image of teaching is depicted as an activity system. While ideal-typical and simplified, the model serves as point of contrast with which the intended practice of the teacher team to be discussed in this chapter may be compared.

The crucial feature of any activity is its object (Leont'ev, 1978). On the standard image, the object of teaching consists of the textbook on the one hand, and of the students on the other hand. The teacher's job is to make these two objects merge, that is, to make the students internalize the textbook so as to be able to produce decent grades and test scores as measures of successful internalization. In order to achieve the expected outcomes, the teacher uses assignments, questions, homework, and tests as instruments. All this happens within the relatively closed community of the school, where a curriculum given from above functions as the supreme rule, enforced by procedures for grading and testing. There is a compartmentalized division of labour, requiring the teachers to work in their self-contained grade-level classrooms. This image of teaching fits comfortably with Cartesian notions of thinking and expertise.

While robust and persistent, this standard image of teaching activity is challenged on multiple fronts. School life is becoming increasingly complex and interconnected. In a study of the teachers of two middle schools, Schwab and her colleagues found that during a work day, the teachers of one school interacted with an average of twenty-five individuals, the teachers of the other school with an average of twenty-nine individuals, not including interactions with students. The authors point out that 'in terms of the sheer numbers of individuals they interact with . . . teachers are as "busy" as senior business executives'. (Schwab *et al.*, 1992, p. 245).

One of the more serious challenges to the standard image of teaching is the introduction of multigrade teacher teams aimed at school-based construction of curricula. In the following, I will bring together two previously separate strands of research and theorizing about teaching: teacher thinking and teacher teamwork. In the case analysed in this chapter, these two meet and converge in joint planning conducted by a team of teachers aiming at the creation and implementation of an integrated global-education curriculum for grades K through 6 in a public primary school in southern California.

The Global-education Team

From the late 1980s, a new wave of teacher teams has emerged (e.g., Maeroff, 1993). This wave is an integral part of attempts at overall restructuring of schools to increase productivity and quality, largely in the spirit of re-engineering taking place in the corporate world (e.g., Hammer and Champy, 1993). As Maeroff (1993, p. 19) puts it, the new teams are supposed 'to deal not only with specific educational problems but also with the dynamics of the change process itself'. Very little research exists as yet on the cognitive and communicative dynamics of these new teacher teams.

The teacher team analysed here was a vertically integrated one, consisting of five teachers responsible for five classrooms covering grades K through 6. The team was initiated and formed by the teachers themselves, with backing from the principal and a group of parents. The team had abandoned regular textbooks; it aimed at creating a new curriculum integrated around the idea of global education. This was a team with a mission and a lot of teacher agency, as Paris (1993) would call it.

The global-education team was preceded by some ten years of an alternative-education programme in the same school. The two teachers of the alternative programme were instrumental in launching the global-education programme in the fall of 1992, after nearly a year of discussion and preparation. The idea of a

Figure 3.3: *Intended structure of the global-education team's activity*

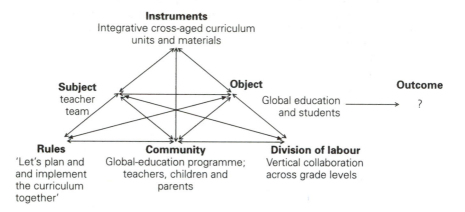

team was an integral part of the new programme from the beginning. The global-education programme occupied a hexagonal building of its own on the school campus. We began to observe and record the team meetings in October 1992.

On the basis of interviews we conducted with the teachers of the team, the structure of the global-education team's activity system as intended by the team members may be sketched with the help of Figure 3.3. I emphasize the word 'intended'; Figure 3.3 is not yet a picture based on observations of the actual practice of the team.

The teachers wanted to create a new kind of educational environment and experience, called global education. In the United States, global education has become a broad movement in recent years, and there is a rapidly growing literature on it (e.g., Kobus, 1983; Tye, 1990; Tye and Tye, 1992). The prominence of the movement is reflected in the fact that the foreword to the recent book by Barbara and Kenneth Tye (1992) was written by Bill Clinton, then the governor of Arkansas.

In spite of this prominence and literature, the teachers we studied did not want to adopt or emulate any of the available programmes. In their interviews, they insisted on the local hands-on creation of their own programme. They made a point of not having come to the idea through literature or courses but through their own, varied practical experiences and personal beliefs. They shared a belief in global responsibility and multiculturalism. But they did not offer prepared definitions of what they were trying to do.

In activity-theoretical terms, the object of the team's activity — the environment and experience of global education — was deliberately fuzzy and emergent. Object here is not to be understood narrowly as predetermined, consciously fixed goal or objective. As Leont'ev (1978, p. 78) pointed out, 'the realized activity is richer and truer than the consciousness that precedes it'. Object defines the horizon of possible actions; it embodies the motive and meaning of the ongoing collective activity. The teachers saw textbooks as restrictive objects; they replaced them with an emergent curriculum to be collaboratively created step by step, as they progressed through the school year. The spirit of such an endeavour was nicely captured by John Dewey.

The plan, in other words, is a cooperative enterprise, not a dictation. The teacher's suggestion is not a mold for a cast-iron result but is a starting point to be developed into a plan through contributions from the experience of all engaged in the learning process (. . .) The essential point is that the purpose grow and take shape through the process of social intelligence. (Dewey, 1938, p. 72)

To achieve the new object, the teachers wanted to use new instruments: integrative, cross-aged curriculum units and corresponding materials. They wanted to include the children and their parents in the community of the global-education programme. They wanted to free their activity from the restrictions of a standard curriculum, replacing it with the simple rule of planning the curriculum together, from the ground up. And they wanted to break the compartmentalized division of labour, replacing it with vertical collaboration across grade levels.

In activity-theoretical terms, Figure 3.2 may be understood as a sketch or a vision of the collective zone of proximal development worked out by the team (see Engeström, 1987, pp. 169–75). The realization of the zone is a lengthy and arduous process of constructive transformation in which collaborative creative thinking plays a key role. In the process of its realization, the vision itself is revised and enriched.

Curriculum Unit as a Cycle of Collaborative Thinking

In the global education team, instruction was planned and structured around integrated topics or curriculum units which included intensive sequences of teaching in mixed-age groups, called 'cross aging' by the teachers. In the summer of 1992, the team drew up a preliminary one-page outline of the topics and activities for the coming school year. The more detailed contents and forms of work in each topic were planned in weekly team meetings as the instruction went on.

The integrated topic planned for November was 'Harvest Celebration'. The team began to discuss and plan the details of this curriculum unit on October 6. They discussed the topic in five successive meetings (10/6, 10/13, 10/15, 10/20 and 11/5). In November, teachers began to discuss issues related to the topic in their own classes. On November 18 and 19, the teachers implemented the intensive core of their plan in cross-aged groups, each teacher working with a group consisting of students from all grade levels from K through 6. On November 23, the team had a sixth planning meeting. On November 24, cross-aged instruction continued. On November 25, all 150 students gathered in a joint celebration where they presented their work and ate various foods they had prepared. On December 8, the team discussed the topic one more time in its meeting.

All in all, the planning, implementation and evaluation of the curriculum unit lasted two months and included seven team meetings. In terms of thinking, such a unit is a cycle or a gradually unfolding web of collaborative problem-solving, planning, execution and assessment. The temporal distribution of thinking embedded in collaborative activity becomes evident in such a cycle.

We video-taped and audio-taped all the seven planning meetings of the team. We also video-taped the events in and around the classrooms during the four days of cross-aged instruction. In addition, we interviewed the teachers and the

Table 3.1: Frequency of types of speaker exchange

Exchange occurrence		
statement followed by a pause	245	40%
simultaneous speech	218	35%
interrupted speech	40	6%
speech w/o preceding pause	116	19%
Total	619	100%

Source: Buchwald, 1993, p. 10

principal of the school. In this chapter, I use transcripts of discourse in the planning meetings as data.

A preliminary analysis of the transcripts (Buchwald, 1993) revealed interesting features of the way the teachers talked in their meetings. While these features are not traditional individual-psychological parameters of thinking, they certainly illuminate the nature of thinking as mediated by talk — the dominant mediational means in the team meetings we studied.

The first feature of talk in the planning meetings was lack of pauses and conventional turn-taking. There was a tremendous degree of overlap and immediate response in the teachers' utterances. The teachers frequently spoke simultaneously, expressed affirmation or disaffirmation during another's speech, or broke in to respond or continue the thought in their own words. Table 3.1, based on a large sample of discourse from three meetings, indicates the frequency of the different types of turn exchange in the teachers' talk.

During these planning sessions, less than half of all turns at talk (40 per cent) were followed by a pause in the discourse. This means that conversational breaks did not occur after an individual utterance or pair of utterances so much as in between clusters of statements, or flurries of talk, coming from multiple participants. A turn at talk in this team may thus be characterized as a collaborative achievement more than an individual chance to speak.

The second feature in the teachers' planning talk was a lack of imperative mood and prevalence of conditional statements. There are three moods in the English language: the imperative, the subjunctive (or conditional), and the indicative. Interestingly enough, Angelika Wagner (1987, p. 165) in her study of 'knots' in teachers' thinking identifies only the imperative and the indicative moods; she does not even consider the role of conditionals in teachers' dilemmatic thinking. In fact, Wagner reduces the 'knots' in thinking to the imperative mood alone.

'A "knot" arises in consciousness if a discrepancy is detected between "what is" and "what *must* be", with consciousness reacting to this with the self-imposed injunction "this discrepancy *must* not exist". Because the discrepancy is already there, as part of consciousness itself, thinking does indeed go around in circles without finding an exit (. . .) Hence, tension arises, with thinking quite futilely attempting to solve a problem it has created itself by continuing to imperate itself that "This *must* not be!" ' (Wagner, 1987, p. 168)

According to Wagner's findings, such self-imperated 'knots' are tremendously common in teacher's thinking, as expressed in in-depth interviews and stimulated recall protocols. While interesting and imaginative, Wagner's work displays the same individualist and Cartesian bias I discussed earlier in this chapter. The 'knots'

Table 3.2:   Relative frequencies of moods in the planning meetings

Verb form occurrence		
Imperative	4	<1%
Conditional	485	43%
Indicative	516	46%
Indicative working as conditional	119	10%
Conditional working as Indicative	7	<1%
Total	1131	100%

Source: Buchwald, 1993, p. 14

were identified solely on the basis of monological responses from individual teachers. No data was collected from collaborative and dialogical thinking.

Findings based on our discourse data are practically opposite to those of Wagner's (Table 3.2). There was a practically total absence of imperatives in the talk of the teacher team. And there was a striking frequency of conditionals. Conditional phrases represent more than half of the total verb forms (53 per cent) if one counts phrases in which indicatives act as part of a conditional string. Questions and statements were stated as possibilities. Statements and recommendations were softened by conditional verbs. Most of each meeting was moved forward by conditionals: 'Perhaps we could . . .'

The heavy use of conditional strings suggests a shared sense of process which includes the tracing of ideas together rather than acceptance of givens from outside or reliance on yes–no decisions. The co-constructed strings of conditionals are instances of joint attention to and extension of ideas, of teachers imagining together. The team worked through potential choices and their possible outcomes. Ideas did not seem to be owned by the teacher who put them forth — it was not his or her obligation to defend them. Examining the transcripts after the execution of the curriculum unit, one sees that there are only very few parts of the overall plan that can be traced back to a single teacher's initiative.

The third feature of the teachers' planning talk was a prevalence of circling back and repetition of issues. An idea or a problem was typically taken up over and over again. Figure 3.4 depicts the discussion segments that dealt with the issue of food preservation (FP) in one team meeting. The segments were not necessarily adjacent to each other; in many cases, other issues were discussed in between the segments depicted. The numbers in the figure represent substantive themes taken up by the teachers in the different segments. The capital letters represent the five pervasive concerns that ran through all the meetings and issues.

A careful reading of Figure 3.4 makes it clear that this is not a case where 'thinking does indeed go around in circles without finding an exit', as Wagner put it. The issue did not return in the same form and with the same content. Repeated raising of the issue allowed it to be considered from various angles and by different teachers. Figure 3.4 shows that food preservation was discussed so as to express and weigh various concerns that may be relevant in the shaping of the topic: from conceptualization of the entire unit to dividing children into groups and selecting appropriate materials.

The entire process of planning and thinking in the team meetings took the shape of a spiral, consisting of various parallel smaller spirals such as the one depicted in Figure 3.4. It was a far cry from models of rational goal-oriented

Figure 3.4: Circling of the issue of food preservation in one meeting

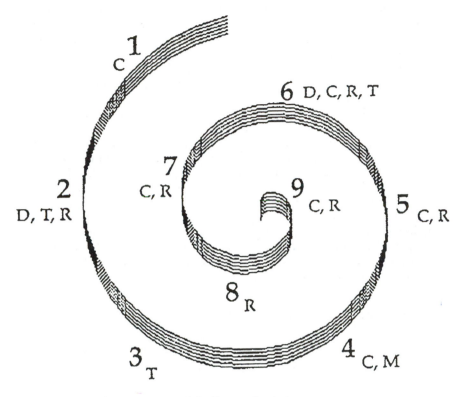

1. FP raised as a prime component of the Harvest Festival.
2. FP considered as a cross-age activity.
3. Concern with the time FP will take.
4. Consideration of foods which might be preserved.
5. FP as one of three main Harvest Festival topics.
6. Discussion of the place of FP within the curricular unit.
7. FP could be an optional activity for any group.
8. Check for consensus that FP will be done by each teacher as he or she sees fit.
9. Reiteration of the relationship of FP to other activities.

Source: Buchwald, 1993, p. 45
Notes: C = Conceptualizing the unit
          D = Dividing children into cross-age groups and subgroups
          T = Use of time
          R = Teachers' responsibilities
          M = Materials

planning that proceeds in a linear order toward a predetermined destination. Rather, the teacher team's thinking progressed like a vessel on a giant potter's wheel, emerging gradually as each teacher shaped it and added to it. The result was robust and sturdy in that the teachers seemed confident and coordinated in the heat of the cross-aged implementation, in spite of having no written plan at all.

Cooperative Formation of a Model for the Curriculum Unit

I will now look more closely into the process of collaborative thinking in the teacher team. A crucial issue in the formation of the curriculum unit of 'Harvest Celebration' was how the cross-aging of the 150 children was going to be accomplished. This issue was more crucial than any specific contents of the unit. In cross-aging, the teacher was to face children from the age of 6 to the age of 12 in his or her classroom, charged with providing meaningful tasks that enable the children of various ages to work together. Cross-aging is a leap beyond the confines of the self-contained single-grade classroom, into the realm of unpredictable interactions. This was at the heart of what the global education team wanted to achieve.

The model for the cross-aged core of the unit was worked out in successive steps in the second, third and fifth planning meeting of the team. Here, I will analyse the first three steps of this lengthy process of collaborative thinking.

The first major step consisted of the formulation of an initial draft model which had the following characteristics: (1) each teacher and classroom has a theme (e.g., wheat); (2) each classroom is divided into five or six groups, each group has its own subactivity within the theme of the class; (3) each classroom is cross-aged. This model was achieved through a number of substeps. First, the teachers encountered the problem of 'gigantic groups' where all thirty students would have to do the same activities in the classroom.

Global-education team meeting #2, 13 October 1992

JW: Could we split up the rooms like, per food type?

BH: Yeah.

LL: Oh, yeah. We could do that. There's five rooms. What if we gave every, like one of the grains to each of the groups?

BH: (Classrooms), right.

LL: But then, then you see, then your groups are gigantic. That means you've got thirty kids in a group!

The problem of 'gigantic groups' was approched by taking up the possibility of dividing each class into three subgroups with slightly different subactivities.

BH: But even if you were doing one grain, maybe you could come up with, you could have three different groups doing the same grain. And maybe come up with three different recipes. One could make a cereal.

LL: a cereal uh huh, uh huh

BH: One could make a pancake or you know a flatbread or something. And the other one could. I don't know, [laughs] come up with something.

LL: make sushi [laughs]

BH: [laughs] Yeah right, (come up) with something.

This idea evoked an attempt to recollect an earlier experience of dividing the students into small subgroups. This, however, led to a momentary confusion and dead end.

> BH: Right. Well, if each of us had a grain and we work (it that) maybe we had three groups, how many groups would we have to have do you remember, maybe ten?
>
> LL: What groups?
>
> BH: When we did the timeline, we had . . .
>
> LL: groups of four people, working to
>
> BH: What did we have? We had twenty-some groups?
>
> LL: Well, there's about, let's see, there's five times, there's about a hundred and fifty kids.
>
> BH: A hundred and fifty kids?
>
> LL: More or less.
>
> BH: And we put four kids in a group, or five. We had five kids in a group. That's five kids in a group; that's thirty groups. Oh God!
>
> LL: Okay. That's unrealistic. If you had, if you have, if we have five teachers . . .

The notion of thirty subgroups was declared unrealistic. However, one of the teachers immediately realized that the seemingly large number is not necessarily unrealistic after all. A realistic division was constructed jointly.

> BH: Well, wait a minute! Thirty kids in a group. I had six in my room. It wasn't unrealistic. It was okay.
>
> LL: Thirty kids in one group. But I'm talking about, if we had five teachers, let's say we had five teachers participating.
>
> BH: 'Kay.
>
> LL: If we divide the kids subsequently into five groups, which gives us *thirty*?
>
> BH: Right.
>
> LL: and inside the thirty we could divide it into three groups and . . .
>
> BH: Right. Well . , even smaller. Ten is too many.
>
> LL: (Maybe. You could divide it into six groups)
>
> JW: (So that one teacher six groups of five)
> That teacher, 'kay one person in that group, then somebody, you could split that thirty (.), the class
>
> ?: Right. Yes. Yes, right.

Thus far, the principle of cross-ageing was not mentioned at all. It now appeared as if in passing. But the attention was diverted to specific contents (raisins).

> JW: Say you had thirty kids, all different grades here
>
> ?: yeah, your room
>
> JW: You could have . , naw, I don't know, maybe you couldn't, but if you're thinking it has all the different grades,
>
> ?: Right.
>
> JW: then maybe you could have some doing raisins, some doing apples, some doing. , you know what I mean?
>
> LL: Yeah, but the trouble is, is that . . .

> I mean what do you mean do raisins? All you do for doing raisins
> is put them out and then every day you come and look at them.
> JW: Aaahh, I see.

Soon the teachers returned to the issue of dividing the students into groups, to draw a summary of the provisional model they had achieved.

> LL: Listen, if we had, if we had five teachers, and each teacher
> takes thirty kids' responsibility. And then within that thirty you've
> got, like, five groups of six, or whatever.
> BH: five groups of six, six groups of five
> LL: And let's say I have the theme wheat. . Wheat.
> JW: Okay.
> LL: Okay. . I need to come up with five activities that we can do with
> wheat. . (in other words) Or six, or whatever (the number is).
> BH: Right, right.

However, this model was still feeble and fragile. It was like a first draft, with little or no mutually constructed concreteness.

Some minutes later, the model was challenged. The teachers envisioned that giving each student in a classroom basically the same topic would become too uniform and rigid. This led to the second major step in the model formation. The second draft model was a radical deviation from the first one. It contained the following principles: (1) each classroom does all the five different themes (e.g., wheat, corn, etc.); (2) each teacher specializes in one substantive theme (e.g., corn) and shares that specialized expertise with the other teachers across all the five classrooms; (3) each classroom is cross-aged.

> LL: But see, once *again* if I've got groups of six, am I gonna ask each
> of those six to do a little bit of research to find out what civili-
> zation used wheat? (. . .) *What* am I gonna have these kids do?
> BH: kids do
> LL: That's right.
> BH: 'Cause usually we have a different topic for each kid.
> LL: Right.
> JW: (Yea.)
> BH: And this way it would be the same. . .

This worry of 'sameness' led to a search for an alternative. The alternative model was gradually worked out.

> JW: That's why it's almost seems like to me: . and I don't know how
> we would do (that) exactly, but it seems like, like, I don't know . . .
> LL: Well, we might want to do it this way and that is, I still have
> responsibility for thirty and I still have responsibility for six groups,
> but I'll have a rice group, a wheat group . . .
> JW: That's what I was thinking.
> LL: a whatever group, a whatever group, but *maybe*?
> JW: in within those thirty?
> LL: Within the thirty

The alternative model began to gain momentum when the idea of each teacher doing exactly the same set of different activities emerged as a labour-saving solution.

JW: That would work. That way you're saying, like in your classroom, you'd have all different grades, but in the sa-, in the other class-room, they'd be doing the same thing, all different recipes or whatever?

BH: Yeah, we'd all be doing the same thing (but) it would be just mixed cross age.

JW: Yeah, that would work.

LL: But I think, I think what we'd be smarter to do is to have all five be exactly the same.

BH: the same, exactly the same

LL: So I'll have the same stuff going on that you have going on and you have going on

BH: Right. We'll all do the same thing for rice. We'll all do the same thing for wheat

LL: but we'll each have different *kids*!

BH: Except for different rooms will have different *kids* doing it.

JW: I see.

BH: 'Cause see then we could (amount of work)

LL: But then see we could save ourselves an incredible amount of work.

JW: I see. Right.

Details of how this model would 'save an incredible amount of work' were elaborated further.

LL: because then one of us could take rice . and research it,

BH: and figure out all the (rice material)

LL: and (get all the activities) and then we would share them. One person would take wheat.

BH: Yeah. That's good.

JW: I see.

LL: One person would take barley. And then we wouldn't be *killing*, I mean, (it isn't like I) have to prepare for six grains!

BH: Right. Yes! That would be *so* much better.

JW: Yeah, that's true.

LL: I could prepare for one grain.

JW: That's a good idea.

BH: Right, right.

The formulation of the alternative model was drafted by three teachers; one teacher had to leave the meeting early and another one was sick. Two days later, the entire team met again. The three teachers presented their alternative model to the two others. The discussion led to the third major step in the model formation. The third model was a return to the first one, only this time with more concrete-ness. It contained the following principles: (1) each teacher and each classroom has a theme (e.g., wheat); each teacher becomes an expert in his or her own theme; (2) each classroom is divided into five or six subgroups; each subgroup has its own subactivity within the theme; (3) each classroom is cross-aged.

The designers of the alternative model presented their idea with enthusiasm and added detail.

Global-education team meeting 15 October 1992, par. 3

JW: And then like LL would be in charge of just corn, and she would get all the information for *all* of us

LL: about corn. And then one person would get all the information about wheat. And one person would get all the information about whatever. So what *if* we decided to do it cross-age, what we'd do is we'd, we'd fan the kids out, so what, there's five of us, right? Yeah, we'd have each each one of us in the five would have a cross-age section. So I'd have thirty kids in my room, but they wouldn't all be my own kids. (Some of yours.) And then inside that group, I would have ( ) and one about wheat and one about rice and one about corn or whatever it is. And so would you and so would you and so would you.

JW: But one teacher would only have to do all the stuff for corn.

LL: Mmhmm.

JW: And they'd give all their information to LL, to TS, to me, to you, to BH. And then you would maybe do wheat, and you'd give all your information, so we'd each have . . .

LL: It would cut down on the amount of work.

The alternative model was first questioned by TS, one of the teachers who was absent from the previous meeting.

TS: So you're like expert group, and you would teach first the information to your own class, and then they disperse then and do it with the other kids?

LL: Well see, we could do it that way, too. And that's just another way to do it.

TS: -( ) one teacher does the planning and just hands it and you'd say, 'Oh, you're gonna have five kids in your class doing corn and this is the activities they're doing.'

JW: Right. That's what we were thinking of. That way, you could do all the research and gather everything for I could do wheat, and you could do rice, you could do . . . I don't know, whatever . . . and then you we'd all give the other information to each of us. So we'd end up with four, like *I* would end up with *your* information on wheat, TS's information on rice, and then . . .

Next, JL, the other teacher who was absent, added a further question. She first received an immediate answer explaining the virtues of the alternative model.

JL: Right. So then why would you need all four, if . . .
JW: Because we want to cross-age.
LL: Because inside one group . . . If we did cross-age, inside my class-
      room, I would have a group for rice, a group for wheat, a group
      for corn, a group for whatever the grains are? So I might have four
      or five groups that *inside* themselves were cross-age. So the oldest
      kids would be, be able to read the information that I had managed
      to collect about corn. The oldest kids would become the experts in
      the group, and then help the other people do the activities about
      corn.
JW: See what I mean? [quietly]

JL then continued questioning the alternative model somewhat vaguely. Her
doubts were now picked up and clearly formulated by JW, one of the teachers
who created the alternative model.

JL: I was thinking yeah, if there is like, cross-age groups but like all
      the kids for who are are . doing the wheat are in one room like
      gathering.
      [BH comes back in. There is some indistinguishable talk.]
      We'll just have, just go ahead and go on. I'm not thinking (exactly;
      that's all right).
JW: Well, you're just thinking why, why should we have the kids, why
      shouldn't we just have all the wheat in one room? That's what
      you're saying?
JL: (That's) because the expert is in that room. But . . .

LL, another originator of the alternative model, immediately adopted JL's
implicit suggestion.

LL: Yeah, that makes sense. We could do that way, too.
JL: And then still have cross-age groups.
JW: Why why are we thinking (corn before)?
LL: Yeah. . So then you'd have, so we'd have a wheat person. And
      you'd have . you know, one fifth of the kids, that would be wheat?
JW: all
JL: Right.

It was realized by the teachers that in spite of the original intention, the
alternative model would not save labour, due to the burden of sharing one's
special expertise across all the classrooms. A return to the first model now seemed
natural.

LL: That would be fine. Be easier.
JW: Yeah, that would be fine. Yeah.
JL: (How does that sound?)
TS: And you wouldn't have to (share) your information with someone
      else.

JL: (you see), I think it would be easier if you're in the one room with the one teacher.

TS: Yeah.

After this, the teachers drew up a list of the five different themes: rice, wheat, corn, hunting, and gathering. They conducted a lottery to decide who gets which theme. This ritual allocation and division of labour, artifactually embodied in lottery tickets with names of the themes written on them, represented a major consolidation of the model.

A particularly interesting feature of the third step was the ease with which the originators of the second, alternative model gave up their idea and adopted the implicitly suggested return to elaborating the first model. In fact, the originators were instrumental in formulating a critique of their own model — a critique only very vaguely implied in the utterances of the two other teachers. It seems that in spite of their enthusiasm, the originators of the second model were operating very much in a tentative, conditional mode which kept doors wide open to doubts and further alternatives. The behaviour of the originators cannot be explained away on grounds of a desire to please senior colleagues; one of the originators was herself the most senior teacher of the whole team.

Conclusion

The general character of the teacher team's discourse may now be summed up. The recurring pattern of their discourse was a spiral or a 'potter's wheel' with constant circling back and repetition of issues. This pattern was not consciously problematized or developed — it functioned as if 'behind the backs' of the participants. The mediating instruments used by the participants were primarily linguistic, conditional strings being the most prominent among them. External material artifacts such as written texts, diagrams, etc., were scarcely used, the lottery tickets being a notable exception.

In Figure 3.3 earlier in this chapter, I presented the intended structure of the activity of the global education team. What do the empirical data and the analysis presented above tell about the structure of that activity as it was actually practised?

On the basis of the analysis, we may now distinguish between two layers of instruments in the teacher team's activity: the 'what' instruments (integrative topics and materials) and the 'how' instruments, consisting of oral planning primarily with the help of conditional strings (for a conceptualization of 'what' and 'how' instruments, see Engeström, 1990, pp. 188–9).

These 'how' instruments may be seen as both a strength and a weakness. The use of conditionals was robust and powerful in keeping the doors of thought open to alternatives and in providing for 'imagining together'. On the other hand, the exclusive reliance on talk as a medium may eventually make it difficult for the team to create and keep up a collective memory to be used as a resource when similar or related curriculum units are planned and implemented again in the coming years. The systematic rejection of prepackaged curriculum materials was a deeply held principle in the team. But without some form of documentation designed as a working alternative to prepackaging, the team members may simply become overburdened.

The emergent object of global education as a new type of educational environment and experience pulls the teachers into a poorly charted zone of experimentation and innovation. Insistence on talk as the only 'how' tool may restrict and disturb the team's journey through its collective zone of proximal development. On the other hand, the very same tension may also become a source of innovation in the journey.

Note

1   The research reported in this chapter was conducted within the project 'Learning and Expertise in Teams and Networks', funded in part by the Academy of Finland. Claire Buchwald, Adrian Cussins, Ritva Engeström, Pentti Hakkarainen and Dana Peterman collaborated with me in the collection of the data. Claire Buchwald was instrumental in the transcription and early analysis of the data. I express my thanks to the teachers of the global education team for their generosity and patience.

Rerefences

BAKHTIN, M.M. (1982) 'The dialogic imagination', Austin, University of Texas Press.
BILLIG, M. (1987) 'Arguing and thinking: A rhetorical approach to social psychology', Cambridge, Cambridge University Press.
BUCHWALD, C. (1993) 'Collaborative curriculum construction without a textbook', Paper presented at The Fifth Conference on Ethnographic and Qualitative Research in Education, Amherst, MA, June 5.
CALDERHEAD, J. (1987) 'Introduction', in CALDERHEAD, J. (Ed) *Exploring Teachers' Thinking*, London, Cassell.
CLARK, C.M. (1986) 'Ten years of conceptual development in research on teacher thinking', in BEN-PERETZ, M., BROMME, R. and HALKES, R. (Eds) *Advances of Research on Teacher Thinking*, Lisse, Swets and Zeitlinger.
CLARK, C.M. and PETERSON, P.L. (1986) 'Teachers' thought processes', in WITTROCK, M.C. (Ed) *Handbook of Research on Teaching*, Third edition, New York, Macmillan.
CLARK, C.M. and YINGER, R.J. (1987) 'Teacher planning', in CALDERHEAD, J. (Ed) *Exploring Teachers' Thinking*, London, Cassell.
COLE, M. and ENGESTRÖM, Y. (1993) 'A cultural-historical approach to distributed cognition', in SALOMON, G. (Ed) *Distributed Cognitions: Psychological and Educational Considerations*, Cambridge, Cambridge University Press.
DAVYDOV, V.V. (1991) 'The content and unsolved problems of activity theory', in *Multidisciplinary Newsletter for Activity Theory*, 7/8, pp. 30–5.
DEWEY, J. (1938) *Experience and Education*, New York, Macmillan.
ELBAZ, F. (1990) 'Knowledge and discourse: The evolution of research on teacher thinking', in DAY, C., POPE, M. and DENICOLO, P. (Eds) *Insights into Teachers' Thinking and Practice*, London, The Falmer Press.
ENGESTRÖM, Y. (1987) *'Learning by Expanding: An Activity-Theoretical Approach to Developmental Research*, Helsinki, Orienta-Konsultit.
ENGESTRÖM, Y. (1990) *'Learning, Working and Imagining: Twelve Studies in Activity Theory*, Helsinki, Orienta-Konsultit.
ENGESTRÖM, Y. (1992) 'Interactive expertise: Studies in distributed working intelligence', *Research Bulletin 83*, University of Helsinki, Department of Education.
GALEGHER, J., KRAUT, R. and EGIDO, C. (Eds) (1990) *Intellectual Teamwork: Social and Technological Bases of Cooperative Work*, Hillsdale, Lawrence Erlbaum.

HAMMER, M. and CHAMPY, J. (1993) *Reengineering the Corporation: A Manifesto for Business Revolution*, New York, Harper.

HARRÉ, R. and GILLETT, G. (1994) *The Discursive Mind*, Thousand Oaks, Sage.

HARGREAVES, A. (1993) 'Individualism and individuality: Reinterpreting the teacher culture', in LITTLE, J.W. and McLAUGHLIN, M.W. (Eds) *Teachers' Work: Individuals, Colleagues, and Contexts*, New York, Teachers College Press.

HARGREAVES, A. (1994) *Changing Teachers, Changing Times: Teachers' Work and Culture in the Postmodern Age*, New York, Teachers College Press.

HUTCHINS, E. (in press) *Cognition in the Wild*, Cambridge, The MIT Press.

KOBUS, D.K. (1983) 'The developing field of global education: A review of the literature', *Educational Research Quarterly*, 8, pp. 21–8.

LEONT'EV, A.N. (1978) *Activity, Consciousness, and Personality*, Englewood Cliffs, Prentice-Hall.

LEONT'EV, A.N. (1981) *Problems of the Development of the Mind*, Moscow, Progress.

LORTIE, D.C. (1975) *Schoolteacher: A Sociological Study*, Chicago, The University of Chicago Press.

MAEROFF, G.I. (1993) *Team Building for School Change: Equipping Teachers for New Roles*, New York, Teachers College Press.

MARKOVA, I. (1982) *Paradigms, Thought and Language*, Chichester, Wiley.

MARKOVA, I. and FOPPA, K. (Eds) (1990) *The Dynamics of Dialogue*, New York, Harvester Wheatsheaf.

PARIS, C.L. (1993) *Teacher Agency and Curriculum Making in Classrooms*, New York, Teachers College Press.

RESNICK, L.B., LEVINE, J.M. and TEASLEY, S.D. (Eds) (1991) *Perspectives on Socially Shared Cognition*, Washington, DC, American Psychological Association.

SALOMON, G. (Ed) (in press) *Distributed Cognitions*, Cambridge, Cambridge University Press.

SAMPSON, E.E. (1993) *Celebrating the Other: A Dialogic Account of Human Nature*, New York, Harvester Wheatsheaf.

SCHWAB, R.G., HART-LANDSBERG, S., REDER, S. and ABEL, M. (1992) *Collaboration and Constraint: Middle School Teaching Teams*, in TURNER, J. and KRAUT, R. (Eds) *CSCW '92: Sharing Perspectives*, Proceedings of the Conference on Computer-Supported Cooperative Work, New York, ACM.

TYE, K.A. (Ed) (1990) *Global Education: From Thought to Action*, 1991 Yearbook of the Association for Supervision and Curriculum Development, Alexandria, ASCD.

TYE, B.B. and TYE, K.A. (1992) *Global Education: A Study of School Change*, Albany, State University of New York Press.

VYGOTSKY, L.S. (1978) *Mind in Society: The Development of Higher Psychological Processes*, Cambridge, Harvard University Press.

WAGNER, A. (1987) '"Knots" in teachers' thinking', in CALDERHEAD, J. (Ed) *Exploring Teachers' Thinking*, London, Cassell.

WEICK, K.E. (1976) 'Educational organizations as loosely coupled systems', *Administrative Science Quarterly*, 21, pp. 1–19.

WERTSCH, J.V. (Ed) (1981) *The Concept of Activity in Soviet Psychology*, Armonk, M.E. Sharpe.

WERTSCH, J.V. (1991) *Voices of the Mind: A Sociocultural Approach to Mediated Action*, Cambridge, Harvard University Press.

WITTGENSTEIN, L. (1953) *Philosophical Investigations*, Oxford, Basil Blackwell.

Chapter 4

The Creativity of Action: Pragmatism and the Critique of the Rational Action Model[1]

Hans Joas

Introduction

Today 'action' is a central concept of philosophy and of almost all the disciplines that concern themselves with human beings. In economics, for example, the theory of rational action is undoubtedly the paradigmatic core of the discipline, in spite of the fact that the exact logical status of the assumption of rational action has always been the object of controversies. In psychology early in this century the radically reductionist notion of 'behaviour' replaced the earlier dualism of physiological research, on the one hand, and introspective studies of human consciousness, on the other. But during the last decades, the cognitive turn of behaviourism has increasingly opened up the perspective of founding psychology on a theory of action instead of behaviour. In sociology the mainstream classics like Max Weber or Talcott Parsons dealt extensively with the action — theoretical foundations of their discipline. The same is true for the originators of competing sociological approaches, like G.H. Mead and Alfred Schütz. In many recent debates of social theory the topic of action is absolutely crucial. Let me just mention debates like that on the general social-scientific importance of economic models of rational action, on a possible revival of Weber's or Parsons' theories, on Habermas' theory of communicative action or on Giddens' theory of structuration. In philosophy twenty years ago Richard Bernstein attempted to show that the most important approaches of modern thought, namely analytical philosophy, pragmatism, existentialism and a Marxism which is no longer understood as a teleological philosophy of history are united in their attempt to conceptualize the active character of the human being. In our days, in which post-structuralism and the revival of Nietzsche and of Heidegger's later writings articulate a skeptical and ambivalent attitude toward human agency, it may be less plausible to see a convergence of philosophical currents in the topic of action. But those approaches can be characterized by their attempt to emphasize the pitfalls of an activist bias in western culture, and hence they are not without an essential connection to the topic of action itself.

The fact that there are so many debates about action theory going on in various disciplines should not lead to the conclusion that an integration of the action theories in these disciplines or at least an integration of these debates is already on the way. On the contrary! One of the major difficulties of the present situation in the field of action theory is that many contributions do not take note of the existing diversity at all. Sociological action theory, for example, permanently moves between the poles of rational action and the normativist critique of this rationalist approach. This makes the debate in sociology richer than in economics, but still poorer than in philosophy and psychology. In those two disciplines and in somewhat marginal parts of the sociological tradition we can detect a third possibility beyond rationalist and normativist assumptions, namely, a theory of the *creativity* of human action. The purpose of the first chapter of a book I have written under this title is to trace the genesis and history of action theory and to make understandable the reasons why creativity was, it is true, not totally neglected in the works of the sociological classics, but became marginalized in the process of the codification of their theories. In the second chapter, titled 'Metaphors of Creativity', I address the main approaches within social philosophy to conceptualize creativity. Here I discuss the paradigms of 'expression', 'production', 'revolution', 'life', and 'pragmatic intelligence and reconstruction'. The third chapter delineates the fundamentals of a theory of the creativity of action, and the fourth one draws conclusions from such a revised theory of action for macrosociological theory as well as for a sociological diagnosis of our time. As it is obviously not possible to present all this in this chapter, I will restrict myself to parts of the third chapter of my book, i.e., the contours of an action theory which takes the creativity of human action seriously.

The Rational Action Model

The rational action model and its normativist critique suffer from a common deficiency. They both produce a residual category of non-rational action. This is an unintended consequence of taking rational action as one's point of departure. Every such approach subsumes the phenomenal variety of actions under an evaluative scheme. Sociology has always had a tendency to define different types of action on the basis of their specific difference from rational action. The typological principle behind Max Weber's famous distinction of four types of action lies in the gradual abandonment of the rationalization of more and more dimensions of action. Thus only purposively rational action satisfies completely the conditions for being termed 'action'. In value-rational action, consideration of the consequences of action is omitted; in affectual action, consideration of values; and in traditional action, consideration even of ends. The ideal remains an action that rationalizes ends, values, and consequences of action. This holds true independently of the exact determination of the notion of rationality. If rationality is conceived in the narrow sense of a maximization of efficiency in the achievement of goals, then emotional and spontaneous forms of behaviour will belong to the same category of non-rationality as morally reflective behaviour. But the same dilemma can be found when we conceive of rationality in a Kantian way; then morally reflective behaviour will be called rational, but amoral orientation toward one's own interests is put into the category of non-rationality. Even Habermas, whose communicative notion of rationality certainly is the boldest and most promising new approach in the field of a comprehensive understanding of rationality, develops his types of action out of his types of rationality — and this leads to a very poor version of action theory.

But what is the alternative, the way out of this dilemma? The alternative cannot consist in mere empirical research about the properties of everyday action, because in spite of the merits which a microsociological opening of the black box of empirical action processes has, there is the danger of losing every connection with the problem of the rationality of action. My proposal is therefore different. I propose a 'genetic reconstruction of the tacit assumptions within the idea of rational action'. All action theories which depart from rational action assume at least three things — whether they have a narrow or a comprehensive, a utilitarian or a normativist or a communicative notion of rationality. They assume, firstly, the actor as being able to act in a purposeful manner. Secondly, they assume the actor as being able to control, to dominate or to instrumentalize his or her own body. And thirdly, they assume the autonomy of the individual actor toward his or her fellow actors and toward the environment. A low degree in the ability of an actor to concentrate upon purposive action, loss or a low degree of control over the body, loss or renunciation of one's individual autonomy — from the perspective of rational action all these phenomena diminish the probability that an actor or an action will be classified as rational. The proponents of these approaches know very well that empirical actions mostly do not fulfill the assumptions of their rational action model. But they are compelled to ascribe the restricted validity of their assumptions as a deficiency not to their own theory, but to the actors themselves. A similar problem arises with respect to the trivial fact that human beings are not rational actors from the beginning of their lives, the date of their birth on. From the perspective of rational action child development is nothing but the process in which the ability of rational action is achieved. According to the proponents of this position a genetic analysis will not teach us anything new about the structure of action and agency. No empirical knowledge about the development of action abilities can add anything to the analytically fixated type of rational action.

I am not saying this in order to deny the empirical fruitfulness of rational action models in the analysis of social phenomena. What I do call in question, however, is the ambition to extend the rational action model to ever new areas of research without prior clarification of its inherent assumptions. It is necessary to elaborate what we mean when we speak of the teleological character of human action, of the particular corporeality and the original sociality of human agency. Such a procedure opens up a vista toward an appropriate understanding of the creativity of human action and allows a contemporary reconstruction of core ideas from the pragmatist and the so-called expressivist traditions.

The Critique

My first step is the introduction of a non-teleological notion of the intentionality of human action. Let me explain what that means. Many classical sociologists, e.g., Max Weber, have declared the notion of goal, end or purpose, and of means as being absolutely crucial and unavoidable categories for any analysis of human action. The most important sociological critique of this apparent truism came from Niklas Luhmann in his book with the title *The Notion of Purpose and the*

Rationality of Systems. This book begins with a critique of Weber's ideal type of bureaucracy and rational organization. This ideal type presupposes the existence of clear-cut goals structuring the organization or the existence of organizations structured in order to achieve goals of any kind. On the basis of extensive empirical research in the sociology of organizations Luhmann denies the fruitful character of the rationalist ideal type. He proposes instead to examine the *function* of goal-setting in organizations. In a next step he applies this very idea to the relationship between action and goals. Everyday action is not structured according to clearly separated goals and means nor according to means-end-chains in which goals can always be means for other goals. The means-end-scheme is, for Luhmann, an interpretation of the original fluidity of human action in terms of a causalistic framework in which the actor himself is put into the position of cause.

If we compare this causalistic interpretation with the ideas of the ancient Greeks, for example the Aristotelian philosophy of action, it soon becomes apparent that such an interpretation of action is anything but self-evident. However, the modern mind has great difficulty in accepting the ancient idea of the *telos* as a moment of maturation and completion intrinsic to an action. In the transition from antiquity to modernity, the meaning of the concept of purpose has been rendered radically subjective. Common to modern interpretations is the extraction of a stable goal from the flow of action. The causalistic interpretation is given a more liberal form when we say that numerous causes underlie all action, and that every action causes numerous effects. Yet this leaves the interpretational model used virtually unchanged. The distinguishing feature of Luhmann's reformulation is that his inquiry is directed toward the function of a causal interpretation of action in general, and of the means-end-scheme in particular, *in relation to human action.*

In both cases, he sees the function as being to provide the actor with an overview of events. With reference to the causal interpretation of human experience in general, this means that its function consists in 'systematizing the experiential and behavioral potentialities that manifest themselves in natural experience and interpreting them in such a way that they become available for the purposes of comparison and thus accessible to rationalization'. (Luhmann, 1968, p. 29). With reference to the interpretation of action according to the model of ends and means, Luhmann claims this model fulfills a selective function for perceiving and evaluating the consequences of actions. He begins by disputing the usefulness of the idea that actors orient themselves toward a uniform value system which is divorced from reality. Like the pragmatists and the phenomenologists, Luhmann too refers to the dynamics of natural experience, which tells us very clearly that the significance of values for our action depends on the degree to which they can be realized and on the level to which other values are satisfied. This enables him to regard it as the function of the concept of purpose to evaluate the consequences of actions:

> The concept of purpose denotes that effect, or complex of effects, which is supposed to justify action, i.e., it always describes no more than a part of the total complex of effects. Its 'subject' is not to bring about these specified effects, but rather purpose denotes their value in relation to the value of the secondary effects (including the effects of other possible actions, which we must pass up once we have committed ourselves to

something else). To set a goal is to state that the value of the intended effects is sufficient to justify the action, *regardless of the value or non-value of the secondary or forgone effects of other actions*. The concept of means describes the same value-relationship from the other side of the disadvantaged values. It starts from the causes which are appropriate to the achievement of the intended effect, and states that we can afford to ignore the value implications of those consequences of these causes that are extraneous to the purpose. (Luhmann, 1968, p. 44)

In pursuing this line of thought, Luhmann focuses his functionalistic gaze not only on organizations but also on the dynamics of human action. The question as to the function of ends within systems of action applies to both the one and the other.

It may be surprising for you to hear that Luhmann's reasoning on the dynamics of human action and on the function of the interpretation of action in terms of means and ends goes back to the pragmatist philosopher and educational theorist John Dewey. The decisive difference between Luhmann's and Dewey's critiques of the means-end-scheme is that Luhmann uses it to justify his radically functionalist systems theory whereas Dewey develops an action-theoretical alternative to the means-end-scheme. His crucial term for that alternative is 'genuine instrumentality'. Dewey's starting point is the idea that we should not simply take for granted the definition of ends as anticipations of future conditions which we want to bring into being.

He contrasts actions in pursuit of *externally set* goals, and actions infused with meaning, as postulated for example in the context of his theory of art and religion. This critique takes the form of an immanent critique to the extent that Dewey shows the categories 'ends' or 'goals' and 'means' to be in no manner self-evident as they appear to be. Dewey's first step is to claim that it is necessary to distinguish between the goals and the results of actions. This may sound trivial, as any actor knows that many of his or her goals remain unfulfilled, or that the results of his or her actions may differ considerably from goals he or she was actually pursuing. However, Dewey means more than this simple difference between goals and results. In his worldview with its radical 'presentistic' metaphysics the results of present actions do not exist at all because they still lie in the future (see Dewey, 1958; Mead, 1932). The conception of goals as anticipated future states does not adequately describe their role in present action because, as anticipations, they belong to the present. If we only dream of the future, we are not acting. Dewey therefore introduces the concept of the 'end-in-view' in order to define the role of goals in the organization of present action. The significance of this conceptual innovation becomes clear when we consider the second step of the critique. Dewey speaks of a reciprocal relationship between an action's end and the means involved. In other words, he does not presuppose that the actor generally has a clear goal, and that it only remains to make the appropriate choice of means. On the contrary, the goals of actions are usually relatively undefined, and only become more specific as a consequence of the decision to use particular means. Reciprocity of goals and means therefore signifies the interaction of the choice of means and the definition of goals. The dimension of means is by no means neutral in relation to the dimension of goals. No earlier than when we recognize that certain means are available to us do we discover goals which had not occurred to us before.

Thus, means not only specify goals, but they also expand the scope for possible goal-setting. 'Ends-in-view' are not, therefore, vaguely conceived future situations, but concrete plans of action which serve to structure present action. They guide us in our choice between various possibilities of action, yet they themselves are also influenced by our perception of these possibilities. Dewey therefore defines a goal or aim in the following terms:

> Specifically, it means foresight of the alternative consequences attendant upon acting in a given situation in different ways, and the use of what is anticipated to direct observation and equipment. A true aim is thus opposed at every point to an aim which is imposed upon a process of action from without. The latter is fixed and rigid; it is not a stimulus to intelligence in the given situation, but is an externally dictated order to do such and such things. (Dewey, 1916, p. 129)

This rounds off the argumentation. Externally determined goals are excluded from the reflective processes that are intrinsic to action. Instead they are fixed at a level above the processes of action and it is this which degrades the means of action to the status of pure means. In Dewey's writings on ethics it becomes clear that his critique of fixed goals applies not only to external but also to self-imposed compulsion. Every justification of an end as a value *per se* conceals from the actor the further consequences of his definition of goals and choice of means, as though in some miraculous way these would not occur or could be ignored (Dewey, 1939). Dewey's orientation is not, however, toward a blind respect for values and a blinkered pursuit of goals, but rather a pragmatic participation in collective action in which all values and all goals are potential objects of reflection and discussion. Despite the significance his educational theory attaches to the role of play, Dewey rejects the common tendency to distinguish play from work on the grounds that the former is goal-free. According to Dewey, play most certainly does involve goals in the sense of an inner regulation of action. It does not consist of random movements, but requires exceptionally sharp concentration and often deeply preoccupies the child. However, the goal orientations involved in play are not fixed externally and maintained irrespective of inner resistance to them. Those who play can be said to be free because they are able to abandon or redefine the current goals if their actions no longer promise fulfillment. The goals of actions do not stand for something to be preserved beyond the limits of the play. In a psychological sense, this description can also apply to work, no matter how protracted the chains of ends and means may be here.

> Both are equally free and intrinsically motivated, apart from false economic conditions which tend to make play into idle excitement for the well-to-do, and work into congenial labor for the poor. Work is psychologically simply an activity which consciously includes regard for consequences as part of itself; it becomes constrained labor when the consequences are outside of the activity as an end to which activity is merely a means. Work which remains permeated with the play attitude is art . . . (Dewey, 1916, p. 241 f)

Dewey's critique of the means-end-scheme as a tool for interpreting human action is, in other words, motivated by his refusal to accept a form of action like work, carried out under external or self-imposed compulsion, as a prototype for a theory of action. For Dewey the crucial issue is the difference between goals which are external to the action and prescribed, and goals which emerge in the course of the action itself but which can also be revised or abandoned. The pragmatist's skepticism regarding any blurring of this distinction coincides here with the objections of thinkers influenced by the philosophy of life to the means-end-scheme (see Tönnies, 1923, pp. 235–70; Simmel, 1918, pp. 37–45, Heidegger, 1987, pp. 114 and 279 ff). Thus Tönnies also addressed himself to the problem of the universal applicability of this model, and concluded that there were two cases in which it stood in obvious contradiction to the actor's own experience: when a person acts on an inclination or a whim, he or she no more distinguishes between ends and means than when performing ingrained habitual actions. Both cases correspond exactly to the pragmatist's ideas on meaningful action and action that has descended to the level of unreflected routine. Georg Simmel goes even further. In his metaphysical work, written toward the end of his career, Simmel views human freedom as lying precisely not in humankind's capacity for purposive action but rather in our capacity to break with purposiveness. Indeed, he defines humans as 'non-purposive' beings, as beings delivered from purpose. But it was Heidegger who provided the most radical demonstration of the impossibility of defining human life as a whole in terms of a chain of ends and means. After all, Heidegger argued, we do not rush from one action to the next in order to reach the goal we have been striving for at the end of our lives. If we wish to understand our relationship to ourselves and to our lives as a whole we need to invoke categories of a totally different nature, categories which Heidegger defines as 'for the sake of', as opposed to 'in order to', and which he attempts to grasp more fully via his analysis of our relationship to death. If we summarize these admittedly quite discrete arguments showing the limited applicability of the means-end-scheme, we find that neither routine nor meaningful, neither creative nor existentially reflected action can be accounted for using this model. Nothing remains, therefore, of the apparent self-evidence of taking this model as the starting point for developing a theory of action.

But the destruction of the deceptive character of the means-end-scheme is only a first step even within this area of an elaboration of the notion of intentionality. At least two additional steps are necessary: One has to develop an alternative understanding of intentionality and then one has to provide an explanation for the ability of actors to act rationally in a way wrongly generalized by the rational action model. In my book I have tried to develop a notion of intentionality out of our pre-reflective embeddedness in situations and a hypothesis on the development from 'wishes' to 'goals'. In this part I rely mostly on Donald Winnicott's theory of transitional objects, play, and culture which allows to understand how the creative act of setting goals presupposes the constitution of a reality considered to be independent of the actor, but presupposes as well the preservation of the actor's ability to dream and wish that reality were different.

Instead of explaining these steps in more detail here I would like to discuss the two other tacit assumptions in the rational action model. I called the instrumentality of the body the second tacit assumption. Many action theories do not refer to the specificities of the human body at all. In a sort of theoretical prudishness the body is simply ignored. There are several reasons why such ignorance is harmful for action theory. A first reason is that every action theory today has to grapple with the reproach that action theory in itself represents a culturally specific or gender-specific way of theorizing, i.e., that it suffers from an activist bias. In order to escape these reproaches action theory has to include passivity, sensitivity, receptivity, imperturbality (*Gelassenheit*) in its notion of the relationship between the human being and his or her environment, and this presupposes the inclusion of human corporeality. Another reason arises out of the problem of an instrumentalist restriction of the body's role. The body is seen as a technical instrument in models of rational action, as completely disciplined in models of normatively oriented action, as mere medium for expressive intentions in models of communicative action. The historical anthropologies of Norbert Elias and Michel Foucault can be considered attempts to trace the historical processes in which such an instrumentalist relationship to the body has arisen. Such a cultural history of the rational actor is a parallel to the ontogenetic reconstruction of the tacit assumptions in the model of rational action. But Elias and, above all, Foucault tend to overgeneralize the results of this history in the sense of ever-increasing discipline. Foucault's bodies have no faces, as Giddens has aptly put it. We have to imagine instead unstable balances of instrumental and non-instrumental relationships to our bodies. Bodily control on the front stage is interrupted by the release of these controls on the back stage. Action theory has to explain the development of control *and* of the ability to loosen this control, i.e., intentional forms of discipline and of reducing the discipline. To give you an idea of what I have in mind let me just mention the phenomena of 'passive intentionality' and 'meaningful loss of intentionality'. We can call 'passive intentionality' those forms of action in which the body is intentionally released from control. My favourite example is the process of falling asleep. We all know that the intention to fall asleep — understood as 'active' intentionality — defeats itself. But we all have the ability to realize this intention by accepting and sponsoring the pre-reflective intentions of our body. The same is true in processes of creative problem-solving. In order to solve a problem we should not insist on a given type of action but open up toward new impulses arising out of the free interplay between the body and the situation. Examples from sexuality can easily be added. The 'meaningful loss of intentionality' is to be found in those forms of action in which we lose the ability to act rationally, because the ambiguity of a situation or its emotional quality are so overwhelming that the actor loses his distance to the situation and to his own actions. Laughing and weeping are cases in point.

These reasons may make plausible the necessity of an anthropological basis for the theory of action. But they do not show the direction in which such a theory has to be developed. Again, I can only select a small part of the pertinent argument. The part I select concerns the problem of the development of the 'body-image'. This term refers to the way the body is subjectively given to the actor. One's own body is not a material object on the same level as other material objects in the world. The 'body-image' is usually defined as the consciousness of the actor about the morphological structure of his or her body, its parts and its attitudes, its movements and its boundaries. One can reconstruct the history of research about the development of the body-image in four phases. The first phase consisted in an attempt to examine the origins of the human ability to localize sensations originating in one's body and to regulate the movements and attitudes of the body. The findings indicated that there must be a special neurological mechanism of high flexibility which allows to represent the wholeness of the body. In the second phase the neurophysiological reductionism of the first phase was superseded. The Austrian-American psychologist Paul Schilder emphasized the fact that there must be a *psychological* representation of the body as a unit. He criticized the so-called *Gestalt* psychologists because they treated the holistic character of the body-image as given. Explicitly taking sides with the pragmatists he began to examine the development of the body-image and its constitution in the actions of individuals. The third phase consists mainly in the extensive analyses of the phenomenological philosopher Maurice Merleau-Ponty. More than Schilder he tries to integrate the cognitive and the affectual dimensions in the constitution of the body-image and to examine the permanent change of the body-image under the influence of ageing, or one could add, under the influence of illness, pregnancy or intimacy. In a fourth phase for which we can already find hints in Merleau-Ponty's later writings and also in Mead's work the constitution of the body-image is connected to the development of the communicative abilities of the child. If one can show that an instrumental relationship to one's body presupposes the constitution of the 'permanent object' and that the 'permanent object' presupposes elementary abilities of role-taking, as G.H. Mead has attempted to do, then it would become clear that the relationship between actors and their bodies is shaped by the structures of interaction in which an actor develops. We can treat our own bodies like a mother who sensitively registers all signals from the child and kindly accepts them, but we can also treat our bodies like an instrument which we subsume to our conscious purposes.

If the actor's body is not immediately given, but only via a body-image, and if this body-image is the result of an intersubjective process, then we find sociality right in the core of human agency. I speak of 'primary sociality' which is to say that sociality in this sense is not the result of conscious interaction, but precedes the ability to act as an individual.

This refers to the third tacit assumption of the rational action models. It is the least tacit of the three assumptions I am attacking here insofar as critical voices on this point have always been quite frequent and in a certain sense even constitutive for the discipline of sociology. For socialization research the question of the social conditions for the genesis of the self, of autonomous individuality are crucial. Only the narrow versions of rational action simply presuppose the autonomy of individual actors and ignore the problem of the constitution of their autonomy. The normativist models are connected to a theory of the internalization of norms, and the theory of communicative action itself aims at a notion of primary intersubjectivity. Therefore I will not develop this point in any detail. But I would like to discuss one possible objection against my thesis of primary sociality. The objection is that sociality is only a genetic, but not a structural precondition of human action. To refute this objection one has, however, to leave the leisurely paths of socialization research and face the eruptive forms of sociality in which the boundaries of the self are shattered. There are two main approaches to conceptualize the self-transcending experiences or primary sociality in mature persons. One goes back to romantic speculations about the possiblity of a return to Dionysos, and of the Dionysian as an evasion from the cultural aporiae of the modern age. This found its most stimulating expression in Nietzsche whose passionate interest in the self-enhancement of the creative personality sensitized him to the tension between creativity and the exclusionary mechanisms of a self which depends on closure and the maintenance of consistency. And Nietzsche was willing to sacrifice identity for the sake of creativity, or, to put it better, to consider creative self-enhancement as a liberation from the coercion to be a determinate, and that is, restricted individual. The other version allowed for an integration of creativity and the formation of a consistent self and considered Dionysian experiences as a form of the religious experience which collectivities need for their revitalization. This found its classical form in Durkheim's analysis of the elementary forms of religious life. Durkheim's analysis of collective effervescence and of the origins of the sacred do not refer to the genesis of obligatory rules or norms, but to the genesis of values and world-constitutive ideals. The birth of the religious idea lies for Durkheim in the experience of a loss of self-identity. For him the experience of self-transcendence is not a primitive or irrational marginal phenomenon of sociality, but the constitutive basis for any affectual social attachment to other individuals, collectivities or values. From this attachment flow our deepest motives and the cohesion of our personalities. Hence we have never reached action ability once and for ever, but can feel the permanent necessity to reconstruct our identity faced with the unanticipated events of life.

The three tacit assumptions of rational action models which I tried to bring to light here characterize the main dimensions in which a theory of the creativity of action has to be developed. Moreover, they are also the main dimensions in which the contemporary debates on 'post-modernity' can be called provocative for the area of action theory. This is true in at least three aspects. To be skeptical toward an activist attitude to the world, to demand that people are able to sit back and let things happen, is to challenge the presupposition that all behaviour is purposive and forces us to break with a narrowly teleological understanding of intentionality (see Sloterdijk, 1989). To focus attention on the body, on the disciplining of the body and the resistance it offers, is to challenge the presupposition that the body can be instrumentalized for the purposes of action and forces us to construe a non-instrumental relationship to the body.[2] To pour scorn on the belief in a substantive self is to challenge the presupposition of autonomous individuality and forces us to accept that identity does not reside in a static condition of always remaining the same person, but rather in an active, indeed creative process of addressing events that befall us and impulses that are alien to the self, and in a willingness to be open to other identities.[3] This is why rationalistic pathos gets one nowhere in the post-modernism debate. Instead, the sociological theory of action must show itself capable of countering the charges and of revising its own position in the light of post-modernist critique. The common denominator for such 'post-modern' revisions is the notion of creativity. But there are two divergent ways to understand creativity today.

Whereas pragmatism, on which my proposals are based, tries to locate creativity within everyday human action and finds in scientific creativity one of the most elaborate cases of this potential, *Lebensphilosophie* and its post-modern revival opposes creation to everyday life and normal science. Whereas pragmatism superseded the Cartesian dualism, *Lebensphilosophie* turned these dualisms around. From Schopenhauer on we find the projection of creativity onto non-human nature. A 'will' is assumed in nature which subsumes human intentionality and rationality to the status of being mere instruments of this metaphysical will. This is a theory of creativity which has lost the connection to the problem of action. It is quite logical that Schopenhauer propagated the renunciation of will as man's salvation. Nietzsche's case is more intricate insofar as he gave an activist turn to this idea of creativity which had lost its connection with everyday action. For him creativity was not part of the permanent reorganization and reconstitution of habits and institutions, but arbitrary production of values or meanings and uncontrolled play. The result of creativity in Nietzsche is the creative personality, not a changed world or social order. He isolates an interest in a more and more creative personality from the intersubjective and objective frameworks in which creative intelligence is naturally embedded. In spite of dealing with the problem of the creativity of action, Nietzsche's approach does not solve the problem, but makes it unsolvable. Creativity for him is the matter of exceptional individuals and their deeds and not a dimension of all action of all human beings. Creativity in the sense of genius is thus 'not creative in the sense of positive generation. It thrives on a negative dialectic which only conveys the sensation of creative freedom by destroying all concrete positions and merely serves to open up the creative universe of possibilities by abolishing existing realities; indeed, it is this alone which it sets out to achieve. It is the kind of genius that, in its abstract claim to absoluteness, is its own end. It forgoes all actuality for the sake of unlimited potentiality' (Schmidt, 1985, p. 165). The difference between Nietzschean post-modernism and pragmatism in their understanding of creativity is thus not simply an obsolete object of interest for historians of ideas. Instead, this ambiguity of creativity marks in my eyes an essential dividing line in today's social theory and cultural situation, at least among those who do not assume that rational action models are the most appropriate for the understanding of the processes of human action. And I do hope and believe that people who are mostly interested in teacher thinking and action must feel closer to the 'creative' and 'intersubjective' notion of human action as I have briefly outlined it here.

Notes

1 This text is based on my book, (1992), *Die Kreativität des Handelns*, Frankfurt am Main, Suhrkamp.
2 This seems to have been the tendency in Foucault's later development. In his books on the history of sexuality he examines, under the label of an aesthetic of existence, possibilities of a person's non-instrumental relationship to him- or herself.
3 In his critical appraisal, Terry Eagleton formulates the post-modernist critique of the concept of identity as reducing the subject to 'a dispersed, decentred network of libidinal attachments, emptied of ethical substance and psychical interiority, the ephemeral function of this or that act of consumption, media experience, sexual relationship, trend or fashion. The 'unified subject' looms up in this light as more of a shibboleth or straw target, a hangover from an older liberal epoch of capitalism, before technology and consumerism scattered our bodies to the winds as so many bits and pieces of reified technique, appetite, mechanical operation or reflex of desire. Terry Eagleton (1985), 'Capitalism, modernism and postmodernism', *New Left Review*, 152 pp. 60–73, here p. 71. I fail to understand, therefore, how Koslowski can arrive at his conclusion that a return to a substantial theory of the self is a feature of post-modernism. See Peter Koslowski (1987), *Die postmoderne Kultur: Gesellschaftlich-kulturelle Konsequenzen der technischen Entwicklung*, Munich, p. 49 ff.

References

DEWEY, J. (1916) *Democracy and Education*, New York, Macmillan.

DEWEY, J. (1939) *Theory of Valuation, Chicago*, University of Chicago Press.

DEWEY, J. (1958) *Experience and Nature*, New York, Dover Publications.

HEIDEGGER, M. (1987) *Being and Time*, Oxford, Basil Blackwell.

LUHMANN, N. (1968) *Zweckbegriff und Systemrationalität*, Tübingen, Mohr-Siebeck.

MEAD, G.H. (1932) *Philosophy of the Present*, La Salle, Ill, The Open Court.

SCHMIDT, J. (1985) *Die Geschichte des Genie-Gedankens in der deutschen Literatur, Philosophie und Politik 1750–1945*, Vol 2, Darmstadt, Wissenschaftliche Buchgesellschaft.

SIMMEL, G. (1918) *Lebensanschauung: Vier Metaphysische* Kapitel, Munich, Duncker und Humblot.

SLOTERDIJK, P. (1989) *Eurotaoismus: Zur Kritik der Politischer* Kinetik, Frankfurt/Main, Suhrkamp.

TÖNNIES, F. (1923) 'Zweck und Mittel im Sozialen Leben', in *Erinnerungsgabe für Max Weber*, Vol 1, Duncker und Homblot.

Part 2

Research Issues

The shift from mind to practice, as discussed in the Introduction, may affect many of the assumptions made within teacher-thinking research. It will have implications for theory development, methodological consideration as well as for ethical concerns. Three of the four contributions in this section can be related to this.

Donald Freeman introduces aspects of linguistic theory. Since teacher-thinking research rests so heavily on language as the tool to reveal teachers' knowledge and learning, the assumptions made concerning language are important to reflect on. Freeman is critical of the way language is customarily dealt with within teacher-thinking research, carrying certain assumptions which can be traced to the roots of teacher-thinking in the process–product paradigm. He advocates a view of language as an expression of the interaction between researcher and teacher rather than an expression of the teacher's 'inner thoughts'. He suggests a combination of this representational view and a presentational view of language. While the former focuses on what is said, the latter focuses on how it is said. The social view of language that Freeman presents affects the interpretation of teachers' voice as well as of how meaning is constructed. The idea of mutual construction of knowledge by researchers and teachers becomes problematic since they belong to different speech communities.

Geert Kelchtermans in his contribution describes in detail a study of teachers' professional biographies which is very valuable as it reveals the research praxis, rendering it visible and also possible to imitate as well as to criticize. With regard to the question of speech communities, it is worth noting how the dialogue between teacher and researcher was influenced by the researcher's visit to the teacher's classroom. The impact of this on their conversation is evident in expressions like 'you know how things are done here', thereby creating another basis for their interaction, since the teacher can rely on the researcher's knowing enough about his or her speech community. Kelchtermans' contribution also shows how teachers can contribute to the construction of knowledge, as well as how the researcher has to do some of the construction him/herself, albeit in collaboration with his or her own research colleagues.

Naama Sabar points out that the ethical questions have been neglected in the discourse on teacher-thinking research. She discusses 'partnership' and 'risks to the informants' as well as the level of awareness concerning ethical questions among researchers. Her contribution is based on interviews with the twelve Israeli teacher-thinking researchers. Consciousness regarding ethical questions did not rate very high among these researchers — or rather had not been explicitly formulated.

However, the interviews themselves raised the level of ethical consciousness, which itself makes the contribution a good example of how research not only intervenes in professional work but can actually contribute to professional development.

One aspect of 'partnership' concerns how involved the participating teachers should — and can — be and how far research objectives can be shared. In this, Sabar follows Clandinin and Connelly, asserting that the highest level of ethical awareness implies mutual construction of knowledge (between researchers and teachers). In relation to this position the Israeli researchers are considered to be some 'steps behind' the ideal development. However, in view of the fact that teachers and researchers belong to different speech communities, the whole idea of mutual construction becomes somewhat problematic, as suggested in the Introduction.

The fourth contribution is in a way not about teacher-thinking research, but rather about the consequences of this and other empirically oriented research traditions for an evaluation of different didactic models. Since didactics is a strong and important part of teacher-education programmes, this is an important issue to raise. Per F. Laursen discerns three different didactics: functionalistic, rationalistic, and reflective. He finds the reflective model only in accordance with what we know about teachers' work and knowledge, although he argues that certain aspects of teachers' work make a reflective didactic model problematic, since such a model misses how teachers' work is governed by institutional factors and because teachers' practice does not 'talk back'. By his contribution, Laursen raises important issues which in turn give rise to other questions: Does Schön's idea of second-order reflection also include institutional frames? Is it 'true' that practice does not 'talk back' in teachers' work? Shoshana Keiny's contribution in this book is one example of the contrary.

Chapter 5

The Use of Language Data in the Study of Teachers' Knowledge[1]

Donald Freeman

Abstract

This chapter examines the assumptions that underlie the use of language data in the study of teachers' knowledge and proposes an alternative approach to analysing such data. Arguing that, to date, teachers' words have been assumed to 'represent' their thinking, the chapter outlines the *representational* view which has been adopted in such research in which language data is taken as isomorphic to participants' thoughts, beliefs, knowledge, and feelings. However, research can benefit from work in linguistics on the nature, form, and social dimensions of language and its relation to thought. From this perspective, a *presentational* approach is proposed which focuses on the interrelationship between what is said in the data about the teacher's inner world, the language used (or not used) to say or 'present' it, and the context — both virtual and actual — of its 'presentation'. The chapter lays out the two views and argues through that their integration researchers can examine, and find evidence of, particular processes of thinking and change.

Introduction: Representational versus Presentational Uses of Language Data

Any study of what teachers know depends on an analysis of what they say. This relationship between the inner world of the teacher and the language which the teacher uses to express that world has provided the foundation for the study of teachers' knowledge, a domain in which I include teacher thinking, teacher learning, and any examination which focuses on what Walberg (1977) called 'teachers' mental lives'. This chapter briefly examines the assumptions underlying language data in the development of such research and proposes an alternative approach to data in the study of teacher knowledge.

To date research on teachers' knowledge has assumed, largely on an intuitive basis, that words can 'represent' thought. In this 'representational' view of language data teachers' words are taken as isomorphic to their thoughts, beliefs, knowledge, and feelings. Thus what teachers think is assumed to be evident in the language they use in oral interviews, in the written documents they produce, and in the language generated through other data-gathering procedures.[2] This assumption that language represents thinking has dominated research on teachers' knowledge, influencing both its methodologies and the development of its theoretical constructs, and has thus served to anchor the establishment of the field.

While treating language in this intuitive manner may have been acceptable while research in teachers' knowledge was establishing itself, it is no longer appropriate or defensible to ignore what is known about the nature of language. Research on teachers' knowledge can benefit from work in linguistics on the nature, form, and social dimensions of language and its relation to thought. A perspective that investigates how data is presented *in* language can preserve the cognitive and sociopolitical foundations of such research while at the same time recognizing and working more fully with the complex nature of language data as language.

A 'presentational' approach to language data focuses on the interrelationship between what is said about the teacher's inner world, the language used (or not used) to 'present' it, and the context — both virtual and actual — of its 'presentation'. The presentation lies in the intralinguistic and interlinguistic relationships in the data and has three basic dimensions: the choice of words or the *expression* which relates what is said with how it is said; the interlocutors linked by those words or the *voice* (what is said to whom and therefore how may be heard and understood); and the communities from which those words are drawn or the *source* (what is said and where it comes from). Thus in presentational analysis the teachers' words are examined for where they come from and how they relate to one another on the levels of form, function, and reference.

Strengthening Validity: Studying Processes of Thinking and Change

The representational and presentational approaches to language data can complement one another in the study of teachers' knowledge and their integration can enhance data analysis and deepen interpretation. Such an integrated analysis allows researchers to examine the processes of thinking and change which are evident in the language itself. In so doing, it reframes questions of validity. When teachers' language is taken to represent their inner worlds, the actual processes of learning and change are difficult to identify. Researchers can make statements about outcomes — that learning and change have or have not occurred — however there is little direct evidence of the processes themselves. Thus validity becomes a matter of trust in the meanings represented in the data and differences in analysis or interpretation of data can become attacks on the veracity of individual participants in the research process (see Mishler, 1990; also Maxwell, 1992; Connelly and Clandinin, 1990). To challenge data or interpretation within a representational framework is to argue that someone must not be telling the truth.

With the addition of presentational analysis, language itself becomes the focus. Such analysis can show evidence of learning and change by tracing patterns in linguistic relationships. Integrating representational and presentational analysis can show not only *what* is being learned or what is changing, but *how* it is being learned or how it is changing. Thus the basis of validity is broadened and discussion is shifted to matters of interlinguistic and intralinguistic analysis. Within this integrated framework, validity becomes a judgment of how linguistic analysis supports the meanings which are identified in or interpreted from the language data.

The Evolving Role of Language

To understand the integration of the two approaches, it is worth reviewing how the representational approach to language evolved into the dominant framework in the study of teachers' knowledge. While neither explicit nor planned, this evolution came about through a mixture of principled commitment to an aim and an intuitive approach to meeting that aim. As a field, the study of teachers' knowledge sought to position the teacher as the subject and the vehicle of study and thus to give voice to experience, perceptions, and understandings which had hitherto been overlooked or excluded in studies of teaching (Pope, 1991). This commitment arose out a sociopolitical and an epistemological concern to represent teachers' own perspectives on their practice and what they know (see Elbaz, 1991). Thus to some degree, research on teachers' knowledge was intended to counter what was seen as the colonization of teachers' experience by research practices which characterized the teacher as one variable within the classroom.

By taking teachers' — concerns, interests, and knowledge as its central focus, research on teachers' knowledge sought to create a different locus within educational inquiry which would address a perceived inadequacy. The creation of this frame raised a methodological challenge however. If researchers intended to uncover teachers' inner worlds, how could they gain access to those worlds? Language quickly and easily became the vehicle through which such access was gained. Thus data was collected, and analysis was undertaken, into teachers' worlds, beliefs, thoughts, personal practical knowledge, and so on. This more-or-less intuitive assumption about the nature of language data quickly became embedded in the procedures and conceptual structures of research on teachers' knowledge and has shaped both its methodology and findings.

Perhaps for this reason, the role of language has been, on the whole, overlooked in the study of teachers' knowledge. When language has been considered, it has been looked at in one way. Researchers have acknowledged the compelling ability of language, through the categories it creates, to shape the conceptual architecture of research (see Bowers, 1987 cited in Elbaz, 1991). This sociopolitical and epistemological argument has focused on the relationship between researcher and subject as well as on issues of power and participation (see Britzman, 1991; also Connelly and Clandinin, 1986). However this wider debate has diverted critical attention from the foundational assumption that language can refer to aspects of the teachers' inner worlds and thus language data can 'represent' thought.

To understand the evolution of this assumption, one must return to the process–product paradigm (Dunkin and Biddle, 1974) which, as the established norm in educational inquiry, extended certain assumptions of stability, regularity and predictability to classroom life. Within the process–product view, teachers' work was categorized in terms of behaviour and activity, and teaching and learning were seen as sequences of thought linked to action within which patterns with predictable outcomes might be uncovered (Gage, 1963). Inquiries within this paradigm sought out external, behavioural indicators which could be measured, compared, and traced. In a certain sense, language became such a behavioural indicator providing a window into thought.

Arguments about the incompleteness of the process–product view of teaching and learning developed on several fronts. There was concern over the push of prescriptivism in which teachers were cast as implementers of research findings, while teaching itself was hardly examined. Methodologically there was also concern for the hermeneutic worlds which were being overlooked in such research (Shulman, 1986). However, even as the concepts and methodologies of qualitative research took hold in various forms of educational inquiry, the basic focus remained on teaching and learning. Behaviour was no longer the exclusive area of attention; instead researchers examined classrooms as realms of meaning, as social and interpersonal domains within which the teacher's cognitive world and meanings were generally included.[3] Despite this major shift in methodology and conceptual framework however, teachers continued to be viewed as one element within the ecology of the classroom.

In focusing on meaning and interpretation, the qualitative paradigm opened research to questions of proprietorship. In hermeneutic data collection and analysis, the issue was not only meaning, but *whose* meaning? To force this question, the place of the teacher in research had to be addressed.[4] In a 1991 article, Elbaz (1991, p. 1) outlined the conceptual categories into which this original impulse evolved, arguing that 'teacher thinking, the culture of teaching, and the personal, practical knowledge of teachers' now comprise research on teachers' knowledge. However, while the loci of research were differentiated, the aim continued to be much the same: to provide within the research process a means and forum for the expression and examination of teachers' views and experiences of their worlds. Elbaz (1991, p. 10) explained this aim in terms of voice, a point to which I will return later, writing that 'Students of teacher thinking have all been concerned to redress an imbalance which had in the past given us knowledge of teaching from the outside only; many have been committed to return to teachers the right to speak for and about teaching.'

Finding a Conceptual Structure

Although the self-declared aim of research on teachers' knowledge brought with it a clear focus on the teacher and her world, from its inception the field lacked commonly agreed-upon methodological procedures or a shared conceptual framework. This created a central dilemma: How could one establish teachers and their worlds as the core of a research agenda and at the same time define for them what those 'mental lives' comprised? On the other hand, how could one launch a field of inquiry, especially one with such a clearly defined allegiance to the individual person of the teacher, without some notion of what one was looking at? Some sort of a bridge was needed which could offer access to the teacher's world without defining what one might find within that world. As a starting point, it seemed reasonable to posit what one was looking *at*, while leaving open what one was looking *for*; to suggest the form without defining its content. What was needed was an a priori conceptual framework that was essentially content-free. This bridge was supplied by the construct of decision-making.

The two major literature reviews (Clark and Peterson, 1986; Shavelson and Stern, 1981) covering the first decade of the field, cast decision-making and the distinction between preactive and interactive decisions (originally noted by Jackson, 1968, pp. 151–2) as their organizing frameworks. The strength of construct seems to lie in the fact that it was largely imported from studies on medical diagnosis (see Kagan, 1988).[5] Insofar as the aim of such research was to establish the place of the teacher in understanding classroom teaching, it seemed logical — at least in retrospect — to borrow from a professional community in which the practitioner plays a central and uncontested role; medicine offered the vision of such a community.[6]

Like any choice of this nature, the extended use of the decision-making construct in the first decade of research was not entirely benign. While the early emphasis grew out of the dual aim to put teachers' 'mental lives' at the heart of the enterprise and to invoke some methodological direction and coherence, it also defined certain key assumptions in the research process. Decision-making inherited, and thus extended, a process–product view of the world which separated thought from action. Within this dichotomy of inner and outer, the teacher's thinking and her private inner world were revealed to the researcher through the skilled use of hermeneutically oriented methodologies.

Language provided the key by which to create an external map of this internal landscape. The teacher could tell, explain, confirm, reflect and thus 'represent' her thoughts, judgments, decisions, and ideas in public words to the researcher, who could then in turn study and analyse them in order to make sense of that internal world. Thus the decision-making construct began to separate the teacher's thought from her language, as her language became a means of documenting her thought and telling the researcher what was in her mind. For the teacher to talk *about* her thinking, her words had to be taken as representing her mental processes.

By the mid-1980s, research on teachers' knowledge grew more diverse and decision-making as an a priori construct was no longer as central. Under the rubric of 'personal practical knowledge', the second generation of researchers began to pursue the use of narrative (Clandinin and Connelly, 1987; Clandinin, 1986; Elbaz, 1983) and biography (Butt and Raymond, 1987) as vehicles to study thought. This movement aimed to redress some of the dichotomies which had surfaced in the first generation of research between the teacher's cognitive world and her classroom practice, between researcher and teacher/subject, and between thought and action. To reunite these dichotomies, Elbaz (1991, p. 3) summarized the integrated view of the second generation of research on teachers' knowledge as a commitment to the teacher's story. For this work on narrative and biography, the story is not that which links teacher thought and action, for thought and action are not seen as separate domains to begin with. Rather, the story is the very stuff of teaching, the landscape within which we live as teachers and researchers, and within which the work of teachers is seen as making sense (Carter, 1993).

As research methodologies, narrative and biography largely resisted the dichotomous approach to thought and action inherent in the decision-making framework. Likewise they addressed the distance and disequilibrium in the roles of researcher and teacher-as-subject which often accompanied the first generation of research. However advocates of narrative continued to emphasize the representation of the teacher's world in and through language data, although that representation focused on story (see Carter, 1993) or collaboratively developed narratives (Connelly and Clandinin, 1986) rather than on documenting the content of teachers' decisions.

Table 5.1:   Content, form and frame of reference of language data in the study of
teachers' knowledge (1975 — present)

Generation of research	Content	Form (research Genre/ linguistic Form)	Frame of Reference
'First' generation (1975–85)	• Individual discrete descriptions of thought — planning, explanations of activities, etc.	• *Genre*: Decisions — preactive and interactive • *Form*: Brief descriptive or propositional statements	• Draws on medical diagnosis and clinical decision-making (see Kagan, 1988)
'Second' generation (1985–)	• Integrated passages merging the teacher's background and present practice, thinking and classroom activity, also researcher and teacher/participant	• *Genre*: narratives; stories; biographies • *Form*: Extended passages of language	• Draws on underrecognized/ valued forms of knowledge and knowing (see Carter, 1993; Elbaz, 1991)

When teachers' knowledge was viewed as decision-making, some status accrued indirectly to both teachers and to the research community through connection of the construct to medicine and physicians' decision-making. The form of language data was posited a priori as decisions, expressed as statements, while the content was supplied by the teacher/participant. In the use of narrative, biography, and story as research vehicles, the form was argued to be a naturally occurring one (Bruner, 1990), expressed in extended passages of language. Content and form develop together, often through researcher–teacher collaboration (Connelly and Clandinin, 1990). With this form of language data, status inured to the research process through reference to unrecognized and undervalued forms of knowledge and knowing (Carter, 1993; Belenky, Clincy, Goldberger and Tarule, 1986). These linkages to feminist theory logically supported the sociopolitical attention to classroom teachers, the majority of whom in north America are women.

The two generations of research differed in their approaches to data analysis however. In decision-making studies, the principal activity lay in categorizing decisions as propositions about the teacher's inner world and tracing their development and interrelations. Data collection and analysis were thus separated into sequential activities. Studies in narrative, on the other hand, sought to emphasize coherence and integration with increased attention to devices such as images (Clandinin, 1986; Elbaz, 1983) and metaphors (Munby, 1986), and to collaboration between researcher and teacher in developing and defining them. In narrative studies, the conventional distinction between data gathering and analysis was blurred as the collection and interpretation of data became iterative and even symbiotic processes. Intended to integrate the teacher's words, actions, and classroom environment into a jointly interpreted whole, these devices of narrative analysis were not exclusively verbal. They often drew on interpretations of the teacher's behaviour, manipulation of teaching materials, and classroom environment (as, for example, with teachers' images), and they depended heavily on language as a shared means of expressing the teacher's inner world.

Although the use of narrative broadened the kinds of data and how it was obtained and analysed, the underlying assumption that language data (whether field notes, interviews, journals, or co-constructed and co-analysed narratives) represented the teacher's world persisted. Ironically, the intense commitment of research to uniting teachers' inner cognitive worlds with their outer worlds of action in this second generation seems to have deepened the basic representational premise that language can express the personal and idiosyncratic natures of those worlds. As Elbaz (1987, p. 501) noted in commenting on Clandinin and Connelly's (1987) review of studies of teachers' personal practical knowledge: 'What we know of [a teacher's] practice is actually researcher assertion: *we have access to practice only through the language we use to formulate what we have seen.*' (my emphasis)

This brief analysis has examined how the representational approach to language data — the assumption that language can represent teachers' 'mental lives' — took root in the study of teachers' knowledge. Both the cognitive structure of decisions of the first generation of such research and the integrated experiences of thinking and doing displayed in narrative in the second generation shared a commitment to this representational view. Driven by a concern to recentre research on the teacher, her understandings and her experiences which arose to counter the predominant emphasis in educational inquiry, and the accompanying logical commitment to hermeneutic methodologies which could make known that internal world, research on teachers' knowledge assumed that language data could represent thought processes. The study of teachers' knowledge has thus far been well-served by this representational approach to language data. Through it, research has achieved the important aims of featuring the teacher centrally in research and of creating the beginnings of a shared framework for such inquiries. It is, in fact, due to these successes that we are in a position to reconsider the nature of language data itself and to expand the methodological approaches used in its analysis.

A Presentational Approach of Language Data

The presentational view assumes that language is both the vehicle and the substance of participants' meanings. It is the medium out of which these meanings are constructed and through which they are conveyed, and these two dimensions are so inextricably bound together that one cannot examine one without considering the other. Thus in this presentational approach, the teacher's words are taken for what they are as well as for what they say. To work with language data one must look at not only *what* is said but *how* it is said. This is, however, more than a study of what linguistic units such as words or phrases mean or even of overarching meanings such as metaphors or images; it is an examination of the relationships embedded in, and created through, the language itself. It entails a technically focused study of the structural relationships within a segment of language, a study which augments, and thus contributes in validating, the representational reading of that data. In such a combined analysis, the representational question, *what* does this data mean, is not sufficient; it must be balanced by its presentational counterpart, *how* is this data meaning?

Presentational analysis is organized around three concepts: linguistic value and syntagmatic and paradigmatic relationships among language items (de Saussure, 1978/1916), socially constructed voice (Bahktin, 1981), and the related concepts of Discourses (Gee, 1990) and of conceptions of practice (Freeman, 1993; 1992). As theorists, De Saussure, Bahktin, and Gee share certain assumptions about the nature of language: They view it as a social system to which individuals gain access and through which they are collectively defined. Thus the study of language, and by extension of language data, examines its systematicity and the connections created within and through it. Meaning is a function of contrasts within the system and among elements of different systems. These shared assumptions about language — that it is systematic, that it is collective before it is individual, and that it gains meaning through the presence or lack of contrast — all centre on the notion of relationship. Thus at the heart of the presentational view is the study of how particular language data presents such relationships, in other words how it means. This entails the three dimensions of *expression, voice,* and *source.*

From Structural Linguistics: The Dimension of Expression

Structural linguistics has investigated the ways in which language functions as a system, gaining meaning through two primary contrasts: what is said in relation to what is not said, and what is said in relation to what precedes and follows it. The former are referred to as 'paradigmatic' or associative contrasts; the latter as 'syntagmatic' ones. A simple example illustrates these two axes of contrast. In the statement 'I am going to the store,' the paradigmatic contrasts include, 'I' versus 'you' or 'they', 'am going to' versus 'went to', 'store' versus 'bank' or 'hospital', and so on. These paradigmatic contrasts exist in principle; as one element is used, it precludes the use of others.

Syntagmatic Contrasts

	I	am going to	the	store.
Para	*You*	am going to	the	store.
	They	am going to	the	store.
digmatic	I	*am going to*	the	store.
	I	*went to*	the	store.
contrasts	I	am going to	the	*bank.*
	I	am going to	the	*hospital.*

The syntagmatic contrasts on the other hand unfold in the linear development of the statement, 'I / am / going / to / the / store.', with each choice limiting subsequent ones.[7]

The observation of the interlocking nature of paradigmatic and syntagmatic contrasts, while relatively simple, has profound implications. In attending to the system of relationships in language, structural linguistics redefined how language could mean. The notion of meaning as coming through reference — that words represented things in the inner or outer world — was challenged by the concept of linguistic value. Contrasts create linguistic value; their boundaries are arbitrary and gain meaning through social agreement. Thus a word means by *what it is not* instead of by *what it is*, and these values depend on shared conventions. As de Saussure (1978) argued:

> The arbitrary nature of the sign explains why the social fact alone can create the linguistic system. The community is necessary if [linguistic] values that owe their existence solely to usage and general acceptance are to be set up; by himself the individual is incapable of fixing a single value. (de Saussure, 1978, p. 113)

This view challenges the primacy of the individual user of language. Rather than choosing words to mean certain things, individuals enact parts of the system of language, generating meaning through the social agreements in which they participate. Think, for example, of a conversation among colleagues in which someone uses a term which one or two people do not recognize: that portion of the conversation is meaningless to those people even though they may well know its referent in the world yet not know the term itself. So language depends on a speech community to create and sustain meanings. Access to those meanings, the linguistic contrasts to which that speech community gives value, comes through participating in the community as a user of its language.

The challenge to the referential notion of meaning brought about by structural linguistics is a substantial one. Research on teachers' knowledge has been predicated on the notion that language data can stand for something outside itself, that talk can represent the inner world of the teacher. The concept of meaning as created through the social fact of arbitrary linguistic value shared by a speech community contradicts this view. Because it is virtually impossible to define the limits and membership of the speech community in which a meaning is shared, it would be equally difficult to be certain that language data mean the same things to researcher and teacher. Regardless of their collaborative intent, researcher and teacher come from different speech communities. Therefore the language data which results from their interactions (through interviews, stimulated recalls, co-constructed narratives and the like) is unique to their relationship. The researcher has obtained words which both create and express that situation with the teacher. Those words may be about something else but they are equally a product of the social relationship that creates them. One cannot avoid the social world out of which the language is woven and which it pictures, which leads to the second concept, the translinguistic concept of socially constructed voice.

From Translinguistics: The Dimension of Voice[8]

As much as it is used, the concept of voice remains a messy one in educational research generally and in the study of teachers' knowledge in particular. The term means many things, but principally it seems to refer to three interrelated sets of ideas. 'Voice' is an epistemological stance about the source of knowledge and understanding (e.g., Britzman, 1991, pp. 23–7); 'voice' is a sociopolitical stance about who is doing the speaking and for what purpose (e.g., Freedman, Jackson and Boles, 1986); and 'voice' is a methodological stance about what lies in the data to be heard, recognized, and advanced through analysis and the reporting of research (Carter, 1993). Collectively and individually these stances find their way into research on teachers' knowledge where they have become inextricably interwoven as Elbaz (1991) demonstrates in the following statement.

> Thus the language we have to talk about teaching has been not only inadequate but systematically biased against the faithful expression of the teacher's *voice* [*as an epistemological stance*]. Recognition of this has given rise to efforts to present teachers' knowledge in its own terms, as it is embedded in the teacher's and the school's cultures. In a sense, the research on teacher thinking constitutes a developing conception of *voice* [*as amethodological stance*] and an ongoing attempt to give *voice* to teachers [*as a sociopolitical stance*]. (Elbaz, 1991, p. 11, my emphasis)

The translinguistic view of voice, from the work of Bahktin (1981) and more recently Wertsch (1991, 1985), differs from these three stances. Here voice is a social and not an individual phenomenon. Individuals assume, participate in, and are constituted by the various voices available to them. As Wertsch (1991, p. 49) notes in discussing voice as authorship, 'In Bahktin's view, the notion of sole, isolated authorship is a bogus one. An essential aspect of his construct of dialogicality is that multiple authorship is a necessary fact about all texts, written or spoken.' In this view, voices, like language, exist in social communities and in the proces. of self-expression people take them on: Wertsch (1991) continues:

> Throughout his analysis, Bahktin stressed the idea that voices always exist in a social milieu; there is no such thing as a voice that exists in total isolation from other voices. . . . [M]eaning can come into existence only when two voices come into contact: when the voice of the listener responds to the voice of the speaker. (Wertsch, 1991, pp. 51–2)

Thus voices are relationships created and sustained in and through language. From this perspective one does not think of individuals' selecting words to express their own meanings. Rather, individuals create themselves through the voices they use and thus identities depend on mutual recognition.

This social view of voice is clearly at odds with the idea of giving voice to individual teachers as Elbaz argues for. Rather the social view assumes that, because they do not belong to individuals, voices cannot be sought out, acknowledged, or valued in that way. Voices exist in and as a social medium. To understand them researchers must accept that what they hear is a function of who they are as individuals within the social community. Their roles are their voices, and those exist only in relationship to one another. (see Mishler, 1986, p. 7)

The dialogical nature of voice means that it is always mutual (see Cazden, 1989). No matter how egalitarian it seeks to be, the researcher–teacher dyad creates a unique voice and relationship which differs from other voices/relationships in which these individual participate, such as for the teacher among peers in the teachers' room or at a parent–teacher conference, or for the researcher among colleagues at a professional meeting. David Hargreaves makes a similar observation in a 1977 article on teacher decision-making.

> When teachers are asked to display their values (to researchers, parents, colleagues, etc.), they doubtless feel constrained by that situation to express

their ideals and to assert a strong degree of coherence, consistency, and integration among those values. *Practice will not be a simple reflection of those values because practice arises in a very different situation which has a quite different structure and set of constraints.* (Hargreaves, 1977, p. 17, my emphasis)

Thus the voice of teachers' knowledge is not so much displayed through the research process as it is created for the researcher-teacher relationship, an artifact of that context.

Some research on narrative in teachers' knowledge has acknowledged the central role of the teacher–researcher relationship in creating a voice (Connelly and Clandinin, 1990), although it has generally claimed the relationship as the foundation of epistemological and sociopolitical voice. In the narrative view, the teacher–researcher dyad creates the possibility and the vehicle for the teacher to voice what might otherwise be unheard, and thus the teacher's inner world is brought out, through co-narration or co-construction, in the research process. The assumption is that the teacher's world is there to be revealed in language. In the view which Bahktin proposes however, that voice is created on occasion of the researcher–teacher meeting for the purpose of their collaboration, out of utterances which each person in effect borrows from existing social voices.[9] Thus voice is a statement about the relationships found within a portion of language. To understand language — and by extension language data — one must investigate the frames of reference, or sources, and interplay of those relationships, how those frames are blended together.

From Social Linguistics: The Dimension of Source

If the concept of voice as a socially constructed phenomenon is to be useful in empirical investigations, it needs to be placed within a broader structure. If voice is a fabric of language, one needs to examine the references and sources for the various threads out of which it is woven. The notion of speech community provides only a partial answer. In positing speech community as a source, language is seen as social before it is individual. However a speech community is an extremely complex notion since it is not confined to a particular geographical place or a specific time. Consider, for example, the various speech communities among users of electronic mail. Displacement is one issue; participation is another. We can and do take part in multiple speech communities simultaneously.

One approach to defining speech communities has been to see them as modes through which people participate in life, rather than as groups of language users. The speech community defines the form of participation and people become members through their increasingly proficient participation in that form. Cognitive psychologists Lave and Wenger (1991) argue that these modes of participation define who a person is:

Activities, tasks, functions, and understandings do not exist in isolation; they are part of broader systems of relations in which they have meaning. These systems of relations arise out of and are reproduced and developed within social communities, which are in part systems of relations among persons. *The person is defined by and defines these relations.* (Lave and Wenger, 1991, p. 53, my emphasis)

Since people can and do participate in multiple forms of life through schools, work, places of worship, family, neighbourhood, professional groups, and so on, they take part in multiple speech communities or what social linguist James Gee has called 'Discourses.'

In studying the development of literacy as a form of social participation, Gee (1989, pp. 6–7) has advanced the idea of Discourses[10] which are 'ways of being in the world, . . . forms of life which integrate words, acts, values, beliefs, attitudes, and social identities . . .' Each Discourse provides participants with 'an identity kit which comes complete with [ways] to act, talk, and often write, so as to take on a particular social role that others will recognize', (Gee, 1990, p. 142). These two characteristics are critical. First, Discourses are by their nature complete and totally defining. Second, they must be mutually recognizable to participants in order to be invoked and sustained. So Discourses are social practices which define, and are defined by, their participants.

Discourses are also plural. Gee notes that 'each social institution commands and demands one or more Discourses and we acquire these fluently to the extent that we are given access to these institutions and are allowed apprenticeships within them' (1989, p. 8). Discourses are learned through participation; because people take part in many social practices, they are learning and sustaining many competing Discourses simultaneously. These Discourses are evident in both written and spoken language, as well as in body language, dress, and pragmatic styles of interaction, among other things. Thus one can look to, and analyse, these externals for evidence of the various Discourses which may be in play when a person participates in a particular situation.

In this way, the concept of Discourses suggests a means through which to approach the presentational dimension of language data. Through examining such data for evidence of the Discourses, or speech communities, within it, the researcher can begin to identify what is being presented and how. However, such examinations are complicated by the fact that each Discourse requires mutual understanding. Therefore the researcher–teacher/participant dyad is critical to reading the Discourses in a passage of language data since that reading will depend, in large part, on the researcher's life experience. The truth or accuracy of the data is not implicit in it, nor is it confirmed through a process of triangulation or reference to an external world; instead it comes from the mutuality of recognition and understanding it inspires in those who hear or read it.[11]

As a theoretical framework, the concept of Discourses suggests how speech communities function as frames of reference for socially constructed voices. Further the fact that people participate simultaneously in various communities suggests a mechanism for understanding the relations and interactions among those voices. Thus a 'presentational' approach examines language data for how it means by analysing the 'voices' created by the particular researcher–teacher dyad and the 'Discourses' from which those voices are drawn. This is done in part by laying out the structure of 'syntagmatic and paradigmatic contrasts' in the data. Limitations of space here do not allow for illustration of these concepts, however, Freeman (1993, 1992) provide examples of such analysis.

Presentational analysis leaves open, however, what such data can say about participants' intentions or reasons for doing what they do. The causal relation between language and action, on which the study of teachers' knowledge turns, remains inaccessible to the researcher since intention is an internal matter and therefore impossible to confirm in external data. In a representational approach to such data, the teacher's reasons are taken as given in her words; in a presentational approach, the language is studied in relation to itself so that the teacher's reasons are analysed through the language in which they are expressed. The interaction of different Discourses within the data can reflect something about the teacher's intentions; here the final concept of 'conceptions of practice' becomes useful.

I have suggested elsewhere that the teacher's conception of practice provides a way of thinking about this complex meeting of Discourses (Freeman, 1993) which appears not only in the research setting but also as Hargreaves (1977) recognized in any teaching situation. The conception of practice provides a bridge among the individual's internal sense-making, the socially constructed meanings which he or she uses, and his or her actions in the world (Freeman, 1993). It is implied in the Discourses which the individual uses. Presentational analysis focuses on observations of the presence, absence, and interrelation of these Discourses within a passage of data, and thus inferring the teacher's conception of practice in that situation.

Conclusion

The theoretical argument for a presentational approach to language data has six parts. First, language is, by nature, a collective fabric of social relationships built upon contrasts. Second, these contrasts create and sustain particular linguistic values, or distinctions, which are meaningful for a given social community. Third, using language is a matter of participating in a social community, one which is not necessarily defined by specific time or place but which recognizes itself in action, through participation. Fourth, therefore language which is not mutually recognizable to speaker and hearer is essentially meaningless; it goes unheard and unacknowledged because speaker and hearer are not participating in the same social community. You may hear the words, and yet not hear what they mean, as, for example, when you visit someone's home and do not follow the family aspects of the dinner table conversation. There are clearly degrees of recognition or mutuality, and these reflect our sense of being partially or more fully understood by another speaker.

Fifth, language use is more than a matter of simply choosing words to express one's meaning; it involves creating mutual recognition among users. A person chooses words for social — not individual — purposes, to be recognized, not simply to communicate. And sixth, for these reasons the study of language in any form must include the study of the relationships within it. These are relationships of *expression* in contrast or linguistic value, of *voice* and mutual relationship, and *source* of frame of reference or Discourses and social communities invoked. Together these relationships present how the particular words mean.

In view of this theoretical argument, the use of language data bears re-examination particularly when that data is said to document the speaker's inner world, as it is in the study of teachers' knowledge. The intuitive, representational way in which language data has been used in such research vastly simplifies its nature as language. Although it has supported the creation of this field of inquiry and has thus served important sociopolitical and epistemological aims. Representational analysis overlooks what is known about the fundamentally social character of language in creating and sustaining meaning. For this reason, the study of language data in teachers' knowledge needs to be expanded to encompass *how* that data means. With the integration of presentational analysis, the use of language data becomes more complex and more appropriate to its character as language. Language data can continue to represent teachers' 'mental lives' even as the construction of those representations is analysed. By looking at, rather than simply through, language data, researchers who study teachers' knowledge can document development and change in teachers' 'mental lives' and hence build a fuller and more complex view of what teachers know.

Notes

1 Preparation of this chapter was supported by a grant from the Spencer Foundation.
2 See Clark and Peterson, 1986, pp. 259–60 for a discussion of such procedures.
3 Two works, Jackson's *Life in classrooms* (1968) and Lortie's *Schoolteacher: a sociological study* (1975), were seminal in reframing this research agenda. Both took classrooms and schools as naturally occurring environments in which to study teaching and teachers' lives.
4 In the mid 1970s, major research panels, of the US National Institute of Education (NIE, 1975) and in England of the Social Sciences Research Council (Eggleston, 1979; Sutcliffe, 1977) articulated this shift in focus. These reports are generally taken as inaugurating the field of teacher cognition.
5 Mackay and Marland (1978) write that the concept of teacher as decision maker was popularized in the early 1970s before any substantial research had been carried out on it. The very early research made no reference to medical problem-solving (see Shavelson, 1973 as an example); in fact, Shulman and Elstein (1975) appear to introduce the medical connection to 'clinical decision-making'.
6 The apparent envy with which teaching has looked to medicine for constructs which would lend it authority, particularly in professionalization, is intriguing (see Labaree, 1992).
7 For a fuller and very clear discussion, see Butt, 1990.
8 For a full discussion of translinguistics, see Doe, 1988, pp. 183–260.
9 Willinsky (1989) makes a related observation, suggesting that even in narrative research which proceeds collaboratively, the researcher-dyad generates 'the press for narrative unity' that may not be actually present in the data or felt by the teacher.
10 Gee uses the capital 'D' to distinguish these Discourses from small 'd' discourse, which are sequential passages of spoken language with which applied linguists work.
11 Mishler's (1990) discussion of trustworthiness as a criterion for validity offers an interesting perspective related to this point.

References

BAHKTIN. M. (1981) *The Dialogic Imagination*, Austin, TX, University of Texas Press.
BELENKY, M., CLINCY, B., GOLDBERGER, N. and TARULE, J. (1986) *Women's Ways of Knowing: The Development of Self, Voice, and Mind*, New York, Basic Books.
BOWERS, C.A. (1987) *Elements of a Post-Liberal Theory of Education*, New York, Teachers College Press.
BRITZMAN, D. (1991) *Practice Makes Practice: A Critical Study of Learning to Teach*, Albany, State University of New York Press.

BRUNER, J. (1990) *Acts of Meaning*, Cambridge, Harvard University Press.

BUTT, D. (1989) *Talking and Thinking: The Patterns of Behaviour*, Oxford, Oxford University Press.

BUTT, R. and RAYMOND, D. (1987) 'Arguments for using qualitative approaches in understanding teacher thinking: The case for biography', *Journal of Curriculum Theorizing*, 7, 1, pp. 62–93.

CARTER, K. (1993) 'The place of story in the study of teaching and teacher education', *Educational Researcher*, 22, 1, pp. 5–12, 18.

CAZDEN, C. (1988) *Classroom Discourse: The Language of Teaching and Learning*, Portsmouth, NH, Heinemann.

CAZDEN, C. (1989) 'Contributions of the Bakhtin circle to "communicative competence"', *Applied Linguistics*, 10, 2, pp. 116–27.

CLANDININ, D.J. (1986) *Classroom Practice: Teacher Images in Action*, London, The Falmer Press.

CONNELLY, M. and CLANDININ, D.J. (1986) 'On narrative method, personal philosophy, and narrative unities in the study of teaching', *Journal of Research in Science Teaching*, 23, 4, pp. 293–310.

CONNELLY, M. and CLANDININ, D.J. (1990) 'Stories of experience and narrative inquiry', *Educational Researcher*, 19, 5, pp. 2–14.

CLANDININ, D.J. and CONNELLY, M. (1987) 'Teachers' personal knowledge: What counts as "personal" in studies of the personal', *Journal of Curriculum Studies*, 19, pp. 487–500.

CLARK, C. and PETERSON, P. (1986) 'Teachers' thought processes', in WITTROCK, M. (Ed) *Handbook of Research on Teaching* (3rd edition), New York, Macmillan Publishing, pp. 255–97.

DOE, J. (1988) *Speak Into the Mirror: A Story of Linguistic Anthropology*, Lantham, MD, University Press of America.

DUNKIN, M. and BIDDLE, B. (1974) *The Study of Teaching*, New York, Holt, Rinehart, and Winston.

EGGLESTON, J. (1979) 'Editorial introduction: making decisions in the classroom', in EGGLESTON, J. (Ed) *Teacher Decision-Making in the Classroom: A Collection of Papers*, London, Routledge and Kegan Paul, pp. 1–7.

ELBAZ, F. (1983) *Teacher Thinking: A Study of Practical Knowledge*, New York, Nichols Publishing.

ELBAZ, F. (1987) 'Response to Clandinin and Connelly', *Journal of Curriculum Studies*, 19, 6, pp. 501–2.

ELBAZ, F. (1991) 'Research on teacher's knowledge: The evolution of a discourse', *Journal of Curriculum Studies*, 23, 1, pp. 1–19.

FREEMAN, D. (1992) 'To make the tacit explicit: Teacher education, emerging discourse, and conceptions of teaching', *Teaching and Teacher Education*, 7, pp. 439–54.

FREEMAN, D. (1993) 'Renaming experience/reconstructing practice: Developing new understandings of teaching', *Teaching and Teacher Education*, 9, 5/6, pp. 485–98.

FREEDMAN, S., JACKSON, J. and BOLES, K. (1986) 'Teaching: An Imperilled "profession"', in SHULMAN, L. and SYKES, G. (Eds) *Handbook of Teaching and Policy*, New York, Longman, pp. 261–99.

GAGE, N.L. (Ed) (1963) *Handbook of research on teaching*, Chicago, Rand McNally.

GEE, J. (1989) 'Literacy, discourse, and linguistics: Introduction', *Journal of Education*, 17, pp. 5–17.

GEE, J. (1990) *Social Linguistics and Literacies: Ideology in Discourses*, Philadelphia, The Falmer Press.

HARGREAVES, D. (1977) 'A phenomenological approach to classroom decision-making', *Cambridge Journal of Education*, 7, 1, pp. 12–20.

JACKSON, P. (1968) *Life in Classrooms*, New York, Holt, Rinehart and Winston.

KAGAN, D. (1988) 'Teaching as clinical problem-solving: A critical examination of the analogy and its implications', *Review of Educational Research*, 58, 4, pp. 482–505.

LABAREE, D. (1992) 'Knowledge, power, and the rationalization of teaching: A genealogy of the movement to professionalize teaching', *Harvard Educational Review*, 62, 2, pp. 123–54.

LAVE, J. and WENGER, E. (1991) *Situated Learning: Legitimate Peripheral Participation*, New York, Cambridge University Press.

LORTIE, D. (1975) *Schoolteacher: A Sociological Study*, Chicago, University of Chicago Press.

MACKAY, D. and MARLAND, P. (1978) 'Thought processes of teachers', ERIC document (pars. 151–328).

MAXWELL, J. (1992) 'Understanding and validity in qualitative research', *Harvard Educational Review*, 62, 3, pp. 279–300.

MISHLER, E. (1986) *Research Interviewing: Context and Narrative*, Cambridge, MA, Harvard University Press.

MISHLER, E. (1990) 'Validation in inquiry-guided research: The role of exemplars in narrative studies', *Harvard Educational Review*, 60, pp. 415–42.

MUNBY, H. (1986) 'Metaphor in the thinking of teachers: An exploratory study', *Journal of Curriculum Studies*, 18, 2, pp. 197–209.

NATIONAL INSTITUTE OF EDUCATION [NIE] (1975) 'Teaching as clinical problem-solving', *Report of Panel #6; National Conference on Studies in Teaching*, Washington, DC, National Institute of Education.

POPE, M. (1991) 'Anticipating teacher thinking', in DAY, C., CALDERHEAD, J. and DENICOLO, P. (Eds) *Research on Teacher Thinking: Understanding Professional Development*, London, The Falmer Press, pp. 19–33.

DE SAUSSURE, F. (1916/1978) *A Course in General Linguistics*, BALLY, C. and SCHEHAYE, A. (Eds), Glasgow, Fontana/ Collins.

SHAVELSON, R. (1973) 'What is *the* basic teaching skill?', *Journal of Teacher Education*, 24, 2, pp. 144–51.

SHAVELSON, R. and STERN, P. (1981) 'Research on teachers' pedagogical thoughts, judgments, decisions, and behaviors', *Review of Educational Research*, 51, pp. 455–98.

SHULMAN, L. (1986) 'Paradigms and research programs in the study of teaching', in WITTROCK, M. (Ed) *Handbook of Research on Teaching* (3rd edition), New York, Macmillan Publishing, pp. 3–36.

SHULMAN, L. and ELSTEIN, A. (1975) 'Studies in problem-solving, judgment, and decision-making: implications for educational research', *Review of Educational Research*, 3, pp. 3–42.

SUTCLIFFE, J. (1977) 'Introduction to the "Volume on classroom decision-making"', *Cambridge Journal of Education*, 7, 1, pp. 2–3.

WALBERG, H. (1977) 'Decision and perception: New constructs for research on teaching effects', *Cambridge Journal of Education*, 7, 1, pp. 12–20.

WERTSCH, J. (1985) 'The semiotic mediation of mental life: L.S. Vygotsky and M.M. Bakhtin', in MERTZ, E. and PARMENTIER, R. (Eds) *Semiotic Mediation: Sociocultural and Psychological Perspectives*, New York, Academic Press, pp. 49–71.

WERTSCH, J. (1991) *Voices of the Mind: A Sociocultural Approach to Mediated Action*, Cambridge, Harvard University Press.

WILLINSKY, J. (1989) 'Getting personal and practical with personal practical knowledge', *Curriculum Inquiry*, 19, 3, pp. 247–64.

Chapter 6

Biographical Methods in the Study of Teachers' Professional Development

Geert Kelchtermans

Abstract

In this chapter a concrete narrative-biographical research procedure for the study of teachers' professional development is presented. Through collecting and analysing teachers' career stories I aimed at understanding how teachers developed a personal interpretive framework (encompassing a professional self and a subjective educational theory) by which they perceive their job situation and act in it. Apart from the description of the research procedure, I discuss a number of methodological issues and their specific appearance in biographical research: the central role of the research relation; the production of autobiographical data as an interactive process of creating meaning; specific ethical issues and finally the question of the quality norms in biographical research. Throughout the chapter I strongly invite fellow researchers to be more explicit about the concrete methodological procedures they use in the publications on their research. I conclude that descriptive and reflective papers on concrete research designs constitute as valuable a contribution to the discussion on the scientific forum as do reports on research findings and theoretical conclusions.

Introduction

Biographical and narrative approaches have become an important 'stream' in research on teaching during the last decade (e.g., Sikes, Measor and Woods, 1985; Goodson, 1992; Huberman, 1989; Kelchtermans, Schratz and Vandenberghe, 1994). Very often, however, the publications on these studies remain very vague about the concrete procedures for data collection and analysis. When starting my own study on teachers' professional biographies, I felt often frustrated by this lack of information in the literature. Sharing methodological reflections and experiences is of crucial importance to develop grounded research procedures in a certain field of study. That's why I want to present in this chapter a reflective account of my own research practice, hoping that it will function as an inspiring and constructive contribution to a more general discussion on qualitative research methodology. After situating the aims of the research project, I describe the procedure, called 'stimulated autobiographical self-thematization'. Further I focus on some specific methodological issues in narrative-biographical research.

A Study on Teachers' Professional Development

In my study I was interested in teachers' professional development, namely the qualitative changes in teachers' professional behaviour throughout the career. I wanted to understand how teachers give meaning to their experiences and how these experiences influence their practice. The teachers' perspective thus is central in this study. Therefore I made teachers reflect on their career to reconstruct their 'professional biographies' (the story in which the career experiences retrospectively are organized). From these professional biographies or career stories I reconstructed the teacher's 'personal interpretive framework'. This framework encompasses two important (and interwoven domains). First there is the 'professional self': the way a teacher sees him- or herself as a teacher, his or her self-representations. The second domain is the 'subjective educational theory': the personal system of knowledge and beliefs a teacher uses to execute the job. Both result from the dynamic interactions between the teacher and the professional environment (organizational context, colleagues, parents, pupils, the local community, etc.). In other words, I collected teachers' career stories and reconstructed from them the professional self and the subjective educational theory, conceived of as indicators for the professional development. Professional self and subjective educational theory were used as sensitizing concepts, according to the grounded theory-approach (Glaser and Strauss, 1967).

Since the conceptual framework and the results of the study have been discussed at length elsewhere (Kelchtermans, 1993a and 1993b; Kelchtermans and Vandenberghe, 1994), I will confine myself here to the methodological discussion.

The Research Procedure

Overview of the Research Procedure and Specific Techniques

In the research procedure I combined several research techniques: a questionnaire, a cycle of biographical interviews, school and classroom observations, interviews with key informants (e.g., principal, colleagues, etc.) and (of lesser importance) analysis of documents (e.g., school papers, brochures etc.). Before starting the project, the entire procedure for data collection as well as data analysis was described in a detailed research scenario (Kelchtermans, 1990). The cycle of biographical interviews is very central in the procedure. The research procedure can be characterized as a stimulated autobiographical self-thematization. The procedure aims at making teachers look back, reflectively, at their own career (autobiographical) and to stimulate them to 'thematize' their experiences (see below).

In a preparatory questionnaire (PQ) the respondents were asked to reconstruct their formal career chronologically. After indicating the period at the teacher-training college, they wrote down for every school year since then, the school and grade they had taught. These data provided the researcher with a general image of the respondent's career that was used as a starting point for the interviews.

A cycle of three biographical interviews was developed during a pilot study (Kelchtermans, 1993b; Kelchtermans and Vandenberghe, 1994) and refined for the main study. The option for biographical interviews (open, narrative) was obvious since I wanted to acknowledge the subjective perception and the narrative character of the professional biography. Because I was also interested in comparisons between the career stories, I used a semi-structured interview form. The interviews were organized in a *cyclical* way: every interview was followed by an analysis that provided topics for the next interview. In other words, the interviews were *cumulative*, meaning that every interview revealed new pieces of the 'life puzzle' (Cole, 1991, p. 14). The interviews took place at the respondent's home.[1]

The observations in school and classroom (OBS) and the interview with the principal aimed mainly at gathering additional information on the professional context of the interviewees. All respondents were observed in their classroom while teaching on at least three occasions for half a day. During these observations I spent the entire day in the school. This allowed me to informally observe the school life. In the interviews, following the observations, the respondents often referred to these school visits, e.g., when talking about a pupil or concrete aspects of school life. The implicit message then was 'you saw how we handle those things' or 'you've been around, so you know how things are done here'. The observations further allowed me to ask specific questions by referring to experiences or observations during my presence in the school. In short, the observations provided the researcher with an image of the reality the teacher talked about.

A central role in the research procedure was given to the research log (NOT). I reported on every contact with the respondents and wrote down reflections on every interview, school visit or phone call with a respondent. This reflection was supported by checklists with questions in the research scenario. Using these lists I documented my observations on the interview situation (presence of other persons; specific non-verbal reactions to certain questions by the respondent; description of the interview location; etc.) or the content of informal talks before and after the recorded interviews, during the school visits, etc. Special attention was given to the respondents' reactions or statements at the arrival or leaving of the researcher. These utterances often set the tone for the interview or indicated themes the respondent currently was concerned about (Measor, 1985, p. 20). Also after the tape recorder was turned off, the respondent often revealed key information (Woods, 1985, p. 20).

A second series of reflections that were documented in the log concerned the teacher's personal experience of the interview/observation visit by the researcher. How did he or she feel? Which thoughts flashed through his or her mind during the sessions? Did he or she make silent commentaries or develop preliminary interpretations? Did he or she hesitate to ask certain questions? etc. However, the research log was more than just an additional source of information. It was also an important instrument to document the actual research process. Practical decisions, made during the data collection or analysis, were written down in the log. In the same way I reported on difficulties, encountered during the research process and the way they were solved. Further the log contained the preliminary interpretive ideas or developing insights. This way the log complemented the general instructions and rules in the research scenario, with the story of the research process with every individual respondent. Figure 6.1 gives an overview of the research procedure and the specific techniques used.

Figure 6.1: Autobiographical Self-thematization — The Research Procedure

Time	Interview (at home)	Analysis	Observation (in school)
		PQ	
Week 1	I1 → NOT1		Contacting the principal
Week 2		AN1 (analysis I1)	
Week 3			Interview principal + OBS1
		AN1' (analysis OBS1)	
Week 4		P2	
Week 5	I2 (+L1) → NOT2		
Week 6		AN2 (analysis I2)	
Week 7			OBS2
		AN2' (analysis OBS2)	
Week 8	(L2)		
Week 9			OBS3
		AN2" (analysis OBS3)	
		SYN	
		(sent to respondent)	
Week 10		P3	
Week 11	I3 → NOT3		
Week 12		AN3	
		SYN2 = Professional Biographical Profile	

The Data Collection

Data were collected from ten experienced Flemish primary-school teachers (fifteen–twenty-five years of classroom experience) in four different schools. From every school I had two or three teachers in the research group. Six respondents were male, four were female. Only when the entire procedure was finished with respondents of one school, I started the process in the next school.

During the first interview (I1) the respondent's career was explored chronologically. The data from the preparatory questionnaire (PQ) on the formal career were used as a guide to encourage teachers to tell their career story (Denzin, 1970, pp. 235–7). At the end of I1 the respondents received a log formular (L1) and were asked to write down any remarks, ideas or additional information that came up in their minds afterwards and seemed relevant to the themes of the first interview.

All interviews were tape-recorded and transcribed word for word. As a general rule of thumb for the transcription I aimed at minimal loss of information (e.g., by also including comments on paraverbal behaviour, like silences, intonation, etc.). Further the protocols (interview transcriptions), as well as the field notes from the observations, were coded. The code list was developed during the pilot study (Kelchtermans, 1993b; Kelchtermans and Vandenberghe, 1994) and adapted for the main study. The codes were primarily descriptive: they summarized the content of the text fragment. Apart from these descriptive codes, I also used a limited number of interpretive codes, that referred to aspects of professional self and subjective educational theory. The use of these codes presupposed a further interpretation of the text fragment in terms of the conceptual framework. The fragmentation of the transcription protocol during the coding, was based on the meaningfulness of the text fragments. The function of the codes was to indicate the global content of the fragments and to make it possible that fragments about the same topic were brought together for interpretation.

In the first analysis step (AN1) I identified the 'Information gaps' (see Woods, 1985, p. 21). Gaps in the chronology, unclear passages (too few details, descriptions too vague) and 'white spots' (aspects of school life that hadn't been thematized yet) were identified, by careful reading of the protocol.

Next I read the text once again, looking for indications of professional self and subjective educational theory. This resulted in preliminary interpretations. Then I introduced the relevant information from the research log in the analysis. Finally the results of AN1 led to a synthetic memo.

Shortly after the first interview, the first classroom observation (OBS1) and the interview with the principal took place. The observations were made in the respondent's classroom, but the school life was also observed more informally during lunch pauses, breaks, etc. The interview with the principal addressed topics of school organization, number of pupils and teachers, contacts between school and environment, etc. Through this interview I collected information about the school context. Sometimes the researcher received a 'school newspaper' or a brochure about the school. For practical reasons, this interview was not tape-recorded; the researcher took as many notes as possible (field notes).

AN1 and OBS1 constituted the basis for the preparation of the second interview (P2). This interview consisted of two parts. The questions in the 'respondent specific part' related to the topics from the first interview. The information gaps and tentative interpretations were translated into questions and presented to the respondent. I asked for further explanation or specific details. The second, 're-spondent un-specific part' consisted of a series of questions that were identical for all the respondents. The central notions of the conceptual framework constituted the basis for these questions.

The second interview (I2) started with a discussion about the eventual notes on the log formular. Further, the questions from the respondent specific and the respondent unspecific part were presented. The interview and the data analysis of I2 were analogue with I1. Also at the end of I2 the respondent received a log formular (L2). On the formular, the questions from the respondent unspecific part were repeated. As with L1, the second formular was also meant as a kind of 'safety net' for eventual relevant information, the respondent might remember after the interviewer had left. The formular had to be sent back to the respondent before a specific date. I mention here that the logs were only very rarely used by the respondents. Probably this can be explained by the fact that autobiographical reflection was quite unusual for the respondents. When the researcher was absent, the most important incentive for that kind of reflection was missing. Further, the informal talks during the observation visits functioned as complementary contact moments between researcher and respondent.

The second analysis step (AN2) was executed in analogy with the first (AN1). The data from the interview with the principal and the observations were also coded and prepared for further analysis. On the basis of OBS1, OBS2 and OBS3, the interview with the school leader, AN1, AN2, the log formulars and the research log (NOT) a synthesis text was written. This text was constructed along a fixed structure, based on the conceptual framework (Kelchtermans, 1993b). This structure reflected also the steps in the interpretation process: starting with the formal career data, I reconstructed the professional biography. These professional biographies were then analysed in terms of professional self and subjective educational theory. Here I also included data on the actual professional environment (macro, meso and microlevel).

This interpretive transformation of the data is described by Woods as dis-tilling 'the essence of the biography into more manageable form, retaining the teacher's "ordinary" language for the most part, but organising the material in a sociologically meaningful way' (Woods, 1985, p. 23; see also Huberman, 1989, p.40). By using extensive quotations from the interviews, I tried to meet Woods' demand to maximally keep the spontaneous talk of the teachers in those syn-theses.[2] At the same time control by the respondent became possible through this summarizing document (Woods, 1985, p. 22). About one week before the final interview, the synthesis text was sent to the respondent, who was asked to read it very carefully and critically append any remarks or comments.

For some respondents I also prepared a respondent-specific part for the third interview, because the data from earlier interviews or observations weren't clear enough yet or because of certain interpretations that needed to be controlled by the respondent.

The synthesis text was the basis for the third interview (I3). In the first part of that interview, the synthesis text was checked page by page and the comments of the respondent were collected. The third analysis step (AN3) was the same as the former ones. The information from interview 3 and the reflective notes of the researcher were added to the synthesis text. This way I got the professional biographical profile (PBP), a document containing all relevant information about one respondent (including reflections and interpretations by the researcher) in a structured and condensed form.

The Data Analysis

The data were analysed in two steps. The vertical analysis consisted of the sequence of interpretive data transformations during the collection process, and resulted in the professional biographical profile (see above). The professional biographical profile, in its final textual form, had two important functions. First there is the 'communicative function'. The text determined the form in which the data became accessible for others. It constituted the medium through which the research data and their analysis were communicated towards the external world. Further the text had an 'argumentative-rhetorical function', since it aimed at convincing the reader that the career stories were correctly presented and that the interpretations were plausible. This implied that the text had to contain sufficient evidence (e.g., fragments of transcription protocols or field notes) to ground the statements and to argue for them. That is why I composed the profiles as 'thick descriptions', so that 'thick interpretations' became possible (Geertz, 1973).

It is clear that the writing of the professional biographical profiles was a very crucial step in the entire research procedure (see also Atkinson, 1991; Clifford, 1986; Wolcott, 1990). This writing implied much more than a mere technical process of reporting. Although the different steps in the analysis were depicted in the research scenario and the content of the different text sections was pre-structured by the conceptual framework, still a creative process of composing a coherent text by the researcher was necessary. Writing is an intensive, reflective conversation with the data, including sustained interpretive analysis and careful phrasing. The research scenario included a list of general 'rules of thumb' as a guide for the writing process in the research scenario: careful phrasing (avoiding ambiguity), staying close to the original transcripts (use quotations), continuous checking of the interpretations, avoiding judgments (non-evaluative attitude), etc.

Before I sent the profiles to the respondents, a colleague — not directly involved in this research project — read them over very carefully and commented on the text draft as an outsider.[3]

Since the textual structure of the professional biographical profiles was identical for every respondent, the profiles constituted the basis for the next step, the 'horizontal analysis'. In this horizontal analysis the professional biographical profiles were systematically compared, using the technique of 'constant comparative analysis' (Glaser, 1969). In the study this concretely implied a cyclical repeated pattern of close reading, developing more general interpretations and controlling these interpretations by confronting them with the data. First the profiles were read through entirely, to get a general overview. Next I compared all the text sections in the profiles one by one for every respondent. In a final integral reading of the profiles I checked that no data were 'forgotten' during the comparative analysis. This horizontal analysis resulted in a set of recurring patterns and common themes among the professional biographies of the respondents (see Kelchtermans, 1993a).

Critical Methodological Issues in Narrative-biographical Research

In this section I will adress a number of specific methodological issues in biographical research. I will identify the questions or problems and describe how I coped with them.

The Research Relation as the Pivot of Biographical Research

In biographical research the relation between researcher and respondent pervades every aspect of the research process: it determines the quality and the quantity of the information gathered (Cole, 1991; Measor, 1985). A very important condition for establishing an appropriate relation is a feeling of trust towards the researcher. Only a respondent who feels safe and perceives the researcher as trustworthy, will be prepared to share his or her autobiographical story. The relation of trust should permit that 'teachers feel sufficiently free and relaxed to be "themselves"' (Woods, 1985, p. 14). To achieve this, I explained from the start to the respondents how the research process would evolve and what I expected from them (Plummer, 1983, pp. 90–3). The respondents were also told how they had been selected for the study. Further the professional background of the researcher was clarified and I promised confidential treatment of the data. Moreover at the end of every session the researcher invited questions or remarks on the research process.

Trustfulness is further enhanced by the reciprocity in the relation. Collecting biographical data should not be a 'one-way-traffic', but rather a process of 'mutual storytelling' (Connelly and Clandinin, 1990, p. 4; Woods, 1985, p. 14). In this process of mutual storytelling, it is important to gain credibility in the eyes of the respondent. This can be accomplished 'through sharing relevant personal anecdotes' (Cole, 1991, p. 12). During the frequent contacts (interviews, observations, informal talks) I was often asked questions about the background of my study (why studying this topic this way?). But respondents were also interested in my opinion about specific situations in the school. They wanted to identify common acquaintances or asked questions concerning my hobbies, family life, etc. Normally these questions were answered honestly, without giving up my role however. I remained alert for the possible influence of my utterances on the teacher's story. The contents of these more informal exchanges were documented in the research log. Experience showed that, especially after the second interview, the respondents felt the need to know more about the researcher. It was as if the balance of giving and taking in the research process had to be restored. I found myself confronted with the subtle task of engaging myself as a person far enough in the relation (to remain credible and to get relevant data), with the risk of going too far and influencing the content of the interview too much (see e.g., Munro, 1991, p. 10).

This already indicates the importance of the affective dimension in the research relation. Biographical research implies more than a pure cognitive exchange of objective descriptive answers to informative questions. Both parties in the meeting observe and listen to each other and build a personal image of the other. This image is also evaluative. More concretely this meant e.g., that the researcher felt more sympathy for some respondents or appreciated some classroom practices more than others. The same was true for the respondents: some of them liked the researcher more then others, and this determined their commitment to the research process. I had to cope with still other relevant feelings: discomfort or uncertainty during the first meetings with a respondent; enthusiasm when hearing certain stories, but also indignation and anger with other anecdotes.

Non- or paraverbal signs are also very important in this respect. Eye contact, smiling, concerned or surprised wrinkling of the eyebrows, etc., are highly relevant, because respondents want affirmation and reassurance (Measor, 1985, p. 62). After all, they are sharing rather personal experiences and thoughts with a stranger.

Methodologically this affective dimension is not an easy matter. On the other hand, it is of no use to deny or minimize it. Moreover, the character of trust and the implied familiarity with each other are necessary conditions for successful biographical research. The interplay between the emotional and the intellectual is an essential element and should thus be made public (Ely *et al.*, 1991). As a qualitative and certainly as a biographical researcher one is forced to aknowledge these affective aspects and recognize them as essential in the collection and interpretation of the data. The only way to control these aspects is permanent self-reflection by the researcher (Denzin, 1970, p. 11). The affective dimension therefore was explicitly present in my log notes.

Summarizing, the **researcher's role** during this biographical study can be characterized as active, interested and non-evaluative listening and observing. The attitude toward the respondent was above all one of empathy, acknowledgment, appraisal and loyalty (Woods, 1985, pp. 20–1). The respondent's story was listened to with alert openmindedness. In biographical research the researcher as a person is the essential research instrument. It is the reflective commitment of his or her social behavioural and interpretive competencies, that make it possible for the researcher to explore and understand the world as experienced by the respondent (Bergold and Breuer, 1987, p. 40).

The Character of the (Auto)biographical Data Production: An Interactive Process of Creating Meaning

Autobiographical data are produced in a social setting (interview) where the respondent is stimulated by the researcher to look back reflectively on the personal career. This setting influences the production of the data. The respondents tell their story to the researcher, or more generally to the implicit audience they assume behind the researcher. The respondents' expectation of what will happen to the information they provide (e.g., the degree to which it will be made public) determines his or her telling (Angrosino, 1991, p. 1; Polkinghorne, 1988, p. 164).

Hoeppel emphasizes the 'intention to communicate' (Mitteilungszweck), inherent to autobiographical data (Hoeppel, 1983, p. 311). One writes an autobiography with an image of the reader in mind or tells it to a listener. More or less conscious motives and intentions play a role throughout the story and influence what is told and what not and the way it is told. Biographical data thus are inherently intersubjective: they arise out of an interactive communication context, where the storyteller retrospectively shares his or her experiences with a listener. A reflection about the influence of the interview context on the data therefore must be part of the data analysis. In the study this was included in the systematic reflection in the research log by the interviewer, after every interview. This reflection was again guided by a checklist, provided in the research scenario (Kelchtermans, 1990). This list contained questions like:

- How would you characterize the interview relation?
- Were there a lot of laughs? Why?
- Were there critical moments during the interview (e.g., refusals to answer, painful silences, etc.)?
- Did you have questions in mind, you didn't dare to ask? Why not? How could they be addressed in the next meeting?
- Were there moments of significant emotional reaction?
- Were there other people present during the interview? Who? When? Do you have indications that their presence influenced the interview? If yes, how?

On the other hand the storytelling as such already has a meaning for the respondent. Bahrdt believes that people have their reasons for recalling the different experiences during their lives and putting them into a meaningful order. This way they create the history of their personal life, a history that can be told to an audience. In the act of storytelling the story is constituted and developed (Bahrdt, 1982, p. 24). Through telling his or her story, the respondent obtains it as his or her (developing) story. This constitutes the inherently *subjective* character of autobiographical data: they are about a personal understanding of experienced situations. There is always a tension between the facts and the personal interpretation. Autobiographical data consist in the idiosyncratic linguistic presentation of the subjective mastering of objective facts (Schulze, 1979, p. 53). Thus it is important to realize that autobiographical stories don't inform about facts and events, but about experiences and their meaning for the storyteller. It is not a matter of truth, but of 'truth for me' as storyteller. Biographical approaches reveal subjective realities, ideas, feelings, experiences.

Ethical Issues in Biographical Research

Qualitative research in general, and biographical research in particular have a clear ethical dimension (Plummer, 1983, pp. 140–5). 'A life history does deal with intimate material, and carries a high ethical load as a result' (Measor and Sikes, 1992, p. 223). The researcher finds himself or herself in 'face to face relationships with other human beings in which ethical problems of the personal as well as the professional are bound to arise' (Soltis, 1989, p. 127).

A first problem in the biographical research was the question of 'intrusiveness'. How deep is one allowed to 'dig' into the personal life experiences of the respondent? During the study I learned that respondents were willing to share their experiences in a detailed, straightforward and outspoken way. For an experienced interviewer it is quite easy to make people tell more and even more personal things about themselves than they first intended to. Therefore Measor and Sikes talk about the 'coaxer' role of the biographical researcher, since the respondents are always to some degree 'seduced' to share their life history (Measor and Sikes, 1992, p. 221).

On the other hand, the private and personal worlds were very relevant for the research interest. The dilemma thus was: How can I collect sufficient information for a reconstruction of the teachers' story, the roots of professional self and sub-jective educational theory, without penetrating the private sphere in an improper way? I don't think there are simple solutions to this dilemma. The researcher has to rely on his or her social sensitivity and tact. Respect for the respondent and integrity should steer his or her behaviour. Thirst for sensation and other dubious curiosity are absolutely to be avoided. As a rule of thumb I never asked questions about the private sphere directly or explicitly. When the respondent happened to bring about these themes, the utterances were explored until the reseacher clearly understood what was meant and how these private experiences were linked to the professional biography.

The 'trustfulness' in the research relation also has ethical implications. The data provided by the respondent had to be handled with discretion. From the start I emphasized that the data would be treated *anonymously* and in a confidential way. I made special efforts to guarantee that the identity of the respondents wouldn't be released. Therefore I consequently used pseudonyms or general descriptions to make the data anonymous, without diminishing their informative strength and clarity. Perfect anonymity however, cannot be obtained (Plummer, 1983, p. 144). This once again created a dilemma. On the one hand I had to protect the respond-ent's anonymity. But on the other hand I needed extensive quotations of the story to underpin the conclusions. Especially if one wants to show the interplay of biography and context, thick descriptions are necessary and demand extensive information. I tentatively solved the dilemma by presenting in the research report only the information needed to ground the interpretations, while using pseudo-nyms and codes for names and places.

The problem of deceiving or exploiting the respondents (Plummer, 1983, pp. 143–5; Thomas, 1992, p. 6) was avoided by correctly informing the respond-ents from the beginning about the aims of the study and the concrete research procedure (see above). The quality of the research relation, as discussed above, was a further guarantee for an ethically correct research process. By using forms of communicative validation (see further), I also provided the opportunity for the respondent to control the data and the way they were made public.

The Quality Norms in Biographical Research

The quality of a scientific study normally is assessed in terms of reliability and validity, as a specification of the more general demand for repeatability. Because both criteria stem from quantitative and positivistic methodology, one could ar-gue that a qualitative, biographical researcher should not bother about them at all. Although I stress the narrative and constructivistic character of the data and the hermeneutical nature of the analysis, I do believe that the requirement for validity and reliability should also be used in this kind of study as guidelines for meth-odological quality.

Reliability refers to the 'repeatability' of the study and to the degree the research outcomes are independent from the research procedure. I conceived of reliability mainly in terms of 'argumentative reliability', namely non-quantitative indications that the research process is repeatable (van Ijzendoorn and Miedema, 1986, p. 499). In this study the *'research scenario'* (Kelchtermans, 1990) was an important means for creating openness about the research procedure. In this document the research procedure was extensively described and legitimated. The research log functioned as a complement for the research scenario and documented the actual research process. This way it is possible for outsiders to trace back the entire research process and the interpretive procedures which lead to the outcomes. Scenario and log contained a detailed description of the selection criteria and actual selection procedure for composing the research group; the different techniques for data collection; the coding procedure (Denzin, 1970, p. 240; Plummer, 1983, pp. 89–91). I am aware that the reliability of the study would have been better if it had been carried out by a research team. During the pilot study this was the case and there I experienced the advantages of 'team triangulation' (Measor and Sikes, 1992, p. 224).

In the research log I also documented my own activities and reflections during the research process. This way it became an important instrument for controlling the subjectivity of the interpreting researcher (Deshkin, 1988). Intuitions, feelings, assumptions etc. were (as far as possible) thematized and written down, to have them available during further steps in the analysis of the data. This subjectivity is an inherent element in interpretative research. Only a systematic and documented reflection process can control that subjectivity and avoid that it biases the research process (Denzin, 1970, p. 11). Apart from describing the research procedure, I also contributed to the reliability by making explicit the conceptual framework that guided the data collection and interpretation (see above; also Kelchtermans, 1993a and 1993b).

·An important further step in enhancing the reliability is the use of 'triangulation', namely using several different research techniques in the study of the same phenomenon. This way the shortcomings of one method can be compensated for by using another (Denzin, 1970, pp. 300–10). In this study I used data triangulation in time, space and person. I gathered data over a longer period of time (several interview sessions and observation visits); at different locations (classroom, school, private home) and with different respondents (at least two colleagues of the same school; the principal). Further I collected data at the level of the individual respondent as well as at the level of interacting individuals (during the observation of the school life). Also the data type (oral, written, observed) was triangulated: I used documents, interviews, observations, informal talks and interviews with other informants.

'Validity' refers to the question how far the collected data, and the insights distillated from them, represent 'reality' (Denzin, 1970; Measor, 1985; Measor and Sikes, 1992; Plummer, 1983; Woods, 1985). The concrete question in this study was: Is the reconstruction of the professional development (in terms of professional self and subjective educational theory) based on the career stories, a correct representation of the way the respondent perceives that development? Can I convincingly argue for the plausibility or credibility of the reconstructions?

Several aspects of the research procedure supported the validity. The research period for every respondent encompassed about three months. Because of this relatively long period of time I was able to collect data in several settings and at several moments. This way I could also control for reactivity and researcher effects. Because of the repeated contacts atypical respondent behaviour because of the researcher's presence was reduced. I also controlled for researcher effects through the lengthy research period, through the systematic reflection in the research log, the explicit instructions in the research scenario and the striving for an unobtrusive use of the techniques for data collection.

Of course the validation of the research findings was also enhanced by the triangulation. By combining ethnographic observations and retrospective interviews, the reconstructions based on the interviews could be confronted with the findings of the observations (e.g., the content of the subjective educational theory). During AN2 I also did a systematic control for internal consistency. When inconsistencies were found in the different data, they were included in the respondent-specific part of the final interview and discussed with the respondent.

The most important technique for validation I used was the 'communicative validation': I tried to show the validity of my interpretations by feeding back the results to the respondents and negotiating a consensus about the interpretations (Terhart, 1982, pp. 153–4). Above I described how I gave the respondents the opportunity to react extensively on the reconstruction of their career story by feeding back the synthesis text. During the writing of this text, I tried to stay as close as possible to the respondent's spontaneous narrative talk. If a respondent didn't agree with the text, I asked him or her to substantiate his or her critique and to propose an alternative formulation. These amendments were included in the final professional biographical profile. Several respondents spontaneously said that they 'recognized' themselves in the text.

The value of communicative validation thus depends on the research relation and the way the finding of a consensus about the interpretation is actually established. Legewie is right in stressing the importance of critically analysing the research situation as a starting point for every validation (Legewie, n.d., p. 10). That is the reason why I gave so much attention to the researcher's role, the research relation and the permanent reflection on it during the data collection.

However, the quality of the communicative validation can be threatened in several ways. Because of his or her social prestige, it is possible that the researcher implicitly (unconsciously) forces his or her interpretations upon the respondent. Because the researcher writes the text, he or she is in a privileged position to shape the narrative and its interpretation (Terhart, 1982 and 1985; Thomas, 1992, p. 7). A solution is the combination of 'consensual' (communicative) and 'empirical' validation. The latter implies the testing of the interpretation by predicting future behaviour from it and researching that future behaviour (Terhart, 1985).

Validity is and remains an important concern for researchers, whether they use qualitative methods or not. I learned that explicit reflection on validity in qualitative (biographical) research procedures, made us more conscious about its complexity and relevance. I believe that sharing the thoughtful ways of handling these 'eternal' questions among researchers, constitutes a main road to improve the quality of (qualitative) research. I further believe that descriptive and reflective papers on concrete research designs constitute as valuable a contribution to the discussion on the scientific forum as do reports on research findings and theoretical conclusions. Therefore this sharing of my research story is an implicit plea for, and invitation to, others to do the same.

Notes

1   The choice of the interview location was left to the respondent. For practical reasons all respondents chose to be interviewed at home. In biographical interviews, it is

of crucial importance that the respondents feel 'safe' (e.g., Woods, 1985, p. 15). The private sphere of their own house, away from the school context, enhanced that feeling of safety. This way the researcher also got information (through informal observation) of the respondent's life outside school.

2   This procedure however also has a 'negative side'. The confrontation with their own, literal statements wasn't always appreciated by the respondents. They felt ashamed about their poor and clumsy looking language. Sometimes it resulted in anger and once even in a conflict because the respondent felt ridiculed by the researcher. An explanation by the researcher of the reasons for the word by word quotation (namely the text was only meant for internal control by the respondent; because of time pressure better editing of the interview fragments hadn't been possible yet) proved sufficient to overcome the resistance or concerns of the teachers. From this experience, I believe it is important to anticipate these feeling in the letter that accompanies the synthesis text.

3   I gratefully acknowledge the dedication with which my wife and colleague Ann Deketelaere took care of this important, but time-consuming task.

References

ANGROSINO, M.V. (1991) *Documents of Interaction: Biography, Autobiography, and Life History in Social Science Perspective*, Gainesville, FLA, University of Florida Press.

ATKINSON, P. (1991) 'Supervising the text', *International Journal of Qualitative Studies in Education*, 4, 2, pp. 161–74.

BAHRDT, H.P. (1982) 'Identität und biographisches Bewusstsein: Soziologische Überlegungen zur Funktion des Erzählens aus dem eigenen Leben für die Gewinnung und Reproduktion von Identität', (Identity and Biographical Awareness), in BREDNICH, R.W. *et al.* (Eds) *Lebenslauf und Lebenszusammenhang*, Freiburg i. Br, pp. 18–45.

BERGOLD, J. and BREUER, F. (1987) 'Methodologische und methodische Probleme bei der Erforschung der Sicht des Subjekts', (Methodological Problems in Researching the Subjects' Perspective), in BERGOLD, J.B. and FLICK, U. (Eds) *Ein-sichten. Zugänge zur Sicht des Subjekts mittels qualitativer Forschung*, Tübingen, Deutsche Gesellschaft für Verhaltenstherapie, pp. 20–52.

CLIFFORD, J. (1986) 'Introduction: Partial truths', in CLIFFORD, J. and MARCUS, G. (Eds) *Writing Cultures. The Poetics and Politics of Ethnography*, Berkeley, University of California Press, pp. 1–26.

COLE, A. (1991) 'Interviewing for the Life History: A Process of Ongoing Negotiation', Paper presented at AERA-meeting, Chicago.

CONNELLY, F.M. and CLANDININ, D.J. (1990) 'Stories of experience and narrative inquiry', *Educational Researcher*, 19, 4, pp. 2–14.

DENZIN, N. (1970) *The Research Act*, Chicago, Aldine.

DESHKIN, A. (1988) 'In search of subjectivity: One's own,' *Educational Researcher*, 17, 7, pp. 17–22.

ELY, M., ANZUL, M., FRIEDMAN, T., GARNER, D. and McCORMACK-STEINMETZ, A. (1991) *Doing Qualitative Research: Circles Within Circles*, London-New York, Philadelphia, The Falmer Press.

FARADAY, A. and PLUMMER, K. (1979) 'Doing life histories,' *Sociological Review*, 27, 4, pp. 773–98.

GEERTZ, C. (1973) *The Interpretation of Cultures: Selected Essays*, New York, Basic Books.

GLASER, B. (1969) 'The Constant comparative method of qualitative analysis', in McCALL, G. and SIMMONS, J. (Eds) *Issues in Participant Observation*, Reading, Addison-Wesley, pp. 216–27.

GLASER, B. and STRAUSS, A. (1967) *The Discovery of Grounded Theory*, Chicago, New York, Aldine.

GOODSON, I. (Ed) (1992), *Studying Teachers' Lives*, London, Routledge.

HOEPPEL, R. (1983) 'Perspektiven der erziehungswissenschaftlichen Erschliessung autobiographischer Formen der Selbstreflexion', (Perspectives for the Use of Auto-biographical Self-reflection in Educational Research), *Zeitschrift für Pädagogik*, 18, Beiheft, Weinheim-Basel, Beltz, pp. 307–12.

HUBERMAN, M. (1989) 'The professional life cycle of teachers', *Teachers College Record*, 91, 1, pp. 31–57.

KELCHTERMANS, G. (1990) *De professionele biografie van leerkrachten basisonderwijs: Onderzoeksdraaiboek*, (The Professional Biography of Primary School Teachers: Research Scenario), Leuven, Center for Educational Policy and Innovation.

KELCHTERMANS, G. (1993a) 'Getting the Story, Understanding the Lives: From Career Stories to Teachers' Professional Development', *Teaching and Teacher Education*, 9, 516, pp. 443–56.

KELCHTERMANS, G. (1993b) 'Teachers and their career story: A biographical perspective on professional development', in DAY, C. CALDERHEAD, J. and DENICOLO, P. (Eds) *Research on Teacher Thinking: Towards Understanding Professional Development*, London, Washington, The Falmer Press, pp. 198–220.

KELCHTERMANS, G., SCHRATZ, M. and VANDENBERGHE, R. (1994) 'The development of qualitative research: Efforts and experiences from continental Europe', *International Journal of Qualitative Studies in Education*, 7, 3. pp. 239–55.

KELCHTERMANS, G. and VANDENBERGHE, R. (1994) 'Teachers' professional development: A biographical perspective', *Journal of Curriculum Studies*, 26, 1, pp. 45–62.

LEGEWIE, H. (n.d.) 'Interpretation und Validierung biographischer Interviews', (Interpretation and Validation of Biographical Interviews), in JÜTTEMAN, G. and THOMAE, H. (Eds) *Biographie und Psychologie*, Heilderberg, Springer.

MEASOR, L. (1985) 'Interviewing: A strategy in qualitative research', in BURGESS, R.G. (Ed) *Strategies of Educational Research*, London, Philadelphia, The Falmer Press, pp. 55–77.

MEASOR, L. and SIKES, P. (1992) 'Visiting lives: Ethics and methodology in life history', in GOODSON, I. (Ed) *Studying Teachers' Lives*, London, Routledge, pp. 209–233.

MUNRO, P. (1991) 'Multiple "I's": Dilemmas of Life History Research.' Paper presented at AERA-meeting, Chicago.

PLUMMER, K. (1983) *Documents of Life*, London, Allen Unwin.

POLKINGHORNE, D. (1988) *Narrative Knowing and the Human Sciences*, Albany, NY, State University of New York Press.

SCHULZE, T. (1979) 'Autobiographie und Lebensgeschichte', (Autobiography and Life History), in BAACKE, D. and SCHULZE, T. (Eds) *Aus Geschichten lernen*, München, Juventa, pp. 51–98.

SIKES, P., MEASOR, L. and WOODS, P. (1985) *Teacher Careers: Crises and Continuities*, London, Philadelphia, The Falmer Press.

SOLTIS, J. (1989) 'The ethics of qualitative research', *International Journal of Qualitative Studies in Education*, 2, 2, pp. 123–30.

TERHART, E. (1982) 'Interpretive approaches in educational research: A consideration of some theoretical issues with particular reference to recent developments in West Germany', *Cambridge Journal of Education*, 12, 3, pp. 141–60.

TERHART, E. (1985) 'The adventure of interpretation: Approaches to validity', *Curriculum Inquiry*, 15, 4, pp. 451–64.

THOMAS, D. (1992) 'Getting up the Nose of the Truffle Hunter: Some Possible Critiques of Teacher Narrative Research', Paper presented at the Annual Conference of the British Educational Research Association, s.l.

VANIJZENDOORN, M. and MIEDEMA, S. (1986) 'De kwaliteit van kwalitatief onderzoek', (The Quality of Qualitative Research), *Pedagogische Studiën*, 63, 12, pp. 498–505.

WOLCOTT, H.F. (1990) 'On seeking and rejecting: Validity in qualitative research', in ELSNER, E.W. and PESHKIN, A. (Eds) *Qualitative Inquiry in Education: The Continuing Debate*, New York, Teachers College Press, pp. 121–52.

WOODS, P. (1985) 'Conversations with teachers', *British Educational Research Journal*, 11, 1, pp. 13–26.

YOUNG, B. and TARDIF, C. (1992) 'Interviewing: Two sides of the story', *International Journal of Qualitative Studies in Education*, 5, 2, pp. 135–45.

Chapter 7

Ethical Concerns in Teacher-thinking Research

Naama Sabar

Abstract

The purpose of this chapter is to identify and study ethical aspects of teacher-thinking research in an attempt to enhance the research community's awareness of this issue. It pertains both to the design and implementation stages of studies and relates to anticipated as well as unexpected events in the course of research. In order to focus our thinking and to identify distinct problems, we set out to create an inventory of ethical problems and dilemmas which arise in teacher-thinking research by studying the attitudes toward ethical issues of most of the professionally recognized members of the Israeli teacher-thinking research community (twelve researchers) through semi-open interviews. The findings are organized and presented according to the major categories that emerged from the responses: 1) Awareness of ethical issues; 2) The nature of the partnership; and 3) The meaning of intervention. The fact that our study has put researchers into the traditional position of their subjects, may also cause them to view these questions from a different standpoint, an experience which in itself may be of value.

Ethical Concerns in Teacher Thinking[1]

There is a school of thought which claims that a qualitative research paradigm demands a special ethics code because of the special relationship between researcher and subject (e.g., Cassell and Wax, 1980; Bogdan and Biklen, 1982; Soltis, 1990; Marshall, 1992). Actually, increasing agreement with this view in recent years led to the special session at the 1993 meeting of the American Educational Research Association devoted to ethical issues in qualitative research culminating in a special publication (Mathison, Ross and Cornett, 1993).

This chapter identifies and discusses ethical concerns in teacher-thinking research both as a methodological aspect of this field and in its broader philosophical implications. It pertains both to the design and implementation stages of studies and relates to anticipated as well as unexpected events in the course of research.

Prologue

In the past two years, we have been engaged in a study of the educational absorption of young Russian immigrants in Israeli schools. Two schools were studied in depth, using intensive observations and interviews, focusing on teachers' perceptions of the immigrants and their behaviour. At the end of the first semester during which we studied the schools, before the summer vacation, we summed up our initial experiences for a research proposal. The principal of one of the schools was very anxious to find out about our preliminary findings and urged us to show them to her. We gave her the report, noting the fact that it was a pilot and in no way identified the school, and asked for her comments before the new school year began, when we hoped to launch the actual study. The principal seemed to feel that we hadn't sufficiently emphasized the objective difficulties facing teachers who dealt with new immigrant pupils, and that the teachers in the other school we were studying had come out somewhat better in the report. She was both defensive and aggressive, and didn't want us to continue studying her school because we didn't serve her purpose. We had to make an enormous effort to convince her to change her mind, which she ultimately did. The whole incident raised a number of questions in our minds: How frank should we be with our informants? Should we have shown her the findings before finalizing them? To what extent should we share our objectives? We began to consider how to present the final report, including the judgmental aspects which are part of any research, with minimal offence to the principal (who would doubtless expect to see the report), yet without affecting the credibility of the research and the clarity of its conclusions. We then decided to look further into some of the ethical aspects in similar studies. While in other fields, such as law, medicine and psychology, ethics codes have long existed, education, except for the areas of testing and measurement (Joint Committee on Standards for Educational Evaluation, 1981), did not until recently have such a code (ESAERA, 1992). Teacher-thinking research in particular, because of the central role of the teacher informant as the direct subject of the research and the source of reflections yielding personal narratives (Elbaz, 1993), and where the researcher 'penetrates' the teacher's mind in a way that may have ethical consequences, deserves special attention.

The purpose of this chapter is, thus, to advocate special attention to ethics through specification and modification and greater attention to codes of ethics relating to teacher thinking. By creating an inventory of the variety of issues and concerns as seen by teacher researchers, we hope to enhance the research community's awareness of ethics in teacher-thinking research and contribute to its professionalism.

Literature Background

The few explicit examples of scholarship on these topics deal with questions of integrity as well as questions of ethics in general in teacher thinking.

Two major problematic issues can be distinguished among the ethical questions raised in the literature: the question of the informant as a 'true partner' in the narrative approach, and the nature of the risks to the research and the informant.

Partnership

The domain of true partnership between the teacher and the researcher encompasses questions which can be divided into two groups.

The Relationship Between the Researcher and the Teacher Informant

Commitment to research authenticity — How can the desire of the teacher to receive feedback after any observation or interview be reconciled with the need to avoid influencing the informant's behaviour? Are the teacher's solitude in the classroom and his or her need for feedback from an adult exploited by the researcher? Is it the researcher's role to be helpful to the teacher and if necessary, to intervene in the observed situation, or is it merely to describe observed behaviour?

Researchers who have dealt with these questions include Cochrane-Smith and Lytle (1990) who, in their paper advocating cooperative research, make the following statement: 'Cooperative research provides valuable insights into the interrelationships of theory and practice, but like more traditional interpretive research, often constructs and predetermines teachers' roles in the research process, thereby framing and mediating teachers' perspectives through researchers' perspectives' (p. 3).

Gudmundsdottir (1992), with reference to issues of integrity, points out that 'informants are often keen to please their researchers . . . The scene is set for compelling [teachers'] stories that sparkle in their narrative truth' (p. 6). A similar caution regarding the meaning we give to stories while ignoring the forces that play on their construction, is raised by Carter (1993). Clark (1991) points out that the stories tell more about the researchers and their narrative competence than they do about the research site or the informants.

Cooperation Between Researcher and Informant

Another aspect of the domain of partnership is the commitment to cooperation between researcher and informant — What is a *truly* informed partnership? How is this partnership defined? What level of mutual agreement between teacher-informant and researcher is needed? Can the interdependence between the teacher and the researcher be controlled? Should it? Whose is the definitive interpretation of the data? Should there be partnership in interpretation of the findings, in reporting the research?

Studies dealing with some of these questions include that of Cornett and Chase (1989) who identify several primary ethical concerns, among them the nature of free informed consent and Scheurich (1992) who notes that 'interviewees are not passive subjects, they are active participants, active controllers of the interaction. They . . . often use the interviewer as much as the interviewer is using them' (p. 11). He also points out that 'the interviewee is under the spotlight, while the researcher's life remains hidden' (p. 10).

McCutcheon (1990) defends the teachers' right to veto elements of the data collection as well as the form of the final report, and specifically the conclusions. On the other extreme, we find Eisner's view that 'in the final analysis, the decision to disseminate or publicize should rest with the researcher ... Giving someone else the right of approval or disapproval ... is to undermine the competence of the writer whose name is on the work' (Eisner, 1991, p. 115).

Risks to the Informant

Regarding the risks to the informant and to the credibility of the research, e.g., biases and problems of truthfulness, the following questions arise: Can the researcher explain to the teacher/informant the extent of his or her vulnerability as a result of this kind of research? To what extent is the researcher responsible for, or capable of, mending damage caused to the teacher's self-image, or, alternately, for bringing about a positive self-image, resulting from exposure? What should be done if significantly negative aspects arise in the study? Can abuse of thick data by teachers' superiors be avoided? What are the implications of the fact that the researcher always views the particular teaching practice through his or her own pedagogical knowledge? How does the researcher's personal experience and knowledge of teaching interact with the informant, e.g., Reinharz's (1984) 'experiential' view? By whose benefit is the research motivated?

Few studies relate to questions of risk; among these are the following: Ayers and Schubert (1990), for instance, discuss the researcher's dilemma when he or she sees something harmful happening in the classroom and they question what should be done in such situations. Burgess (1989) and Shulman (1990) discuss ethical consequences which hinge upon the question of anonymity versus visibility. Cornett and Chase (1989) also identify as primary ethical issues the protection of confidentiality in the case of thick description and the potential negative effects of intensive and extended scrutiny as weighed against potential positive effects.

When discussing the ethical issues researchers face in dealing with possible harm caused by the research, a number of moral theories should be considered. The moral aspect reflects on the issue of damage to the individual as opposed to the advantage to society as a whole. Major ethical theories are either based on principle, e.g., utilitarian and deontological theories; or on virtue, e.g., communitarian theories (Mathison *et al.*, 1993). The utilitarian view argued that damage to an individual is only justifiable if future benefit or prevention of greater damage can be proven. The liberal rights point of view holds that one cannot justify causing an individual harm solely for the benefit of society (Hart, 1962). Rawls claims that 'rights secured by justice are not subject to political bargaining or to the calculus of social interests' (Rawls, 1971, p. 4). Thus, the teachers' right to privacy should be viewed as his or her prerogative.

Though some of the above questions have, as we see, been raised in the literature, a systematic and comprehensive study of ethical concerns in teacher-thinking research has not yet been designed. Clearly, the different status existing between the teacher and the researcher has implications for many aspects of the research, e.g., the partnership, responsibility, accreditation, immediate benefits, etc.

There are several ways to study ethical questions. The mini-study described below was carried out in an effort to find out to what extent the teacher-thinking researcher is aware of ethical issues, and whether the researcher encounters them when doing research.

The Study

A dozen teacher-thinking researchers (who comprise almost the entire Israeli research community in this area) were asked to participate in a short interview on 'Ethical issues of teacher thinking'. All agreed without hesitation. Seven of the twelve researchers were female and five were male, four were in their late 30s or early 40s and the rest were 50 and above.

The interviews, consisting of four probing questions, were semi-open and lasted about an hour; they were recorded with the researchers' consent. The interviewees were encouraged to reflect on their own ideas, give vignettes or examples of their own encounters with ethical issues and raise new questions regarding ethical concerns and their awareness of these in research. The transcripts were analysed qualitatively, using emic and etic categories (Goetz and Le Compte, 1984). Analyses were validated by two expert judges. The findings are organized and presented according to the major categories that emerged from the responses rather than by frequency, since even a single response is viewed as representative of the researchers' thinking. Frequency is noted only in those cases where it was felt to be significant.

Findings and Discussion

Most of the researchers' responses in the interviews could be grouped into three areas: awareness of ethical issues; the nature of the partnership between researcher and informant teacher and, the meaning of the researcher's cognitive intervention. The majority of the interviewees responses dealt with the two latter areas of concern. It is interesting to note that some questions which were raised in the literature were dealt with differently in the interviews. For example, the question of risk was dealt with in the literature from one aspect, and in the interviews from another; questions like that of partnership were given similar expression in both the literature and the interviews, and others, in the area of awareness of ethical issues, were rarely found in the literature, but did arise in the interviews.

Awareness of Ethical Issues

Only two of the interviewees indicated that they had specifically given thought to ethical issues in teacher-thinking research prior to the interview. All others either responded that they did not think that there was a special problem, or that they had not previously thought about it in any organized way. Two even expressed surprise at our raising the question. Yet all had a well-defined research philosophy with ethical premises which they carry with them in any area they explore.

Some argued that the accepted ethical norms for research in any of the social sciences extend to teacher-thinking research as well. For example, one researcher said, 'If you as a researcher have integrity and honesty, these norms always guide your research . . . We all act so as not to harm the teacher . . . There is no basic difference among the various schools of methodologies.' Another interviewee said, 'I think that it is like ethical problems in other research areas. When you work with people there are ethical problems . . . I haven't thought of it till now.

I can only give you my intuition.' Or 'I don't think that there is anything special about teacher thinking, nor is it different from children's thinking or other cognitive interventions.' Or 'In education in general we are dealing with what "ought to be" and this is already in the realm of ethics. When we try to expose organized cognitive norms, we are dealing with ethics and morality.'

Some, however, said that they sensed intuitively that some ethical problems were quite specific to this area: 'When you study a teacher you get into his guts and thus you have to go along with him to some extent.' Or 'When you intend to go deeply into the teacher's mind, you're taking a certain risk, you create intimacy . . .' Or 'You illuminate flaws in the teacher's thinking and thus shake the fragile stability created by the teacher.'

In spite of the initially low level of awareness, as the interviews progressed, all the interviewees recognized weightier ethical concerns in this area, and came up with examples from their own experience. For example, the most basic question of research in general, 'To what extent are we allowed to turn private knowledge into public knowledge?' was translated into a question relevant to the field: 'It often happens to me that I want to use stories that teachers told me informally, and then I stop myself and ask "who gave me permission to use it?"' This dilemma, reflecting the tension existing between honesty and increased professional knowledge versus commitment to the informant, is similar to the dilemma of physicians, lawyers, journalists, etc. One of the findings was that researchers who study teachers' subject-matter knowledge seem to encounter fewer ethical and related problems than those who work on general teacher-thinking subjects such as teachers' beliefs or biographies. Is this because beliefs and attitudes are affective and thus have greater ethical implications than the cognitive area of subject knowledge?

The variety of responses we received seem to indicate that the level of awareness may be related, among other factors, to age and experience. There were differences between the responses of younger and less experienced researchers and those of veteran researchers, with the exception of one experienced researcher who responded like the younger group.

Those who responded that they hadn't considered the issue before or that they didn't see any difference between teacher-thinking research and other research areas with respect to ethics were all highly experienced veteran researchers, with implicit ethical norms. This may be the reason why at first they didn't consider teacher-thinking research different or exceptional. However, through the examples they themselves generated, many of them came to recognize the emphasis, the weight and the practical expression that ethical issues have in this particular area of research. It should be made clear that regardless of their attitude to our questions, all the researchers expressed their commitment to an ethical code in research in general.

We have seen that many of the researchers' responses varied in the level of their moral judgments. Younger, less experienced researchers are more open and sensitive to ethical issues and more willing to speak out about their concerns and to voice their doubts. This may be so since they are the product of a different academic era, more doubting and more collaborative. Another explanation might be that due to their relative youth in the field, they have not yet tacitly internalized their knowledge of research ethics in a way similar to that of their more experienced colleagues.[2]

Recognition of ethical issues is a process that develops over time and with experience, and demands research maturity of the field. Teacher-thinking research is a relatively new field of study that has developed over less than a decade (Lyons, 1990). Clearly, basic concerns such as conceptual issues will be the first to occupy the research community, then followed by methodological refinements. Ethical issues will be dealt with only later, both as part of the methodological concerns and in terms of philosophical considerations. In that respect, ethical issues make up the 'cream' of any research area.

Most of the interviewees eventually came up with at least one instance of encountering an ethical problem specific to the field. This may indicate that the interview itself raised their ethical awareness. Since they make up the Israeli teacher-thinking community, we may say that this community is gradually coming to realize that special thought should be given to building up an ethical code for this relatively new area of research. In this respect, the Israeli group seems to be in line with the educational research community at large, in view of the fact that ethical standards for educational research as delineated by the American Educational Research Association (AERA) have only recently emerged (ESAERA, 1992).

Increased awareness of specific ethical issues enables researchers to take these into consideration while designing and implementing their research. However, this may be problematic; Marshall (1992) points out that desirable as it may be to plan and pre-consider for ethical purposes, this is often difficult and may be impossible due to the process-oriented nature of ethnographic research. Still, drawing the attention of the research community to this area and bringing it to public discussion will hopefully serve as another step in the direction of 'research maturity' and will comply with the purpose of this study.

The Nature of the Partnership

Great variability appears regarding the issue of teacher informants as research partners, in the sense often used in the literature (i.e., Connelly and Clandinin, 1986; Lather, 1986). However, most remarked immediately that in their experience this partnership was limited and commented on its restrictions. Of those who disagreed with this notion of partnership, one even called it a 'hypocritical way of looking at this relationship'. Researchers' interpretations of the partnership varied from the most basic perception of teacher informants as 'contributors to the body of knowledge' (the majority of the responses), through the view of teacher informants as 'partners in interpretation' which emphasizes the mutuality and the collaborative nature, to the ultimate view, in which teachers are 'partners in constructing a case study' (only one).

Two aspects of the informants' view of the partnership arose from the interviews: that of differing status between researcher and teacher, and the various views found regarding the mutuality of the partnership.

Differing Status
Several researchers commented on the difference in position between the researcher and the teacher. Among these were the following remarks: 'Each one comes to the interaction with a different status; the teacher contributes his or her story and the researcher classifies and defines the new knowledge'; 'It is important for

the researcher to avoid communicating a sense of superiority . . . This leads to alienation . . . You can't pretend that you are interested in the teacher's opinion if you are not, teachers sense it immediately . . .' This difference stands out especially in those cases where researchers use student teachers as informants. Four of the interviewees mentioned this difference in status, but only one raised the problem of the researcher's position of power *vis à vis* student teachers.

A few researchers commented on the fact that it is almost always one side who does the questioning, for example: 'This one-sidedness creates a feeling that the teacher is being tested, that we are on opposite sides of the fence, especially since we question them on subject-matter knowledge not always during the period when they are teaching the specific topic in class . . . It is not necessarily at their fingertips at the time of our study and thus they may feel uneasy.'

While at the beginning of the interaction between the researcher and the teacher, the latter is at an advantage since the study depends entirely on his or her willingness to share his or her story, after extracting the information from the teacher there is a definite shift of power to the researcher. A few of the interviewees noted that 'the researcher has an advantage in every respect, he gets the publicity while the teacher remains anonymous', or as one younger researcher put it: 'I'm not afraid to remove the wall between the researcher and the teacher. I see turning our teachers into teacher-researchers as an ideal . . . This will improve their teaching . . . but this is not what happens in teacher-thinking research . . . What exists today is more a philanthropic attitude: "We have come from the university to help you".' It seems that what bothers this researcher is not the inequality of roles which is legitimate and should not be problematic, but rather the patronizing attitude of the researchers toward the teachers.

The different status of the researcher and the teacher seems not to be a problem as long as each respects the other and keeps his or her promises. Since keeping promises is most important, each side needs to know exactly what the contract entails. According to contract theory, a good contract will describe the relationship between the parties and state clearly under what conditions it is entered into and how and to what extent it can be changed. The contractual aspect of the problem of ethical standards in research derives its philosophical and moral base from liberal philosophy which believed firmly in the 'sanctity of contract' (Salmond, 1947). This is the ultimate expression of one's right to freely relinquish freedom by binding oneself to a mandatory contract. In our case, the teacher, and certainly the student-teacher, is clearly in a weaker position *vis à vis* the researcher.

An additional concern linked to the issue of differing status was the extent to which researchers felt ready to reveal the true purpose of the study to the teacher in order to obtain informed consent. When you are supposed to share the research objectives with the informant before receiving his or her consent to carrying out the study, you face the problem of research truth. Most of the researchers were ready to reveal only part of the truth, justifying this as a way of minimizing the effect of bias on the teachers. Only those who studied pedagogical subject-matter knowledge had no problem sharing the research objectives with their teachers. One researcher referred to the partnership by saying: 'Anyone who does not know the true research objectives can't be called a real partner.' Such a comment leads us to reflect on an additional question: Is it legitimate to lie for the good of the research? Our immediate reaction is an unconditional no, in line with Erickson (1982) who states that one is never justified in using deception for research purposes;

however, there are instances when it may be preferable not to expose the whole truth.[3] This sometimes justified hesitancy in disclosing research objectives may act as a limiting factor in the definition of the partnership itself.

Mutual Construction of New Knowledge

A most surprising picture emerged concerning the researchers' view of informants operating as partners in the research, of their interpretation and the possibility of shared reporting. It would be natural to expect researchers who use open observations followed by interviews as part of a qualitative paradigm, to view the informants' interpretations as an integral part of the interpretive research approach. However, mutual construction of new knowledge (by researcher and teacher) was mentioned by only two researchers and even they did not perceive of it in terms of Connelly and Clandinin's (1986) 'narrative approach', where new knowledge construction is a joint venture.

Lincoln and Guba (1989) firmly advocated the right of the respondant/participant to 'shape that information's use and to assist in formulating the purposes to which they will lend their names and information. To do less is to violate, to intrude and to condemn to indignity' (p. 236). On the other hand, McCutcheon's (1990) view that the teacher/informant has the right to veto the final form of the report seems to us and to some of the researchers who referred to this issue as being a bit extreme. In general, there is little commitment to accepting the teacher's interpretations or endorsement of his or her statements and insights prior to publication. This seems to reflect a double standard considering that such low commitment is not in keeping with researchers' current caution regarding their own conference papers on which they so often stipulate 'Do not quote without permission.'

Even among researchers who accepted the idea that informants construct new knowledge together with researchers, most did not consider asking for the informant's interpretation of the findings before publication, not to mention the idea of publicly acknowledging the teacher's contribution. Only two, after being asked, considered the possibility of doing so in the future. All justified their stand by pointing to the advantage for the teacher of anonymity. Most said they had no objections to showing teachers both the interpretation and results before publishing the report. However, few actually took this initiative, and those who worked with student teachers added that by the time the report was ready the informants would often be unreachable. Others noted that this was sometimes the case with practising teachers as well, given the lengthy interval between data collection and publication.

One researcher drew a distinction between the teacher as a research object and as a partner in constructing new knowledge, when she said, 'If you approach research in the sense of "I have come to study you", this is not a partnership, but if you mean it in the sense of "Let's build the story together", as in the narrative method, that is a partnership.' Another researcher went to an extreme when she viewed the whole research encounter as a 'mutual collaboration'. In her view, the interdependence was such that the theory of action (the new knowledge) constructed in this research should be viewed as a joint endeavour.

It seems that the willingness of researchers to accept the teacher's comments on the researchers' interpretations may in part depend on the stage of the study; the farther it progresses, the less the researchers ask the informant to comment on the interpretations. Another factor is the feeling of some researchers that teachers tend to express opinions, attitudes, which they believe the researchers expect to hear, an aspect which complicates the issue of teachers' shared interpretations. One researcher recently performed a study in which she asked her student-teacher informants to endorse each step of the interpretation as the study progressed, a procedure she took from MacDonald (1976), however, even she did not ask the latters' consent to the final report, 'because it doesn't work that way'.

Regardless of the researcher's position *vis à vis* the teacher's interpretations, clearly the researcher must indicate the teacher's statements as primary sources, while the researcher's interpretations are secondary. It is important to emphasize that most of our interviewees expressed reservations regarding the teachers' rights at the reporting stage. One might ask if the fact that the Israeli research community lagged behind leading north American researchers in adopting the qualitative paradigm may have affected their attitude in this matter, regardless of the fact that the younger researchers were exposed to interpretive approaches during their formal training. (One wonders if this fact may contribute to the more open, equal, democratic stance taken by younger researchers.) Clearly, there is room for both the conservative, researcher-dominated kind of research and the researcher–teacher partnership kind. The former, which we found to be more prevalent, unknowingly embraces Eisner's (1991) stand denying the teachers' right of approval, as quoted above. Our findings indicate that there is a need to refine and crystallize the definition of the expression 'the teacher as research partner'. It is time to come out of the slogan stage to the point where the researcher and the teacher define together for each case what kind of partnership is intended and where and what kind of responsibility this entails (Mackwood, 1993). Based on our findings, such a definition would include the following components which may be relevant to any subject of study, but have emerged very distinctly in our particular field:

- readiness to share the research objectives with the teacher/informant;
- the level of independence and responsibility given to teachers/informants concerning the research design, its implementation and eventual feedback; and
- the weight and place given to the teacher/ informant's interpretation.

Above all, there must be honest acceptance of the fact that without either of the two partners, there could be no research and no new knowledge in this area could be constructed. This is the true meaning of a mutual process. Our findings, on the other hand, indicate that currently in Israel the notion of partnership has only very limited meaning and is highly asymmetric. This asymmetry should not pose an ethical problem as long as both parties know what to expect and there is mutual respect.

The general question which emerges from these findings on both aspects of partnership — that of differing status, and that of mutual construction of knowledge — is 'When and under what conditions do researchers accept teachers as partners?' Researchers' attitudes on this question vary. This variability doesn't indicate that there are preferred ethical relationships. What is most important is the mutual respect between researcher and teacher, and not their different status.

As this mini-study shows, 'mutual construction of knowledge' in Connelly and Clandinin's (1986) sense seems to be the highest level of partnership in research. However, most of our researcher-informants do not reach this level: The teachers' share in this partnership is the contribution of their story and only to a small degree their interpretation. Beyond this, controlling the interviews, organizing and classifying the data, generating the knowledge generalizations, writing up the report and taking responsibility for its content — all these are performed by the researcher and it is he or she who gets the credit, the praise and the criticism.

The question of reciprocity is dealt with in different ways in various fields: the researcher takes knowledge from the informant; reciprocity may be through acknowledgment, remuneration or therapeutic value. Even 'having another pair of adult eyes in the lonely classroom', as teachers often say, may be beneficial. In participatory research, researchers reciprocate through advocacy, shared power and emancipatory action. As Mathison *et al.* (1993) point out, 'Seldom does the exchange of commodities create an equally beneficial situation for all involved' (p. 4).

Intimate questioning of the teacher on the one hand, and no accreditation on the other, is often justified by referring to the protection of teachers' anonymity. Researchers offer teachers anonymity as protection from potential negative consequences, such as the effect on their status, their self-confidence, etc. But in fact the thick description which characterizes this kind of research may lead to identification, e.g., of the school (especially in relatively small educational systems), without prior consent having been either requested or given, a fact which adds to the complexity of the problem (Shulman, 1990). In addition, when the teacher remains anonymous, the story is 'given' to the researcher who adds his or her interpretation, and often the fact that the story basically 'belongs' to the teacher is obscured. One alternative is to accept the teacher as a recognized partner who is expected to give up anonymity while the researcher, on his or her part, relinquishes exclusiveness of credit.[4]

The Meaning of Intervention

Another concern raised by researchers referred to the effect of intervention during data collection, as an outgrowth of the relationship between the researcher and the teacher informant. While all researchers are primarily interested in describing existing cognitive structures, mental models, pedagogical content knowledge, attitudes or beliefs of teachers or student teachers, they are aware that the resulting descriptions do not strictly reflect their informants' knowledge. Some even raised the often quoted question: 'Whose story is it — the teacher's or the researcher's?' Obviously obtaining teachers' knowledge from their stories entails some kind of intervention. Such intervention was referred to as intruding on the informant's privacy and affecting his or her current knowledge. As one of our subjects said, 'Questioning the teachers, regarding, for example, how they connect content and pedagogy (logically or associatively) in their pedagogical content knowledge involves penetrating their minds more than you originally intended or expected.'

One researcher said, 'Even the teacher's reflections during the interviews change and contribute to his or her knowledge.' Other comments referred to the intended or unintended guidance which researchers give teachers through their questions. For example, 'If we spot a "wrong" concept we lead the teachers in the direction we want them to take their students until they get it right . . . They gain a lot this way.' Such comments are a principal test of researchers' ethics. The more the researcher serves as a guide, the greater the effect on the teacher's 'genuine knowledge' (which actually does not exist).

The central question raised by some researchers in this respect was, 'What is the role of research and the researcher in education?' As one researcher remarked: 'Can there be pure research in education without intervention? I doubt it.' Another researcher began by asking, 'Is our role only to describe or should we intervene as well?' One researcher explained the dilemma, one of the most difficult problems facing researchers in the behavioural sciences, thus: 'I believe that because in educational research we deal with what "ought to be" (and not just with what is) we must consider the question of our right to intervene, to cause change.' A well-defined statement of the opposite attitude came from another researcher: 'Our function is to expose, not to correct. Change is not part of our role definition.'

It is possible, therefore, to view attitudes and intervention as a continuum. At one end of the continuum, we have a description of the teacher's knowledge generated without any prior intent to intervene. In this case, the research setting itself causes the teacher informant to say things he or she may not have thought of otherwise. In the centre of the continuum, the researcher intends to intervene through asking guiding questions which cause the teacher to reflect and reorganize his or her thinking. The other end of the intervention continuum is reached when the questioning is expressly designed to achieve change. Here the teacher's awareness and readiness to participate is crucial, since in this case the desire to implement change is the result of a normative comparison and probable dissatisfaction with an existing situation.

The first two views, in which the role of the researcher is primarily to describe, are the more common ones in methodological conceptualization. Even in this role, the researcher's presence often affects the response of the informants. While the first two levels may result in unplanned change, the third intervention explicitly aims at change and this raises ethical issues related to the teacher's consent and willingness to participate in the study. Ethical concerns which are submerged at the first stage surface at the third. In the second and third stages, communication becomes more complex and demands greater sensitivity since the aims of the change and of the study itself may be affected by the way the communication is carried out.

Obviously such intervention cannot be carried out without the teacher's consent. However, even when such consent is obtained at the time that the researcher approaches the teacher, it is not always clear whether it really reflects the teacher's comprehension of what the implications of the study may have for him or her. One researcher gave the following example: 'Intervention may lead to a change in a teacher's conventionally established way of thinking and may introduce uncertainty even with an assertive teacher.' In respect to the researcher's ongoing questioning of the teacher, another researcher noted: 'Teachers do not realize, when granting their consent to the researcher, that they are exposing themselves to a situation where they are put to a test. No one likes to be tested.' The teacher probably agreed to being questioned, but not to being tested. This statement raises the problem of to what extent the consent an informant gives reflects a real understanding of what is behind the requests agreed upon.

We can see that different kinds of intervention have various implications on the issue of consent:

- intervention explicitly aimed at change requires prior consent;
- teachers may not fully comprehend what they are consenting to; and
- teachers may feel they are being tested rather than questioned.

The interviewees' statements raise serious ethical issues. What, in fact, is the role of the researcher? Does the researcher's role end with exposing the teacher's knowledge, after organizing and interpreting the data? Shouldn't this kind of research, in which the positions of the researcher and the teacher are asymmetrical, make the teacher eligible for help from the researcher? As one of the researchers said, 'The researcher exposes new knowledge and gets the credit while the teacher is stuck with the problems.' Most of the interviewees believe that helping the teacher after the study is part of the researcher's role. In this respect, they perceive the researcher as a clinician. If this view is accepted, the question arises as to what form the help should take, and how long it should last. Another view expressed by one of the researchers was that though responsibility for this help should lie with the researcher, in practice, it should be carried out by somebody else.

A researcher should be aware of whether a proposed study calls for minimal intervention or for intervention which aims at creating a defined change. Accordingly, the ethical implications should be considered as well, bearing in mind the need for formal written consent by the participants, which in turn requires a description of research objectives and of what this will entail for the participant.

Conclusion

An attempt has been made here to engage in an exploratory study intended to encourage a systematic approach to ethical awareness in studying teacher thinking. An expansion on researchers' views of partnership, and a report on how the international community of teacher-thinking researchers views the teacher–researcher relationship can be found elsewhere (Sabar, 1994). It is only natural that the next stage of the current research be to study teacher-informants' views on ethical issues in teacher thinking. Justification for such an approach derives from studies (i.e., Rudduck and Hopkins, 1985; Cochrane-Smith and Lytle, 1990) which have found that teachers' participation in research is needed to increase professionalism and raise the level of teaching. Since researchers' behaviour from the standpoint of ethics contributes to the socialization of teachers into research, even greater attention should be given to ethics. Teachers and researchers should be aware that since some ethical issues are not easily resolved, they require consideration prior to embarking on the research. Younger, less experienced researchers were found to be more open and sensitive to ethical issues, more willing to speak out about their concerns and to voice their doubts.

As teacher-thinking research practice shows, the time may be ripe for the second generation of researchers to espouse ethical specifications and modifications based on the current democratic perceptions of listening to the teacher's voice and accepting teachers as partners. This perception of collegiality could alter conservative attitudes without lessening the credit of the research community. And finally, in an era when true consent is required even for trivial actions, informant endorsement of their statements when used as data should become part and parcel of any research procedure.

We believe that the code of professional ethics guarding the relationship between professional and client in general, e.g., teacher–pupil, physician–patient, lawyer–client, etc., is unsuited to teacher-thinking research where the teacher is more like the researcher's partner than a client or patient. The relationship between researcher and teacher, however, has a different basis:

- The teacher usually doesn't approach the researcher to request 'treatment'; the initiative comes from the researcher who thus needs the teacher's consent.
- The researcher's desire to build the relationship with the teacher stems from his or her interest in a phenomenon which he or she wishes to describe and clarify. It is only later that the relationship may develop into one of 'treater–treated' or of cooperation.
- Unlike clients in other fields, who may not be well-educated or even illiterate, teachers are educated professionals with some knowledge of research methods to which they were exposed during their studies.

For these reasons, the teacher can't be treated as a regular 'client'. However, he or she deserves the protection that clients of other fields get, and should not be treated as just another 'case'. In reality, however, as we noted above, due to difference in status and vulnerability, the teacher is not a true partner. Clarifying the meaning of partnership in its limited conceptual framework may contribute to cooperation based on honesty and mutual respect, i.e., sharing the results before publication is a must, though sharing the research objectives at the initial stages is not always desirable. Detailing such specific ethical issues in this area is of extreme importance. Only in 1992 was an ethical code for educational research defined by AERA (ESAERAs, 1992). Since high-status fields such as medicine and law have long had ethical codes and ethical committees to enforce them, establishing such a committee for the field of education may increase the awareness of our members and contribute to raising the status of the field of education (Sabar and Gibton, in press).[5] Clearly issues of ethics have not been sufficiently considered by the educational research community and much of what we do is done intuitively. In the best case, researchers' behaviour in this area is based on codes of ethics carried over from researchers' training in other areas such as psychology, sociology, etc., and it is high time that we define our rules and regulations according to our own field of action and research.

Notes

1   The author wishes to thank Dr N. Shafriri, Dr Y. Tamir and Mr D. Gibton for their comments and critiques of this chapter, and the intellectual stimulation they contributed.

2   I like this explanation which was suggested to me by Gunnar Handal.
3   In reality, codes of ethics enable the researcher, if not to lie, then to hide information from the subject as long as it is disclosed at the debriefing stage.
4   The right of the teacher to remain anonymous and maintain his or her privacy, or to be credited and appear in print stems from the agreement reached by the parties. Initially, each has two basic rights: the right to privacy, and the right of ownership of the product of one's work. However, each can, if he or she so desires, give up these rights, if by so doing, other aims are achieved (i.e., the advancement of science).
5   In judging the level of professionalization among the various professions, it seems that the higher the status of the profession, the greater its members' awareness of ethical issues, the longer it has had an ethical code, a committee of ethics, etc., which then contribute further to the status of the profession. It is therefore not surprising that, from this point of view, education has low status.

References

APA (1982) *Ethical Principles in the Conduct of Research with Human Participants*, Washington, DC, APA.

AYERS, W. and SCHUBERT, W. (1990) 'Qualitative Research: Do the right thing', Paper presented at the annual meeting of AERA, Boston, MA.

BOGDAN, R.C. and BIKLEN, S.K. (1982) *Qualitative Research for Education: An Introduction to Theory and Methods*, Boston, Allyn and Bacon.

BURGESS, R.G. (Ed) (1989) *The Ethics of Educational Research*, East Sussex, The Falmer Press.

CARTER, K. (1993) 'The place of story in the study of teachers and teacher education', *Educational Researcher*, 22, 1, pp. 5–12.

CASSELL, J. and WAX, M. (Eds) (1980) 'Ethical problems in fieldwork', Special issue of Social Problems, 27, 3.

CLARK, C.M. (1991) 'Real lessons from imaginary teachers', *Journal of Curriculum Study*, 23, 5, pp. 429–34.

COCHRANE-SMITH, M. and LYTLE, S.L. (1990) 'Research on teaching and teacher research: The issues that divide', *Educational Researcher*, 19, 2, pp. 2–11.

CONNELLY, F.M. and CLANDININ, D.J. (1986) 'On narrative methods, personal philosophy, and narrative unities in the story of teaching', *Journal of Research in Science Teaching*, 23, 4, pp. 293–310.

CORNETT, J.W. and CHASE, S. (1989) 'The analysis of teacher thinking and the problem of ethics', Paper presented at the annual meeting of AERA, San Francisco, CA.

EISNER, E. (1991) *The Enlightened Eye: Qualitative Inquiry and the Enhancement of Educational Practice*, New York, MacMillan.

ELBAZ, F. (1993) 'Knowledge and discourse: The evolution of research on teacher thinking', in DAY, C., DENICOLO, P. and ROPE, M. (Eds) *Insights into Teacher Thinking and Practice*, London, The Falmer Press.

ERICKSON, K. (1982) 'A comment on disguised observation in sociology', *Social Problems*, 14, pp. 366–73.

ETHICAL STANDARDS OF THE AMERICAN EDUCATIONAL RESEARCH ASSOCIATION (ESAERA) (1992) *Educational Researcher*, 21, 10, pp. 23–6.

GOETZ, J.P. and LE COMPTE, M.D. (1984) *Ethnography and Qualitative Design in Educational Research*, London, Academic Press.

GUDMUNDSDOTTIR, S. (1992) 'The Interview as a Joint Construction of Reality', Paper presented at the annual meeting of AERA, San Francisco, CA.

HART, H.L.A. (1962) *Law, Liberty and Morality*, Stanford, CA, Stanford University Press.

JOINT COMMITTEE ON STANDARDS FOR EDUCATIONAL EVALUATION (1981) *Standards for Evaluation of Educational Programs, Projects and Materials*, New York, McGraw Hill.

KLEINBERGER, A.P. (1979) *Introduction to Educational Philosophy*, Tel Aviv, Yahdav (in Hebrew).

LATHER, P. (1986) 'Research as praxis', *Harvard Educational Review*, 56, 3, pp. 257–77.

LINCOLN. Y.S. and GUBA, E.G, (1989) 'Ethics: A failure of positivistic science', *The Review of Higher Education*, 12, 3, pp. 221–40.

LYONS, N. (1990) 'Dilemmas of knowing: Ethical and epistomological dimensions of teachers' work and development', *Harvard Educational Review*, 60, 2, pp. 159–79.

MACDONALD, B. (1976) 'A political classification of evaluation studies', in HAMILTON, D. *et al.* (Eds) *Beyond the Numbers Game*, London, MacMillan.

MACKWOOD, G. (1993) Personal correspondence.

MARSHALL, P.A. (1992) 'Research ethics in applied anthropology, IRB', *A Review of Human Subject Research*, 14, 6, pp. 1–5.

MATHISON, S., ROSS, E.W. and CORNETT, J.W. (Eds) (1993) 'A Casebook for Teaching about Ethical Issues in Qualitative Research, Qualitative Research SIG', American Educational Research Association.

MCCUTCHEON, G. (1990) 'Conflict About Conflict: Between a Rock and a Hard Place', Paper presented at the annual meeting of AERA, Boston, MA.

RAWLS, J. (1971) *Theory of Justice*, Cambridge, MA, Belknap-Harvard.

REINHARZ, S. (1984) *On Becoming a Social Scientist: From Survey Research and Participant Observation to Experimental Analysis* (2nd edition), New Brunswick, NJ, Transaction Books.

RUDDUCK, J. and HOPKINS, D. (Eds) (1985) *Research as a Basis for Teaching: Readings from the Work of Lawrence Stenhouse*, London, Heinemann Educational Books.

SABAR, N. (1994) 'Teacher and Researcher: What Kind of Partnership is it? Ethical Implications', Paper presented at the annual meeting of AERA, New Orleans, LA.

SABAR, N. and GIBTON, D. (in press) 'Needed: Directing to knowledge and ethical code-some comments on the professionalization of teaching', in AMOS, B.A. and TAMIR, Y. (Eds) *Professionalization of Teaching*, in the Series of Education and Society, Ramot, Tel Aviv (In Hebrew).

SALMOND, J. (1947) *Jurisprudence* (10th edition), WILLIAM, G.J. (Ed) London, Sweet and Maxwell.

SCHEURICH, J. (1992) *A Postmodernist Review of Interviewing: Dominance, Resistance and Chaos*, Columbus, OH, The National Center for Science Teaching and Learning.

SHULMAN, J.H. (1990) 'Now you see them, now you don't: Anonymity versus visibility in case studies of teachers', *Educational Researcher*, 19, 6, pp. 11–15.

SOLTIS, J.F. (1990) 'The ethics of qualitative research', in EISNER, E. and PASHKIN, A. (Eds) *Qualitative Inquiry in Education*, New York, Teachers College.

Chapter 8

Teacher Thinking and Didactics: Prescriptive, Rationalistic and Reflective Approaches

Per F. Laursen

Abstract

Didactic theories do not correspond to the fundamental realities of teaching as viewed from the perspective of the research on teacher thinking and sociology of teaching. The classical prescriptive and rationalistic approaches to didactics conflict so much with the realities of teaching that they should be either abandoned or viewed as limited approaches to the practice of teaching. Also, some aspects of the reflective approach suffer from a naive optimism because they do not recognize the institutional frameworks and because they overestimate the possibilities of feedback on student learning.

Introduction

Didactics is the field of educational theory that provides guidelines and tools that are used to develop the practice of teaching. The term didactics in English educational terminology is rarely used and has for some decades been viewed as old fashioned while it is much more commonly used in other languages. In some languages there has been a revival of the term 'didactics' during the last few years — I hope that this will also happen in the English educational terminology.

Traditionally research on teacher thinking does not give any guidelines on how the quality of teaching should be developed. Lately there has been a noticeable trend in the research on teacher thinking to contribute to the development of the quality of teaching as it is carried out in practice (Pope, 1993, p. 28). The main contribution that research on teacher thinking can yield to didactics is that it can tell us what the realities are that didactics want to reform. Therefore, it is important to keep in mind the question: What consequences does research on teacher thinking have for didactic theory?

Research on teacher thinking has inspired new trends in didactics and it has made it possible to understand why more traditional approaches have failed to influence the practice of teaching. When we talk about didactics it is important that its theories do not conflict with the fundamental realities of teaching and education. If theories conflict with reality teachers will view the theories as irrelevant and these theories have no possibility to contribute to the development of the quality of teaching. In this chapter I will try to answer the following questions:

- Do the dominant didactic theories correspond to the fundamental realities of teaching as viewed from the perspective of the research that has been done on teacher thinking and sociology of teaching?
- If not, how can the theory of didactics be developed to have a greater respect for these realities?

I will focus on the recently popular approach to didactics, the reflective approach. I will also briefly sketch answers to the two questions concerning the more traditional prescriptive and rationalistic approaches.

Didactics

Didactic theories can be classified according to their approach to two fundamental questions concerning the practice of teaching:

- Do the didactic theories give concrete and precise, or abstract and procedural guidelines for teaching and planning of lessons?
- Are they based on analyses of actual teaching practices or not?

Looking at the historical development of didactics with these questions in mind three different basic didactic approaches stand out: prescriptive; rationalistic; and reflective.

The prescriptive theories are the classical theories of teaching and they give concrete and precise guidelines on how to teach and how to plan lessons. They are not based on an analysis of the actual teaching practices but focus on ideals. They totally dominated educational theory until the beginning of this century.

Rationalistic theories first appeared during the early decades of this century and they suggest abstract and procedural guidelines on how to teach and primarily on how to plan lessons. Like the prescriptive theories they are not based on an analysis of the actual teaching practices but instead they focus on rationalistic principles and theories of learning.

Reflective theories can be traced back to John Dewey and have been dominant during the last decade. They provide very abstract guidelines for teaching. These theories are the only ones based on an analysis of the teaching practices. The analysis, however, is not always adequate, as I shall argue as part of my thesis.

The Realities of Teaching

In this chapter I critically analyse the above three approaches according to the following criteria: Do prescriptive, rationalistic and reflective theories conflict with the main research findings on teacher thinking and on the sociology of teaching?

The results and conclusions of teacher thinking and sociology of teaching research are too extensive to give a detailed summary. However there are some generally accepted points which are of fundamental importance to didactic theory. The following points are based primarily on Clark and Peterson (1986), Halkes and Olson (1984), Lortie (1975), Olson (1991), and Strømnes and Søvik (1987).

- Teaching is an institutionalized activity and the organizational framework highly influences the teaching practice.
- Teaching is a routinized activity guided by practical, often tacit, knowledge. The teachers' repertoires of routines are of great importance to the practice of teaching.
- The teachers' thoughts concerning planning, evaluation and the actual practice of teaching represent several forms of rationality. The means-ends rationality is one form but it does not exclude or even overpower other forms of rationality.
- Teaching is to some extent guided by feedback from students. Feedback is generally not about student learning but about their activity and the teacher's ability to control the situation.

Have the theories of didactics — prescriptive, rationalistic and reflective — taken these points into consideration?

The Prescriptive Approach

In the history of educational and didactic thought the prescriptive approach has prevailed. Until the turn of the century this approach was dominant. Most applications of the prescriptive approach are based on religion, political ideology or philosophical anthropology; 'consequences' for educational practice have been deduced from these ideologies. All the great classics of the history of educational thought represent this kind of thinking.

More recently applications of the prescriptive approach have been proposed based on social movements, for example women's liberation, the ecological movement and various peace movements. These newly proposed movements represent the classical prescriptive rationality: concrete and precise guidelines for teaching based on value principles found outside education itself.

When the prescriptive theories are confronted with the realities of modern teaching a fundamental problem becomes evident: Teaching does not seem to be guided to any considerable extent by prescriptive principles of the kind proposed by the applications.

Of course moral intentions and standards of professional ethics play an important role in teaching. This is because moral intentions and ethics are more inherent in teaching and education and based more on personal experience (Lortie, 1975, p. 79) and practical principles (Clark and Peterson, 1986, p. 290).

The flaw in the implicit logic of the prescriptive approach is the asssumption that general value principles will 'filter down' through the different levels of decisions about teaching and ultimately guide the actual teaching practice in the classroom.

Due to the institutionalized and routinized character of teaching the applications of the prescriptive approach do not work. It would appear that in order for the prescriptive approach to guide teaching practice it will be necessary to change the institutional framework of teaching. There is also some empirical evidence to suggest that if the institutional setting of a school is reformed according to prescriptive principles then a new teaching practice with new effects will result (Illeris, 1991).

Thus it is reasonable to conclude that prescriptive approach to teaching is in fundamental conflict with the realities of teaching.

There is one more reason for the inadequacy of the prescriptive approach. In modern societies there are many conflicting value systems and many social movements. It is impossible to give any convincing and acceptable reason for choosing one of the value systems — Christianity, women's lib, environmental movement, peace movement, socialism — over another as the ideological and philosophical basis for teaching practice.

The Rationalistic Approach

The rationalistic approach to teaching developed early in this century in the context of behaviourism. The behaviouristic influence tried to transform theories of learning into methods for efficient teaching. This endeavour has, to some degree, been successful but the behaviouristic theories are still limited to teaching methods — they say little about aims and content of instruction.

It seems impossible to behaviourism to give concrete and precise prescriptions concerning aims and content. The rationalistic solution to this problem was to focus on a more abstract 'scheme of thinking' (Taba, 1962, p. VI). The fundamental principles of this scheme were suggested by R.W. Tyler (Tyler, 1949) who recommended that the teacher make decisions concerning the following four areas when preparing lessons:

* purpose;
* selection of learning experience;
* organization of learning experience; and
* evaluation.

In the transition from the prescriptive to the rationalistic approach the focus shifted from the content and aims of teaching to the planning of it.

Several studies of teacher thinking have compared the way teachers plan their courses against the 'Tyler rationale'. The results indicate that more experienced teachers do not plan according to the Tyler-tradition. They do not plan linearly beginning with the purpose as recommended by Tyler. Teachers tend to think cyclically and focus more on content and methods than on purposes (Clark and Peterson, 1986, pp. 263–6).

The rationalistic approach does not respect the fundamental realities of teaching — that is the institutionalized and routinized character of teaching and the plurality of rationalities in teacher thinking. Teaching practice is only to a modest degree a rational process aiming at clearly defined purposes. Clark and Peterson, 1986, provide support for these assertions when they argue that planning of teaching is 'selection, organization and sequencing of routines' (p. 260) that are adapted to the institutional framework.

The rationalistic approach used to be viewed as a general theory of teaching practice. Now it must be considered a partial theory relevant only for one aspect of teaching practice and the planning of it. Still the rationalistic approach should not be totally abandoned — teaching is an intentional process and its content and methods must be relevant to its purpose. Curriculum planning requires thinking about ends and means even though it is of little relevance in the classroom routine.

Paralleling the decline of the prescriptive approach there is a cultural trend that marks the decline of the rationalistic approach. There is a general tendency for the so called 'post-modern cultures', or 'late modernity', to view man's rational control over his environment as less realistic now than it was in the 1950s and 1960s. In other words teaching practice is seen as being wiser than the theoretical models trying to rationalize it.

The Reflective Approach

When it is impossible to prescribe teaching practices and when the rational planning models are of only modest validity, what can theories do to enhance the quality of teaching? During the last ten years the most common answer to this question has been that theoretical models can help teachers reflect on their practice. In the United States of America especially the concept of reflective teaching has dominated discussions about teacher education and teaching practice.

Different authors have used the concept of reflective practice in different ways. However the theory of D.S. Schön (Schön, 1983; 1987) has inspired most authors in this field.

The theory of Schön claims to be a general theory of professional practice but his empirical material is primarily from the architectural, medical and psychological fields. Except for discussing how to teach the above professionals in their respective fields Schön makes almost no reference to teaching as a profession. Therefore, whether or not Schön's theory is an adequate theory of teaching is a central question to the analysis of the reflective approach. I shall argue that the theory is inadequate in relation to teaching in two central ways: it underestimates the institutionalized and routinized character of teaching and it overestimates the possibilities of relevant feedback.

This does not mean I want to abandon the whole concept of reflexivity. Several sociological authors have stressed that reflexivity is a central psychological, cultural and social phenomenon in 'late modernity' (e.g., Giddens, 1984; Luhmann, 1984; Giddens, 1990). There seems to be no alternative to viewing teaching practice and other forms of professional practice as reflectively monitored action (Giddens, 1984, p. 5 ff). Reflectively monitored action is guided by a form of practical consciousness which the agent, more or less, can explicate and make up his mind about.

The general concept of reflective practice is, no doubt, relevant to teaching, too. Unfortunately, D.S. Schön's theory is too general to give an exact analysis of teaching practice. Some of the reservations I have about Schön's theory will be expanded upon in the following section.

The Problem of Social Reproduction

The first problem concerning Schön's theory of the reflective practitioner relates to his view of the social role of the professional.

Today most professionals work in large organizations. The classical socio-logical theories noted that

> the involvement of professionals in complex organizations . . . has forced very substantial modifications in the way in which professional services are run . . . (Parsons, 1968, p. 542).

This statement, of course, is particularly true when teachers are the professionals of interest. Most teaching takes place in large educational institutions and most institutions make decisions about the aims and content of instruction. The insti-tutional framework of schools can be viewed as a structure which is both con-straining and enabling to teaching (Giddens, 1984, pp. 169–80). It is constraining in the sense that many valuable educational activities are impossible to carry out in the schools because of the large number of students, the lack of equipment and the limited timetable available. On the other hand it is enabling in the sense that the structures and routines of the school make it possible to accomplish educa-tional objectives.

This means that the work to be done and the problems to be solved by teachers are more or less defined by the institutional setting in which teaching takes place. Empirical research on the relationship between the institutional frame-work factors and the teaching practice itself supports these general sociological points (Lundgren, 1972).

The educational system plays a fundamental role in society and is deeply involved in many political, social and moral issues such as equality.

These aspects of teaching practice are not well reflected in Schön's theory. He recognizes that the understanding of a problematic situation is part of the teacher's professional competence and that many problematic situations involve conflicts among values (Schön, 1987, pp. 4–6), but he emphasizes what the professional can do to understand and solve the immediate problems of his job. As noted by S. Adler the reflection advocated by Schön will not involve the fundamental issues of teaching:

> Curriculum content or goals are not necessarily questioned. Schön stresses practitioner knowledge or 'knowledge-in-action', not necessarily the ana-lytic application of, for example, social science knowledge. (Adler, 1991, p. 146)

Schön views the professional as a person who has to understand and solve prob-lems. He does not see the professional as sharing responsibility for the institu-tional setting and for the way the institution functions in society. It does not mean that Schön's analysis of the epistemology of teaching practice is wrong but, that it is incomplete. The French sociologist P. Bourdieu (1989) has analysed many types of professional and everyday practices and he has stressed that a practice often is both intelligent, flexible, open towards feedback and so on, *and* at the same time socially reproductive without the knowledge of the agent. The prac-titioner will often be unable to see the constraints of the institutional setting on his professional practice: 'Practical mastery is learned ignorance' (p. 19). A. Giddens has made almost the same point. Although the practices of daily and professional life are reflectively monitored it is often impossible for the agent to grasp the total consequences of his actions. They will almost always have unintended consequences and they will often be socially reproductive (Giddens, 1984, p. 293 ff).

The Problem of Feedback

According to Schön the starting point of reflection-in-action is when our routines do not work:

> Routine responses produce a surprise — an unexpected outcome, pleasant or unpleasant, that does not fit the categories of our knowing-in-action . . . Surprise leads to reflection within an action-present . . . Reflection gives rise to on-the-spot experiment . . . (Schön, 1987, p. 28)

This 'reflective conversation with the materials of a situation' (Schön, 1987, p. 31) is fundamental to the theory because it is considered the central point of artistry.

Schön's main cases are from architectural designs and he compares all other professional practices to design process whether it is musical performance, psychoanalysis or consulting. In the design process most of the reflective conversation with the situation takes place in 'virtual worlds' (constructed representations of the real world of practice) where experimentation is easy and without severe consequences. According to Schön every profession has a virtual world which is the medium of reflection-in-action (p. 77).

K. Jordell (Jordell, 1987, p. 160) notes that this point is overly simplified by Schön. There seems to be fundamental differences between the role the virtual worlds play in professions. It is not easy to answer questions about the virtual world and the medium of reflection concerning teaching practice. Teacher education uses Schön's reflective practicum as a kind of laboratory experience but what about in the actual practice of teaching?

The most obvious parallel to the sketchpad of the designer is the lesson plans of the teacher. But there is no parallel concerning feedback. Schön demonstrates the designer's likelihood of receiving a lot of good and relevant feedback when he is drawing. He can conduct hypothesis-testing experiments on paper. That is much more difficult to do when a teacher plans instruction. When planning lessons the experienced teacher can imagine what might happen if he or she does this or that, but the feedback from the lesson plans is minimal.

There seems to be no virtual world that acts as the medium of reflection-in-action in teaching practice. The only medium is the actual classroom teaching itself.

Lortie said in his classic work on sociology of teaching (Lortie, 1975, p. 142) that most teachers find it very difficult to know the effect of their work because they receive little feedback on student learning. Lortie, therefore, wrote about 'the intangibility of teaching' and this point has been supported by other research on teacher thinking.

Teachers, of course, do get some feedback from the situation and from their students. However the feedback is not about student learning. The feedback is primarily about whether the situation in the classroom is under the teacher's control or not and whether or not the students are actively engaged (Halkes and Deykers, 1984, p. 157). The 'surprise' that Schön suggests will lead to reflection appears when the teachers lose control over the situation or when the students are completely passive. The surprise does not appear when students have not learned anything.

Teaching is not regulated mainly by feedback about student learning but is a routinized activity (Lowyck, 1984, p. 10; Clark and Peterson, 1986, p. 275). In this regard, Olson (Olson, 1991, p. 16) has concluded that teaching is too complex an activity to be named reflection-in-action in the sense Schön talks about it. I would propose a more cautious conclusion than Olson.

Teaching cannot be compared to designing because virtual world experiments cannot be conducted in teaching. Teaching is a routinized flow of activity. It is guided by feedback, but by feedback that concerns teacher control and student engagement in learning. It is not about the student learning. Schön's analysis of the professional design process cannot without modification be applied to teaching practice.

To summarize this critique of Schön's theory, teaching is not a kind of professional artistry guided by feedback on the student learning. Rather, teaching is a routinized and institutionalized practice guided by the organizational framework of the school.

Three Instances of the Reflective Approach

I selected the following three typical and current applications inspired by the reflective approach:

- G. Handal and P. Lauvås: *Promoting Reflective Teaching*, 1987;
- D.R. Hellison and T.J. Templin: *A Reflective Approach To Teaching Physical Education*, 1991 and;
- J.W. Brubacher, C.W. Case and T.G. Reagan: *Becoming a Reflective Educator*, 1994.

I conducted an analysis of the books in order to answer the questions: Do these authors recognize the realities of teaching as socially reproductive, guided by the framework of the school, and offering limited feedback on student learning?

The two American books by Hellison and Templin and Brubacher *et al.*, stress the importance of responding to the 'larger issues of society'. They raise questions about the 'political, moral and social implications of what and how we teach' (Hellison and Templin, 1991, p. 4).

One of the main purposes of the book by Brubacher *et al.*, is to inspire teachers to become 'good ethical decision makers' (Brubacher *et al.*, 1994, p. 128). So far so good; but perhaps the awareness of values and the readiness to make ethical decisions are only minor aspects of the professional qualification. What, in my judgment, is more important is being able to analyse the relations between the institutional setting and the practice of teaching. If teaching is primarily a routinized and institutionalized practice, and if the routines are more or less determined by the institutional setting the important qualification is to be able to see the connections between setting and practice. Then the teacher becomes qualified to alter the setting and create better possibilities for new teaching practices.

The Norwegian authors (Handal and Lauvås) are much more aware of the importance of the institutional framework factors but are more interested in educating teachers to exploit the 'free space' within the system (Handal and Lauvås, 1987, p. 23).

It is of great value that teachers are taught to make ethical decisions and that they can exploit the free space within the institutional framework. Yet, what remains lacking in the reflective approach to teaching practice are concepts and strategies to educate teachers so that they can develop and reform the institutional framework. Teachers should be seen as responsible, not only for their own teaching, but also, as sharing a responsibility for the school as an institution and for trying to reform the socially reproductive role of education.

Concerning the question about teacher knowledge of student learning all three books reflect the importance of the teacher receiving knowledge about the learning results. Handal and Lauvås note that the results often differ from the intentions (*ibid.*, p. 81) but they tend to want to draw teacher attention to the classroom process rather than to the learning results. Hellison and Templin recognize this problem and the importance of solving the problem (Hellison and Templin, 1991, p. 141) and they propose several methods for evaluating teaching practices and programmes. They do not, however, seem to recognize the research that indicates it is very difficult for teachers to be aware of student learning. Hellison and Templin and Brubacher *et al.*, share a certain naive optimism; they presume the problem is solved if teachers simply learn about methods of evaluation.

This optimism bears resemblance to the fundamental attitude of the rationalistic approach — the teachers just need to learn how to use planning models to prepare their courses and lessons. But what the research of the last twenty-five years ought to have told us is that the practice of teaching cannot be reformed simply by instructing teachers to use theoretically developed models and methods.

The education community should admit that the theory of teaching has a hitherto unsolved problem (Marton, 1993): How can teacher awareness focus on student learning and how can teachers obtain knowledge of the ongoing student learning in the classroom? The three books as representatives of the reflective approach express a tremendous progress in comparison to the rationalistic approach when it concerns recognition of the realities of teaching.

Two fundamental problems still seem to be unsolved:

- How do teachers become educated so that they can reform the institutional frameworks of teaching practice and transform the social role of education?
- How can teachers get in contact with student learning?

Conclusion

The purpose of the article was to answer two questions:

- Do the didactic theories correspond to the fundamental realities of teaching as viewed from the perspective of the research that has been done on teacher thinking and sociology of teaching?

> - If not, how can the theory of didactics be developed to have a greater respect for these realities?

The answer to the first question is mainly 'no'. It is generally accepted that the prescriptive and the rationalistic approaches conflict so much with the realities of teaching that they should be either abandoned or viewed as limited approaches to the practice of teaching. Also, some aspects of the reflective approach suffer from a naive optimism because they do not recognize the institutional frameworks and because they overestimate the possibilities of feedback on student learning.

The second question, of course, cannot be given any complete answer in this chapter; only a few principles can be stated. Reflective theories of teaching must simply start with a critical analysis of the actual routinized practices of teaching going on in our schools. The relationship between the institutional framework and the teaching practices must be emphasized because the reform of institutional settings often is a prerequisite to the reform and development of teaching practices. The critique of teaching and its institutional framework must be based on principles and standards inherent in the field of teaching and education. Also, teachers must be educated to work collaboratively on reform of the institutional framework and on changing the socially reproductive role of education.

References

ADLER, S. (1991) 'The reflective practitioner and the curriculum of teacher education', *Journal of Education for Teaching*, 17, 2.

BOURDIEU, P. (1989) *Outline of a Theory of Practice*, Cambridge, Cambridge University Press.

BRUBACHER, J.W., CASE, C.W. and REAGAN, T.G. (1994) *Becoming a Reflective Educator*, Thousand Oaks California, Corwin Press.

CLARK, C.M. and PETERSON, P.L. (1986) 'Teachers' thought processes', in WITTROCK, M.C. (Ed) *Handbook of Research on Teaching* (3rd ed.), New York, MacMillan Publishing Company.

DAY, C., CALDERHEAD, J. and DENICOLO, P. (1993) *Understanding Professional Development*, London and Washington, The Falmer Press.

GIDDENS, A. (1984) *The Constitution of Society*, Cambridge, Polity Press.

GIDDENS, A. (1990) *The Consequences of Modernity*, Cambridge, Polity Press.

HALKES, R. and DEYKERS, R. (1984) 'Teachers' teaching criteria', in HALKES, R. and OLSON, J.K., *Teacher Thinking*, Lisse, Swets and Zeitlinger.

HALKES, R. and OLSON, J.K. (Ed) (1984) *Teacher Thinking*, Lisse, Swets and Zeitlinger.

HANDAL, G. and LAUVÅS, P. (1987) *Promoting Reflective Teaching*, Milton Keynes, SRHE and Open University Press.

HELLISON, D.R. and TEMPLIN, T.J. (1991) *A Reflective Approach to Teaching Physical Education*, Champaign, Ill, Human Kinetics Books.

ILLERIS, K. (1991) *Pædagogikkens betydning*, København, Unge Pædagoger.

JORDELL, K.O. (1987) 'Teachers as reflective practitioners?', in Strømnes and Søvik, *Teachers Thinking*, Flataasen, Tapir.

LORTIE, D.C. (1975) *School-Teacher*, Chicago and London, The University of Chicago Press.

LOWYCK, J. (1984) 'Teacher thinking and teacher routines: A Bifurcation?', in HALKES, R. and OLSON, J.K., *Teacher Thinking*, Lisse, Swets and Zeitlinger.

LUHMANN, N. (1984) *Soziale Systeme*, Frankfurt, Suhrkamp.

LUNDGREN, U.P. (1972) *Frame Factors and the Teaching Process*, Stockholm, Almquist and Wiksell.

MARTON, F. (1993) 'On the Structure of Teachers' Awareness', Keynote address delivered at the 6th International Conference on Teacher Thinking, Gothenburg.

OLSON, J.K. (1991) *Understanding Teaching*, Milton Keynes, Philadelphia, Open University Press.

PARSONS, T. (1968) 'Professions', in SILLS, D.S. (Ed) *International Encyclopedia of the Social Sciences*, New York, The Macmillan Company and The Free Press, 11 and 12.

POPE, M. (1993) 'Anticipating teacher thinking', in DAY, *et al. Understanding Professional Development*, London and Washington, The Falmer Press.

SCHÖN, D.A. (1983) *The Reflective Practitioner*, New York, Basic Books.

SCHÖN, D.A. (1987) *Education the Reflective Practitoner*, San Francisco, Jossey-Bass Publishers.

STRØMNES, Å.L. and SØVIK, N. (1987) *Teachers Thinking*, Flataasen, Tapir.

TABA, H. (1962) *Curriculum Development*, New York, Harcourt, Brace and World.

TYLER, R.W. (1949) *Basic Principles of Curriculum and Instruction*, Chicago and London, The University of Chicago Press.

Part 3

Teachers' Thinking and Action

Each of the four articles in this part deals in its own way with the relation between thinking and action.

The main issue in Mikael Alexandersson's chapter is how teachers reflect on their own practice. His approach is a phenomenological one and the key concepts he is dealing with are reflection and intentionality. Alexandersson's intention is to describe how people perceive, conceive, experience or understand different phenomena in the world. Alexandersson focuses more closely on teachers' awareness, and consequently it may be worthwhile to read it in the light of Marton's keynote address, Chapter 2.

The contribution by Greta Morine-Dershimer and Peggy Reeve deals with metaphoric language. It is a descriptive approach examining the potential value of identifying what they call desirable metaphors for teaching and learning. They examine different assumptions underlying teachers' metaphoric language. One central question is whether changes in teachers' metaphors also will change their beliefs and behaviour.

Helmut Fischler's chapter deals with differences between intention and action. He examines how student teachers in physics education perceive the differences between pupils' everyday understanding and scientific understanding. Fischler deals with the question of how discrepancies between teachers' pedagogical ideas and their teaching practice arise in actual lessons. The chapter also discusses consequences for teacher education.

Maria de Fátima Chorão C. Sanches' chapter discusses teachers' cognitive styles and a possible correspondence between their cognitive style and preferential pedagogical practices. The article focuses on creativity styles. Kirton's 'adaptation — innovation' theory is Sanches' point of departure. Cognitive styles are studied both for teachers as individuals and as members of a group.

Chapter 9

Focusing Teacher Consciousness: What Do Teachers Direct Their Consciousness towards During Their Teaching?

Mikael Alexandersson

Abstract

This chapter reports a study that focuses what teachers experience in their teaching. The study is carried out within the framework of phenomenology and primarily concerns consciousness and intentionality. A phenomenographical approach has been used to describe and analyse the experiences of twelve primary teachers. A stimulated recall method was used to remind the teachers of their own thought processes during a previous lesson. The findings indicate that the teachers comment upon similar aspects of their practice — above all, capturing their pupils' attention and developing the pupils' thinking or creating a sense of community in the class. However, although the teachers direct their consciousness towards similar aspects, they do so in three qualitatively different ways: the act of consciousness is directed towards the activity itself; the act of consciousness is directed towards aims of general character; and the act of consciousness is also directed towards a specific content.

Introduction

This chapter is a summary of a study where the ways in which primary school-teachers reflect on their everyday work were studied (Alexandersson, 1994). The main aim was to describe what teachers experience in their teaching. The teacher experience of his or her own teaching is an expression for an interaction between the teacher and the teaching itself. When this relation here is described, it is represented by the way it appears to the teachers. The central research issue in this study is 'What do teachers direct their consciousness towards during their teaching?' A related purpose is to illuminate teachers' awareness in relation to their conception of their own working methods.

The Theoretical Framework

One way to focus the central issue in this study is to take the point of departure in phenomenology. Phenomenology investigates that which appears to someone. When something appears in our consciousness (when we experience something), the appearance occurs in a world which is historical, cultural and social. At the same time, however, we are historical, cultural and social beings. As Merleau-Ponty (1965) expresses it, a meeting between the individual and the world takes place with every act of consciousness. That meeting is the very condition of our existence. When we experience something in our existence, we do not experience isolated properties of an object, but we experience these properties — both functional and valuational — simultaneously, and we interpret their significance. My consciousness structures that which I experience but *what* my consciousness constructs depends upon my previous experiences. Experience consists of all the special thoughts, memories, emotions, expectations, etc., which the experience elicits in us. As far as the present study is concerned, when a teacher experiences teaching it is an expression of an 'interaction' between the teacher and the teaching itself.

The theoretical foundation for the study is related to the phenomenological concepts of 'reflection' and 'intentionality'. Reflection is here being used in terms of phenomenological reflection. The purpose of reflection is to try to grasp the essential meaning of something. According to van Manen (1990, p. 77) 'the insight into the essence of a phenomenon involves a process of reflectively appropriating, of clarifying, and of making explicit the structure of meaning of the lived experience'. The phenomenological concept — intentionality — could be defined to be 'the directedness of an act to an object'. According to Ihde (1986) intentionality is the correlation between the mode of consciousness and the object.

This study is carried out within the framework of a qualitative research approach called phenomenography (Marton, 1981, 1988). Phenomenography attempts to describe and understand how people conceive, experience, perceive or understand different aspects of the world. This is done by investigating people's conceptions. From a phenomenographic point of view a conception is a way of seeing something. Phenomenography is based on the assumption that the conceptions of a single object differ among people. Differences in conceptions are explained by the fact that different people have different experiences due to their different relations to the world. People then make different analyses and arrive at different knowledge about the object concerned. Phenomenographic research attempts to describe these differences. There are three strategically important ways in which phenomenography is framed. In the context of the present study, these are as follows:

- There is a search for understanding variation in what teachers direct themselves towards in their own practice.
- Instead of applying a model of description defined in advance, there is an attempt to explore the meaning of the variation in directedness.
- There is an aim to find a meaning of the variation in directedness, by studying the teachers' experience of teaching.

The Selection Process of the Teachers and the Data Collection

In qualitative studies, a general theoretical research problem is to find an acceptable point of balance between the requirement of a great range of variation and the requirement of a manageable empirical foundation. If the range of variation is too broad, the empirical foundation will be too confusing and difficult to handle. In the present study, the choice of teachers was made with the goal of achieving a balance between these two demands. The range of variation, for instance, includes a distribution relating to number of years of teaching experience, to a variation in the aim of the teaching, and also to the fact that the school context in itself should optimally vary in the teacher study. When considering generalization in connection with the phenomenographical approach, this means that the conceptions which are attained shall cover as many qualities within the phenomenon as possible.

In order to optimize the possibilities of varying the methodology in the study, the choice of thirty teachers was made from the primary school. The teachers were well recommended and respected for their teaching ability at their own school. This criterion included a range in different working methods. Technically a teacher in primary school can vary his or her method within most subjects. Most subjects in primary school can also comprise different proficiency factors, leading to a variation as regards verbal and visual performances. The educational material at this stage has a kind of layout that makes the methods vary considerably. Further, the variation of content in the teaching should not be constant in the study. With a variation also here, the following analysis could be made on a more general level. The selection process for this investigation can be described as purposeful sampling (Patton, 1990) together with what is known in ethnography as theoretical sampling.

In this study, data collection was limited to one occasion per teacher, but information was gathered on a continuous basis, with no predetermined limit to the number of teachers who would participate in the study. The data was processed on a continuous basis, which meant that I gradually became saturated with information. When my ongoing analysis no longer disclosed new dimensions in the material, I therefore discontinued the collection of data. This occurred after twelve occasions. Glaser and Strauss (1967) term this effect of data collection on the investigator as theoretical saturation. The collection of data took an average of half a day for each teacher, and each session comprised three stages: videorecording, limited to one lesson, which varied between forty and sixty minutes; commentary, in which the teacher commented freely upon the documentary film (This stage constitutes the main source of information for this study.); follow-up discussion, a semi-structured interview for following up and examining more closely issues communicated in the commentary stage and for formulating general questions about the classroom teaching.

The purpose of video-recording the lesson was to stimulate the teacher's thinking about the completed lesson, to remind the teacher of his or her own thinking (the stimulated recall method, see Calderhead 1981; Peterson 1982). The question this study addresses — Towards what do teachers direct their consciousness when they teach? — indicates that the interest lies not in the video-recording as such, but in teacher thinking about the instruction which has been carried out. In other words, the focus is on what the teacher thought about during his or her teaching. The teacher was therefore requested to respond to the following three questions:

- What were you thinking about during the sequences you are now viewing?
- What were you doing?
- Why did you do what you did in that particular way?

Because the teachers could control the video-recorder by remote control during the commentary part, they could choose the sequences they wished to comment upon (389 sequences altogether). Thus, they were able to stop the film to give spontaneous reactions to what they saw. That which was communicated through commentary is an intentional expression of what the teachers experienced in their own practice. In their descriptions of different occurrences, an intentionality lies in their way of giving shape to 'that which appears' to them. That which they experience does not exist in explicit form but must be interpreted at a later stage on the basis of the totality to which their descriptions belong. The unstructured part was followed by a semi-structured interview. The purpose was to deepen and problematize the unstructured part. Teachers were asked the following questions:

- When commenting on certain aspects, scenes, incidents or sequences, why did you choose just those?
- Were you aware of your own acting and what was happening?
- Please describe your intention and in what way was this documented hour a part of a whole?
- How would you define your own working methods and of what importance are they to you?

A preliminary interpretation of how the teachers experience their own teaching was made simultaneously with data collection. To some extent, this interpretation directed the follow-up discussion which took place shortly afterwards. The interpretation was also an unavoidable part of the processing of the transcriptions of the commentary and follow-up and of the review of the video-recording. The analysis and interpretation of the commentary and follow-up discussion was divided into four phases, each having a different objective:

- to familiarize myself with the data and gain an overall impression;
- to note similarities and differences in the statements;
- to determine descriptive categories for conceptions; and
- to examine the underlying structure of the system of categorization.

Results

The central finding in this study is the identification of the 'direction-related' dimension. When the teachers directed their consciousness towards different aspects in the recorded teaching sequences, major qualitative variations could be identified as shown in Table 9.1. The twelve teachers showed all three variations of directedness, but the main feature in each commentary could be located in one of them. A statistical analysis of quotations — 581 altogether — was carried out in relation to these three categories of description. The contents of the quotations

Table 9.1:   Qualitative variations in the direction-related dimension:
Three qualitative main categories

A.   Consciousness is directed towards **the activity** itself
B.   Consciousness is directed towards **aims of general character**
C.   Consciousness is directed also towards **a specific content**

Table 9.2:   Subcategories in main category A

A1.   How the pupils are developed socially
A2.   How a deep communication and relation is growing
A3.   How the pupils are being noticed
A4.   How to teach pupils to listen
A5.   How a systematic teaching leads to activity
A6.   How structured and balanced teaching is performed
A7.   How I think and how the pupils think

were examined both linguistically and for content, which resulted in a quantitative description of variations as regards the direction of consciousness. From the statistical point of view the quotations encompass three main component parts. These component parts were clearly separable; there was an activity and there was an object acted upon. The object could be stated in more general terms as aims of indefinite character and in more specific terms as a fixed and limited content. The findings indicate that, when commenting one specific instance, it was not natural that the teachers described the wholeness, i.e., their directedness in general was not towards a specific content in relation to a general aim and activity.

1   **Main category A**: Consciousness is directed towards the activity itself (seven teachers)

What the different conceptions in this category had in common was the fact that consciousness was firstly directed to various aspects and situations which took place in the activity itself. There was no evident direction towards any general or concrete aim when the different instances were commented. Reflections consequently did not go beyond the visible activity. Apart from the topic of the content, it was the actual situation — the ongoing activity — which was commented upon. One can mention two levels of comments with the qualitative content, one level where only the activities in the different instances were described — the teachers referred to what was happening — and one level where the teachers explained what was happening. At the latter level the explanations were completed by statements about causal connections or about previous motives for their own or the pupils' activities. The analysis of the teachers' statements resulted in various conceptions forming a foundation for seven subcategories (see Table 9.2).

One recurrent theme was the question of how a deep, social relationship with the pupils might be developed. When this theme was in focus, general or distinct aims were rarely drawn from the activities which were then noticed. In order to explain causes behind different sequences, the teachers based their explanations on experiences which had reference to an outside classroom situation — for instance to the pupils' social home situation. In several subcategories consciousness was directed towards situations where the teacher was helping pupils to discover knowledge themselves. When those situations were commented, statements often dealt with the importance of the fact that the individual pupil should have the possibility to develop his or her own thinking. In the following statement we can recognize the characteristics when the directedness is towards the ongoing process, i.e., how the teacher reflects upon his or her own thinking as well as upon the pupils' thinking: 'I am trying to find out how they think here and how I am thinking. So I got some seconds there and took the opportunity. Something like that I was thinking.'

Another striking feature was the fact that the consciousness was directed towards the teacher's own way of structuring and organizing the lesson. On this occasion the importance of systematic planning in order to make the lesson successful was emphasized. Through a stable and consistent structure on the lesson it would be possible to more effectively control the pupils' activities. Connected to the teacher's own part was also the effort to establish deep communication and a relationship with the pupils. Irrespective of the fact that the relationship was of social or of intellectual character, it could, according to the teachers, lead to an increase in the pupils' general understanding and learning.

The teachers in this main category had difficulties in commenting on the meaning of method in a distinct way. They preferred to refer to the possibility that the method should result through the development of cooperation between teacher and pupils during the lesson. As the method was more important than the content, the teacher's instruction could be separated from what was instructed about; i.e., what the pupils learned regarding content was not the main point in the instruction. They should rather learn methods which provided them with the independence they need when seeking knowledge. Methods in teaching were mentioned as a way to establish contact in terms of a good relationship with the pupils. One could trace the teacher's intention as being the capture of the attention of the pupils. In this perspective, the method became analogous to activities which satisfy the teacher's own needs and interests. Irrespective of arranged methods of any kind, the ultimate aim with the methods was to catch the pupils' attention.

In its concrete content, the method could be compared to areas like reading-methods and writing-methods, or to activities like developing pupils' thinking and ability to make reflections. When cognitive activities were commented, it was the variations in reflection and not the content in itself which were focused. Method was stated, partly as a means to organize the lesson so that the pupils should learn by being active themselves, and partly so that the pupils by their own discoveries might develop their thinking. In this way, the method was meant as a support to the pupils' cognitive development.

2 **Main category B**: Consciousness is directed towards aims of general character (four teachers)

Teachers within this main category have a general attitude to the aims of different activities. In their directedness a forward leading aim can be found which goes beyond the activity itself, but does not aim at a specific outcome of the activity. The comments mostly deal with the fact that the actual activity has an aim of general character. Nearly half of the total amount of quotations can be assigned to descriptions of general aims. However, in the quotations there is no direction towards any specific content. The descriptions of aims are expressed at a more

Table 9.3: Subcategories in main category B

B1. Aims for the present conversation
B2. Aims for the open attitude in the teaching
B3. Aims for the teacher's active discipline
B4. Aims for catching the pupil's attention

general level. The teachers have given reports of the situations rather than analyses. Four qualitative different conceptions can be distinguished concerning the content in direction of consciousness (see Table 9.3). The content in the descriptions of general aims concerned the teacher's ambition to develop relationships, to create high activity or to activate the pupils' thinking. The various methods which, directly or indirectly, were explicated in the commentaries and correlated to the clarification of method conceptions, made in the semi-structured interview, were really directed towards these descriptions of general aims. The recorded teaching sequence brought, throughout, thoughts on different principles for raising pupil activity. The directedness was towards visible, action-related situations which came from both the teacher as well as from the pupils. This started comments about the importance of action for education and knowledge in general. Reflection concerning the pupils' learning was on very few occasions related to a fixed content but rather more to thinking as an activity. Thinking was, in this perspective, one of several activities in the teaching process. The following statement below demonstrates the characteristics of the directedness in the category: 'The aim is here to bring thoughts and questions with them, so that they all the time feel forced to activate a thinking process. That is the purpose of this question.' In the same way as in the previous main category, teachers held a more general attitude to the conception of method. They conveyed a certain irresolution in clarifying the method conception, and they connected the conception, at first hand, to their own activities and not to the pupils' learning. However, there was one divergence. The method conception seemed to be more reflected upon by teachers, in this main category.

3 **Main category C**: Consciousness is directed also towards a specific content (one teacher)

This third direction-related main category differs from the other two by the fact that consciousness is directed not only towards the activity in itself or towards a general aim, but also to a specific content. The direction of the quotations towards a general aim and towards a specific content regarding the present situation comprises two-thirds of the total number of quotations from the twelve teachers. A content-related discussion is principally always preceded by focusing the activity and/or the aims of general character. The present activity — alternatively the aim for this — is connected to content-related intentions for the teachers' own activities as well as for the acts of the pupils. Of the twelve teachers only one represented this direction-related main category. The outstanding feature in the teacher's direction of consciousness corresponds essentially to the category 'to activate the pupils' thinking'. The qualitative conception is contained in the subcategory shown in Table 9.4. The teacher's comments concerned mainly the reflection activity of the individual pupil and his or her ability to verbalize the reflection or to describe

Table 9.4: Subcategory in main category C

C1. That the pupils learn a specific content

---

the reflection in a concrete action. Consciousness was then directed towards the way in which the pupil expressed his or her action in relation to a fixed content. There was an evident direction in the teacher's comment to produce a synthesis of, on the one hand, the pupils' reflection and action and, on the other, the teaching content. Reflection, action and content were consequently integrated. They were mutually dependent on each other and on each other's conditions. The three aspects in question were also expected to be correct. Neither in the unstructured interview nor in the follow-up discussion was there any statement which pointed out that a pupil's verbalized thought — in spite of quality — should be accepted and passed by the teacher. When the three aspects formed a correct totality, they were accepted. From this point of view the development of the pupils' thinking processes will become a part of a large totality. The following statement shows this reasoning concerning the activating of the pupils' thinking. The characteristics for this statement are the obvious directedness towards the pupils' learning of a specific content.

> I'm walking to them all to see if they all know what a triangle is. Then some were a bit uncertain of it. They managed to make a loose angle, because then the whole of it is like an angle for him, but later when it is fitted in the triangle . . . If they are a bit away on the wrong track. Then I choose to walk between all of them and ask them to show me the angle.

If there was a connection between thought and action of the pupil, according to the teacher, that could mean an increase in the possibilities for the pupil to 'think right'. The 'inner method', i.e., the pupil's cognitive activity, was comprehended as internalized in the pupil's consciousness. The 'outer method', in terms of way of directions, became then means to facilitate and support such cognitive activities which could mean that the pupil's thought and action would be integrated into a totality. In this way, the method technically took a more remote place in the teacher's own consciousness.

Summary

In Table 9.5 the results of the qualitative analysis and the statistical analysis of the contents of the quotations in each qualitative category are presented. In the horizontal heading the three statistical categories represent what the teachers made comments about. In category 1 the quotations are about activities — the present is described and explained. In category 2 the quotations are also about general aims for the activities and in category 3 the quotations include specific contents in relation to the aims and the activities. The statistical analysis revealed that the teachers in each qualitative category emphazised different component parts. For instance, the seven teachers which comprise main category A have their main feature in the statistical category 1. Out of a total of 347 quotations only fourteen

Table 9.5: Number of quotations in each qualitative main category

Qualitative Main categories	Statistical Categories			No. of quotations
	1	2	3	
A. Consciousness is directed towards the activity itself (7 teachers)	266 (78)	67 (18)	14 (4)	347
B. Consciousness is directed towards aims of general character (4 teachers)	87 (51)	52 (30)	32 (19)	171
C. Consciousness is directed also towards a specific content (1 teacher)	23 (37)	12 (19)	28 (44)	63
Total no. of quotations	376 (65)	131 (22)	74 (13)	581

Note: (Per cent)

(4 per cent) were in category 3. On the other hand, 266 quotations (78 per cent) were located to the statistical category 1.

The overview above indicates that, of a total of 581 quotations, 376 (65 per cent) concerned the activity — either the ongoing process or the function of the teacher's own activity in the classroom. In 131 quotations (22 per cent) the directedness concerned aims of general character and in 74 quotations (13 per cent) a specific content.

An issue of central importance is how the three main categories stand in relation to the group of teachers and the subject taught, which formed the object of the analysis. Regardless of school, grade, subject of instruction and content of subject, the teachers commented upon similar aspects of their practice — above all, capturing their pupils' attention and developing the pupils' thinking or creating a sense of community in the class. However, although the teachers direct their consciousness towards similar aspects, they do so in qualitatively different ways. Thus, the subject or subject matter does not determine the directedness of the teachers in this study. Data was collected upon a single occasion for each teacher and from a specific research perspective. If a different classroom session had been documented, different results would have emerged for each individual teacher. I can confidently state that the three main categories — and possibly others — exist irrespective of the concrete teaching context. These categories appear upon different occasions, and teachers — regardless of the grade or subject they are teaching — can then be carriers of the structural content in each category. On the other hand, I cannot claim that the distribution among the three categories reflects teachers in general. The distribution of quotations within the categories and the distribution of teachers among the categories are only valid for the unique occasions on which data was collected.

Conclusion

It is not possible to argue that these differences in directedness are general for teachers in primary school, but on the contrary the results show that this kind of different directedness among teachers in their own teaching process may take place. In fact, how the teachers reflected upon their own practice points out the fact of obvious variations in directedness. One could say, that the overarching theme in this study indicates that highly skilled teachers are not necessarily driven by the aim that their pupils should develop certain specific understanding, knowledge or skill; the teachers were in general not directed towards some specific content of the pupils learning. The study also points out differences in the way in which the teachers comprehended their own working methods. With regard to this study, it seems to be a correspondence between how consciousness was directed and the conception of working methods. When directedness pointed towards some specific content for the pupils' learning, the method technically took a more remote place in the teachers' consciousness. When the activity itself was in focus, the method was more important than the content. The outcome in terms of specific understanding, knowledge or skill was not the main point when different methods were used in the teaching process.

The general picture is quite clear and could be summarized in the following way: A specific content does not appear to be a major driving force for the teachers' activity. The teachers in general were not oriented towards specific learning aims and they rarely focused on means-ends relations. Since aims, goals, content and means-ends relations are not emphasized, the teachers' directedness in terms of awareness does not correspond to Lortie's conception of 'technical knowledge' or to Schön's description of 'technical rationality' (Lortie, 1975; Schön, 1983; 1987).

An important strategy in the research field focusing on the practical rationality is to provide a basis for understanding the different ways in which teachers reflect upon their own practice. Such a description may not only contribute to understanding of structure of consciousness, it will also contribute to increase the understanding of teachers' professional knowledge. One important issue for the future is the understanding of why teachers' directedness varied in the way it did according to this study. In using Marton's words (Marton, 1993) 'What are the factors that may have contributed to the erosion of content in schools?'

References

ALEXANDERSSON, M. (1994) 'Metod och Medvetande' (Method and Consciousness), Doctoral dissertation, Göteborg Studies In Educational Sciences 96, Göteborg, Acta Universitatis Gothoburgensis.

CALDERHEAD, J. (1981) 'Stimulated recall: A method for research on teaching', *British Journal of Educational Psychology*, 51, 2, pp. 211–17.

GLASER, B. and STRAUSS, A. (1967) *The Discovery of Grounded Theory: Strategies for Qualitative Research*, New York, Aldine Publishing Company.

IHDE, D. (1986) *Experimental Phenomenology*, New York, Putnam.

LORTIE, D. (1975) *Schoolteacher. A Sociological Study*, Chicago, The University of Chicago Press.

MARTON, F. (1981) 'Phenomenography — describing conceptions of the world around us', *Instructional Science*, 10, pp. 177–200.

MARTON, F. (1988) 'Phenomenography: Exploring different conceptions of reality', in FETTERMAN, I.D. (Ed) *Qualitative Approaches to Evaluation in Education*, New York, Praeger.

MARTON, F. (1993) 'On the structure of teachers' awareness', Keynote address delivered at the 6th International Conference on Teacher Thinking held in Gothenburg, August 10–15.

MERLEAU-PONTY, M. (1965) *Phenomenology of Perception*, London, Routledge and Kegan Paul.

PATTON, M.Q. (1990) *Qualitative Evaluation and Research Methods*, Newbury Park, California, Sage Publications.

PETERSON, P.L. (1982) 'Beyond time on task: Students' reports of their thought processes during classroom instruction', *The Elementary School Journal*, 5, pp. 481–91.

SCHÖN, D.A. (1983) *The Reflective Practitioner: How Professionals Think in Action*, New York, Basic books.

SCHÖN, D.A. (1987) *Educating the Reflective Practitioner*, San Francisco, Josey-Bass Publishers.

VAN MANEN, M. (1990) *Researching Lived Experience. Human Science for an Action Sensitive Pedagogy*, Ontario, The Althouse Press.

Chapter 10

Studying Teachers' Thinking About Instruction: Issues Related to Analysis of Metaphoric Language

Greta Morine-Dershimer and Peggy Tarpley Reeve

Abstract

This study investigated the potential value of a descriptive approach for identification of 'desirable' metaphors for teaching and learning.[1] Lessons taught by ten secondary-education majors were identified as more or less successful in terms of pupils' active engagement. Transcripts of student teachers' stimulated recall interviews were analysed to identify their individual patterns of metaphoric language use, then the patterns exhibited by six students who taught the most and least successful lessons were compared. Differences in their use of metaphoric language are identified and discussed in cross-case comparisons.

Introduction

In recent years a number of researchers have investigated aspects of teacher thinking by examining the metaphors for teaching and learning held by prospective and experienced teachers. One approach to this research is based on an exploration of images that are implicit in the natural use of metaphoric language exhibited by teachers in descriptions of their practice (Morine-Dershimer, 1983; Mostert, 1992; Munby, 1986; 1987). Another approach involves studies that examine explicitly stated teaching metaphors prompted by interview questions or other data collection tasks initiated by researchers (Bullough, 1991; Carter, 1990; Tobin, 1990).

Some researchers (e.g., Wubbels, 1992) have suggested that prospective teachers' preconceptions of teaching can be changed (improved) by analysing and revising their metaphors for teaching and learning, and a number of researchers have reported on such attempts (Bullough and Stokes, 1993; Marshall, 1990; Weade and Ernst, 1990). For the most part these attempts have involved asking prospective teachers to identify metaphors that reflect their images of themselves as teachers, and then to consider alternative metaphors. These attempts to change prospective teachers' images of teaching would seem to be based on three related assumptions: 1) that some metaphors or images of teaching are more appropriate than others, or more apt to contribute to effective teaching practice; 2) that prospective teachers, or the researchers and teacher educators seeking to promote change, have some

150

knowledge that will help them to identify a more or less appropriate image or metaphor; and 3) that a change in their metaphors for teaching will influence prospective teachers' underlying beliefs and, eventually, their behaviour. These assumptions need to be critically examined. That is the issue addressed by this chapter.

To address these assumptions, we first return to the distinction between the two approaches to research on metaphors for teaching and ask which approach might be expected to be most revealing of tacit beliefs and perceptions, the natural metaphoric language used to describe one's teaching, or the explicit metaphor generated in response to an assigned task. This study is based on the assumption that the natural use of metaphoric language will be the more accurate reflector of teachers' underlying conceptions. Thus we consider the three assumptions from the perspective of that particular approach.

It is clear from the literature that researchers tend to believe that some metaphors or images of teaching are more appropriate than others. Munby (1987), for example, has identified several metaphors which seem to be pervasive in teachers' natural use of language to describe their practice, including 'lesson as a moving object', 'mind as a container', and 'attention as a commodity'. He has also observed that teachers' sense of curriculum is often articulated in terms like 'content to be covered' (Munby, 1990). Munby appears to consider these common metaphors to be constraining to teachers' thinking, and generally undesirable images.

Certainly, these images appear to conflict with the constructivist views of teaching and learning that currently guide many efforts to improve teacher education (e.g., Anderson, 1989a; 1989b). However, Lakoff (1987) argues that many of these types of images derive from kinesthetic image schemas which are an important basis for all our abstract conceptualizations. If his theory is valid, these images are not necessarily negative, and they could be very, very difficult to change.

One recent descriptive study by Mostert (1992) has identified subtle differences in experienced teachers' use of these common metaphors. For example, with regard to 'lesson as a moving object', some teachers he interviewed talked about leading their pupils through the lesson, while others described themselves as moving through the lesson together with their pupils. Is one sense of 'lesson as a moving object' more appropriate than another, or should both be considered equally undesirable? And how might we reasonably answer this question?

To address these concerns, we set out to investigate the potential value of a descriptive approach to answer a more general question. We asked: Are there patterns of metaphoric language used by prospective teachers to describe their teaching that are associated with variations in the success of the lessons they have taught, when success is measured by the extent of pupil engagement in the lesson?

Method

Participants

Participants in the study were six secondary-education majors in the final year of their teacher-education programme. Using an extreme-case sampling strategy (Patton, 1990), we selected these six students from a group of ten who taught lessons identified as more and less successful in terms of pupils' active engagement. Three taught lessons rated as most successful, and three taught lessons rated as least successful. The six participants exhibited considerable variety in demographic characteristics (gender, ethnicity, subject-matter specialization).

Procedures for Identifying Successful Lessons

The first means for identifying successful lessons involved pupil responses to the lessons. At the end of each lesson pupils were asked to write down on a 5x7 card 'a key idea' of the lesson, and 'two things you heard anybody saying during the lesson'. In prior studies (Morine-Dershimer, 1991) the phraseology in pupil statements of 'key ideas' tended to emphasize pupil responsibility for learning (pupil-oriented key-idea statements) in more pupil-centred lessons, while pupil reports of hearing side conversations rather than comments on lesson content were associated with pupils' off-task behaviour during the lesson. In this study, pupil responses to the three most successful lessons differed significantly from their responses to the three least successful lessons in two ways (Artiles, Mostert and Tankersley, 1994). Pupils reported proportionately more pupil-oriented key-idea statements in the more successful lessons than in the less successful lessons. Pupils also reported hearing more side conversations in the less successful lessons than in the more successful lessons. In short, pupil responses indicated that pupil engagement was much higher in the more successful lessons.

The second means of identifying successful lessons involved analysis of interactive behaviour. The ten video-taped lessons were coded according to the 'Beginning Teacher Assistance Program' (BTAP) system, developed for the purpose of evaluating first-year teachers in Virginia. Based on research on effective teaching, this objective observation system organizes teaching behaviour into fourteen competencies, and indicates which competencies have been demonstrated by a given teacher. In this study the three most successful lessons differed from the three least successful lessons in terms of both the number and type of competencies demonstrated (Artiles, Mostert and Tankersley, 1994). Student teachers in the three most successful lessons demonstrated most of the competencies related to teacher attention to pupil performance, while student teachers in the three least successful lessons demonstrated very few of these competencies. Differences in organizational and presentational competencies were much less pronounced.

Data-collection Procedures

Data on participants' natural use of metaphoric language to describe their teaching practice came from their comments on their interactive thinking in these lessons. Following each lesson, the student teacher was interviewed using a stimulated recall procedure (Morine and Vallance, 1975; Morine-Dershimer and Oliver, 1989). In an introductory portion of the interview, the student was asked to explain his or her plan for the lesson, and to describe the class of pupils being taught. The video-tape of the lesson was then played, and the student was asked to stop the video-tape at any point where he or she was 'aware of making a decision or noticing something particular about the pupils'. Whenever the video-tape was stopped, the interviewer asked, 'what were you thinking about or noticing here?' All interviews were audio-taped and transcribed.

Data-analysis Procedures

Data analysis involved the identification and categorization of the metaphoric language contained in the transcripts of the stimulated recall interviews. The initial categories were derived from six kinesthetic image schemas identified by Johnson (1987) and Lakoff (1987). These are (in order of their frequency of use by participants in this study): the 'Source–Path–Goal' schema, the 'Container' schema, the 'Compulsive Force' schema, the 'Centre –Periphery' schema, the 'Link' schema, and the 'Part–Whole' schema. These schemas are displayed in Table 10.1, together with their structural characteristics as described by Lakoff and Johnson, and illustrated by examples of associated metaphoric language exhibited by student teachers in this study. An additional category was derived from the metaphor of 'attention' as 'commodity', identified by Munby (1987), and expanded to include 'time' as 'commodity' (Mostert, 1992). One further category emerged from analysis of the data, which revealed a Performance metaphor used by several of the student teachers. Examples of the metaphoric language associated with these latter two categories are also included in Table 10.1.

Results

For purposes of this chapter, we present two sets of paired cases. The first pair of cases involves lessons taught by two post-graduate students, one a more successful English lesson taught by a female, the other a less successful mathematics lesson taught by a male. The second pair of cases involves lessons taught by two fifth-year students. For subject-matter contrast here, we selected a more successful science lesson and a less successful social-studies lesson. Both members of this pair were female, and both were minority students. For each pair we present a brief cross-case comparison, then we draw some conclusions from the two sets of cases.

Anne and Chip

Anne, a post-graduate student completing a two-year programme for the Master of Teaching degree in English education, was student teaching in a rural high school. She was interviewed about a lesson that she taught on poetry interpretation to a class of eight 11th and 12th graders in a humanities elective course, pupils she described as 'the brightest kids' in the county, while also noting, 'they're a little bit lazy.'

Chip, a post-graduate student completing a two-year programme with a major in mathematics education, was teaching in a high school located in a small city. He was interviewed about a lesson that he taught on inequalities and constraints to a class of twenty-two college-bound 10th and 11th graders, a class he described as 'all very bright', while adding that 'they don't seem to be all that excited about math. . . . it's hard to get them to interact.'

Table 10.1: *Metaphoric schemas used as categories*

Schema	Structural Elements	Examples
Source–Path–Goal	starting point, destination, route and direction	I want them to read and see how the poets *convey* ideas. We're *nearing the end* . . . now we're *finishing up*. This is the content we'll be *going over*.
Container	Interior, boundary, exterior	They can *pick up* things on their own. It *holds* a little more interest. Whatever comes *into his mind*, he speaks.
Compulsive Force	force, object, movement/change	I did *drag* them into it. I *push* the kids. It's quite a *battle*.
Centre–Periphery	centre as basic core, periphery (dependent on the centre)	I *focus* on him. But I always kind of *edge in* there.
Link	two or more entities, a connector or 'ties'	I try to make some *connections*. I think I'm gonna try to finish and *tie everything together*.
Part–Whole	whole, parts, configuration/separation	It gives me the chance to *gather* my thoughts. We *broke it up* and did smaller things.
Time and Attention as Commodities	giving, paying, trading time and attention	They don't like to *spend a lot of time* doing that. She was still *paying attention*.
Performance	students or teachers as actors on the stage	I didn't really *play it up*. They were *taking on the teaching role* themselves.

Anne and Chip were similar in that both saw their pupils as bright, though somewhat reluctant to contribute in class. Given this perception, Anne planned a lesson that involved small group work, organizing the class into dyads and giving each pair a selected poem to read and interpret. Toward the end of the class each pair of pupils read their poem aloud and shared their interpretation with the class. Chip's lesson, in contrast, was mainly lecture and demonstration, with limited discussion from pupils.

While Anne and Chip were fairly similar in the categories of metaphoric images they used to describe their teaching, they were quite different in the subtle shadings of language use within each schema. Anne's images depicted her intention of sharing responsibility for lesson development with her pupils. Chip's images reflected a concern with, and an uncertainty about, his own performance. These differences are noted and illustrated in Table 10.2.

The images of teaching and learning revealed by Anne's natural use of metaphoric language in describing her thinking about her lesson included pupils as an integral part of the instructional process, and as active contributors to that process. This was consistent with her interactive behaviour, for she demonstrated all seven competencies related to teacher attention to pupil performance. Pupil perceptions of the lesson also reflected this view, as pupil reports of what they heard being said in the lesson were strongly focused on classmates' comments about their interpretations of the poems they had read.

The images of teaching and learning revealed by Chip's natural use of metaphoric language failed to include pupils as a prominent part of his lesson. Pupils likewise failed to include themselves as important participants in relation to lesson content. Only one pupil reported hearing a comment by another pupil about the content of the lesson, while more than one-third reported hearing classmates' side conversations, a pattern indicative of off-task behaviour. Observable interactive behaviour was consistent with these reactions. Chip failed to demonstrate any of the seven competencies associated with teacher attention to pupil performance.

Anita and Candace

Anita, a fifth-year student in science education, taught in a high school in a small city. Her biology lesson was taught to a class of eighteen pupils who were mostly college-bound 10th graders, with a few selected 9th graders. The biology curriculum for this class was 'fast paced', and Anita described her pupils as 'a good class . . . generally interested in learning'.

Candace, a fifth-year student in social-studies education, also taught in a high school in a small city. Her lesson was taught to a class of nineteen 10th–12th graders in an elective course on international relations. Candace described the class as 'a very vocal and opinionated group . . . very willing to state their ideas and interact in the class setting. . . . They all really like the subject, which is good. And they seem to like each other, too, which is important.'

Anita's planned activities had pupils working in cooperative learning teams. Each team contained an 'expert' who shared information he or she had learned about a certain group of organisms. Each group worked its way through one of three learning centres where they watched and discussed video-tapes and slides,

Table 10.2: Comparison of natural metaphoric language: Two post-graduate prospective teachers

Areas for Comparison	Anne 'Shared Responsibility'	Chip 'Uncertainty'
SOURCE–PATH–GOAL SCHEMA Goal specificity	A goal of mine is to get them to learn how to read poetry.	My plan? I just went through and saw everything I needed to cover.
Belief in pupil ability to construct meaning	If you point out, or lead them a little bit, they're real sharp. I didn't even prepare or write down what I thought should be answers for these poems. I thought I'd just let them go. He's my fastest student; he has lots of lightbulbs going on . . . I always try to stop and acknowledge the lightbulbs.	I felt like they would be lost as to my intent. I needed to define linear programming, then go on to the problem . . . After I had gone through a word problem, and gotten a little bit of their feet wet . . . I do try to get them involved, just to keep them on their toes somewhat.
Sense of language as 'vehicle' to convey meaning	We talked about how authors convey through language what they're trying to say. Now I want them to see how the poets convey idea.	You want to use a precise language . . . to convey what you want to say right to the T . . . There are times when I wish (my) language would flow a tittle easier.
Sense of ability to manage progress toward goal	I had a student who was pretty much lost (with writing poetry about love), and I had her do a poster (instead).	That threw me off there for a second, so I had to grab my bearings.

Schema		
CONTAINER SCHEMA Where information is 'held'	They caught on to the variety of poetry (in the examples).	I knew the whole process so it was just a matter of thinking off the top of my head what I had done last night.
How ideas are 'extracted'	He picked out the important idea of his poem.	I didn't want to just tell them ... Ideally, I would try to draw it out of them more.
	I double-checked to make sure she got it (the meaning of a line of a poem), because it's one of those things that you could easily miss.	They aren't at all questioning, but they seem to pick up on (the math content).
COMPULSIVE FORCE SCHEMA Source and direction of pressure	They have been pushing me about defining harder words. I push the kids ... (to) share stuff (read their writing aloud).	I had the time breathing down my neck.
TIME AND ATTENTION (COMMODITY) SCHEMA Sense of time/attention management	We looked at the poem, and I really took time with it. The question for me as a teacher is how do you budget your time.	I was wondering how long to give them to read (a math problem).
PERFORMANCE SCHEMA Sense of who are major actors	I think they like having an audience ... having someone stand there and be interested in what they're doing. I talk to him ... about channeling his energy more, and being a little more aware of, and in control of, his presence in the classroom.	I feel like there's just a lot of rough edges ... I found it hard to go out there every day and be very smooth. It's just a matter of practising my routines and working them in.

guided by information and questions on a worksheet Anita had produced and distributed, while she circulated and assisted the groups.

Candace's lesson dealt with a spectrum of political positions (reactionary to radical). She described different positions along this political spectrum, then drew a graphic model of the political spectrum on the board, and had pupils discuss how to label and where to place public figures (e.g., Saddam Hussein, George Bush, Margaret Thatcher, Karl Marx) in terms of their political positions. The discussion included lively comments and arguments, as well as two lengthy digressions from the main topic.

Both Anita and Candace saw their pupils as bright and interested in learning, and both planned lesson activities that involved active pupil participation. They exhibited no major differences in the types of metaphoric images they used to describe their teaching, or in the order of predominance of their use of these images, but differences were evident in the ways these two prospective teachers framed the content of their metaphors. Anita's language emphasized pupil involvement, while Candace's images emphasized pupil control. These differences are depicted in Table 10.3.

Anita's use of metaphoric language painted a picture of an active teacher with involved pupils. This pattern was fairly consistent with data on her interactive behaviour during the lesson, as well as pupils' responses to the lesson. She demonstrated four of the seven competencies associated with teacher awareness of pupil performance and five of the seven competencies associated with organizational and presentational skills. Fewer than one-third of her pupils reported hearing side conversations during the lesson, a proportion that could be considered surprising given the independent group work that characterized the lesson activity. The other pupils almost all reported hearing comments about the content of the lesson made by their classmates.

Candace's language of control was more revealing of her concerns than of her accomplishments, according to the data on her interactive behaviour during the lesson and the pupils' responses to the lesson. Despite a preoccupation with 'focus' and with questions as the vehicle to focus the students and move the lesson along, Candace demonstrated only one of the seven competencies of presentational and organizational skills. She also demonstrated only one competency in the area of teacher attention to pupil performance. Furthermore, despite her emphasis on pupils paying attention, the pupils' responses to her lesson showed a clear lack of attention to the content of the lesson. More than three-fourths of her pupils reported hearing classmates' side conversations during the lesson, a pattern indicative of off-task behaviour and lack of pupil engagement.

Conclusion

The cases described here (as well as the cases of the two other participants in this study, whose lessons and language are not reported here) demonstrate that it is possible to identify differences in the patterns of metaphoric language used by prospective teachers in discussing their practice. Furthermore, the patterns of metaphoric language identified here were related to the teachers' patterns of interactive behaviour, as well as pupil responses to the lessons that they taught. What do these findings mean for the assumptions that we set out to examine — the

Table 10.3: Comparison of natural metaphoric language: *Two fifth-year prospective teachers*

Areas for Comparison	Anita 'Involvement'	Candace 'Control'
SOURCE–PATH–GOAL SCHEMA Sense of long-range purposes	We started out the unit about two weeks ago. I can see how this unit is going to be really useful down the road.	We'll do this quickly, we'll get through it, we'll discuss it, and then we'll go on. I've been very laid back and easy going, it's just like, whatever, we'll do whatever.
Belief in pupil ability to construct meaning	(I was) trying to give them a little bit of direction about what they needed to do for the day, and then pretty much just letting them go. Usually there are a few other things that end up popping up as we go along.	I go through the lesson, putting the information on the board a step at a time, so that they would have to keep up with me. None of them were the answers I was looking for, so I decided to pretty much ignore them and keep trying to refocus.
Sense of ability to manage progress toward goal	I know that as I go through time, I just keep learning more and more.	I was concerned about how it was gonna go.
CONTAINER SCHEMA What 'holds' pupil interest	I think that studying the insects held a lot of interest for them.	If I do it . . . a step at a time, they're constantly involved in it.
How ideas are 'extracted' or taken in		Usually I don't try and draw her out a lot, because she's kind of shy. A couple of people picked up on the idea that you can be conservative and liberal. At the same time, they weren't really grasping any of the staff I was talking about. I don't spoon feed them a lot, so when I do, it's okay.

159

Table 10.3: Continued

Areas for Comparison	Anita 'Involvement'	Candace 'Control'
COMPULSIVE FORCE SCHEMA		
Sense of restraint	I usually give them time to get into it, then I go around and poke my nose in. I try to give them a little space and see what they can do on their own before I jump in.	I did drag them into it. Do I address it (a pupil's question) or do I just blow if off?
TIME AND ATTENTION (COMMODITY) SCHEMA		
Sense of time/attention management in use of force	One thing … that I want to spend more time on next year is long-term goals. They don't like to spend a lot of time (listening to lectures).	If I give him a certain amount of attention, it keeps him focused. I did it on purpose to antagonize her … but she was still paying attention, and that was what I wanted to do.
LINK SCHEMA		
Sense of content linkages	I just try to make some connections between the different groups that they're studying now (and broad topics — evolution, etc.)	I think I'm gonna try and like finish and tie everything together.
PERFORMANCE SCHEMA		
Sense of who are major actors	My role … has been to sort of go around to each of the groups and just make sure that they're getting the things that they need to get out. So (the pupils) were taking on the teaching role themselves.	
UNIQUE IMAGE ('Stereo system')		
Sense of interference with 'hearing the music'		If they don't feel like they're getting any kind of feedback, positive feedback, they turn off. I guess I was turning all that out cause I don't remember hearing that.

assumptions on which teacher educators' attempts to change prospective teachers' metaphors for teaching appear to be based?

The first such assumption seems to be that some metaphors or images of teaching are more appropriate than others, or more apt to contribute to effective teaching practice. Participants of both the more and less successful lessons in this study used the same kinesthetic image schemas in roughly the same order of frequency. The 'Source–Path–Goal' schema was predominant in the descriptive language of all of these prospective teachers, and the 'Container' schema was also prevalent for them all. Thus the 'lesson as a moving object' and 'mind as a container' were images used by these teachers regardless of the apparent success of the lessons they were discussing.

While the basic kinesthetic image schemas occurred in the natural language of all these participants, the shades of meaning with which these images were expressed did differ. And these differing shades of meaning within particular schemas *were* related to the success of the lesson, when success was measured by interactive behaviour supportive of pupil engagement and pupil responses indicative of pupil engagement in the lesson. Thus, based on this study, a more acceptable first assumption might be stated as: prospective teachers' ways of *expressing* common metaphors of teaching are related to their success in promoting pupil engagement in lessons.

The second assumption on which change efforts appear to be based is that the researchers and teacher educators seeking to promote a change in teachers' metaphors have some knowledge that can help them to identify a more or less appropriate image or metaphor for teaching. For participants in this study, the ways of expressing common metaphors that were most closely associated with successful lessons were expressions that emphasized pupil involvement and shared responsibility for development of knowledge. Thus the perceptions revealed by the natural metaphoric language of the more successful teachers were perceptions of teaching and learning that fit well with the constructivist views currently guiding the efforts of many teacher educators to improve the preparation of teachers. Based on this study, then, an appropriate second assumption might be stated as: researchers and teacher educators seeking to promote change in prospective teachers' metaphors do have some available knowledge that could help them to identify ways of expressing common metaphors that may be indicative of potential for success in promoting pupil engagement in lessons.

The third assumption apparently supporting change efforts is that a change in their metaphors for teaching will influence teachers' underlying beliefs and, eventually, their behaviour. While this study shows relationships between interactive behaviour and the shadings of metaphoric language used by prospective teachers to describe their teaching practice, it was not designed to provide evidence about whether a change in metaphoric images would contribute to a change in either behaviour or beliefs.

This third assumption is more complex than our initial statement of it would indicate. When unpacked, it contains a set of contributing assumptions, which include the following:

- underlying beliefs influence behaviour;
- a change in underlying beliefs may precipitate a change in behaviour;
- underlying beliefs may be tacit;

- a belief must be consciously acknowledged before it can be consciously changed; and
- generating an explicit metaphor that reflects an image of oneself as teacher may serve to bring tacit beliefs to a level where they can be consciously acknowledged.

The results of this study suggest that an examination of the natural use of metaphoric language to describe teaching can provide a viable alternative route to accomplishing the goal of bringing tacit beliefs to the surface, where they can be systematically questioned. Prospective teachers could be alerted to the nuances of language used to describe teaching in relation to several of the common kinesthetic image schemas. They might begin by comparing statements made by various teachers with information presented in a format similar to that in Table 10.4. After exploring the perspectives on teaching revealed by these examples of language use, they could move to examining the metaphoric images in their own descriptions of teaching, to identify the themes pervasive in their own language. Researchers could then test whether such an examination contributed to any change in behaviour. Until a series of such studies are carried out, the third assumption must remain untested.

There are clear limitations to this study, given the small number of participants and the single lesson taught by each of them. It is worth noting, however, that the extreme-case sampling strategy, and the development of paired cases for analysis, served to identify clear patterns of relationship between language use, teaching behaviour, and pupil engagement in lessons. The systematic variation in characteristics of the teachers and the teaching settings in the paired cases described here provided interesting additional information about factors that were *not* related to variation in metaphoric language use, or to lesson success. These included: subject area taught (English/social studies versus math/science); academic level of the teacher (undergraduate versus graduate student); ethnic background of the teacher (minority versus majority culture); and type of class taught (elective course versus required college entrance course). Each of the variations in every one of these factors was associated with both more and less successful lessons, as well as with metaphoric language patterns that both acknowledged and denied the importance of pupil contributions to development of lesson content.

This result lends useful support to the premise that the language and behaviour observed in this study were both manifestations of some underlying teacher beliefs rather than outward teacher or setting characteristics. The results of the study as a whole serve to indicate the value of teachers' natural use of metaphoric language in revealing underlying teacher beliefs. We recommend more studies of this type, in the belief that they can contribute useful and interesting information to the field of research on teacher cognitions.

Note

1 This study was supported in part by the Commonwealth Centre for the Education of Teachers, Curry School Education, University of Virginia.

Table 10.4: *Metaphor: Lesson as movement along a path (Examples from student teachers' comments about their lessons)*

H	ANITA	ANNE	CANDACE	CHIP
	• I was trying to give them a little bit of direction about what they needed to do, and then pretty much just letting them go.	• I lead them a little bit.	• ...going through the lesson, putting the information on the board, a step at a time, so that they would have to keep up with me.	• I went through and saw everything I needed to cover.
		• ...just so that I'm not doing all the directing.		• I felt like they would be lost.
	• At the beginning I usually back off a little bit, and let them get started.	• When my kids do group work, I let them go, but I always kind of edge in there.	• The information we've been covering...has been really high level thinking skills.	• After I had gotten a little bit of their feet wet. ...
	• I can see how this unit is going to be really useful, down the road.	• I didn't even prepare what I thought should be answers for these poems — I thought I'd just let them go.	• I just wanted to find out where they stood.	• I wanted to keep them on their toes.
	• As I go through time, I keep learning more and more.	• I just try to get it to flow.	• This is a lot of the content that we'll be going over.	• ...stopping to see where I wanted to go next.
	• Usually there are a few other things that come popping up as we go along.		• I'd like to get through this relatively quickly.	• I got into the flow with talking about why it works.
			• That's what I was gearing the questions toward.	• That threw me off there, so I had to grab my bearings.
			• They're gone on me — they've gone in another direction.	

References

ANDERSON, L. (1989a) 'Classroom instruction', in REYNOLDS, M.C. (Ed) *Knowledge Base for the Beginning Teacher*, For the American Association of Colleges for Teacher Education, Oxford, Pergamon Press.

ANDERSON, L. (1989b) 'Learners and learning', in REYNOLDS, M.C. (Ed) *Knowledge Base for the Beginning Teacher*, For the American Association of Colleges for Teacher Education, Oxford, Pergamon Press.

ARTILES, A.J., MOSTERT, M.P. and TANKERSLEY, M. (1994) 'Assessing the link between teacher cognitions, teacher behaviors, and pupil responses to lessons', *Teaching and Teacher Education*, 10, 5 (in press).

BULLOUGH, R.V., Jr. (1991) 'Case studies as personal teaching texts', Paper presented at the annual meeting of the American Educational Research Association, Chicago.

BULLOUGH, R.V., Jr. and STOKES, D.K. (1993) 'Analyzing personal teaching metaphors in preservice teacher education as a means for exploring self and encouraging development', Paper presented at annual meeting of the American Educational Research Association, Atlanta.

CARTER, K. (1990) 'Meaning and metaphor: Case knowledge in teaching', *Theory into Practice*, 29, 2, pp. 109–15.

JOHNSON, M. (1987) *The Body in the Mind*, Chicago, University of Chicago Press.

LAKOFF, G. (1987) *Women, Fire, and Dangerous Things*, Chicago, University of Chicago Press.

MARSHALL, H. (1990) 'Metaphor as an instructional tool in encouraging student teacher reflection', *Theory into Practice*, 29, 2, pp. 128–32.

MORINE, G. and VALLANCE, E. (1975) *Special Study B: A Study of Teacher and Pupil Perceptions of Classroom Interaction* (Technical Report No. 75–11–6), San Francisco, Far West Laboratory for Educational Research and Development.

MORINE-DERSHIMER, G. (1983) 'Tapping teacher thinking through triangulation of data sets', (R&D Report No. 8014), Austin, University of Texas, Research and Development Center for Teacher Education.

MORINE-DERSHIMER, G. (1991) 'Learning to think like a teacher', *Teaching and Teacher Education*, 7, 2, pp. 159–68.

MORINE-DERSHIMER, G. and OLIVER, B. (1989) 'Examining complexity of thought in secondary student teachers', in LOWYCK, J. and CLARK, C.M. (Eds) *Teacher Thinking and Professional Action*, Leuven, Belgium, University of Leuven Press.

MOSTERT, M. (1992) 'Metaphor in special education teachers' language of practice', Unpublished doctoral dissertation, Charlottesville, VA, University of Virginia.

MUNBY, H. (1986) 'Metaphor in the thinking of teachers: An exploratory study', *Journal of Curriculum Studies*, 18, pp. 197–209.

MUNBY, H. (1987) 'Metaphor and teachers' knowledge', *Research in the Teaching of English*, 21, pp. 377–98.

MUNBY, H. (1990) 'Metaphorical expressions of teachers' practical curriculum knowledge', *Journal of Curriculum and Supervision*, 6, pp. 18–30.

PATTON, M.Q. (1990) *Qualitative Evaluation Methods*, Beverly Hills, Sage.

TOBIN, K. (1990) 'Changing metaphors and beliefs: A master switch for teaching?', *Theory into Practice*, 29, 2, pp. 133–40.

WEADE, R. and ERNST, G. (1990) 'Pictures of life in classrooms, and the search for metaphors to frame them', *Theory into Practice*, 29, 2, pp. 133–40.

WUBBELS, T. (1992) 'Taking account of student teachers' preconceptions', *Teaching and Teacher Education*, 8, 2, pp. 137–49.

Chapter 11

Concerning the Difference Between Intention and Action: Teachers' Conceptions and Actions in Physics Teaching

Helmut Fischler

Abstract

Various experiences in teacher education show that student teachers' decisions during the lesson do not follow general and subject related pedagogical theories which are offered to them in teacher training. The orientations which are actually effective are rooted in pedagogical everyday ideas. These ideas typically develop long before teacher training and influence the way the student teachers think about teaching. For the subject related training, this situation results in considerable problems which are described in two case studies. In both cases, teacher training did not take into account the solidity of the already existing conceptions and therefore failed to correct them. In the following, methods and results of investigations are described, the goal of which is to find prospective physics teachers' conceptions and their real orientations in physics teaching.

Introduction

In a longer interview before his teaching practicum in physics, a student expresses his conceptions of teaching and learning. During this interview it becomes clear that he knows the special conditions of physics learning to a considerable extent. Pupils come to the lesson with concrete ideas about physical phenomena and with concepts which are influenced by everyday understanding. In the lesson the pupils are confronted with the scientific concepts. The notion 'work', for example, has totally different connotations in both areas of experience. Therefore learning demands that the pupils grapple with the new ideas against the active background of the already fixed preconceptions. The teacher has to support this process in that he does not judge pupils' ideas as incorrect, but rather gives the pupils the opportunity to compare both views and to understand them in their specific context. The position of the student is clear: he would like the pupils really to understand physics and he intends to give them sufficient opportunities for the discussion of their ideas.

In one of his first teaching lessons during the teaching practicum, the student demonstrates, however, a behaviour that decisively contradicts his previous statements: he does not react to wrong contributions of the pupils, and he impatiently addresses different pupils if the correct answer does not come. He mostly calls on those pupils whose contributions help to keep the lesson moving.

In previous courses within his subject-related educational training the student received a great deal of information about the enormous importance of these everyday ideas for physics learning. He became acquainted with investigations that reveal the complex network of everyday and scientific concepts and the efforts required of the pupils to see through the complexity, at least at a low level.

The student has not only become familiar with this fact as an important part of the psychological basis of science learning, but also with several practical consequences of teaching. He has connected this knowledge with many learning situations, and he is convinced that he, as a teacher, has no alternative but to apply it if he wants the pupils to be successful in learning physics.

In the actual teaching lesson, however, this knowledge no longer seems to play a role. How does such a discrepancy between his pedagogical ideas and his teaching actions arise? Are the stated pedagogical principles only superficially taken on by the student? Does he mention them only because he thinks such statements are expected of him? Or does he in fact hold this view, but in the concrete planning and teaching of the lesson, other principles become stronger against his will?

Subject-related Educational Theories and Everyday Thinking

The situation described is surprising only for someone who has naive illusions about the practical efficiency of theoretical knowledge. Investigations have revealed that teachers' decisions in the planning phase and during the lesson seldom follow rational models of decision-making that have a great significance in teacher training. The teacher does not question the pedagogical theories as to their possible contributions when he or she has to cope with the demands of planning and to solve the problems that arise during teaching. He or she refers to such theories only in official situations, for example, for a demonstration lesson within the final examination.

Nevertheless his or her teaching is not without theory. Each teacher has orientations of action, whose sources are embedded in pedagogical everyday ideas and which, in teachers' judgment, passed the test many times. And so the prospective teacher as a trainee does not deem it necessary to exchange his or her knowledge about acting for the results offered by subject-related pedagogical science.

In teacher training one may complain of the stability of the pedagogical everyday theories because they call into question the efficiency of teacher training. However, this complaint cannot be the only response. If teachers' trainers want the prospective teachers to think about their preconceptions and connect them with the knowledge presented by pedagogy, it is necessary to carry out investigations that reveal everyday theories. Therefore the domain of teachers' thinking is an important research subject for improving teacher education.

In the many research projects on teachers' thinking the aspect of subject-related factors does not play a remarkable role. This is largely because psychologists have carried out this general research. On the whole the influence of subject-related factors on teachers' orientation of acting is regarded as being very small. A stronger emphasis on such factors is especially realized in research projects on mathematics (Leinhardt and Smith, 1985; Bromme, 1981). The natural science subjects are seldom integrated into such investigations.

Generalized statements about teachers' orientations of planning and acting are scarcely possible. Besides the teaching subject itself there are still other factors that induce special conditions; teachers' experience and the school level are especially significant in this context. One of the few results that has been confirmed and is independent from these special conditions is the very intensive orientation of the teachers towards their prefixed ideas about the appropriate teaching process (Bromme and Brophy, 1986). Most of the teachers begin the lesson with an 'image' of this process including their activities as well as pupils' reactions. The latter were considered primarily with regard to their contribution to a successful lesson that proceeds without any friction. With this orientation pupils' learning problems and the question of an acceptable selection and transformation of the teaching material have essentially less significance for teachers' decision-making. Differences exist, however, between teachers who have different levels of professional experience. Novices show a stronger concentration on the continuation of the teaching process than do experienced teachers. As a rule the latter have developed a repertoire of routines for ensuring the activity flow. This repertoire makes it easier for them to become aware of the learning problems of individual pupils (Leinhardt and Greeno, 1986; Borko and Livingston, 1989). On the other hand, the attention of novices is directed towards the whole group, whereby pupils' participation, the interest shown, and their behaviour form important criteria for the teacher's evaluation of his or her teaching (Housner and Griffey, 1985).

What are the consequences of this generally observed orientation for teachers' decision-making in lessons on a specific subject? Are there subject-specific characteristics? Do other subject-related orientations come into play?

For physics teaching the activity-flow orientation of student teachers and in-service trainees has been completely confirmed (Fischler, 1989). This orientation is most obvious in how teachers view the function of the experiment, which is regarded almost exclusively as a means to achieve activity flow. It integrates the pupils actively into the teaching process and gives the weaker and less interested pupils an opportunity to participate. The successful completion of the procedure and of the evaluation of the experiment provides a conclusion, which establishes a visible sign of a successful lesson. In this orientation, which strives for a continuous flow of activities, the significance of the experiment as a method of inquiry or as an aid to learning recedes into the background.

Identifying Subject-related Factors

There are some reasons to suppose that both the subject-related instructional possibilities for designing the lesson and the specific learning factors have an influence on the effective orientations of teachers' acting in a teaching situation. The conditions of physics learning described above make demands on the teacher, that cannot be compared with those made in other teaching subjects. Teachers' reactions to these requirements are certainly formed by general pedagogical orientations, but also by judgments and views which can be regarded as a result of the subject-related aspects of teacher training. Decisions about the selection of particular teaching topics, instructions during pupils' experimental work, responses to pupils' questions and reactions to their learning problems are activities which are influenced by the teachers' knowledge of the subject as well as by their position *vis-à-vis* subject-related teaching problems.

The knowledge of subject-related pedagogical principles does not necessarily lead to a teaching lesson created according to these basic statements. This is not only a characteristic of the case-study described at the beginning of this chapter, but a recurring experience in the various phases of teacher training. There is similar disparity in the connection between the extent and intensity of the knowledge of the subject on the one hand and teaching competence on the other, although it is plausible to assume that greater subject competence imparts the self-confidence needed as an important precondition for successful teaching. But research findings did not reveal any definite example of this aspect. It can be observed that an accumulation of knowledge does not always produce a better insight into the structure of the subject. When questioned, even advanced students show that they often superficially take in the physical and mathematical formalism for a long time without having changed their everyday understanding (Nachtigall, 1990). Leinhardt and Smith (1985) report about positive effects of teachers' basic mathematical knowledge on their teaching: The knowledge of mathematical structures help the teachers to go beyond the purely calculating level when they treat elementary subject matter (for instance fractions). Hashweh (1987) found that physics teachers with greater subject knowledge have a wide repertoire of approaches to problem-solving and of available examples, whereas teachers without this qualification are unsure of their competence and therefore much more dependent on textbooks and other supports, a situation that results in a limited approach to teaching.

There are contradictory reports on possible effects of the knowledge level held in the subject. Presumably, factors on the level of personal judgments are more likely to affect actions; they are connected with the background of knowledge acquired, which is individually assimilated integrating already existing ideas about the goals and purposes of teaching the subject. Therefore subject-related subjective theories, as an accumulation of views and attitudes concerning teaching, combine subject-related and general pedagogical knowledge with personal concepts about the characteristic features of successful teaching.

Admittedly it has until now been merely a plausible hypothesis that subject-related influences underlie teachers' orientations of acting. One can also hypothesize the formulation of single factors making up these orientations. The knowledge of these factors could present a detailed picture of these orientations and would give the opportunity to regard teaching in the light of ideas and intentions. In the few publications concerning this problem there are mainly three variables mentioned that are likely to have an impact on the thinking and acting of physics teachers:

a   conceptions of the nature of science (physics);
b   conceptions of the goals and purposes of physics teaching; and
c   conceptions of learning and teaching physics.

In the following article the possible connections between these conceptions and teachers' decision-making will be discussed. The next section deals with the question in reference to the group of variables (a) whether a specific understanding of the nature of physics influences teachers' content-related and instructional decisions. For the intentions and goals of teaching (b) such an influence can certainly be assumed, but its concrete effects are still unknown and have to be looked at more carefully. This is also the case with the variables in (c). The section 'Learning problems and teachers' decision-making' presents possible connections.

The analytical approach does not hinder the view of more general characteristics if the categories of observing and questioning are appropriately open. Teachers often apply metaphors to describe teaching and learning processes and especially their own role within these processes (e.g., teacher as an information transmitter or as a person who takes care of the pupils). These metaphors have proved to be interesting indicators for the positions and attitudes that are held (Briscoe, 1991; Tobin and Fraser, 1989), but often they are only the beginning of an investigation about the subject-specific shaping of the 'pictures' used.

Processes of Inquiry and Models of Teaching

On each level of physics teaching the scientific process of inquiry should be a model for the instructional techniques. This may be a very old statement, but it still can be read in modern texts on physics education. Besides the questionable nature of this statement, it is more problematic that 'the physical-research method' is not described anywhere. The numerous scientific theoretical discussions in recent years have shown that no single method exists. However, a different view prevails at school. Fixed structures are provided by strict series of observation, hypothesis, experiment and conclusion (during the discovery of a physical connection) and planning, procedure, observation and explanation (during an experiment). It is difficult to determine whether such decisions should reflect the supposed reality of physical research or whether they are justified for instructional reasons.

Therefore, the concrete decisions made by a teacher during a lesson do not necessary reflect his or her concept of the nature of science. But on the other hand it can be assumed that, for instance, a rigid opinion about fixed rules of discovering knowledge will act on teachers' decision-making, especially if their goal of teaching emphasizes the transmission of a closed canon of laws and theories. It is difficult to imagine a teaching situation where the teacher, being convinced of a universal scheme for the processes of scientific inquiry, would allow his or her pupils to choose their own way in which they want to work on new physical problems. But the extreme alternative is also not realistic, i.e., that a teacher, who knows that scientific inquiry does not always follow a special model, would dictate to the pupils how they should prepare, carry out and evaluate an experiment. Intensive instructional arguments for an appropriate teaching process must exist if this tension between the teachers' intention and their practice is to be managed. It is clear that there are good reasons for a teaching process which is closely directed by the teacher. Teaching is not just a sequence of learning situations, but a series of events including conflicts. These events require decisions which do not refer to the learning processes alone. Therefore even extreme discrepancies between the basic intentions for acting and their concrete realizations are not surprising in any individual case.

The results of investigations made up to now are discouraging. Reflections on the nature of science are, as a rule, not a part of the planning process and do not play any role in teachers' decision-making during the lesson (Duschl and Wright, 1989). Neither teachers' behaviour nor pupils' knowledge show a connection with teachers' knowledge and their conceptions (Lederman and Zeidler, 1987). Experts presumably are more successful than novices in bringing together their conceptions and their actions (Brickhouse, 1990; Brickhouse and Bodner, 1992).

Pedagogical Intentions and Instructional Decisions

Various prescribed programmes (for instance a syllabus) restrict teachers' decisions concerning the teaching topics. But nevertheless, in each lesson the teacher has to make decisions about many details for which he or she alone is responsible and which are certainly influenced by his or her basic pedagogical concepts. Giving opportunities to the pupils for experimental work on their own or emphasizing aspects of application are decisions that bring to light teachers' goals for physics teaching. These goals could be, for example, the intention to let the pupils have the experience of the demanding but productive experimental work, or the belief that physics teaching will help the pupils understand the technical environment.

In addition to the unclear knowledge about possible connections between teachers' concepts and their actions, in this field of interest one can also construct a situation with contradictory components: A teacher regards pupils' experimental work as a chance to promote autonomous acting, to let them have the experience of the advantage of working in groups, and to train the ability of working experimentally. In the teaching lesson he or she does not integrate the pupils into the process and carries out the experiments without their participation. Is it possible that a teacher can deal with such a contrast? Which conditions are necessary so he or she can manage it?

The results of investigations made up to now draw an ambiguous picture. The attempts to identify teachers' conceptions about the processes of teaching and learning are quite new (Hewson and Hewson, 1988; Freire and Sanches, 1992). The characteristic features found in this research are still categorized in very different ways, so that results are hardly comparable.

Learning Problems and Teachers' Decision-making

It is hardly questionable that a close connection exists between teachers' concepts of learning and their decision-making during a teaching lesson. Through the successes of the subject-related research in determining subject-specific learning conditions, the physics teacher does not have to depend on general psychological knowledge. He or she can integrate research findings that directly refer to his or her teaching topics. Whatever themes are presented to the students, they already know a great deal about them, but embedded in non-physics contexts of everyday experience. These well-known subject-related preconditions often present stumbling blocks to understanding physics. These barriers remain insurmountable if it is not possible for the pupils to grapple with both frameworks of meaning.

The finding common to all investigations shows that teachers are mostly not aware of these misconceptions held by pupils. This observation does not surprise those who know everyday life at school. Science teachers regard the learning process mainly from the standpoint of knowledge transfer; as experts in teaching they have to present physical topics in a convincing manner and with skilfully arranged instructional techniques. According to this image their view about the pupils' role is a very passive one. Learning is a mere intake of the knowledge offered by the teacher. Contrary conceptions that hold a constructivistic view and stress the active role of pupils and the advising function of teachers are not to be found very often.

However closely related the research on pupils' concepts and the instructional consequences are, insight into these connections in no way guarantees the corresponding teaching decisions. Johnston (1988) reports on an extreme case: Two teachers actively participate in the development of a physics curriculum that consequentially aims at taking into account the pupils' concepts. In the teaching lesson, however, doubts quickly arise, whether the discussion of pupils' contributions leads to the end desired, that is, to the acceptance of the 'correct' theories by the pupils. So the directions given by the teacher were substantially stricter than required by the pedagogical conception developed by the teachers themselves. In teacher training the conceptualization of programmes that only intend to transmit knowledge may be insufficient. This is maintained by Hewson and Hewson (1987) who could determine in special seminars using questionnaires that meaningful changes of teachers' conceptions occurred. But they were sceptical about the possible practical effects of this change of orientation. On the way from intention to action there are several barriers. It is an important task of teacher training to uncover and overcome these constraints.

A Study of Two Beginning Teachers

From the great number of student teachers and beginners who were investigated under the aspects described above, two cases will be chosen. These cases are very typical for a whole body of results and illustrate the problems of teacher education against the background of the complex 'teachers' thinking' extremely well.

The reconstruction of the conceptions bundled up in the groups (a), (b) and (c) is achieved by various methods: written and oral reactions to given statements, to teaching situations described and to a video-taped teaching lesson deliver broad information about the respective individual view.

(a) In order to determine the student teacher's 'conception about the nature of science', the investigation could profit from numerous questions that have been used on many different arrangements of questionnaires (Schmidt, 1967; Kimball, 1967/8; Andersen, Harty and Samuel, 1986; Lederman, 1986; Koulaidis and Ogborn, 1989). When selecting the questions, care was taken that about a third of these refer to the functions of experiments within physical inquiry, because a close connection is assumed between the teaching decisions and the attitude towards the functions of experiments. In addition to these questions items were chosen which presumably could best be connected with certain aspects of the behaviour of the teacher. Such variables can be assigned to the following subscales:

a1   process orientation (science is a process of dynamic and creative research);
a2   comprehension of scientific method (there are many methods of science); and

a3   conception of reality (propositions of scientific theories cover only some aspects of reality).

(b) 'Conceptions concerning goals and purposes of physics education' are identified using open questions as well as ratings of statements presented. Especially the reaction to the description of pupils' extremely negative judgment about physics teaching provides information about the intention with which the teacher plans to confront his development. 'What should physics education look like so that it is suitable for someone living in our society as it is today and as it will be tomorrow?' (Häussler *et al.*, 1988). During a broad Delphi-investigation, the IPN (Institute for Science Education) in Kiel asked numerous persons the characteristics of this physics education. In this study the central features found in the IPN study are presented to the teachers who are then requested to put them into an order of priority so that the goals which they primarily intend to pursue become apparent.

(c) The teachers make statements about 'conceptions of science teaching and science learning' as a response to direct questions and as comments on given learning and teaching situations.

c1   With the help of a number of tasks the study attempts to determine a valid picture. The first task consists of a number of questions put to the teachers which they are requested to answer freely. These answers are then assigned to the following assertions (Pope and Gilbert, 1983):

  • Teaching is a process of cultural transmission.
  • Teaching has to guarantee an 'organic growth' which happens mainly without outside influence.
  • In teaching, an environment has to be created which enables the students to deal actively with the problems introduced to them.

c2   One of the teaching scenes show how a teacher, at the end of a sequence about the basic notions of mechanics (mass, volume, density), is confronted with pupils' explanations which demonstrate that they did not understand anything (HEWSON and HEWSON, 1987). In this task ten possible teacher reactions are provided. The teachers' answers indicate the degree to which they regard learning in a constructivist point of view (learning as conceptual change).

c3   In an absolutely open interview situation the teachers are finally asked to comment on a video-recorded teaching section: At the beginning of a teaching sequence a teacher is trying to interest the pupils in the phenomena of pressure and in the connection between this quantity and those of force and area (by means of many demonstrations). Without the teacher being aware of it the variety of activities is concealing the problems in learning with which pupils obviously struggle. Does this recording show a lesson in which students' learning problems are considered?

Central to the part of the investigation relating to teaching are recordings of lessons and interviews along the line of the recordings. In a combination of qualitative and quantitative methods of text analysis the structures of acting are reconstructed by the researcher with the teacher's assistance and the patterns of arguments are analysed by the interpreter of the text. Determination and representation of decisional structure are thoroughly described elsewhere (Fischler, 1989).

Conceptions, Intentions and Actions: Results of a Case-study (I)

In the teaching situation described in the beginning of this chapter, the beliefs and intentions stated by the student teacher and his concrete behaviour differed widely. Before the lesson he had described his opinion about the process of physics learning by expressing ideas that show the reception and assimilation of the knowledge which was taught in subject-specific pedagogical courses. If this view was not mentioned only as a declared belief without his being convinced of it, it became a substantial part of a 'subjective theory' about appropriate learning processes in physics. Nevertheless, in the concrete teaching lesson 'subjective theories', which were different from those held before, guided his behaviour. As the case-study points out, these effective theories obviously were developed long ago and remained unchanged in teacher education. They promise the teacher a better and faster solution for teaching problems and help him to carry out a teaching process that is acceptable for him.

The detailed investigation of the motives for replacing the intentions of action during the teaching process has to begin with efforts to establish more precisely the student teacher's conceptions, which have been described as subjective-specific factors of influence. The evaluation of the responses to questions about the nature of science revealed the picture of a teacher who is open-minded towards the various positions about the nature of science, without being tied to a special dogma. It is true, in his opinion, that particular sequences often can be observed in the process of physical inquiry, but it is not possible to subordinate researchers' creativity and imaginativeness to fixed rules. Measurements are not at all results on their own: often one can interpret them in different ways or they are an outcome of experiments which were planned with definite expectations. Not only experimentally gained data are important for the process of acquiring new knowledge, but also the intellectual background that lead to an experimental plan or to the interpretation of measurements.

In his statements about the teaching goals he regards as essential, the student teacher constructs a balance between an orientation towards physics as a science, on the one hand, and an emphasis on environment-related topics on the other. This position can be called pluralistic.

In response to the lesson ended with a total failure, the student teacher's reaction is very pupil-oriented. Obviously a mere repetition does not make any sense, and it would certainly not be realistic to tell the pupils to learn at home what they have missed at school. Ideally the teacher's decision should not push the subject matter to be taught to the fore, but he should find out through patient questioning and listening what understanding was achieved and, above all, what the barriers to learning are. Plainly recognizable in this reaction is the belief that physics teaching is an arduous process of changing concepts, in which everyday ideas get new meanings that contradict normal experience (for example to carry a bag horizontally is not a physical work).

Decisions During the Lesson

During a teaching practicum the student teacher conducts a lesson on the theme 'resonance'. His planning largely corresponds to the ideas he expressed previously. Phases with clearly preconstructed teacher activities are followed up by periods in which the pupils can mark out and formulate their contributions to the lesson largely on their own. In the actual lesson the last part of this planning is completely disposed of. From the beginning the lesson is very strongly teacher-concentrated. During the experimental demonstration as well as in the evaluation the teacher attempts to initiate discussions with the pupils. However, he quickly gives up because the pupils do not react in accordance to his expectations.

For the explanation of the phenomena of resonance in the spring he needs simple references which were used in the previous lesson. 'On what factors does the oscillation period depend?' None of the pupils answers. 'But we have already done it, surely you must know that.' His disappointment about this lack of knowledge finally becomes so great that he asks the pupils fewer and fewer questions and thus gives them fewer chances to actively get involved in the lesson. Only a few pupils help the teacher by giving acceptable answers without hesitating for a long time. The teacher concentrates on these pupils when the failure of the others is indicated by long pauses or by contributions that are not understandable at once.

Comments After the Lesson

Which factors became so powerful in class that they repressed the teacher's conceptions? Of course the student teacher has recognized this discrepancy between his statements before the lesson and his decisions in the lesson. His first comment is somewhat of an apology, intended to explain his behaviour during the whole lesson. He was impatient when his expectations were not immediately fulfilled, in the lesson as well as in other situations. Several comments on single scenes show that this attitude alone cannot be responsible, but that other factors in the form of situationally specific orientations of acting dominate and at best strengthen general dispositions.

Statements repeatedly made during the whole interview particularly stress the following orientations of acting:

- **Activity-flow orientation**

I felt a little pressured.

Actually, I wanted to make progress.

First of all it was important for me that the lesson continued.

The teacher gave these reasons in order to justify that he has integrated only those pupils whom he regarded as being competent into the teaching process and that he has carried out the essential phases of the lesson alone. The statements point out the efficiency of the 'activity-flow orientation', i.e., the intention to keep the lesson moving and to realize the planning of the teaching periods that are a part of the picture of the whole teaching process. In such an orientation, since the learning processes are of secondary importance, they are no longer included in the aims of the teacher, because he concentrates primarily on ensuring a continuous flow of activities.

- **Completion orientation**

   I wanted to achieve a certain completion, especially the experiment should be completed. I think, experiments should be a part of physics teaching.

For his actions from the middle of the lesson on, the teacher formulates explanations that refer to the end, which is staged as a completion of the teaching process instead of as a learning process. Not only the execution of the experiment, but also its evaluation should be 'managed', the latter best concluded with a summarizing sentence that demonstrates to the pupils that the lesson has ended successfully with a visible result. As a beginner, the teacher obviously needs this feeling of success for confirmation that he has not failed. In his opinion the pupils also need this final signal to give them the impression that they have learned something. This kind of experience is necessary to maintain the motivation for learning.

- **Conceptions about teaching and learning under the scheme offer–reception**

   . . . Anyway, the pupils know all this, resonance, too. The regular teacher has told them that again and again. Therefore I subconsciously thought, well, now I'll continue. The lack of participation I interpreted as pupils' boredom.

Reproachfully and repeatedly the student teacher complains that the pupils should have known some facts, because they have been treated in previous lessons.

   We had some exercises the lesson before, and so I thought that it would be presented [by the pupils] spontaneously.

The activity-flow orientation underlying the actions becomes so dominating that conceptions of physics learning, which the teacher thought he had overcome, were reactivated. They fit better into the shaping of the teaching process than constructivistic views, which are scarcely compatible with fixed ideas about the intended teaching process. Supposedly, this orientation replaces the teacher's fundamental readiness to respond to the pupils' ideas and contributions. His views expressed in the interview before the lesson are superficial and do not hold up against the actual behavioural orientations. Even his ideas of physics teaching no longer hold. His reproach against the pupils, as quoted above, that they could not remember the topics which they had already been dealt with, is repeated in the interview after the lesson. This view shows one misunderstanding which comes from the idea that considers learning as a unique process which comes about almost automatically and which only requires the presentation of the subject. The content has been treated, and the pupils, according to the teacher's memory, participated actively, therefore it can be assumed that they have learned it.

This simple scheme, offer – reception, is complemented by the second misunderstanding: the teacher's view about pupils' contributions. They are mainly seen to have a function for the process of the lesson. His disappointment that the pupils did not respond to his questions, is for him not a cause to think about possible learning problems, but more an expression of his dissatisfaction with the disrupted teaching process. The teacher regards pupils' contributions mainly from the viewpoint of their possible function to promote the teaching process, and not from the standpoint of successful or failed learning processes.

> Our university studies probably spoil us, as far as the subject is concerned. Here, the contents are presented to us, and we have to learn it. It is difficult, but it works.

His own experience of learning physics at the university is transferred to the learning situation at school. Maybe these experiences are not totally positive, but on the whole the student teacher regards his studies as successful. He can cope with the demands; he enjoys physics; and the successful learning motivates him.

It is difficult to judge whether the teacher's assumption is correct, that his teaching and learning experiences at the unversity have a bad influence on his decisions in the classroom. It is also an open question whether competence in, and enthusiasm toward, the subject support a particularly teacher-oriented lesson. The teacher's comment at least suggests that such connections exist.

The teacher displaces not only his conception of teaching and learning under the pressure of the orientations that are now dominating the teaching process, but also his position about the nature of science, that the process of physical inquiry cannot be submitted to a fixed model. Under this condition the only perception possible for the pupils is that physical knowledge can be gained with definite methods.

Case-study (II): Congruences

The connection between intentions and actions is much closer with a teacher in the second phase of teacher education after his university studies. From the beginning of the lesson his decision-making corresponds to the subjective theories that he has mentioned before the lesson. For this teacher strong rules govern the processes of physical inquiry, only in this way can an objective description of nature be reached. Physics teaching should promote the understanding of these connections by doing exercises with systematical problem-solving, in which the mathematically formulated law is an important goal. The conceptions about teaching and learning are definitely teacher-oriented. Spontaneously the teacher reacts to the learning problems presented in the fictive teaching situation. A repetition, perhaps with additional explanations and experiments, would be the only appropriate instructional technique to insure successful learning for the pupils.

His decisions during the lesson are along the same line as his conceptions:

- The teacher does not take an appropriate notice of pupils' 'wrong' contributions; he attributes negative judgments to them. For him, only a particular physical truth exists. Subjective views and individual interpretations are not justifiable even as an intermediate stage.

- He calls on those pupils from whom he expects 'correct' answers. For him, a continuous activity flow is more important than broad acquisition of knowledge.
- Often he criticizes the pupils' poor engagement and their lack of knowledge. If they do not accept the teacher's offer, it is obviously their failure.

In both case-studies different conceptions about the analytically determined areas (nature of science, goals and teaching and learning) apparently lead to comparable orientations of actions. A smooth transition from conceptions to decision-making occurred in the second case, whereas in the first example the same situation was effected by a break between intention and action, that the teacher deemed necessary under the concrete conditions of teaching. On the surface, the decisions made during the lesson are in both cases comparable, as the descriptions of teachers' behaviours show. The detailed analysis of the interview texts before and after the lessons yield, however, fundamental differences in the way teachers made their decisions. In the second case, the teacher's remarks before the lesson show hardly a trace of his subject-related pedagogical training. All efforts to make him sensitive to the learning problems of the students obviously failed. How could this have happened? Should not all teachers have experienced the particular difficulties of learning physics as students themselves? It is obviously possible that the attitude achieved by prospective teachers at the end of their education makes them more attuned to the teaching of the subjects which they studied at the university than simply to the learning difficulties of the students. Investigations into socialization through the subject matter indicate that especially the studies of physics and chemistry promote such a development which the subject-related pedagogical training cannot correct. Pedagogical ideas run up against the brick wall of the subject matter.

The remarks made by this teacher after the lesson confirm this hypothesis. He concentrates on the body of the laws of physics which are to be taught without regard to the learning problems of the students. The overwhelming amount of material and the connections made by the system of physics make it impossible, according to his opinion, to worry about students' conceptions. As shown by the interview, these conceptions are not taken seriously during the lesson. The respective remarks of the students are for him a sign of lacking knowledge, about which he complains bitterly after the lesson.

The wall created by the subject is broken through by the student teacher. However he faces a second challenge: the class as a whole, into which the individual students disappear. That his pedagogical efforts fail has more to do with the fact that during the lesson orientations become effective which are aimed not at the individual student, but rather at the entire class. The intention to observe the problems of learning is replaced by the belief in the necessity of managing the teaching process.

Conclusion: Consequences for Teacher Education

The student teacher began the lesson with the intention of following his concepts about physics learning. These subjective theories have been elicited by the study of the findings of the subject-related educational research and by their practical consequences. However, during the lesson other orientations dominate his actions, which aim at a successful teaching process where external activity-oriented criteria play a more important role than considerations about learning. Grappling with pupils' 'wrong responses', discussion about their contributions that seem to mislead for a moment, and allowing 'action-free' pauses for thinking do not have a place in this orientation.

What sort of assistance can be given during teacher training to ensure that the pupils become the focus of teacher's attention? Particularly, how can a level of teacher competence be attained so that knowledge and fundamental beliefs referring to the research findings about physics learning are not displaced in the concrete teaching situation by orientations that satisfy the criteria of a successful teaching process more than requirements for successful teaching and learning?

Student teachers mainly expect the development of self-assurance from subject-specific pedagogical education. They want to know planning techniques, to become competent and skilful for a rather frictionless teaching process and to attain sureness in handling the physical instruments. For a beginner the necessity of such aids should not be underestimated. However, all preparations that regard the planning of teaching as a draft of a design with different activities (pupils' contributions, experiments, summaries) having a special place in the teaching process tend to equate teaching phases, experimental sequences and the change of pupils' activities with phases of learning. Each conception, wherein a particular period of the planned lesson can be concluded successfully with appropriate instructional finesse and justifiable pressure on pupils, implicitly leads to the assumption that learning processes could also be regarded as completed after corresponding efforts (by teachers and pupils). Research results though confirm what many experienced teachers already know: pupils' knowledge is taken in depending on context. If it is acquired in a certain content-related connection, then it often is not available in a different context.

Openness toward complicated learning processes requires openness in the designing of teaching processes. Of course, planning does not become superfluous. But it should not consist of a detailed plan, rather it should include the planning of possible teachers' reactions to pupils' conceptions and to the learning problems that become evident. The usual instructions for planning do not fulfil this idea. Rather they promote conceptions to which physics teachers are especially inclined. The planning of a teaching process would be an adequate precondition for an acceptable process that can be disturbed severely by action-free phases and be definitely supported by a sequence of visible teachers' and pupils' activities.

In addition to these consequences, which can be regarded as avoidance strategies, one should consider other solutions that refer to a permanent change in teachers' conceptions. These solutions should take into account the special conditions of 'action under pressure'. According to Wahl (1991) the teacher relies on memories in which specific situational classes are linked with definite classes of actions. According to the perception of the situation, those possibilities of acting are actualized which have been previously effective in the course of professional experience. Therefore they were not further tested or thought through at the time, which is not possible in these situations.

Therefore the subject-specific educational training of prospective teachers has to create conditions in which elaborate theories (for instance student teachers' conceptions about learning and teaching processes in physics instruction) can be linked with already existing and effective theories. The preconditions for the success of these changes are considerably bad in the face of the short subject-related educational studies at the university and the relatively long time provided for the growth of orientations of acting. It is highly probable that the way and manner in which the student teacher has experienced and still experiences teaching and learning physics decisively impacts conceptions about the intended teaching process, the desired learning processes and the expected learning results. As a pupil he or she became acquainted with an instructional technique in which every problem was pinned down from the beginning. It was clearly outlined in the posing of the question, with a functioning experiment and its evaluation restricted by the teacher according to time and topic. At the university the still unsolved problems of interpretation and the questions of the principles of inquiry are hardly addressed, so that the picture of a science which can be learned in closed units is never questioned.

The rigid conceptions about the philosophy of science of the teacher in the second case-study hinder his pedagogical access to the subject to be taught. If physics is seen more as a complete system than as a dynamic process, if research methods are assumed to be a rigid canon of rules, and if physical knowledge is regarded as a reflection of reality, then subjective aspects of the process of obtaining knowledge cannot play a role. If this is the case, subject-related pedagogical training is in a hopeless situation. First of all, the point of view regarding the philosophy of science should be changed. The teacher must be made conscious of the fact that physical laws do not exist a priori waiting to be discovered, but rather that they are formulated by people who approach nature with their own ideas and questions. Presumably, a 'conceptual change' concerning the philosophy of science would be a necessary precondition for a pedagogical reorientation.

The two cases described above surely belong to the more problematic cases within the subject-related pedagogical teacher training. Fortunately there are also physics teacher students and teachers who are open to pedagogical ideas and who are also capable of transferring these ideas to classroom. However, the difficulties described show that teacher training is especially characterized by the problematic relation between pedagogical theory and teaching practice.

References

ANDERSEN, H.O., HARTY, H. and SAMUEL, K.V. (1986) 'Nature of science, 1969 and 1984: Perspectives of preservice secondary science teachers', *School Science and Mathematics*, 86, 1, pp. 43–50.

BORKO, H. and LIVINGSTON, C. (1989) 'Cognition and improvisation. Differences in mathematics instruction by expert and novice teachers', *American Educational Research Journal*, 26, pp. 473–98.

BRICKHOUSE, N.W. (1990) 'Teachers' beliefs about the nature of science and their relationship to classroom practice', *Journal of Teacher Education*, 41, 3, pp. 53–62.

BRICKHOUSE, N.W. and BODNER, G.M. (1992) 'The beginning science teacher: Classroom narratives of convictions and constraints', *Journal of Research in Science Teaching*, 5, pp. 471–85.

BRISCOE, C. (1991) 'The dynamic interactions among beliefs, role metaphors, and teaching practices: A case study of teacher change', *Science Education*, 75, 2, pp. 185–98.

BROMME, R. (1981) '*Das Denken von Lehrern bei der Unterrichtsvorbereitung: Eine empirische Untersuchung zu kognitiven Prozessen von Mathematiklehrern*, Weinheim Beltz.

BROMME, R. and BROPHY, J. (1986) 'Teachers' cognitive activities', in CHRISTIANSEN, B., HOWSON, G. and OTTE, M. (Eds) *Perspectives on Mathematics Education*, Dordrecht, pp. 99–140.

DUSCHL, R.A. and WRIGHT, E. (1989) 'A case study of high school teachers' decision making models for planning and teaching science', *Journal of Research in Science Teaching*, 26, pp. 467–502.

FISCHLER, H. (1989) 'Orientations of the actions of physics teachers', *International Journal of Science Education*, 11, 2, pp. 185–93.

FREIRE, A.M. and SANCHES, M.F.C. (1992) 'Elements for a typology of teachers' conceptions of physics teaching', *Teaching and Teacher Education*, 8, 5 and 6, pp. 497–507.

HASHWEH, M.Z. (1987) 'Effects of subject-matter knowledge in the teaching of biology and physics', in *Teaching and Teacher Education*, 3, 2, pp. 109–20.

HÄUSSLER, P., FREY, K., HOFFMANN, L., ROST, J. and SPADA, H. (1988) *Educations in Physics for Today and Tomorrow*, Kiel.

HEWSON, P.W. and HEWSON, M.G. (1987) 'Science teachers' conceptions of teaching: Implications for teacher education', *International Journal of Science Education*, 9, 4, pp. 425–40.

HEWSON, P.W. and HEWSON, M.G. (1988) 'Analysis and use of a task for identifying conceptions of teaching science', Paper presented at the Annual Meeting of the American Education Research Association, New Orleans, LA, April.

HOUSNER, L.D. and GRIFFEY, D.C. (1985) 'Teacher cognition: Differences in planning and interactive decision making between experienced and inexperienced teachers', *Research Quarterly for Exercise and Sport*, 56, pp. 45–53.

JOHNSTON, K. (1988) 'Changing teachers' conceptions of teaching and learning', in CALDERHEAD, J. (Ed) *Teachers' Professional Learning*, London, New York, Philadelphia, pp. 169–95.

KIMBALL, M.E. (1967/8) 'Understanding the nature of science: A comparison of scientists and science teachers', *Journal of Research in Science Teaching*, 5, pp. 110–20.

KOULAIDIS, V. and OGBORN, J. (1989) 'Philosophy of science: An empirical study of teachers' views', *International Journal of Science Education*, 11, 2, pp. 173–84.

LEDERMAN, N.G. (1986) 'Students' and teachers' understanding of the nature of science: A reassessment', *School Science and Mathematics*, 86, pp. 91–9.

LEDERMAN, N.G. and ZEIDLER, D. (1987) 'Science teachers' conceptions of the nature of science: Do they really influence teaching behavior?', *Science Education*, 71, pp. 721–34.

LEINHARDT, G. and GREENO, J.G. (1986) 'The cognitive skill of teaching', *Journal of Educational Psychology*, 78, pp. 75–95.

LEINHARDT, G. and SMITH, D. (1985) 'Expertise in mathematics instruction: Subject-matter knowledge', *Journal of Educational Psychology*, 77, pp. 247–71.

NACHTIGALL, D.K. (1990) 'What is wrong with physics teachers' education?', *European Journal of Physics*, 11, pp. 1–14.

POPE, M.L. and GILBERT, J.K. (1983) 'Explanation and metaphor: Some empirical questions in science education', *European Journal of Science Education*, 5, pp. 249–61.

SCHMIDT, D. (1967) 'Test on understanding science: A comparison among several groups', *Journal of Research in Science Teaching*, 4, 2, pp. 80–4.

TOBIN, K. and FRASER, B.J. (1989) 'Barriers to Higher-level cognitive learning in high school science', *Science Education*, 73, pp. 659–83.

WAHL, D. (1991) 'Handeln unter Druck: Der weite Weg vom Wissen zum Handeln bei Lehrern', *Hochschullehrern und Erwachsenenbildern*, Weinheim.

Chapter 12

Teachers' Creativity Styles and Pedagogical Practices

Maria de Fátima Chorão C. Sanches

Abstract

Designed to address the potential of Kirton's theory to the study of school as an organization, this study purported to illuminate the complexities inherent to the interaction between the teachers' creativity styles and their pedagogical action.[1] The study developed in a twofold dimension: identification of the teachers' styles of creativity; and characterization of their preferred pedagogical practices in the light of their dominant personal styles as adaptors or innovators.

Data revealed a dominant culture of teaching within the discipline group which the teachers who scored as adaptors tended to share in an uncritical manner. In contrast, the innovators tended to influence the discipline group and, consequently, the nature of the teaching culture itself.

While identifying pedagogical characteristics that appear to correspond to styles of creativity, the study may contribute to the understanding of factors that underlie the development of the teachers' professional knowledge.

Introduction

Schools as any other social institution aim at valuable goals through the accomplishment of educational activities which are expected to be performed in known and approved ways according to the dominant educational paradigm. In this sense, teachers as school actors, are expected to adhere to 'bureaucratic expectations' (Hoy and Miskel, 1987), and perform roles in coherence with the schools' organizational nomothetic characteristics. However, one may expect variability regarding personal and professional practices the teachers prefer while interacting with those organizational expectations. In Giroux (1985) terms, teachers may conform, be hegemonic and help reproduce the existing educational paradigm; they may also be critical, go beyond the 'language of critique' and transform, becoming innovative agents. While facing school problems and organizing their pedagogical work, one may expect that teachers differ regarding their personal styles in defining and solving problematic situations. Indeed, being a matter of style, some may have a preference for 'doing things better' while others seek more radical solutions to existing problems.

Based on Kirton's 'Adaption-Innovation' theory (1987a; 1989), the present study addresses the question of a possible correspondence between creativity styles and preferential pedagogical practices. The theory postulates the hypothesis of an 'adaptor-innovator' personality continuum in which people differentiate themselves regarding the following dimensions: generation of ideas, initiation and acceptance of change, ways of defining and solving problems, and decision-making. While stressing that the theory is one of cognitive style rather than capacity or level, Kirton further suggests its relevance for the understanding of a person's preferred way of problem-solving both individually and as a member of a group.

Being part of a larger project, designed to address the potential of the Kirton's theory to the study of school as organization, the study purports to illuminate the complexities inherent to both the interaction between teachers' creativity styles and their pedagogical action, and to the nature of the cognitive context of the teachers' personal and professional development. The study developed in a two-fold dimension: identification of the teachers' styles of creativity; and characterization of their preferred pedagogical practices in the light of their dominant personal styles as adaptors or innovators. Specifically, the following question was researched: Are there differences regarding pedagogical practices among teachers who scored as adaptors and innovators in the Kirton 'Adaptation-Innovation Inventory' (KAI)?

The extension of the Kirton's theory to the study of teachers' pedagogical thinking and action appears to be relevant in several ways. First, being a teacher according to a preferred style, as 'adaptor' or as 'innovator', signifies acting in specific and unique ways either originating innovative pedagogical practices or making them work. Second, developing the ability to recognize personal style of pedagogical thinking may be understood as part of the developmental process of the teachers' professional identity and growth. Third, learning about their personal context of teaching will help understand the other colleagues' personal styles of creativity. In this sense, if the school is to become a space for collegiality, then, the way teachers see themselves and how they relate to colleagues in regard to their pedagogical problem-solving and decision-making styles are matters of great relevance for the domain of teacher education.

The chapter is organized as follows. An account of Kirton's theory is given through the characterization of styles of creativity, followed by the conceptual framework for the data-content analysis and the description of the main themes extracted from the theory. The results are interpreted and discussed in the light of the teachers' professional identity development, and in terms of the role that teaching experience and teaching cultures (Feiman-Nemser and Floden, 1986) might play in the development of a preferred style of creativity. The study offers implications for reframing teacher-education programmes.

Characterization of Creativity Styles: The Innovators and the Adaptors

According to Kirton's theory (1989), creativity styles are determined according to the differential positions individuals may take on the adaptive-innovative continuum. Preferring an adaptive style means 'doing things better' while being an innovator implies 'doing things differently'. Adaptors seek consensus, tend to solve problems within the limits of the existing models or dominant paradigms,

Table 12.1: Characteristics of adaptors and innovators

The Adaptor	The Innovator
• Characterized by precision, prudence, reliability, efficiency, methodicalness, discipline, conformity.	• Seen as undisciplined, approaching tasks from unsuspected angles.
• Concerned with resolving residual problems thrown up by the current paradigm.	• Search for problems and alternative avenues of solution, cutting across current paradigms.
• Seeks solutions to problems in tried and understood ways.	• Queries problems' concomitant assumptions: manipulates problems.
• Reduces problems by improvement and greater efficiency, with maximum of continuity and stability.	• Is catalyst to settled groups, irreverent of their consensual views; seen as abrasive, creating dissonance.
• Seen as sound, conforming, safe, dependable.	• Seen as unsound, impractical; often shocks his opposite.
• Liable to make goals of means.	• In pursuit of goals treats accepted means with little regard.
• Seems able to maintain high accuracy in long spells of detailed work.	• Capable of detailed routine (system maintenance) work for only short bursts.
• Is an authority within given structures.	• Tends to take control in unstructured situations.
• Challenges rules rarely, cautiously, when assured of strong support.	• Often challenges rules, has little respect for past custom.
• Tends to high self-doubt. Reacts to criticism by closer outward conformity. Vulnerable to social pressure and authority; compliant.	• Appears to have low self-doubt when generating ideas, not needing consensus to maintain certitude in face of opposition.
• Is essential to the function of the institution all the time, but occasionally needs to be 'dug out' of his system.	• In the institution is ideal in unscheduled crisis, or better still to help avoid them, if he or she can be controlled.
When Collaborating with Innovators	**When Collaborating with Adaptors**
• Supplies stability, order and continuity to the partnership.	• Supplies the task orientations, the break with the past and accepted theory.
• Is sensitive to people, maintains group cohesion and cooperation.	• Appears insensitive to people, often threatens group cohesion and cooperation.
• Provides a safe basis for the innovators' riskier operations.	• Provides the dynamics to bring about periodic radical change, without which institutions tend to ossify.

and conform to existing rules and social norms. In contrast, innovators appear to be less tolerant of the rules, aim at radical change, and may generate new paradigms. Different styles might have implications in educational and organizational terms. While adaptors are essential people for the ongoing functions, innovators are essential in times of change or crisis. Both are capable of developing creative solutions, however. Indeed they reflect their own personal and differential approaches to problem situations. Other characteristics (Kirton, 1989, pp. 8–9) that differentiate the two creativity styles are described in more detail in Table 12.1.

Some studies, conducted under an organizational perspective, have put in evidence the modes of interaction between people who differ regarding their styles. When the adaptor works with the innovator, he or she tends to be attentive to group cohesion and cooperation, relying on order and continuity, providing safe grounds for the innovator's risky attempts to change. Indeed, the innovator is more concerned with radical change and breaking with accepted theory than with being sensitive to people who may oppose.

Method

The Participants

The general study developed in two phases. First, a national random sample of science teachers was selected to obtain data on creativity styles. The second phase of the study pertained to the characterization of pedagogical practices in relation to the teachers' location on the adaptive-innovative continuum. The part reported here regards the study which involved science junior high-school teachers only. Seven teachers were selected from two urban schools, according to their scores as adaptors or innovators. However, only four teachers accepted to participate; two scored as innovators and the other two as adaptors. All were female, with ages ranging from 31 to 45 years; their teaching experience ranged from seven to eighteen years. One participant had performed the role of head of the discipline group for the last two years; another one had also performed the same function before as well as other organizational roles in school. Regarding their professional status, three participants were tenured faculties while another one had not tenure.

The Measuring Instrument

The measure of the creativity styles — the Kirton Adaptation-Innovation Inventory (KAI) — was developed by Kirton (1976; 1987b) and has been applied in several countries. The KAI inventory is a measure of style of creative problem-solving, not of level or capacity. Repeated factor analysis of KAI established three stable and reliable factors. The first was labelled originality. The innovator pole of this dimension regards proliferation of original ideas. Adaptors prefer to produce fewer ideas, some of which may bring change about, and are considered to be useful, sound and relevant to a specific situation. As Kirton points out, to the extent that measures individual preference for producing ideas, this factor does not pertain to level or capacity.

The second factor — efficiency — is the adaptor pole. It refers to a preference for precision, thoroughness, attention to detail, reliability, and efficiency. The third factor is described in terms of working within the limits of rules and structures. It encompasses a preference for being methodical, prudent and prone to group conformity. In contrast, the innovator pole describes willingness to resist to group pressures and discipline. Scores below the mean are interpreted as the adaptor mode; the innovator mode locates above the mean.

The Interview Procedure

The case method focused on four subjects, differing in terms of their thinking styles, years of experience, and professional status accepted to collaborate in this part of the research. Fifteen science lessons were video-taped for all subjects. In addition, two series of interviews were conducted in two sessions each. Questions addressed both personal and professional data according to the following dimensions:

- motives to become a teacher;
- changes in their professional career and status;
- personal evolution regarding their views of education;
- personal perspectives regarding the ongoing school reform; and
- participation in school projects and organizational roles.

The second interview regarded the lessons video-data, using a 'stimulated recall' procedure combined with a reflexive analysis on the lessons occurrences. Questions referred to the following aspects of teaching:

- the structure of the lesson unit;
- planning; and
- choice of instructional methods.

Interview data were taped, transcribed verbatim, and submitted to content analysis.

Data analysis and interpretation was guided by a conceptual framework which was developed according two interaction dimensions:

1 originality, rule conformity, and efficiency constituted the main categories extracted from Kirton's theory, as described in a previous section;
2 pedagogical dimensions pertaining to the subjects' teaching preferences and school organizational roles performance.

Examination of data was systematic in searching for pedagogical patterns that could characterize and differentiate between the participants' creativity styles.

Pedagogical Characteristics According to the Creativity Styles

The analysis revealed differences among the participants regarding the hypothesis of an association between creativity styles and predominant pedagogical practices. Main differential areas were the following: preferences regarding the teaching methods, approaches to the official curriculum and science content, classroom management, lesson-unit planning, and attitude toward change. The pedagogical emphases pertaining to both the adaptor and the innovative styles are described according to the following categories: efficiency, rule conformity, and originality.

The Adaptor Style

Consistencies in the data regarded the following pedagogical areas: planning, use of textbook, acceptance of the discipline group culture, and methods of teaching.

Figures 12.1 and 12.2 summarize the differential pedagogical characteristics corresponding to both the adaptor and innovator styles.

Rule Conformity
Emerging in reference to professional and school organizational themes, several sources of rules were identified for the adaptor subjects: the discipline group as an organizational structure; the head of the discipline group as an authority figure; the colleagues as professional referents to the extent that they were more experienced teachers or viewed as more knowledgeable; the textbook as approved by the discipline group; and the national curriculum viewed as a working context which was accepted as it had been structured officially. Other areas of rule conformity were the following:

- finishing the science subject-matter programme as determined officially;
- planning according to the sequence established in the official programme; and
- following the instructional sequence as established in the textbook.

The adaptors also appeared to be receptive to the influence of the discipline-group teaching culture while accepting and following both pedagogical decisions and directions from the discipline group uncritically and in a strict manner, as shown in the following categories:

1 definition of the time line for the content per unit and yearly;
2 orientations regarding the methods of instruction, the didactic structure,
  · and the sequential organization of the subject matter; sticking closely to the teaching-units plan organized by the group either for each term or for the whole academic year;
3 reliance on the textbook selected and approved by the discipline group; use of the textbook in the manner prescribed by the group (emphasis on some parts, selection of the schemes, etc.); and
4 developing the evaluation tests together with the group.

On the one hand, these teachers seemed to value both formal authority and pedagogical experience. In a way, they constituted sources of professional learning. Such perspective and a similar mode of learning and acting appeared in common to these participants:

I ask for opinion and accept my colleagues' ideas, those who are more experienced.

We have the group head's opinions, since she is the head and has more experience than me.

I try, I see the students' reactions and I accept the opinions of the other colleagues who have a bit more experience than me and that of the head [The Discipline Group]

On the other hand, a low sense of self-efficacy to teach permeated the data as revealed by feelings of uncertainty regarding the adequacy and effectiveness of

Figure 12.1: *Pedagogical characteristics corresponding to the adaptor style*

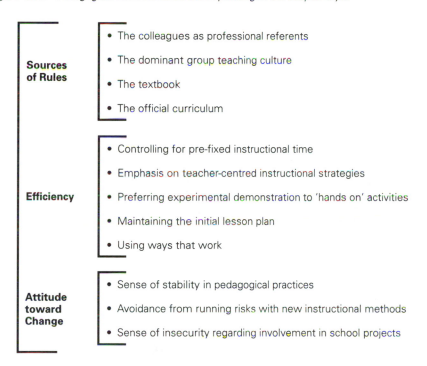

Sources of Rules
- The colleagues as professional referents
- The dominant group teaching culture
- The textbook
- The official curriculum

Efficiency
- Controlling for pre-fixed instructional time
- Emphasis on teacher-centred instructional strategies
- Preferring experimental demonstration to 'hands on' activities
- Maintaining the initial lesson plan
- Using ways that work

Attitude toward Change
- Sense of stability in pedagogical practices
- Avoidance from running risks with new instructional methods
- Sense of insecurity regarding involvement in school projects

some personal pedagogical practices. It appears that guidance from the discipline group and its head also constituted organizational sources of professional security and development.

Efficiency

This feature of the adaptor style was found in two main dimensions of the lessons plan: allocation of instructional time in accordance with both the 'official' curriculum and the discipline group; and an emphasis on more efficient instructional strategies. For the adaptors, time was a prevalent factor to be considered not only regarding the structure of the lessons but also the management of unexpected occurrences in class. As one subject emphasized, 'we always plan the time'. Aiming at reaching a higher level of instructional efficiency, in general, changes to the initial plan implied the regulation of time either within the limits of the lesson unit or the yearly plan. Although allocating the time throughout the whole official programme was decided within the discipline group, the adaptors tended to show a conservative mode of using it. In a teacher's words: 'sometimes, I taught the topic of the programme too fast when compared to other colleagues (. . .) May be I did not spend enough time in clarifying the students' questions.' Or, as another teacher recognized, 'I did not go deeper, regarding some topics of the subject matter programme.'

The teachers' conceptions subjacent to the criteria for determining instructional time and selection of appropriate instructional strategies were associated in

Figure 12.2: Pedagogical characteristics corresponding to the innovator style

Rules
- Critical perspectives regarding school policies
- Planning for flexibility — a 'mental' plan
- Reconceptualizing the official curriculum

Efficiency
- Sharing the instructional time with students
- Emphasis on student-centred instructional strategies
- Preference for 'hands on' activities
- Flexibility regarding the initial lesson plan
- Time to deal with unexpected situations

Attitude toward Change
- Involvement in innovative projects
- Liking to run risks and challenges
- Experimenting new roles and avoiding monotony in classroom

Pedagogical Leadership
- Promoting innovative pedagogical practices
- Initiating change in school
- Influencing the nature of the teaching culture of the discipline group

the data. Some strategies were considered to be more time-consuming than others. Accordingly, the preference for, and selection of, specific instructional strategies tended to obey to the efficiency criterion. Indeed such elements constituted part of the students' learning-efficacy context. This tendency in the data is illustrated through their preference for experimental demonstration in detriment of more student-centred strategies and, specifically of experimental work. Some subjects justified such preference through the following arguments:

> I had to give up because I had not sufficient conditions, got too much noise, they [The students] did not organize the groups (. . .) and I began to see that it was not working at all.

> (. . .) that [experimental work] would take the whole class time and, in the end, a positive benefit would not result from it, and then I changed, I will do it myself , you [the students] do the scheme at your seats (. . .) I thought it would work, and then I had to draw back because it did not

work as I expected (. . .) after this I had to be the one to indicate to them what I want them to see and not let them alone and see by themselves.

(. . .) and I reached the conclusion that the students would not learn anything that way and all that was no more than a waste of time.

Listening to students' opinions . . . each one has his or her own opinion; we lose a lot of time.

Compliance with the official curriculum — while understood and accepted as an organizational norm — associated to being efficient in order to accomplish the entire science programme for the 5th graders. In this sense, the adaptors lived a pedagogical dilemma. On the one hand, they knew that using more student-centred learning strategies motivate the students and raise a higher interest in science. However such strategies were considered to be more time-consuming than didactic methods. On the other hand, planning the instruction to giving more time to 'hands on' science activities and satisfying the answers to all students' questions appeared to be incompatible with their nomothetic context of teaching. The adaptors emphasized two features of this context: there is a discipline programme which the teachers are required to finish; and it is necessary to accomplish the whole programme so that the students acquire a solid knowledge foundation and become ready to go on to the next grade. The efficiency framework is characterized by 'ways that work', as it is illustrated below:

1 Adjusting the global structure of the lesson and readjusting the initial lesson plan in order to end it in time; and managing the instruction time for each instructional unit so that the initial plan be maintained.
2 Preferring teacher-centred methods of instruction in order to prevent or solve discipline problems; and preferring the didactic method of instruction to the students' 'hands on' activities in order to save time and finish the official programme.
3 Using the same lesson plans for all classes belonging to the same grade.

Attitude toward Change
Emphasis on efficiency and a preference for maintaining specific strategies appeared to be associated. What had proved to work well in class tended to become part of the adaptors' pedagogical repertoire. In this sense, efficiency appeared to prevent willingness to risk regarding pedagogical innovation. When asked about the ongoing curricular reform and the possibility of her trying new methods, a participant stated that she did not 'like to risk without being very sure', and that she 'should keep on the same way I have used till now (. . .) I usually guide myself according to what I have already done.'

Willingness to take risks in class opposed itself to a concern with pedagogical efficiency. Moreover, a sense of low self-efficacy (Bandura, 1986) to teach (Ashton, 1986) emerged in the data associated to both a certain insecurity regarding curricular changes and individual initiatives out of the context of the discipline group. As a teacher acknowledged, 'I did not try that yet because . . . well . . . because I am a little afraid of . . . because it might work wrongly.' Or , as another said , 'I don't feel at ease, and it is because of that I don't change, I think that when I consider

the possibility of changing I have to feel very secure regarding what I am doing'
... 'I am afraid of taking the initiative regarding certain new things and then
working wrong and the results being not that positive.'

The Innovator Style

Rule Conformity versus Flexibility
The teachers who scored as innovators on KAI tended to reveal a weak inclination
to conform with the constraints of the context of teaching in that they appeared
to be able to create a classroom climate made of flexibility in order to deal with
contingency. Innovators recognized the limitations imposed on their professional
work by a centralized system. However, unlike adaptors, innovators were prone
to take formal position regarding official policies (for example, in regard to the
debate over the new official instructional evaluation policy), and to lead other
colleagues in supporting their initiatives. Innovators tended not to conform but to
take a critical stand in the face of educational issues, as well as in trying to challenge colleagues who were viewed as 'resistant to change'. In this regard, innovators were leaders in the school pedagogical council and within the discipline group.
To this extent, innovators were influential regarding the nature of the dominant
teaching culture (Feiman-Nemser and Floden, 1986) in the discipline group.

A Mental Plan
Innovators contrasted with adaptors in relation to their conceptions of instructional planning. The following dimensions emerged from the data:

- a minimum of planning as a first approach to the development of innovative projects and pedagogical change;
- flexibility regarding the initial plan; and
- interpretation of unpredictable situations not as a 'violation' of the lesson
plan but as normal events.

In general, the innovators' preference for 'mental' plans associated to flexibility
even beyond the classroom situation. Flexibility and capacity to deal with matters
that were not clear or too explicit characterized the innovators style when working in school projects and planning with other colleagues:

> I have already worked under the orientation of other colleagues ... and
> one was till the last minute without knowing what was going to gener-
> ate, what the result was going to be ... things reached a good result
> although with the double of effort.

> But at the start the people who work in a project must have a span of
> possibilities (...) of course the plan is never rigid, one is advancing, is
> giving structure here and there, sometimes some ways fail and we need
> to move on to other ways. But the drawbacks are less likely to happen,
> less personal anxiety , I think , if things are planned from the beginning.

Strategic Flexibility: Reconceptualizing the Official Curriculum
The innovators approached teaching with a flexibility style in several ways:

- diversifying the methods of instruction;
- developing strategic plans for accommodating possible changes;
- reconceptualizing the subject-matter according to goals considered to be relevant to students; and
- managing instruction to broadening learning goals beyond the knowledge of the subject-matter 'codified' in the official programme.

For the innovators, flexibility signified the possibility of reconceptualizing the discipline content according to a personal mode of being professional. As a participant stated, 'along all these years, I discovered other sequences which are more logical and allow me to finish the programme.' Indeed she had acquired 'enough flexibility that allows me build the entire programme in a personal way.'

Articulating the subject-matter themes in original sequences, structuring the subject-matter and transforming it into personal pedagogical content knowledge (Shulman, 1986; Wilson, Shulman, and Richert, 1987) were typical ways of being innovator in the daily work of these participants:

> And I think, on the other hand, I am not distorting the philosophy underlying the science subject matter . . . Now , all the articulation of the subject-matter . . . because as it is [In the official programme] it is a mere list of contents which for me, as a science teacher, it is useful only as themes , nothing else. And from there . . . well then . . . I do everything with that. It is like having eggs, salt, sugar etc., and it is with these ingredients that I make the cake, the best cake with specific goals . . . I still add two or more things . . . and keep adding.

In sum, while 'turning things around, running away from the official curricular subject matter' the innovators showed a preference for being transformers of the official and centralized school curriculum; in this way, they reflected the convergence of several factors: their personal practical knowledge (Clandinin, 1985; Elbaz, 1983), motivation to study, to experiment and reflect on new ideas, in addition to a sense of professional self-efficacy.

Efficiency versus Educational Relevance
Concern with teaching efficacy was also found in the innovator participants data. However, because efficiency combined with flexibility, it tended to originate different pedagogical practices. Indeed making room for creativity at the implementation of the pedagogical action required 'looking for the unexpected', 'finding connections' and, in the end, 'searching for the unity'. From the innovators' perspective, efficacious practices were not those which guaranteed finishing the official programme by the end of the year, nor were those which conducted the class in a strict obedience to a prior plan. Innovators differentiated from adaptors in that neither the unit plan nor the official subject matter of the discipline constituted formal rules or norm to be followed without personal reflection and consequent transformation. It was at this light that innovators presented a specific definition of teaching efficacy. Embedding their personal science-teaching conceptions and views about educational aims to be achieved by the students, the innovators' practices took different forms, as shown in a participant' words:

> I say efficacious in a double sense. I say efficacious because a class of this type makes things easier and [the students] may develop other things besides knowledge. It is the dialogue. They have learned to wait. Raising the arm means to debate, to disagree with (. . .) In this way they develop the capacity of dialogue, of listening to, and knowing how to use arguments with the colleagues (. . .) It is efficacious because they pay a lot of attention because they want to listen to the colleagues and at the same time I think they memorize better and this facilitates their work. In this area I get good results.

In sum, for the innovators, the strategies selection seemed to obey not an efficiency criterion, as it did for the adaptors, but the educational relevance attributed to the strategy itself. Yet the time allocated to the units of instruction and to the entire programme was a factor the innovators also took into account. In this regard it appeared that flexibility combined with using particular adaptive instructional strategies.

What is the rationale that underlies this situation? To what extent did innovators differ from adaptors regarding the solutions found for the time versus instructional-organization dilemma? Although innovators were also caught in the time — official-programme dilemmas, they faced and dealt with them in specific ways, however. Sharing the class-time management with students, listening to them, and integrating their questions and knowledge were main strategies typical of the pedagogical innovative style. Thinking in action appeared to lead innovators to make essential decisions: increasing the students' participation on the one hand, and paying attention to the subject-matter content in order to focus on the essential points on the other hand. These were the paths through which innovators extended class time for the students to express their interests and ideas.

Defining the Essential in the Lesson Plan
When innovators faced the time versus official-programme dilemma they tended to select adaptive strategies although less frequently than the adaptors and, again, from a different perspective. For the adaptor, time was 'omnipresent' throughout the academic year. In contrast, while introducing the concept of 'open class', the innovators assumed a special learning contract with their students. And, in so doing, these teachers performed a particular role which included 'building bridges towards the synthesis'. As one of them described,

> In a class, what I consider essential is the point where I want to arrive at. As far as the process to get there, although there is a line — there has to be a conducting line regarding the subject matter — sometimes, as it is an open class in which the students give the ideas, things they have, things they know, one has to reflect a little and then I have to get all that in order to build the bridge towards the lesson synthesis.

From such perspective, the teacher becomes the conductor of the 'logical line' which gives meaning and structure to the subject matter. The understanding of a 'structural line' becomes the basic criterion to determine what the essential should or should not be when the time dilemma imposes itself on the innovators. Yet in defining the essential for developing the students' science knowledge, both adaptors and innovators seemed to share the conception of curriculum as 'solid foundation'. In this aspect, the participants shared a concern either with preparing the students who intended to pursue further science studies or with the others who will not learn more science but need preparation for the practical problems of life (See a similar curricular perspective in a study by Freire and Sanches, 1992).

In summary, the adaptive instructional strategies were the following:

1 selecting the essential parts from the official subject-matter programme;
2 managing the program: 'going deeper' in some sections of the subject-matter versus 'going more superficially' for other parts;
3 maintaining specific 'hands on' activities; and
4 introducing more 'economical' instructional strategies as the end of the year approached.

Attitude toward Change
Innovators regarded change as practice infused in their daily teaching. Indeed it appeared to be associated to motivation to continuing learning and self-efficacy to teach. Innovators' action developed in diverse ways: leading change in school, initiating pedagogical activities focusing on school community, and taking part in interdisciplinary projects. For the innovator, considering 'new things, new materials' was understood as an 'incentive' to continuing learning. Indeed, in a participant's words, change 'is a matter of desiring to know things, liking to know, finding out how it is, how it is to be done, how it is to experiment new things'. Introducing change in classroom practices and in school also required a blend of 'having many new ideas' with the capacity of 'going forward' and the will to be 'involved in some [pedagogical] adventures'. As one teacher said, 'in order to change something one has to run the risk; change is not a peaceful thing, and if there are certain things which I think are not well or I am against or they could become better . . . if one does something about it, well . . . that requires change (. . .) that works as a risk doesn't?' Sensed as a permanent professional 'adventure from which is hard to get out from', change appeared to be not 'a superficial attitude but a challenge' and as a source of personal pleasure for these subjects.

In summary, the following categories emerged within the theme of change:

1 openness to the colleagues' ideas;
2 running away from 'things that become monotonous';
3 appetency regarding the new; and
4 considering 'new things, new materials' as motivation to continuing learning.

Conclusion

The study purported to apply Kirton's theory of creativity to the pedagogical domain and to identify teaching practices which might be associated to both adaptive and innovative styles of creativity. Within this theoretical frame-work, the following categorial dimensions were researched: rule conformity; efficiency; and attitude toward change. Differences among the participants regarded pedagogical practices in correspondence to both styles of creativity. A synthesis of the results follows.

A preference for practical pedagogical knowledge, composed of routines and rules of practice (Elbaz, 1983) helped the science teachers who scored on KAI as adaptors cope with current classroom problems. As found in other research studies (Calderhead, 1988; Clandinin, 1985), it was also a knowledge that teachers developed from their personal experience. Indeed the participants also learned to be teachers by experimenting with ideas from their colleagues.

A sense of a pedagogical pragmatism appeared in the adaptors through an avoidance to run risks and a preference for familiar instructional strategies or others which had proved to work well in class. In contrast, the innovators not only diversified the strategies but also selected them according to holistic educational purposes: making the students learning science and contributing to their personal development. In this sense, one may say that while the adaptors' participants were prone to view their work embedded in a 'bureaucratic rationality' (Schön, 1987), the innovators appeared to work within a transformational perspective.

The discipline group constituted a context influencing the nature of the teaching practices for both adaptors and innovators. However, it did not influence their pedagogical practices in the same manner. For the adaptors, the discipline-group rules worked as source of information for solving practical problems. On the one hand, following the yearly plan, such as it was organized by the discipline group, may have contributed to reduce uncertainty, to simplify the complexities of teaching, and to enhance self-confidence in the effectiveness of the lesson results. On the other hand, the discipline group worked as a source of direction while selecting priorities, suggesting curricular emphases, determining goals to students' achievement and, to this extent, influencing these teachers' professional behaviour and science-teaching conceptions (Freire and Sanches, 1992). This analysis converges with results from studies on the functions of planning (Clark and Yinger, 1987). In contrast, the innovators tended to shape the work context itself through the leadership they exerted regarding the culture of teaching within the group.

In conclusion, socialization of students, their behaviours and needs as learners constituted an object of concern for all the participants. However, personal perspectives on the nature of the pedagogical content knowledge (Shulman, 1986) constituted an important dimension that appeared to differentiate the participants regarding their styles of pedagogical creativity. This emphasis required them to think about new pedagogical ways to transform the subject-matter content, and to treat it as a set of suggestions rather than as a requirement imposed by the national curriculum. The adaptors approached the content as an absolute in that changing its sequence was out of question and following it through the end was a requirement. The innovators preferred to emphasize transformation of the content (Wilson, Shulman and Richert, 1987), adopting a critical perspective, becoming reflective in order to change the logical sequence, making their own interpretation of the official curriculum, and adding other topics according to the students' occasional interests. Starting with a 'mental plan' which 'is never fixed', innovators opened space and time in classroom for engaging in pedagogical conversations with students about unpredictable situations (Schön, 1987), revealing, in this way, an understanding of the learning situation as 'reflective conversations'.

While identifying pedagogical characteristics that appear to correspond to styles of creativity as defined in Kirton's theory, the study may contribute to the understanding of the question on the factors that might underlay the development of the teachers' professional knowledge. However, it is important to look at limitations, some of which call for further research. First, the number of participants is small since it was not possible to obtain the participation of teachers whose scores were located on the extremes of the KAI adaptive-innovator continuum. This was particularly the case of participants who scored as innovators. Second, the analysis found pedagogical practices which did not differentiate between innovators and adaptors. To the extent that creativity is made of uniqueness, further clarification of the results justifies a new question: What factors are associated to such similarities? To what extent the similarities or the differences may be understood in the light of the teaching-cultures nature? On the one hand, data revealed a dominant culture of teaching within the discipline group which the teachers who scored as adaptors tended to share in an uncritical manner. As expected, the innovators tended to influence the discipline group and, consequently, the nature of the teaching culture itself. New studies, with a larger number of teachers from other discipline groups will research this further. On the other hand, the participants appeared also to differ regarding both teaching experience and their sense of self-efficacy in some areas of teaching. In this regard, more research will illuminate the question concerning the self-efficacy role on the differences found between the two groups of teachers as innovators or adaptors.

Note

1   This study is part of a research project developed under a grant awarded by the Instituto de Investigação Educacional. We are grateful to Professor Michael Kirton for his advice in the first part of the research project.

References

ASHTON, P.T. and WEBB, R.B. (1986) *Making a Difference: Teachers Sense of Efficacy and Student Achievement*, Longman, New York.

BANDURA, A. (1986) *Social Foundations of Thought and Action: A Social Cognitive Theory*, Englewood Cliffs, NJ, Prentice-Hall.

CALDERHEAD, J. (1984) *Teachers' Classroom Decision-making*, London, Holt, Rinehart and Winston.

CALDERHEAD, J. (1988) 'Knowledge structures in learning to teach,' in CALDERHEAD, J. (Ed) *Teachers' Professional Learning*, The Falmer Press, pp. 65–83.

CLANDININ, D.J. (1985) 'Personal practical knowledge: A study of teachers' classroom images', *Curriculum Inquiry*, 15, 4, pp. 361–85.

CLARK, M.C. and YINGER, R.J. (1987) 'Teacher planning', in CALDERHEAD, J. (Ed) *Exploring Teachers' Thinking*, Cassell Educational Limited, pp. 84–103.

ELBAZ, F. (1983) *Teacher Thinking: A Study of Practical Knowledge*, London, Cross Helm.

FEIMAN-NEMSER, S. and FLODEN, R.E. (1986) 'The cultures of teaching', In WITTROCK, M.C. (Ed) *Handbook of Research on Teaching*, American Educational Research Association, pp. 505–26.

FREIRE, A.M. and SANCHES, M.F.C. (1992) 'Elements for a typology of teachers' conceptions of physics teaching', *Teaching & Teacher Education*, 8, 5 and 6, pp. 497–507.

GIROUX, H. (1985) 'Intellectual labor and pedagogical work: Rethinking the role of the teacher as intellectual', *Phenomenology and Pedagogy*, 3, 1, pp. 20–32.

HOY, W.K. and MISKEL, C.G. (1987) *Educational Administration: Theory Research and Practice*, New York, Random House.

KIRTON, M.J. (1976) 'Adaptors and innovators: A description and measure', *Journal of Applied Psychology*, 61, pp. 622–9.

KIRTON, M.J. (1987a) 'Adaptors and innovators: Cognitive styles and personality', in ISAKSEN, S.G. (Ed) *Frontiers of Creativity*, Buffalo, NY, Brearly.

KIRTON, M.J. (1987b) *Kirton Adaptation-Innovation Inventory (KAI)*, Manual ND Edition, Hatfield, UK, Occupational Research Centre.

KIRTON, M.J. (Ed) (1989) *Adaptors and Innovators. Styles of Creativity and Problem-solving*, Routledge.

SCHÖN, D.A. (1987) *Educating the Reflective Practitioner*, San Francisco, Jossey-Bass.

SHULMAN, L. (1986) 'Those who understand: Knowledge growth in teaching', *Educational Researcher*, 15, 2, pp. 4–14.

WILSON, S.M., SHULMAN, L. and RICHERT, A.E. (1987) '150 different ways of knowing: Representations of knowledge in teaching', in CALDERHEAD, J. (Ed) *Exploring Teachers' Thinking*, Cassell Educational Limited, pp. 104–24.

Part 4

Development of Teachers' Knowledge and Practice

The four chapters within this section of the book in different ways focus on the developmental issue: What can be done to develop in student teachers their knowledge, thinking and practice of teaching? In that way they are truly educational in their intention. However, they relate to different educational situations or phases: the two first ones (Rita Riksaasen and Ora Kwo) deal with pre-service teacher education while the three latter ones (Shoshana Keiny, Tapio Kosunen and Elisabeth Ahlstrand) look at in-service qualification of practising teachers.

To appreciate fully the two Nordic papers in this section (Kosunen and Riksaasen) it is necessary to draw your attention to the central status of a national-curriculum text in the Nordic countries. There is a long tradition for a national curriculum which, although it historically has existed in quite different formats, has an important ideological function of outlining the common curriculum for all pupils at any given level of the school system. This tradition is further strengthened by a strongly centralized school system. The degree to which this curriculum, however, is actually studied and observed by the teachers, vary substantially. In fact one of the core problems has been to get teachers to really take the implementation of the curriculum seriously. Recent development in this field involves an increased demand on local schools and their teachers to engage in developing a local version of the curriculum for their own use in their school.

Even within the two groups mentioned above, the variation is substantial. Looking at the pre-service chapters, Rita Riksaasen is concerned with the influence of the difference in curricula between teacher-education programmes for kindergarten and primary-school teachers. She analyses these in terms of Bernstein's concept of curriculum code and maintains that the difference in curricular codes between the two programmes create a difference in the professional cultures of these programmes. These cultures again influence the students' conceptions of their work as well as their practice. Riksaasen fears that the difference between these professional cultures may complicate future cooperation between teachers from different programmes who may more often have to work together in a new organization of the school for the 6-year olds in Norway, where schooling has traditionally only started at the age of 7.

Riksaasen consequently sees the culture of the training institution as influential in bringing about differences between groups of teachers, and she refers the cultural difference back to the influence of different curricula.

Ora Kwo, on the other hand, takes a view that is more individually oriented. Her study deals with student teachers' practice (instructional behaviour in communication terms) and their thoughts about their practice (in stimulated recall situations) as well as the relationship between the two. Her objective is to check if students, through a seven-weeks period of practice, develop in relation to steps in a stage model of teacher development taken from the novice–expert research tradition.

Consequently Kwo takes teacher education more as a situation for studying the development of (student) teachers rather than as a factor influencing (differently?) development of student competence.

For both pre-service teacher-education chapters we may consequently conclude that while one is studying the effects of different professional cultures on students and the other is studying development of teacher competence during practice periods, neither of them are primarily focused on finding ways or means to improve teachers' knowledge, thinking and practice through their pre-service education.

The three chapters dealing with in-service development of teachers' thinking and practice show some similarity to the ones mentioned above in this respect. They do not either study effects of organized training programmes in a strict sense. Rather they draw their examples either from some sort of curriculum-improvement project or from everyday practice of teacher teams.

In Shoshana Keiny's case teachers participated in curriculum-development groups including persons outside the school and involving confrontation with, and discussion of, activities in industry or community-service activities as possible learning experiences for their pupils. It is demonstrated that these experiences contributed to the teachers' conceptual change as well as to changes in their practice.

Tapio Kosunen relates to the Nordic curricular situation described above. He studies groups of teachers who have — and do not have — experience from previous work with local curriculum development and their conception of the importance of the curriculum and their planning and implementation of teaching in relation to it. Teachers who have previous curriculum-planning experience are found to have internalized the core idea of the national curriculum as well as to demonstrate a more flexible and versatile type of practice. In other words they had developed their thinking and practice as a result of experience with curriculum-development practice.

Elisabeth Ahlstrand's interest lies in the effect of the organization of teachers in cooperative teacher teams in Swedish schools, the allocation of time for these teams to meet and work together, and the discursive practice of the teams during meetings. Although this may be characterized as a form of 'imposed collaboration' the teachers evaluate it positively as it contributes to breaking their isolation and providing mutual support and care. It is, however, more difficult to trace an effect of the arrangement on the teachers' professional development.

Two related observations strike us as interesting:

One is — as mentioned above — that neither of them actually deal with efforts to develop teachers' thinking and practice by means of formal teaching, course participation etc. Development is seen either as a result of teachers' participation in project work or as a result of the way their activities in daily professional life is organized. It is possible that an increased emphasis on principles from situated learning as a way of understanding and designing professional development of teachers, may lead to such ways of in-service training as an alternative to traditional 'coursing'.

The other observation is that it is probably in this section of the book that we may find the clearest examples of studies of teacher thinking and practice, related to different contexts. As mentioned in the introduction to the book, this was planned as a focus for this particular conference. At least some of these five chapters (Keiny, Kosunen, Ahlstrand) look at how the way the teachers' working situation and their experiences are structured, affect the teachers' development of competence. Consequently we see — although in some cases rather implicitly — that structural or 'frame' factors are seen as influential on the thinking as on the practice of teachers. This — in an interesting way — opens up the 'trialectical' interactions of the three factors — thinking, practice and structural context — that it will be interesting to explore further within this field of research.

Chapter 13

Models of Two Professional Cultures: Teacher Training for Kindergartens and Primary Schools

Rita Riksaasen

Abstract

How are kindergarten and primary-school teachers socialized during their education? Will the two groups of teachers have problems collaborating when they work together with 6-year-olds. The article proposes that the kindergarten-teacher students and primary-school teacher students in Norway are socialized into different professional values with respect to caring relationships and that educational knowledge is organized according to different codes in the two professional cultures. The study indicates that different teaching traditions of primary school and kindergarten also can be observed in classroom interaction and supervision during teacher education.

Introduction

How are kindergarten and primary-school teachers socialized during their education? Will the two groups of teachers have problems collaborating when they work together with 6-year olds? These are the priniciple research questions of this study. Socialization is here seen as an interactive process between college teachers, teaching supervisors and students. In this process, the individual becomes both a subject and object, interpreting situations and taking into account other persons' actions.

In this chapter I argue that kindergarten-teacher students and primary-school teacher students are socialized into different professional values with respect to caring relationships and that educational knowledge is organized according to different codes in the two professional cultures. By 'caring relationship' I mean the value of being emotionally close to children under instruction or supervision. 'Professional' is here defined as an occupation for which you need a formal education. This formal education must include theory and standardized training. By 'culture' I mean the dominating understanding of realities, and the profession's values and norms. Norms indicate what the profession stresses and what it looks upon as valuable. A 'code' is:

A regulative principle, tacitly acquired, which selects and integrates relevant meanings, forms of their realization and evoking contexts. (Bernstein, 1987)

The concept of code is inseparable from the concepts of legitimate and illegitimate communication, and it thus presupposes a hierarchy in forms of communication and their demarcation and criteria. We can merely make out a code on the basis of a critical analysis of the formulation about practice and what happens in practice. (Bernstein, 1990)

This project was inspired by the fact that Norway will soon begin offering primary-school education for children 6 years of age instead of the current 7 years. This means that teaching 6-year-olds will become a common task for kindergarten and primary-school teachers. This fact will undoubtedly lead to conflicting opinions among these two groups of teachers as to how this age group is best taught. 'The 6-year-old child experiment' was run in forty-two municipalities in the years 1986–90 (Haug, 1991). Both Haug's studies and my own interviews with participants of this '6-year-old child experiment', indicate that the two groups of teachers had problems collaborating. Haug suggests that the reasons for this difficulty are rooted in two groups' different institutional backgrounds, drawing upon Basil Bernstein's theory that 'the tradition of the school is based on a collection code of knowledge and the tradition of the kindergarten is based on an integration code of knowledge' (Haug, 1991).

The principal goal of this study is to go into the two professional cultures and investigate whether the collaboration problems are caused by a different socialization during education. In Norway, children have up to now begun primary school at the age of 7. Parents had the responsibility for child care before that age. About half of the children have had the opportunity to attend kindergarten, but the parents have paid a high fee for this service. In comparison to countries such as France and England, Norwegian kindergartens have traditionally operated very independently of primary schools. Ideologically, kindergartens have been closely associated with the home and family life and have been dominated by a domestic discourse. The kindergarten ideal has been to be 'a good home' and 'a good family' for the child while the child is away from her mother (Korsvold, 1990). Instead of taking the achievement-oriented school as a model, the Norwegian kindergarten has adopted the caring mother as a model (Kjørholt,1990).

Unlike the primary schools, Norwegian kindergartens have never operated under a work plan approved by Parliament. Such a plan is now in progress, but the professional autonomy of Norwegian kindergarten teachers has traditionally been strong. Kindergartens have accordingly stressed the importance of giving the children unstructured activities and plenty of freedom to play. It is expected that the children will learn indirectly. Development of the child's personality and social skills is very important.

The primary school, too, is interested in children's personal development, but at the same time, it puts stress on teaching children formal knowledge. The Parliament has been involved in school matters by regulating textbooks and curricula.

Primary-school and kindergarten teachers stress different elements in their approaches to their work tasks. It can be argued that it is natural for teachers working with younger children to have a different perspective from those working with older children. The kindergarten teacher has cared for children from 1 to 7 years old, the primary-school teacher has cared for children from 7 to 15 years of age. However, I argue that primary-school teachers and kindergarten teachers still have many working tasks in common because they both work with children. Because the two sets of pedagogues will soon begin to share the task of instructing 6-year-olds, it is useful to study their different professional cultures for their general similarities and dissimilarities.

Methods

This study uses a qualitative method. In August 1991, I established a connection with a beginning class at a college of kindergarten-teacher education and a beginning class at a college of primary-school teacher education. I observed each of these classes for a period of four weeks. To enhance my ability to compare the two, I alternated between the two institutions, staying one week at a time at each. My objective was to 'walk in the students' shoes' as they began their education. During this first year, I interviewed ten students in each class twice. During the next year, I interviewed fifteen college teachers in a kindergarten-teacher college and fifteen college teachers in a primary-school teacher college. Because I did not want to influence future observations, I did not interview teachers from the colleges where I observed. Each interview with students and college teachers was recorded and lasted for about one and a half hours.

The special feature of this method is the alteration between observations and interviews which was designed to control my observations by asking students and college teachers questions about selected episodes I had observed. Generally, it was easy to be an observer in the classrooms. The students took notes and so did I. Nobody noticed that I, for example, took down that the college teacher turned up her nose at a student who talked about *aunts* (employers) in kindergartens. I attended lessons unannounced — when I wanted to. During practice periods, I had to plan the observations and make appointments. Here it was more difficult to take notes. The following demonstrates my method of working.

During the first weeks of education, the kindergarten-teacher students learned a lot of song games during their music, drama, and physical-education lessons. These song games were expected to be a useful working tool when the students attended kindergartens as inexperienced teachers. As I followed the students into practice sessions, I observed what happened to these song games. One day when the children were playing outdoors, two of the student teachers started to arrange games. The children looked very happy. To me, it seemed as if the children were not used to adults taking part in their outdoor play. Later on, when the children pretended to be 'grown-ups' who were outdoors, they stood quietly in a long row along a wall. These observations correspond to other studies indicating that adults usually do not take part in outdoor play. This tendency was reinforced when the teaching supervisor told the student teachers, in effect, 'Oh, you will soon learn not to burn the candle at both ends.'

This observation is a good demonstration of the difference between the ideals and the realities of preschool pedagogy. Later interviews with students about the practise of song games outdoors confirmed my observation. As I interviewed college teachers, I asked about the intent of teaching the students these song games.

Theoretical Framework

Basil Bernstein's theory of the classification and framing of educational knowledge provides the framework for this study. Bernstein argues that educational knowledge is a major regulator of the structure of experience (Bernstein, 1977). Identities are created by the transmission of educational knowledge. In an institution of education, formal educational knowledge is realized through three message systems: curriculum, pedagogy and evaluation. The curriculum defines what counts as valid knowledge, pedagogy defines what counts as the valid transmission of this knowledge, and evaluation defines what counts as a valid realization of the knowledge on the part of those taught. The term 'educational-knowledge code' refers to the underlying principles which shape curriculum, pedagogy and evaluation. The form this code takes depends upon social principles which regulate the classification and framing of knowledge made public in the educational institutions.

The term 'classification' does not refer to what is classified, but to the relationship between categories. Where classification is weak, there is reduced insulation between categories — the boundaries between categories are weak or blurred. The term 'frame' is used to determine the structure of the message system, pedagogy. Frame refers to the form of the context in which knowledge is transmitted and received and to the specific pedagogical relationship between the teacher and taught. In the same way as classification does not refer to contents, so frame does not refer to the contents of the pedagogy, but to the strength of the boundaries between what may be transmitted and what may not be transmitted in the pedagogical relationship. Frame also refers to the relationship between the non-school, everyday community knowledge of the teacher or taught and the educational knowledge transmitted in the pedagogical relationship. The basic structure of the curriculum message system is given by variations in the strength of classification. The basic structure of the pedagogy message system is given by variations in the strength of frames. The structure of the evaluation message system is a function of the classification and frame. The strength of the classification and the strength of frame can vary independently of each other. An organization of educational knowledge which involves strong classification and a strong framing is called a 'collection code'. An organization of knowledge which involves weak classification and weak framing is called an 'integration code'. The characteristic of a code is that it contains principles of guidelines for interpreting the work around us or governing our behaviour.

Knowledge within a collection code is private property. A collection code involves a hierarchical organization of knowledge. A key concept of the collection code is discipline. Discipline means accepting a given selection, organization, pacing, and timing of knowledge realized in the pedagogical frame. The evaluation system places an emphasis upon attaining states of knowledge rather than ways of knowing. Knowledge of education is uncommon sense knowledge freed from the local through various languages of the sciences or forms of reflectiveness. The pedagogy in the collection code tends to proceed from the surface structure of knowledge to its deep structure. According to Bernstein, the pedagogy of the primary school is characterized by strong classification and strong framing. This form of pedagogy he names visible pedagogy. With visible pedagogy, you are involved in transmission of specific skills. The existence of firm criteria makes evaluation rather easy to measure.

In an integration code, various insulated subjects are subordinate to some relational idea which blurs the boundaries between subjects. We can distinguish between two types of integration codes — a teacher-based integration code in which the same teachers blur boundaries between different subjects and a teacher-based integration code which involves relationships with other teachers. Integration reduces the authority of the separate categories, and this has implications for existing authority structures. An integrated code will reduce the discretion of the teacher in a direct relation to the strength of the integrated code. Reduced discretion of the teacher is paralleled by increased discretion of the pupils. With a change from a collection code to an integration code, there is a shift in the balance of power in the pedagogical relationship between teacher and taught. With an integrated code, the pedagogy is likely to proceed from the deep structure to the surface structure. According to Bernstein, preschool/infant pedagogy is characterized by weak classification and weak framing — an integration code. This type of pedagogy he names 'invisible pedagogy'. The teacher's control over the child is implicit rather than explicit. The teacher arranges a context which the child is expected to rearrange and explore. Within this arranged context, the child apparently has wide power over what activities he or she selects, how he or she structures these activities, and the time span he or she allots to them. The child regulates his or her own movements and social relationships. There is reduced emphasis upon the transmission of specific skills. The criteria for evaluating the pedagogy are multiple and diffuse and thus not easy to measure. A basic concept in the invisible pedagogy is play. Play is understood to be not just random activity. Rather, it is an activity from which interpretations, evaluations and diagnoses are derived and which also indicates a progression. Learning by playing is a tacit, invisible act. Its progression is not facilitated by explicit public control.

Different Cultures: Results

Caring Values

Studies indicate that child care in kindergartens differs from that in primary schools, even when both institutions give formal instruction in caring. In kindergartens, the teacher will take a child on his or her knee to comfort him or her when necessary. The working ideal is to look upon the child as an equal, to listen, and to pay attention to his or her psychological as well as physical needs. In the primary school, there is much greater 'distance' between teacher and child. Caring at the primary school can mean, for example, interaction with a pupil by asking him or her a subject question. The teacher 'cares' when he or she 'receives the answer' (Noddings, 1985). We can say that caring varies depending on the context. I think it also varies with the age of the child: a caring relationship between a kindergarten teacher and a small child will often be similar to a caring relationship between a parent and a child. I argue that these caring relationships are emotional in basis, not intellectual, rational, or connected to a professional female or male behaviour. I base this argument on my own observations from an earlier study of physicians. Here I asked questions about the physicians' personal involvement with their patients. A general problem for the physicians was becoming involved with small children. Surgeons felt that it was different to have a child rather than an adult 'on the table' (Rikaasen, 1988). I also believe that the students' desire to be emotionally close to children is often their motivation to become a kindergarten teacher.

This study indicates that primary-school student teachers and kindergarten student teachers begin to react differently towards children at an early point in their studies. When I was in their classroom, I often heard kindergarten student teachers talking about children. In this first class I learned a new notion: 'auntchild' (a child with whom the student teacher had a particularly close relationship). The students often referred to children in their family and talked about them with pride and a smile. When a student brought her newborn baby to class, ten students immediately crowded around her. When told they were going to learn first-aid, the kindergarten student teachers did not look very interested. However, when the college teacher brought three dolls for the students to 'breathe life into', one of the students referred to an adult doll as a 'poor fellow'. When another student saw a baby doll, she exclaimed, 'Oh, a baby'. In other words, while there are undoubtedly exceptions, these students seemed to be oriented towards persons instead of problems. Values such as love for children, the desire to protect them, and a general caring attitude towards people clearly dominated.

The primary-school teacher students less frequently talked about children or pupils they knew. They seemed to be genuinely interested in pupils and they wanted to be good and caring teachers. Most of the time, however, they focused on subjects and learning methods. When I observed a beginning class at a primary school, I detected that a student teacher became embarrassed when a 7-year-old boy wanted to take her hand. In this class, the teaching supervisor was an unusually caring teacher and she encouraged the students to sit with the pupils on their knees. Twice I observed students with pupils on their knees, but the students did not talk or interact with them: the children just sat there.

That kindergarten student teachers and primary-school student teachers differ with respect to how they care for children is not surprising. These student teachers practise in different institutions and are motivated to work with different groups of children. What is surprising however, is that these differing communication structures also seem to exist between students and teachers within the two colleges of education themselves.

Very early in this study, I became convinced that different communication structures between teachers and students existed within the two colleges of education. Although I was not able to measure what I perceived, it was my experience that teacher training for primary school seemed more controlling and directing. In the training for kindergarten teachers, the student–teacher interaction looked more friendly. Here, the students were encouraged to ask spontaneous questions. In my first interviews with the student teachers, I asked how student–teacher interaction at the college they were currently attending compared with such interaction at their previous college. Six out of ten kindergarten student teachers felt that the teachers at their present college were more involved with students and cared more for them. The students reported, for example, that their teachers often chatted with them before they started lessons, asking questions such as 'How are you today?' I frequently heard supportive statements from teachers such as: 'Don't worry, we'll get through the syllabus, just take it easy.' One student suggested that the talk was almost too cosy.

When I asked the same question of the primary-school student teachers, they responded differently. Half of the students complained that lessons were too controlled. The teacher often directed communication. Teachers talked about democracy more than they practised it. One student said that the interaction in her present college was much like it was in her junior college, except that it was easier to ask questions and criticize teachers. A third student characterized student–teacher interaction as pleasant but distant.

These observations and interviews suggest that just as there is a tendency for kindergarten teachers to be emotionally close to the children they care for, there is a tendency for college teachers of kindergarten student teachers to be emotionally close to those they instruct. Similarly, the emotional distance often found between teachers and pupils in the primary school also tends to exist between teachers and students in the college of education of primary-school teachers. This suggests that the atmosphere in the classrooms of colleges of education plays a role in the students' professional socialization.

Visible and Invisible Pedagogy

Norwegian kindergartens practise an indirect method of teaching. The children are responsible for their own learning. This style of instruction also seems to characterize the college of kindergarten teacher education. Both appear to be cases of invisible pedagogy. Primary schools, on the other hand, favour visible pedagogy. There are clear criteria for evaluation, a direct effort is made to teach formal knowledge, and teachers attempt to control what the students learn during practice periods. This hypothesis is based on my observations which show that the two colleges of education indicated what they regarded as good or bad practice in different ways.

In the kindergarten-teacher training, the teachers very seldom talked about bad practice or what they regard as poor work. They focused on what they considered to be good practice. When the college of kindergarten teacher education appointed supervisors in kindergartens, it had no other formal requirements than passing an examination at a college of education. Even if the supervisor has passed the examination with 'a cry of distress', one of them told me, the college will delegate the supervision to her.

If you do not talk about unwanted pedagogical practice, have restricted control over practice, and have weak control over the appointment of supervisors, it can be difficult to promote and direct ideal practice. The students will have the responsibility of defining what is bad practice according to ideals of good practice.

When I observed school-teacher training, I was surprised to hear constant discussion about what was good or bad pedagogical practice. Remarkable also were constant references to the students' past as pupils. Over and over again the students were told that the teaching they had experienced as pupils was probably not good enough. The school of today is better than that. An example mentioned to warn the students was a story about the teacher who asked the pupils to write by dictation and then corrected their writing with a red pencil. Today, pupils are taught to do process writings. You never correct their work with a red pencil when they have just started to go to school.

What is surprising is that this college of education was not worried about using a 'mental' red pencil on students who had just started their studies. Most students had perhaps chosen to be teachers because of their own experience as pupils. Many of these students said they had learned a lot by writing dictations, in spite of the red pencil.

When the college of school-teacher education sent their students to practise, they did so in order to show the students ideal pedagogical practice. The supervisors were considered to be competent pedagogues, and they were often well-educated as to instruction. There was competition to be appointed to these jobs because the payment was rather good. On the other hand, few teachers were appointed and every supervisor thus had about five students. The experience of school practice was thus not realistic.

My study indicates that students in the college of school-teacher training seemed to learn more from teaching-models. Before they began teaching, I observed supervisors advising the student teachers. After the students' teaching, they were immediately evaluated both by supervisor and fellow students. In later interviews, the students were asked questions about supervision, such as, 'Before you began teaching, did your supervisor give you any advice?' All the primary-school teacher students had comments on their workplan before hand. One group of school-teacher students said they made a workplan together with their supervisor. Another group said that the supervisor was too dominant: the students made proposals, but the teacher directed their work by making alternative proposals. She also instructed the students in how to give commands, where the pupils should wait for the teacher when they moved to another room, etc. These students complained that they were not allowed to learn by doing. A third group of students said they made a broad outline of what to do and received advice if there were serious mistakes. The last group of school-teacher students complained of a supervisor who only gave praise. This feedback was really frustrating.

When I asked the same question about supervision of kindergarten-teacher students, only two reponded that they had been given advice before short periods of practise teaching. Half of these students had made a workplan before teaching (*samlingsstund*), but the supervisor did not look at it. Three of the kindergarten student teachers did not make a written plan. Many of the students said that they initially had received some general advice about order and songs before they started to work. All of them observed the supervisor's activity before teaching.

When kindergarten student-teachers had four days of leadership, all of the students had some advice beforehand. Only two of the students complained of a dominating supervisor. The students had to learn by doing and experienced frustrating episodes. Some of the students had restricted information and had to search for a workplan which they finally found. One student looked sad when she told me about her experience on her first day of leadership. The kindergarten was to have baking-day. Because the kindergarten had never had baking on this weekday before, the student was unaware of the event and failed to make the necessary arrangements. The supervisor had wanted to make the point to the student that there was much to take notice of when you are a leader. Information about the baking day had been placed on a wall. Another student cried when she talked about her leadership. One child, who often provoked adults, was frustrated when the student-teacher tried to guide him and refused to do what she asked him to do. The kindergarten teacher just sat and watched the student try unsuccessfully to persuade the boy. Because of this episode everything was delayed and the assistants could not have their lunch on time. This student came to doubt her competence and decided to terminate this education.

When I interviewed college teachers of kindergarten teacher training, I occasionally mentioned these two stressful episodes and asked for comments. A college teacher of pedagogy, who had worked in kindergarten teacher-training for many years, told me that instances of students crying were not unusual.

As supervision seemed to be very different at the two colleges of education, I also mentioned examples of supervision from kindergartens in interviews with college teachers of primary-school teachers. Some of these college teachers were horrified when I told them about how supervision of kindergarten-teacher training is conducted.

The following example is from an interview with a pedagogue at the college of school-teacher training. He has worked as a teacher for many years.

Q: In kindergarten-teacher training, the students have only two hours supervision a week.

A: Oh damn, excuse the expression. That is a gigantic difference.

Q: The students have four days of leadership during their first year of study.

A: That is very different. Practice in teacher training is supervised practice.

Q: Why are you so concerned with supervised practice?

A: Yes but, oh my God, the whole intention with teacher training is to be competent as an autonomous teacher. What counts is ability to reflect. You will not develop that by moving on the surface and pretending to be a teacher.

Q: You will have supervision when you have finished the leadership day.

A: You can do this in different ways. What is important is didactic relational thinking. To state the reason for your own choice of action on the level of intention. You legitimate action. It is by thinking and planning that you legitimate what you choose to do. That you cannot stimulate. Now I am shocked. This is very unthinkable in teacher training. From time to time you might experience episodes like this. But you cannot pretend to be a teacher for three weeks and expect to experience the full strain of being a teacher. This is completely a conscious choice, the development of competence and reflection.

Q: Do you mean a gradual habituation to teaching?

A: No. It is not to habituate. It is education. Practice also is education. It is not an aim to experience the strain of being a teacher. In any case you pretend. Our practice has completely different central goals.

In another interview, the college teacher of pedagogy was 'open' to leadership days, but by this she meant that the students should grow into the teacher role.

Many of the college teachers of kindergarten-teacher training justified the leadership days. Here is an example which indicates how one of them tried to legitimate this supervision. This example comes from an interview with a college teacher appointed to connect theory and practice. She has worked as a kindergarten teacher for many years.

Q: What is the goal of the leadership days during the students' first year of study?

A: To make the students conscious of the nature of leadership and to see if someone does not have the capacity to be a leader. They have to know what leadership is about.

Q: How should a leadership day take place?

A: There should probably be some supervision in advance. We talk about leadership during preparation for practice. We want the supervisor in kindergarten to talk about it too, to comment on the workplan . . .

Q: Students have told me that this is rather a tough experience.

A: It is good for the students to know it is hard, in my opinion. This is a conscious attitude. So many students believe they are going to be with children. They are going to do something else. They have no human right to be kindergarten teachers. The students have to be mature, to dare to find out whether they have the potential to become leaders later on. This is very important. Some students from other colleges of education say they do not want to be leaders after finishing their studies. If several students leave college during their first practice, it is no disaster. I am not ashamed of letting the students be leaders.

Q: Where is the supervisor?

A: At a certain distance, but she is there. She will save the students from disaster. But the students should have the opportunity to discover things themselves. The supervisor or assistants should not tell the student what is wrong at once. This is a hard profession. The students will only experience part of the strain during training.

These observations and interviews strongly suggest that the two pedagogical professions have different opinions about how learning should take place in schools and kindergartens as well as how supervision of college students should take place.

Control of Supervision

Observations and interviews indicate that the training of primary-school teachers involved explicit control of student socialization. This could also be observed when college teachers visited schools during the students' practice. Nine out of ten school-teacher students were observed when they taught. According to observations and interviews, the college teachers often observed the students' supervision during their visit. With the exception of the college teachers of music, the college teachers observed the supervision before they entered into conversation with supervisor and students. The classroom teacher retained responsibility for supervision even when the college teachers were present. The college teachers looked upon the supervisors as well-qualified subject teachers and they wanted initially to be observers when they entered the classroom. Thus these college teachers could control supervision if they wanted to. I don't think this opportunity to control was very conscious and planned.

In the case of the supervision of kindergarten-teacher training, student interviews indicate that the college teachers observed only one out of ten students while they worked with children. Instead, they interviewed students about their experiences in kindergarten, asked questions about the children, and talked about the different tasks the students were going to do during practice. As the college teacher had a dialogue with the student, the supervisor in kindergarten more or less initially was an observer. The college teachers, both the pedagogues and the different subject teachers, thus took the role of the supervisor, reducing their ability to control ordinary supervision in the kindergarten. When I asked a college teacher in this training why she did not want to control supervision in kindergartens and informed her about the possibility, she really thought this was a good idea which could be adopted. But she thought it would be too 'dangerous' for the kindergarten teacher to supervise when the college teacher observed.

As we can see, the college teachers of primary-school teacher training and kindergarten-teacher training want to respect the supervisors. But to do this, they behave in different ways.

Different Teaching of Subjects

In this final section, I will demonstrate differences between the two professional cultures by presenting examples from teaching religious knowledge. This example demonstrates:

- differences between integrating or segregating subjects;
- differences in level of abstraction when presenting knowledge; and
- different classroom interactions between college teachers and students.

In kindergarten-teacher training, I sometimes observed subject boundaries to be blurred and the progression of knowledge more often went from the concrete to theoretical abstractions. In school-teacher training, the subject boundaries seemed sharp and progression of knowledge often went from the abstract to the concrete.

The kindergarten student teachers are often initially invited to ask questions and knowledge was related to work with children or to work in kindergartens. In this training, it looked as if college teachers needed to legitimate the presentation of theory by relating it to professional use. In school-teacher training, general theory or knowledge is often presented first. Students are then invited to take part in dialogues or encouraged to discuss the theme with a fellow student. Also, theory or knowledge is related to work with pupils, but the presentation of theory is not legitimized by explicitly linking it to professional work.

The following is a more concrete example drawn from the teaching of religious knowledge. In both colleges, I observed teaching about the theme 'death'. In school-teacher training, death was taught as a religious theme. When I observed, the college teacher gave a lecture on death related to ethics. The students then were invited to discuss abortion and euthanasia. When I observed teaching about death in kindergarten-teacher training, religious knowledge was integrated with Norwegian.

Consequently the college teacher also had more time for this theme. The teacher started by introducing children's books about death. The students worked with three or four different books in groups, analysing texts and pictures. Then the students were invited to talk about their own first meeting with death and sorrow. The students' own reactions to these events were compared with children's reactions. Finally, the teacher gave a lecture on how death has been described historically in children's literature.

As we can see, the theme 'death' in kindergarten-teacher training was related to practice and to persons (the students' own experience with bereavement). The progression of knowledge went from the concrete (books and the students' experiences with death) to the abstract (how death has been described historically in children's literature). The teacher–student authority relationship was personal throughout the discussion.

In school-teacher training the theme 'death' was taught in an academic way. The level of abstraction was rather high as the connection to the theory of ethics and religious knowledge dominated. The teacher–student authority relationship was hierarchical or positional. When I interviewed college teachers, I wanted to control my observations as to transformation or decomposing of knowledge and the differences I had observed as to teaching about death. I thus asked college teachers of religion the following question: Death is a theme which is taught both in kindergarten and school-teacher training. Can you please tell me how you teach this theme?

The college teachers of school teachers told me that this was not a theme which they spent much time on (as I had also observed). The tradition in this training is not to stress this. Death was talked about as a religious theme. One of the teachers really complained about the curricula which he saw as a miniature of the theoretical study of theology. He wanted to work to change the curricula and he had now started to teach about death and sorrow.

If we want to explain these different methods of teaching about death, we can look at the curricula of primary schools. Here we can see the priority given to teaching children religious knowledge. School-teacher training is preparation for this work. In kindergarten-teacher training, you want to prepare teachers to manage difficult situations like a death among children or their parents, or a divorce, which is a far more dominating problem both in schools and kindergartens.

To see whether my observation was representative, I asked the following question to the college teachers: 'When you think of your own education, is it your experience that you draw upon all of the different components of your education as a college teacher, or are there components of your own education which you use more?' (This was an indirect question. I wanted information about decomposing or transformation of the teachers' own subjects from university).

Twelve out of fifteen teachers of primary-school teacher training answered that they could use parts of their education. A teacher of religious knowledge said, for example, that the Testament was the Testament at the university as well as at this college. With exception of the pedagogues of kindergarten-teacher training, who felt they could use most of their education at this college, the rest of the college teachers had to reorganize their knowledge and to think in new ways. They had to decompose their theoretical knowledge from the university. Kindergarten-teacher training is strictly directed to work with children. Besides, you partly integrate subjects.

Conclusion: Models of two Professional Cultures

To sum up the chapter, let us look at parts of two professional cultures which influence student socialization, that is, at the dominating norms for professional work which are transferred to new members in a direct or indirect way.

My observations suggest that kindergarten teacher training has an invisible pedagogy and an integration code of knowledge. In the introduction, I mentioned the caring relationship between students and children as well as between students and college teachers. This can mean that there is weak framing, where personal relationships and everyday knowledge is included in classroom interaction as well as in kindergartens. In the example of different teaching of religious knowledge, we can observe the integration code in this training in different ways. The insulation between subjects is blurred and the structures of knowledge run from deep structure to the surface. We can also observe that knowledge about death is related to the students' personal experience with bereavement (common-sense knowledge).

Kindergarten-teacher training has a more indirect way of control than primary school-teacher training. This we can observe in the way the college marks good or bad pedagogical practice by mentioning examples of good pedagogical practice. This is an implicit manner of transmission of knowledge. When we look at how the student teachers are supervised, the college teachers interview students during practice and they do not control supervision or observe the students' teaching. The students' leadership days remind me of children's free activities in kindergartens. The students often have to search for information and leadership in a personalized act. In short, learning at this college of education looks to be a more tacit and invisible act than in primary-school teacher training.

In primary-school teacher education I observed a visible pedagogy and a collection code of organizing educational knowledge. Here there is a 'distance' between students and pupils as well as between college teacher and students. The method of control is direct when the college introduces the students to what is good or bad pedagogical practice. The selection of supervisors is strict, the college teachers observe students' skills when they teach, and supervision can be controlled. In the example of teaching religious knowledge, death is taught in a theoretical and academic way. While college teachers of the kindergarten teachers often have to decompose their own knowledge from university, the college teachers of school-teacher training more often can directly transfer their own knowledge. In the interview with the college teacher about the students' leadership days in kindergartens, we can see how he made knowledge of education into uncommon sense knowledge, to a language of sciences and a form of reflectiveness. According to Bernstein, the language of the interview of this college teacher indicates a positional control which is the norm for a collection code, while the language of the college teacher of kindergarten-teacher training indicates the personal form of control which is characteristic of an integration code.

The study can explain why there will be collaboration problems between kindergarten teachers, educated at an institution mediating an integration code, and primary-school teachers, educated at an institution mediating a collection code.

This study supports Basil Bernstein's theory about the organization of educational knowledge. Further research is needed to test this theory more profoundly, but educational knowledge is probably a major regulator of the structures of experiences as to professional socialization.

References

BERNSTEIN, B. (1977) *Towards a Theory of Educational Transmissions: Class, Codes and Control*, Vol. 3, London, Routledge and Kegan Paul.

BERNSTEIN, B. (1990) *The Structuring of Pedagogic Discourse, Class, Codes and Control*, Vol. 4, London, Routledge and Kegan Paul.

HAUG, P. (1991) *Institusjon, tradisjon og profesjon*, Sluttrapport frå vurdeing av 'Forsøk med pedagogisk tilbud til 6-åringar', Møreforsking, Høgskolen i Volda.

KJØRHOLT, A.T. (1990) *Pedagogisk tilbud til 4-7 åringer i et al: internasjonalt perspektiv* (rapp. nr. 18) Trondheim, Senter for barneforskning.

KORSVOLD, T. (1990) *Synliggjøring av barnehagens innhold*, Trondheim, Norsk senter for barneforskning.

NODDINGS, N. (1984) *Caring: A Feminine Approach to Ethics and Moral Education*, Berkeley, CA,

RIKSAASEN, R. (1988) *Men leger er også mennesker*, En intervjuundersøkelse om påkjenninger i legeyrket, Universitetet i Trondheim.

Chapter 14

Learning to Teach: Some Theoretical Propositions

Ora Kwo

Abstract

This chapter relates to research on teachers' interactive thinking and teacher development.[1] Because the ways in which novices develop into experts are inadequately understood, it is important to focus on how student teachers learn to teach. The research reported in this chapter investigated the instructional behaviour and information processing of student teachers during the interactive phase of teaching. The subjects were student teachers majoring in English language teaching in the full-time PC.Ed programme of the University of Hong Kong. Two sets of data were collected weekly over their teaching-practice period. Each subject was first video-recorded in the classroom and then audio-recorded during interview with a stimulated recall procedure. Profiles of basic statistics and qualitative analysis were established for all individuals. Matrices were then set up to describe major patterns and trends. By relating the findings to the current literature, the chapter concludes with some theoretical propositions about learning to teach.

Learning to Teach: Some Theoretical Propositions

To address issues concerning quality in education, an important goal in research is to increase understanding of the processes of teaching. Clark and Peterson (1986) pointed out that teachers' thoughts constitute a large part of the psychological context of teaching, within which curriculum is interpreted and acted upon through teaching and learning. It has in the past been widely assumed that teachers can be programmed to implement desirable curricula effectively. Such approaches in training have often met failure, which has sometimes been blamed on teacher resistance. A narrow focus on teaching behaviour has been inadequate to inform practice. More needs to be known about the ways in which teachers' thoughts are embedded in practice. Parallel to studies of teacher thinking is the pursuit of theories on teacher development. This chapter reports on a study on student teachers' development during teaching practice. It focuses particularly on the relationship between instructional behaviour and information processing, and results are discussed in relation to existing literature. The chapter concludes with some theoretical propositions.

215

Teachers' Thinking

A model of teachers' interactive decision-making was described by Peterson and Clark (1978). Their reports of the cognitive processes of twelve teachers showed that teachers followed the lesson without having to consider alternatives, as they found student behaviour within tolerance. Teachers reported considering altern-ative strategies in only 20 per cent to 30 per cent of the cases across the three days of instruction. This model highlighted the flow of teacher thought starting at a specific point when student behaviour is judged to be no longer within acceptable tolerance limits. It was assumed that when alternative teaching strategies are avail-able, the teacher decides to behave differently to bring student behaviour back within the limits of tolerance.

Joyce (1978–9) proposed a theory of information processing in teaching. He observed that thought patterns of the teachers under investigation were closely aligned to the recitation style of teaching. To keep the classroom running in a relatively orderly fashion, teachers did not normally reflect on alternatives which would considerably change the direction of instruction. Even if they did, the alternatives selected were better characterized as fine-tuning of their original plans rather than major changes in the lesson.

Regarding the cognitive process in arriving at a decision for action, Sutcliffe and Whitfield (1979) reported that the proportion of immediate to reflective decisions was greater for the inexperienced teachers, while experienced teachers far more frequently converted potential immediate decisions into reflective ones. They also stressed (p. 31) that 'the variety of options used in comparable classroom situations by the inexperienced teachers precludes their rational consideration of choice without a necessary reflection time'. Experience tends to influence teachers' reflection time in making decisions.

The findings challenge a common view that teachers' consideration of alter-natives is characteristic of teachers' decision-making. Decision-making could be more appropriately conceptualized in terms of rule-governed behaviour. It is hypothetical that most of teachers' thinking and behaviour rests on routines and automated reactions. Shavelson and Stern (1981) proposed an alternative model that was based on the work of Joyce (1978–9), Peterson and Clark (1978), and Shavelson (1976), on the assumption that teachers' interactive teaching may be characterized as carrying out well-established routines. They argued that routines minimize conscious decision-making during interactive teaching, and therefore that 'activity flow' is maintained. They also argued that routines reduce the information-processing load on the teacher by making the timing and sequencing of activities and students' behaviour predictable within an activity flow.

Although the Shavelson and Stern's model (1981) incorporates the idea of 'routine' as an important concept to explain teachers' decision-making, it still assumes that the only antecedent for the teacher's interactive decision is observa-tion of student 'cues', which are potential stimuli as verbal or non-verbal behav-iour from students. The nature of antecedents was revealed in other studies.

Marland (1977) found that the teacher's judgment that students' behaviour was not within tolerance was not the only antecedent of the teacher's reported interactive decisions. In fact, only 44 per cent of teachers' interactive decisions were noted to be responses to student cues. The majority of teachers' reported interactive decisions occurred in response to other antecedents. In his study of a single teacher, Wodlinger (1980) found that 51 per cent of the teacher's reported interactive decisions had antecedents that originated in the teacher or the environment rather than in the student. Similarly, Fogarty, Wang and Creek (1983) found that student cues were not the only type of antecedent, although they were the majority (64 per cent) of teachers' interactive decisions.

Research on teacher thinking has for some time followed the model of teaching as decision-making. The associated frameworks of conceptualization (Peterson and Clark, 1978; Shavelson and Stern, 1981) help to guide studies deductively, but delimit the extent of observation. The question is whether decision-making as a process comprises a complete and accurate picture of the nature of interactive thoughts. It appears that important teaching action, both mentally and physically, takes place apart from acts of decision-making. The focus of research has only recently departed from decision to a variety of ways to represent the processes of teachers' interactive thinking (see e.g., Mitchell and Marland, 1989). The validity of alternative models has yet to be assessed. Clark and Peterson (1986, p. 278) stress the need for more descriptive studies on how teachers make interactive decisions, in order to form a basis for revision of existing models of teachers' interactive decision-making.

Teacher Development

Research on effective, expert teachers has revealed the complexity involved in information processing, and has contributed to theories about the development of pedagogical expertise. Based on Fuller's model (1969) and comparative studies of the cognitions underlying novice and expert teaching, Berliner (1988) inferred a five-stage model of teacher development with a focus on the cognition underlying teachers' classroom behaviours. The stages are as follows:

1 **Stage 1 — Novice**: At this stage, a teacher is labelling and learning each element of a classroom task in the process of acquiring a set of context-free rules. Classroom-teaching performance is rational and relatively inflexible, and requires purposeful concentration.

2 **Stage 2 — Advanced beginner**: Many second- and third-year teachers reach this stage, where episodic knowledge is acquired and similarities across contexts are recognized. The teacher develops strategic knowledge, an understanding of when to ignore or break rules. Prior classroom experiences and the contexts of problems begin to guide the teacher's behaviour.

3 **Stage 3 — Competent**: The teacher is now able to make conscious choices about actions, set priorities, and make plans. From prior experience, the teacher knows what is and is not important. In addition, the teacher knows the nature of timing and targeting errors. However, performance is not yet fluid or flexible.

4 **Stage 4 — Proficient**: Fifth-year teachers may reach this stage, when intuition and know-how begin to guide performance and a holistic recognition of similarities among contexts is acquired. The teacher can now pick up information from the classroom without conscious effort, and can predict events with some precision.

5 **Stage 5 — Expert**: Not all teachers reach this stage which is characterized

by an intuitive grasp of situations and a non-analytic, non-deliberate sense of appropriate behaviour. Teaching performance is now fluid and seemingly effortless, as the teacher no longer consciously chooses the focus of attention. At this stage, standardized, automated routines are operated to handle instruction and management.

According to Kagan (1992), the stages of this model differ from each other in some fundamental ways, concerning how a teacher monitors classroom events, the degree of conscious effort involved in classroom performance, the degree to which performance is guided by personal experience and the teacher's focus. Developmental trends include the moves towards an unconscious recognition of common patterns, and towards fluid, flexible automated routines, as the teacher can predict events accurately, and as student work and academic tasks ultimately become the major organizing framework of instruction.

Inferring from her review of forty studies of pre-service and beginning teachers, Kagan (1992) yielded consistent themes that partially confirmed and elaborated both Fuller's and Berliner's model. Despite the inconsistency in the studies in terms of a novice's biography, the nature of the particular pre-service programme, and the school/classroom context in which teaching occurred, the behavioural and conceptual development of novice and beginning teachers can be described in five components:

- An increase in metacognition: Novices become more aware of what they know and believe about pupils and classrooms and how their knowledge and beliefs are changing.
- The acquisition of knowledge about pupils: Idealized and inaccurate images of pupils are reconstructed. Knowledge of pupils is used to modify, adapt, and reconstruct the novice's image of self as teacher.
- A shift in attention: As the image of self as teacher is resolved, a novice's attention shifts from self to the design of instruction to pupil learning.
- The development of standard procedures: Novices develop standardized routines that integrate instruction and management and grow increasingly automated.
- Growth in problem-solving skills: Thinking associated with classroom problem-solving grows more differentiated, multidimensional, and context-specific. Eventually, novices are able to determine which aspects of problem-solving repertoires can be generalized across contexts.

Kagan's new model suggests that the novice's initial inward focus constitutes necessary and valuable behaviour, and that the novice cannot progress until the initial self-image is adapted and reconstructed. This contrasts to the implication of Fuller and Bown (1975) that the novice's initial focus on self is a weakness that is best shortened. In essence, the new model inserts a schema theory into the model of Fuller and Bown (1975). Also, it suggests that effective routines integrate class management and instruction. The acquisition of procedural routines, with the resolution of the image of self as teacher, allows the beginning teacher's focus to turn outward to pupils and their learning performance. Finally, the new model confirms Fuller's and Berliner's observations about the inappropriateness of contemporary pre-service teacher-education programmes in their expectation of student teachers' sophistication of performance.

Despite the systematic nature of Kagan's review and the emergence of a theory in teacher development, certain issues remain controversial. Grossman's (1992) major argument against stage theories concerns the implication that earlier stages lead to later stages. She provided counter-evidence and pointed out that having developed classroom routines that work, teachers will not necessarily begin to question those routines. Furthermore, to challenge Berliner's suggestion that 'there may be too little in the minds of preservice teachers about what actions might be realistic, relevant, appropriate, moral, and so forth' (Berliner, 1988, pp. 63–4), Grossman (1992) presented findings to demonstrate that pre-service teachers are capable of reflecting on ethical and instructional issues.

Another dimension of Grossman's critique about stage theories concerns the effect of teacher training on teacher development. Studies were cited to indicate that a training course could influence pre-service teachers' beliefs and knowledge about teaching, even when theoretical issues were addressed before classroom routines had been established. While teacher education was perceived as preparing teachers to challenge current practices and to work for change, arguably discussions of teacher education should be informed as much by normative concerns as by empirical findings.

Kagan's intention (1992) was to go through the learning-to-teach literature to examine whether a coherent and consistent picture of the natural course of teachers' professional development could emerge. Because of the small sample sizes, diverse contexts, and heterogeneous methodology of the studies, the literature might lead to such an idiosyncratic view of teachers that generalization became difficult (Carter, 1990; Richardson, 1990; Kagan, 1992). The grounded method of literature analysis led to the described model, which represented a natural course of advancement of theories in social sciences, as depicted by an integrative perspective (Biddle and Anderson, 1986). A proposed theory does not have to represent ultimate 'truth', but represents the best explanation for those events so far observed. With an integrative perspective, it is healthy to note the contextual variations and alternative observations as emphasized by Grossman (1992). Opposing views essentially reveal the complexity of the phenomena in the process of theoretical maturation.

Research Problem and Questions

In the long-term, research on teachers' interactive thinking and teacher development may be promising to guide experimentation and suggest possible revision of existing models. Meanwhile, the debates signify the need for more studies on basic descriptions of existing phenomena, before the model can be strengthened with convincing hypotheses. As the ways in which novices develop into experts are inadequately understood, it is especially important to strengthen investigation of how student teachers learn to teach during the period of teaching practice.

In studies of effective teachers' schemata in information processing, a recurring question is what makes effective teachers — is it their amount of experience or their level of intelligence? It is important to interpret thinking in the context of teaching for a better understanding of both. As there are limitations to self-reports of teachers from stimulated recall interviews, verbal reports ought not to be the only source of information for understanding how teachers think. Teachers' overt classroom behaviour should also be noted. In order to validate perceptions and explore the relationship between teaching and thinking, data of both the observable and inner acts of teaching should be studied in parallel to each other.

With a belief that descriptive studies should be fundamental before research can confront theoretical generalization, the study reported here focused on the description of student teachers' instructional behaviour and information processing during teaching practice. Specific research questions for the study were:

- How do student teachers develop in their instructional behaviour?
- How do student teachers develop in their information processing?
- How does student teachers' instructional behaviour relate to their information processing?

Parallel to each question were the further questions:

- Are there variations across time?
- Are there individual differences?

'Instructional behaviour' refers to communications in the classroom during a lesson, including teacher talk and student talk as defined by the Teacher Innovator System (TIS), as well as non-verbal behaviours noted qualitatively by the researcher.

'Information processing' refers to the thoughts reported by teachers in the stimulated recall interviews which describe mental activities during teaching. The 'relationship between instructional behaviour and information processing' is inferred from the two sets of descriptions of instructional behaviour and information processing.

Design and Procedures

The subjects were nine student teachers in the full-time pre-service teacher-education programme at the University of Hong Kong, majoring in English language teaching under the direct supervision of the researcher. During the seven-week period of teaching practice, one sample of behaviour was taken weekly from all nine subjects in order to plot their patterns of learning to teach. Two sets of data were collected. Each subject was first video-recorded in the classroom, and then audio-recorded soon after each lesson at a stimulated recall interview which was conducted with the aid of the video-tape. This procedure generated sixty-three video-tapes and sixty-three audio-tapes from nine subjects over the seven weeks of teaching practice.

An inductive approach was applied to data analysis. Both quantitative and qualitative perspectives were taken to describe the student teachers' patterns of learning to teach. Video-recorded data of instructional behaviour were coded according to the Teacher Innovator System (TIS), which originated in Columbia

Figure 14.1: Formulae for TIS indices

$$\text{TTALK} = \frac{\text{Teacher Talk}}{\text{Total Communications}} = \frac{\text{TS1..19} + \text{TQ1..19}}{\text{TS1..19} + \text{TQ1..19} + \text{SS1..19} + \text{SQ1..19}}$$

$$\text{WC} = \frac{\text{Time for Whole Class Teaching}}{\text{Total Class Time}}$$

$$\text{TIS9} = \frac{\text{Information Communications}}{\text{Total Communications}} = \frac{\text{TS9} + \text{TQ9} + \text{SS9} + \text{SQ9}}{\text{TS1..19} + \text{TQ1..19} + \text{SS1..19} + \text{SQ1..19}}$$

$$\text{STR} = \frac{\text{Structuring Communications}}{\text{Total Communications}} = \frac{\text{TS1..8} + \text{TQ1..8} + \text{SS1..8} + \text{SQ1..8}}{\text{TS1..19} + \text{TQ1..19} + \text{SS1..19} + \text{SQ1..19}}$$

$$\text{FB} = \frac{\text{Feedback Communications}}{\text{Total Communications}} = \frac{\text{TS14..18} + \text{TQ14..18} + \text{SS14..18} + \text{SQ14..18}}{\text{TS1..19} + \text{TQ1..19} + \text{SS1..19} + \text{SQ1..19}}$$

Teachers' College and has been validated in over fifty studies of teaching as sensitive to wide variations of teaching patterns (Joyce, 1980). The three major dimensions are 'structuring', 'information' and 'feedback communications'. Within these dimensions are nineteen categories, as shown in Appendix 1. Codes are constructed in terms of teacher question (TQ), teacher statement (TS), student question (SQ), and student statement (SS), plus the appropriate category number. Thus TQ9 refers to a teacher question at the factual level of communication. A TS-14 refers to a statement of approval by the teacher. A SS-6 is a negotiating statement by a student over the planning of procedures. The instrument for classifying student teachers' information-processing thoughts was generated from the reported data in the stimulated recall protocols, known as the Stimulated Recall Analysis System (SRAS), as included in Appendix 2.

To reveal variations across time and among subjects, ratios between sets of categories were utilized. These ratios were referred to as indices. For basic analyses of instructional behaviour, five indices were developed from the Teacher Innovator System (TIS), the formulae of which are presented in Figure 14.1.

For basic analyses of information processing, the indices included the eight major categories and the five most frequent subcategories of the Stimulated Recall Analysis System (SRAS). These indices are distinguished from the SRAS categories, as defined in the formulae of Figure 14.2.

Frequency counts permitted description of basic statistics, which revealed patterns in the variables, and guided qualitative analysis. Profiles were then established for all individuals. Relationships between the variables were further explored through qualitative reviews of individual profiles. Hypotheses were grounded from initial analysis, which guided further analysis. As mentioned earlier, this chapter focuses on the report of the relationship between instructional behaviour and information processing of student teachers.

Figure 14.2: Formulae for SRAS indices

$$\text{Total Thoughts} = T + A + Ch + S + R + E + P + Mcs$$

$$TT = \frac{\text{Text (T)}}{\text{Total Thoughts}} \qquad\qquad PP2 = \frac{P2}{\text{Total Thoughts}}$$

$$AA = \frac{\text{Anticipation (A)}}{\text{Total Thoughts}} \qquad\qquad PP11 = \frac{P11}{\text{Total Thoughts}}$$

$$CCh = \frac{\text{Checking Student Progress (Ch)}}{\text{Total Thoughts}} \qquad\qquad RR7 = \frac{R7}{\text{Total Thoughts}}$$

$$SS = \frac{\text{Silence (S)}}{\text{Total Thoughts}} \qquad\qquad PP6 = \frac{P6}{\text{Total Thoughts}}$$

$$RR = \frac{\text{Receiving Student Response (R)}}{\text{Total Thoughts}} \qquad\qquad PP7 = \frac{P7}{\text{Total Thoughts}}$$

$$EE = \frac{\text{Explanation (E)}}{\text{Total Thoughts}}$$

$$PP = \frac{\text{Planning-Evaluation-Decision (P)}}{\text{Total Thoughts}}$$

$$MMCS = \frac{\text{Miscellaneous (Mcs)}}{\text{Total Thoughts}}$$

Correlation between Instructional Behaviour and Information Processing

Between instructional behaviour and information processing, to find out which showed more variations among the subjects than the other, rank difference of the TIS and the SRAS categories across time were calculated. Using a similarity matrix, the rank-order correlations of the TIS categories by teacher (Table 14.1) indicated consistency among the subjects. Within the broad pattern of recitation, they displayed mild variations in the frequencies of TIS categories. A parallel procedure in obtaining a similarity matrix was followed, when the rank-order correlations of the SRAS categories by teacher were computed (Table 14.2). Ranging from 0.29 to 0.97, with 0.63 as the median, the coefficients revealed obvious variations among individuals. Within the general concern for the flow of the lesson, certain student teachers followed rather similar patterns which contrasted acutely with some others' patterns.

Table 14.1:   *Similarity matrix of teachers in terms of TIS categories*

Teacher	One	Two	Three	Four	Five	Six	Seven	Eight	Nine
One	1.00								
Two	.93	1.00							
Three	.96	.91	1.00						
Four	.97	.97	.96	1.00					
Five	.94	.86	.94	.90	1.00				
Six	.95	.94	.92	.96	.89	1.00			
Seven	.92	.86	.90	.91	.92	.89	1.00		
Eight	.95	.95	.94	.98	.89	.97	.91	1.00	
Nine	.94	.90	.94	.96	.91	.96	.93	.96	1.00

Table 14.2:   *Similarity matrix of teachers in terms of SRAS categories*

Teacher	One	Two	Three	Four	Five	Six	Seven	Eight	Nine
One	1.00								
Two	.43	1.00							
Three	.71	.68	1.00						
Four	.45	.69	.92	1.00					
Five	.79	.52	.81	.64	1.00				
Six	.76	.66	.97	.84	.92	1.00			
Seven	.74	.57	.61	.40	.86	.77	1.00		
Eight	.72	.53	.93	.77	.92	.96	.72	1.00	
Nine	.79	.29	.79	.60	.81	.80	.52	.89	1.00

The two sets of similarity matrices demonstrated that the student teachers varied more in information processing than in instructional behaviour. By correlating the two sets of similarity indices in terms of the frequency rank order of the TIS and the SRAS categories, the Pearson product-moment correlation coefficient was calculated, with a finding of 0.23. This analysis further suggested that if student teachers were very similar in instructional behaviour in terms of the rank order of their TIS categories, it did not follow that they were also similar in terms of their information processing in terms of the rank order of their SRAS categories. This weak correlation presented the difficulty in relating the subjects' profiles of instructional behaviour to those of information processing. Despite the difficulty, active interpretation has nevertheless been made to set up the nine profiles describing the relationship between instructional behaviour and information processing, as already presented in this chapter.

A one-way analysis of variance was performed for the TIS indices using the subject as the independent variable. Only the index WC showed significant difference among the subjects (Table 14.3). In parallel, a one-way analysis of variance was performed for the SRAS indices in a similar procedure of analysis. By contrast, seven indices showed significant difference among the subjects (Table 14.4). With the Scheffe procedure at 0.05 level, teachers One, Six and Eight were identified as the extreme cases. Teacher One had significantly more thoughts than others on anticipating student response (A), whereas teacher Six showed prominent concerns for the next teaching step in the light of student progress (P6). In the case of teacher Eight, her dominant P2 thoughts were accompanied by minimal concerns in A and P6, hence displaying a teacher-centred style. A review of

Table 14.3: Oneway ANOVA on TIS indices among teachers

Index	F-ratio	F max
TTALK	1.36	85.69**
WC	2.23*	7.90
TIS9	1.25	18.55
STR	0.73	62.03**
FE	1.78	6.29

Notes: n = 63 (df = 8,54)
    * P < 0.05
    ** P < 0.01

Table 14.4: Oneway ANOVA on SRAS indices among teachers

Index	F-ratio	F-max	Result of Scheffe Procedure (at 0.05 level of significance)
TT	3.32**	5.55	
AA	3.91**	19.48	Tchr 1 > Tchr 8; Tchr 1 > Tchr 9
CCH	0.53	4.49	
SS	0.84	11.86*	
RR	1.50	18.12*	
EE	2.54*	40.41**	
PP	1.60	9.70	
MMCS	1.50	32.00**	
PP2	4.31**	16.55*	Tchr 8 > Tchr 4; Tchr 8 > Tchr 6
PP11	2.14*	5.56	
RR7	2.73*	98.65**	
PP6	4.72**	25.88**	Tchr 6 > Tchr 2; Tchr 6 > Tchr 8
PP7	2.19*	7.56	

Notes: n = 63 (df = 8,54)
    * P < 0.05
    ** P < 0.01

the one-way ANOVA on the TIS and the SRAS indices affirmed the tendency of the student teachers to differ more in information processing than in instructional behaviour.

Emergence of Major Patterns and Trends

Further analysis is based on methods adopted by Marton and Saljo (1984), when they were in a parallel track exploring the relationships between process and outcome of learning under investigation. By reviewing statistical data for individuals, matrices were tentatively set up to explore major patterns and trends. Following review of the observations made in the nine profiles, these matrices were revised to expose essential details for the major patterns and trends.

Major Patterns

Table 14.5 presents the major patterns in the relationship between instructional behaviour and information processing. Among the TIS indices, WC and FB were

Table 14.5: *Major patterns in the relationship between instructional behaviour and information processing*

| | Information Processing | | | | |
| | Flow of the lesson | | Focus of interaction | | |
	Plan implementation	Spontaneity	Teachers	Students	Problems
Instructional behaviour					
Teacher-centred	T1,T2, T7,T8	T9	T1,T2 T7,T8	T9	T1,T2, T7,T8,T9
Student-centred		T3,T4 T5,T6		T3,T4, T5,T6	T3,T4 T5,T6

found to be strong ones to identify the two major variations in instructional behaviour: teacher-centred and student-centred. The teacher-centred style was characterized by abundance of time for whole-class teaching and a mechanical search for the expected answer at feedback without address of students' unexpected responses, whereas the reverse features were found in a student-centred style. Concerning information processing, two parameters were identified from a qualitative review of the nine profiles: the flow of the lesson and the focus of interaction. For the flow of the lesson, the correlations among the SRAS indices suggested a useful dichotomy of plan-implementation and spontaneity. The focus of interaction refers to the teacher's reported concern while interacting with students in whole-class teaching. Three dimensions emerged from the general distribution of the SRAS categories: teacher, students, and problems. In a further review of the nine profiles, attempts were made to relate major patterns of instructional behaviour to information processing for each individual according to this matrix. Of course, cases of unclear patterns and exceptional features arose, but they were not dominant and could therefore be put aside in the search of major patterns.

Despite the limitations, the matrix succeeded in highlighting the major variations. Five student teachers were noted to be more teacher-centred in their management of class time. They appeared to regard teaching as implementation of the lesson plan with expected pacing and coverage. The communications appeared rushed, and they rarely tackled a wrong response from a student with further interactions. They were generally more concerned about their own intention and performance than the actual responses and progress of the students. Invariably they were conscious of problems arising in the lesson and critical of their own performance. However, they also shared a sense of uncertainty and did not arrive at major decisions to tackle the problems. Interestingly, teacher Nine was an exceptional case for a teacher-centred style. A quarter of her class time was occupied in whole-class teaching, which was the highest of all subjects. She obviously demonstrated reluctance to let students engage in independent work and committed in this sense to a teacher-centred approach. Unlike other teacher-centred subjects, however, she was actively concerned with the spontaneity of the lesson. Although she was also frustrated with uncertainty when encountering problems, her attention given to checking students' progress was higher than average and she demonstrated definite interest in students' performance during her interactions. The contrastive student-centred style of instructional behaviour was

Table 14.6: Major trends in the relationship between instructional behaviour and information processing

| | Information Processing | | | | |
	Flow of the lesson		Focus of interaction		
Instructional-behaviour stability	Pl^1	$Pl{\rightarrow}Sp^2$	Sp^3	$+Sts^4$	Problems[5]
High (T1,T8)	T8	T1			
Medium (T2,T3		T2,T4			
T4,T6,T7,T9)		T6,T7	T3	T6,T7	
Low (T5)			T5		T5

Notes:
1. Consistent concerns for plan-implementation
2. A switch of emphasis from plan-implementation to spontaneity of the lesson
3. Consistent concerns for spontaneity of the lesson
4. Heightened sensitivity to students' performance
5. Consistent awareness of problems

typically portrayed by the other four subjects. They were also commonly aware of problems. They differed from the previous group in the greater abundance of time for students' independent work and their more dominant concern for students' performance. This was revealed in their attention to students' responses and their more interactive discussions with students. Initial but unsatisfactory response was acknowledged and followed by further prompts. Corrective feedback communications were often suspended until students' different responses were solicited and considered. Rather than being merely concerned with their intention as planned, they seemed to conduct the lessons with regard to the spontaneity in the flow of interaction.

Major Trends

Table 14.6 presents the major trends in the relationship between instructional behaviour and information processing. The matrix was formulated from an identification of stability level in instructional behaviour and the adoption of the flow of the lesson and focus of interaction as parameters in information processing. The identification of stability level was based on a review of the range of index scores of the subjects over the seven-week period of teaching practice. Teachers One and Eight had high stability, whereas teacher Five had low stability. The others were noted as of medium stability. Concerning the parameters in information processing, flow of the lesson and focus of interaction were summarized as the major trends.

For the flow of the lesson, three patterns emerged: consistent adherence to the plan, a switch of emphasis from the plan to the spontaneity of the lesson, and consistent concern about spontaneity. It was apparent from the extremes of teachers Eight and Five that the subjects with less stability in instructional behaviour were more alert about spontaneity of the lesson.

It was much more difficult to identify trends on the focus of interaction, as the concerns of the subjects were insufficiently stable. Instead the concerns were rather dependent on the nature of the lesson. If any trends could be captured at all, they could be identified as a heightened sensitivity to student performance and a consistent awareness of problems. Only teachers Six and Seven showed a heightened sensitivity to student performance. Teacher Five again as the extreme case of low stability in instructional behaviour was unique in her consistent awareness of problems.

The matrices derived from the statistical reviews provided a useful framework to accommodate essential details for the identification of major trends. While all teachers were concerned about problems, some managed to depart from the plan and their own performance to be involved in the spontaneity of the lesson and their students' performance. Although the analysis focused on the description rather than the evaluation, by considering the subjects' different emphases, it was possible to interpret the student teachers' patterns of learning over time. This will be discussed in terms of their weaknesses and improvement.

Student Teachers' Weakness and Improvement

While adhering to the plan, the student teachers were critical of their own performance, and were puzzled about why problems arose and how they should be tackled. As the lesson plan had prepared the ground in teaching, the student teachers were likely to assume that adherence to it would keep them from having to make many new decisions. Therefore the initial concern with the plan was natural. Yet unexpected problems were inevitable, and commonly the student teachers shared a sense of helplessness without any major decision or any action which would change the course of the lesson. The fact that they were under assessment as well as supervision should also be considered. While all were striving for the best performance, it was possible that the weaker ones tended to avoid risk-taking, thus maintaining a higher level of stability in their instructional behaviour. However, that possible attitude did not take them away from problems, as they still reported having problems. Problems perceived were usually related to the implementation of the plan and students' involvement rather than spontaneity of the lesson and students' achievement. Little regard was given to optimizing student learning. A natural question to ask concerned how to facilitate individuals to develop themselves during the teaching practice with a consideration of problems.

In order to improve, most student teachers attempted to experiment with different strategies to reduce teacher dominance. On these occasions, they adhered to their plans less strictly, and gave more attention to students' performance. Most of the thoughts about problems and reactions to them were noted in the middle or later part of teaching practice, which was parallel to the pattern of their experimental attempts for more student-centred activities. It was evident that their awareness of problems intensified with a teaching mode which was deviant from routines. The switch of emphasis from plan to spontaneity was a sign of improvement for most student teachers, although the extremes were the consistent adherence to either plan or spontaneity. Interestingly these trends were associated neatly with the levels of stability in instructional behaviour. The student teachers with less stability in instructional behaviour tended to be more consistent in concerns about spontaneity of the lesson and awareness of students' performance and the arising problems. It could be deduced that those student teachers who showed more variations in instructional behaviour and more attention to the spontaneity of the lesson could have learnt more over the teaching practice than the ones maintaining stability in the adherence to the plan.

The identification of student teachers' weaknesses and signs of improvement has presented a basis for depiction of their process of learning to teach. It is alarming to note the possibility that the novelty of the research setting had added incentive to their performance, and that the situation could be worse in an ordinary setting. In addition to a chronic sense of helplessness when encountering problems, the student teachers might even be less sensitive to notice problems without the aid of video-tapes.

Towards some Theoretical Propositions on Student Teachers' Pattern of Learning to Teach

This study confirms that interactive information processing generally follows the pattern of recitation with very few decisions that significantly alter the course of activities that have been established (Peterson, Marx and Clark, 1978; McNair, 1978–9; Clark and Peterson, 1986). Prepackaged textbook materials share dominance with recitation teaching in most observed lessons which do not require extensive information processing during the interactive moves. Of all the forty-three categories in the SRAS captured inductively, only P2, P6 and P7 concern reasoning and decisions. Such findings add weight to the argument against the conception of teacher-as-decision-maker (Yinger, 1986; Mitchell and Marland, 1989), and further demonstrate that teachers' interactive thinking covers more areas than is depicted by the conventional decision-making model.

Student teachers' constant concerns for justification of their teaching steps and tendency to adhere to the planned routines correspond to Berliner's (1988) depiction of novices in his model of teacher development: classroom-teaching performance is rational, and relatively inflexible, and requires purposeful concentration. This study provides strong evidence to confirm the nature of teaching at this stage. In essence, the student teachers are trying to develop, follow, understand and use rules of teaching. Teaching practice was a time in which student teachers felt insecure, and the risks involved in leaving planned routines could be considerable in terms of time loss and pupil misbehaviour. Therefore adherence to plans could reduce the load on interactive thinking and keep them away from having to make many new decisions.

On the other hand, despite adherence to the lesson plan, the process in learning to teach included attempts to move from routines to novelty, when the student teachers attempted to reduce the time on whole-class teaching and become more task-oriented. On these occasions, they paid more attention to learners' performance, with increased thoughts about problems and reactions to them. However, they did not come up with new decisions about how to tackle problems. Without achieving their intentions, many resumed a teacher-centred style with less time for students' independent work and less variety of student tasks. Although data in this study do not clearly address other stages of Berliner's model, they do match two components of Kagan's (1992) account about the behavioural and conceptual development of novice teachers: an increase in metacognition of teaching, and a shift in attention from self to the design of instruction to pupil learning. This study responds positively to theories about stages of teacher development by presenting characteristic problems of student teachers as novices. In view of Berliner's (1988) expert stage of teacher development concerning automated routines, this study provides a close-up picture of the novice stage about the various patterns in the implementation of plans, when they may be in the process of exploring and establishing workable routines.

It could be speculated that student teachers might have to go through a stage of inactive interactive thinking when they are simply concerned with the planned routines, before a stage of active interactive thinking, when they are increasingly aware of learner problems, and struggle to respond to the perceived problems. Progressing further, they might reach a stage of 'improvisation' (Borko and Livingston, 1989, p. 483) when thinking is characterized by 'rapid judgment' and 'transformation' (Doyle, 1977), and problems are tackled promptly and decisively because of their well-developed knowledge schemata, or because there are fewer problems with effective teaching. In fact, the two schemata identified by Marland and Osborne (1990) in avoidance and reaction to problems can illustrate this sophisticated stage, whereas this study provides data about the possible background in the course of such a pattern of development.

Parallel to these speculations, the notion of problem-solving can be better understood. If effective teachers' automated routines could release their conscious processing for specialized purposes and problem-solving that could not be routinized (Doyle, 1979), student teachers' passive reactions to problems and lack of new decisions during interactive teaching as reported in this study could well reflect a stage that planning had not yet led to establishment of workable routines. The recurrence of problems of similar nature could be a consequence to the adherence to plans which were not connected to past experiences. This study sheds light on studies on teachers' planning, and carries significant implications for teacher education, namely that experience by itself would not lead to improvement of practice, and student teachers need assistance to reflect upon the experience.

While further studies would need to clarify whether certain traits in teaching practice are superior to others and consistently identifiable among some teachers across contexts, this study addresses the literature along the Fuller-Berliner-Kagan line of research aiming to identify student teachers' process of learning. With the student teachers' general tendency in adherence to plans and their lack of active information processing with regards to unexpected situations, individual differences and variation across time, however, show possible levels of their attainment. Some theoretical propositions are grounded from the findings, namely that during teaching practice, the dominant recitation mode of teaching establishes the problem-frame — the boundaries within which interactive thinking is operated. Over time, there is an increase in metacognition of teaching along attempts to experiment with student-centred activities. Of course, it is possible that at least part of this increase can be attributed to the research setting itself. The use of video-tapes may have achieved more than the stimulation of recall of interactive thoughts to the extent that student teachers might become more sensitive in perceiving problems. However, it seems also natural that metacognition increases under difficult circumstances in learning to teach. It would be hard to argue that this aspect of learning is singularly influenced by the stimulated recall interviews, though it may be a methodological question for further investigation.

Another aspect of learning to teach concerns a shift in attention from self to the design of instruction and pupil learning, and from plan-implementation to spontaneity of interaction. Attention to learning involvement dominates over that to learning achievement. Despite an increasing awareness of problems, the student teachers generally do not come up with strong decisions which change the direction of a lesson.

While these propositions reflect some possible trend in a conventional setting of teaching practice, they do not suggest that the trend applies to all individuals, nor do they imply any linearity of the nature of the trend. Nevertheless, they contribute to the ongoing dynamic of constructing a theory about student teachers' process of learning to teach.

Note

1. This study greatly benefited from inputs of Bruce Joyce, Beverley Showers, and Ference Marton during their visits to the University of Hong Kong, and over subsequent correspondence.

References

BERLINER, D.C. (1988) 'Implications of studies on expertise in pedagogy for teacher education and evaluation', *New directions for teacher assessment* (Proceedings of the 1988 ETS Invitational Conference, 39–68), Princeton, NJ, Educational Testing Service.

BIDDLE, B.J. and ANDERSON, D.S. (1986) 'Theory, methods, knowledge, and research on teaching', in WITTROCK, M. (Ed) *Handbook of Research on Teaching*, New York, Macmillan.

BORKO, H. and LIVINGSTON, C. (1989) 'Cognition and improvisation: Differences in Mathematics instruction by expert and novice teachers', *Amercian Educational Research Journal*, 25, 4, pp. 473–98.

CARTER, K. (1990) 'Teachers' knowledge and learning to teach', in HOUSTON, W.R. (Ed) *Handbook of Research on Teacher Education*, New York, Macmillan.

CLARK, C.M. and PETERSON, P.L. (1986) 'Teacher's Thought Processes', in WITTROCK, M. (Ed) *Handbook of Research on Teaching*, New York, Macmillan.

DOYLE, W. (1977) 'Learning the classroom environment: An ecological analysis', *Journal of Teacher Education*, 28, pp. 51–5.

DOYLE, W. (1979) 'Making managerial decisions in classrooms', in DUKE D.L. (Ed) *Classroom Management* (Yearbook of the National Society for the Study of Education), Chicago, University of Chicago Press.

FOGARTY, J.L., WANG, M.C. and CREEK, R. (1983) 'A descriptive study of experienced and novice teachers' interactive instructional thoughts and actions', *Journal of Educational Research*, 77, 1, pp. 22–32.

FULLER, F.F. (1969) 'Concerns of teachers: A developmental conceptualisation', *American Educational Research Journal*, 6, pp. 207–26.

FULLER, F.F. and BOWN, O.H. (1975) 'Becoming a teacher', in RYAN, K. (Ed) *Teacher Education* (74th Yearbook of the National Society for the Study of Education), Chicago, University of Chicago Press, Pt. II, pp. 25–52.

GROSSMAN, P.L. (1992) 'Why models matter: An alternate view on professional growth in teaching', *Review of Educational Research*, 62, 2, pp. 171–79.

JOYCE, B. (1978–9) 'Toward a theory of information processing in teaching', *Educational Research Quarterly*, 3, 4, pp. 66–77.

JOYCE, B. (1980) *Teacher Innovator System: Observer's Manual*, Eugene, Oregon, Booksend Laboratories.

KAGAN, D.M. (1992) 'Professional growth among preservice and beginning teachers', *Review of Educational Research*, 62, 2, pp. 129–69.

MARLAND, P.W. (1977) 'A study of teachers' interactive thoughts', Unpublished doctoral dissertation, University of Alberta.

MARLAND, P. and OSBORNE, B. (1990) 'Classroom theory, thinking, and action', *Teaching and Teacher Education*, 6, 1, pp. 93–109.

MARTON, F. and SALJO, R. (1984) 'Approaches to learning', in MARTON, F., HOUNSELL, D. and ENTWISTLE, N.J. (Eds) *The Experience of Learning*, Edinburgh, Scottish Academic Press.

McNAIR, K. (1978–9) 'Capturing inflight decisions', *Educational Research Quarterly*, 3, 4, pp. 26–42.

MITCHELL, J. and MARLAND, P. (1989) 'Research on teacher thinking: The next phase', *Teaching and Teacher Education*, 5, 2, pp. 115–28.

PETERSON, P. and CLARK, C. (1978) 'Teachers reports of their cognitive processes while teaching', *American Educational Research Journal*, 15, 4, pp. 555–65.

PETERSON, P., MARX, R. and CLARK, C. (1978) 'Teacher planning, teacher behavior, and student achievement', *American Educational Research Journal*, 15, 3, pp. 417–32.

RICHARDSON, V. (1990) 'Significant and worthwhile change in teaching practice', *Educational Researcher*, 19, 7, pp. 10–18.

SHAVELSON, R.J. (1976) 'Teachers' decision making', in GAGE, N.L. (Ed) *The Psychology of Teaching Methods* (Yearbook of the National Society for the Study of Education), Chicago, University of Chicago Press.

SHAVELSON, R.J. and STERN, P. (1981) 'Research on teachers' pedagogical thoughts, judgments, decisions, and behavior', *Review of Educational Research*, 51, pp. 455–98.

SUTCLIFFE, J. and WHITFIELD, R. (1979) 'Classroom-based teaching decisions', in EGGLESTON, J. (Ed) *Teacher Decision-Making in the Classroom: A Collection of Papers*, London, Routledge and Kegan Paul.

WODLINGER, M.G. (1980) 'A study of teacher interactive decision making', Unpublished doctoral dissertation, University of Alberta, Canada.

YINGER, R.J. (1986) 'Examining thought in action: A theoretical and methodological critique of research on interactive teaching', *Teaching and Teacher Education*, 2, 3, pp. 263–82.

Chapter 15

Teachers' Professional Development as a Process of Conceptual Change

Shoshana Keiny

Abstract

This chapter is about School Based Curriculum Development (SBCD) as a means of enhancing teachers' professional development, where professional development is viewed as a continuous process of conceptual change. According to our hypothetical model, conceptual change is a process that occurs in two interdependent contexts; a social-theoretical locus which is a reflective group where teachers can voice their different ideas of teaching and through a dialectical process of reflection, reconstruct their pedagogical knowledge, and a practical context, or the teachers' actual practice, where he or she can experiment their new ideas and reflect on (or in) their experience (Gorodetsky, Hoz and Keiny, 1993). There is no necessary sequence between the two loci, they are mutually dependent and the interplay between them is instrumental in the development of a new conception, namely in teachers' professional development. The study draws its ideas from a 'comprehensive community school' project, where teachers involved in SBCD, construct curricula units which use the local industrial plants as well as community institutions, as learning resources. The teachers' conceptual change was traced through their changed concept of 'school=community relationship', and their new understanding of learning as an interaction with reality.

Introduction

School innovations aim to improve education by introducing radical changes in students' learning. School projects which are Action Research (AR) oriented, in particular, involve the teachers themselves in the process of change, by taking responsibility to develop their own knowledge as a basis for action. The underlying assumption of AR projects is that a transfer of responsibility or ownership from top to bottom, or from management to the teacher entails a conceptual change in the teacher's role, a paradigmatic shift from the idea of teaching as a theory applying activity, towards teaching as a theory generating one (Ebbutt and Elliott, 1985; Elliott, 1992; Stenhouse, 1975). Teachers as theory generators are more apt to cultivate the capacity of their students as learners, in the sense of taking more responsibility for their learning as a knowledge-construction process.

Table 15.1: Teachers' statements at the beginning of the project, conveying their 'Instrumental Role Conception'

	Instrumental	**Developmental**
General orientation	technical rationality	reflection in action
Epistemological aspect	objectivism: knowledge is an external entity	constructivism: knowledge is a subjective construction
Task ownership	teacher	student
Assumptions about the learner	passive, has to be controlled i.e., external motivation	active, initiative internal motivation
Teacher's responsibility	instruct, transfer knowledge	promote the students' learning process by providing opportunities for direct interaction with knowledge
Goals and learning	achievements as products of learning	learning as a process

Thus AR school projects can be viewed as sites for experimenting with new ideas, reflecting upon them and reconstructing new theories of teaching (Schön, 1983), which, in turn, bring about improved, more meaningful learning in the classroom.

Teachers' conceptual change, which is the focus of this chapter, has become an umbrella for various ideas, depending upon what is meant by conception. 'Conception' has been used interchangeably with ideology, philosophy, 'personal knowledge', world view, basic principles, belief, perspective opinion, and subjective theory. All these terms convey a notion of 'comprehensive organized body of knowledge' a person holds at a given moment. In our working definition of the term, conception is not regarded merely as a cognitive term; it consists of schemes of concepts, developed as a result of actions and interactions with the world, yet it is anchored in the person's beliefs and basic assumptions, and in a way unknown to us, also influences action (Gorodetsky, Hoz and Keiny, 1993)

Teachers' conception of their role is part of this general structure. It reflects their beliefs or basic assumptions about the pupil (learning and teaching); about society or the goals of education; and about knowledge.

In my previous work I referred to the teachers' role in terms of two alternative conceptions: instrumental and developmental (see Table 15.1), showing that participation in AR school projects brought about a transfer from instrumental to developmental orientation (Keiny, 1985; Keiny and Dreyfus 1989; Keiny, 1993).

My aim in this chapter is to show that this change of role conception reflects a higher-order change (Bateson,1978). Bateson defines learning on level II as second-order change, which implies understanding the way a working system functions and restructuring previous knowledge; third-order change he refers to as 'metalearning' or to learning about learning (ibid.). We interpret this high-order learning in terms of high awareness of the teacher to the process, and his endeavour to promote his or her students' higher levels of learning as well as their ownership and responsibility for learning.

Moreover, by reflecting on their practice and scrutinizing the effect of their teaching, teachers shift their focus from merely observing relationships or feedback mechanisms within the classroom (or the school as institution), 'to include in their observations themselves as observers too'. In von Foerster's words they shift from first-order cybernetics to second-order cybernetics (Von Foerster, 1992). This self-reflective enterprise forces them to recognize themselves as observers and accept responsibility for their observations, explanations and interpretation, to the way they build their systems of knowing and acting epistemologically (ibid.). This process of teachers' conceptual change will be illustrated by using an AR school project as a case-study.

The comprehensive community school (CCS) project, was aimed to involve teachers in the construction of their own model of a community school; a school that extends its boundaries to include its natural and sociocultural environment as learning resources. Such an endeavour required a new way of thinking about school, with respect to subject matter, teaching strategies and the learning process. It also entailed a change in the conventional conception of school–community relationship.

The idea was thrown to the principal of the comprehensive school in Yerucham, a small developing town in the Negev, and was accepted with enthusiasm by him and a team of leading teachers. They managed to interest people from the community in the CCS project, and involve them in collaborative teams, such as an industrial team; chemical team; community team, etc. Each team, facilitated by a trained graduate, indulged in school-based curriculum development (SBCD) activity, with the aim of constructing curriculum units that link the learning process with the different institutions of the community.

The team facilitators (who were supervised by me) were sensitive to the unique setting of the teams, adapting themselves to the diverse modes and pace of learning rather than clinging to a rigid model of teamwork This approach was justified retrospectively, for it left space for the participants' initiative to contribute as partners.

Thus three different strategies of learning came into play:

1   learning through a direct encounter of the participants with the industries or institutions as working places;
2   learning from their students' experiences in these working places; and
3   peer-learning in the teams through a 'dialectical process of reflection' (Keiny and Dreyfus, 1989).

All team meetings were recorded, transcribed and content-analysed.

In the next part of the chapter I shall focus on the industrial team, which consisted of teachers of mathematics, technology, sociology, management and secretarial studies, as well as community representatives from three different industrial plants (see Figure 15.1). By following the team's learning process, a clearer insight of the teachers' conceptual change could be gained.

The Industrial Teamwork

At the beginning of the project the teacher participants of the team revealed an instrumental orientation, in terms of their implicit epistemologies and their

Figure 15.1: The comprehensive community-school plan

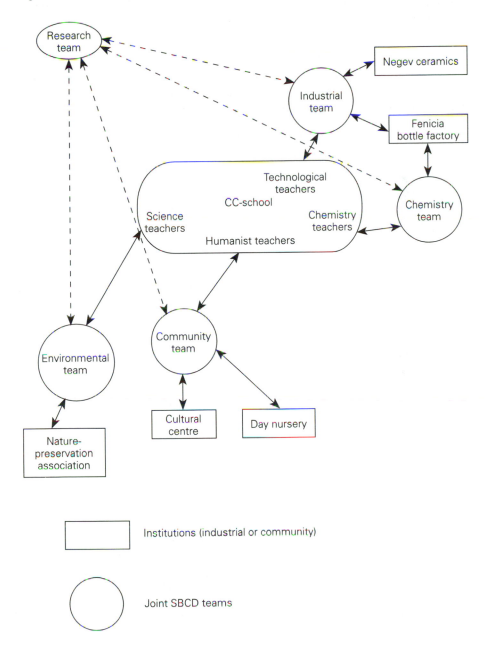

Table 15.2: Teachers' statements, conveying their 'Instrumental Role Perception'

Epistemological aspect: Objectivism: knowledge as an external entity	• . . . My teaching is highly structured . . . that is how I manage to transmit a lot of material. I call this effective teaching. • My main interest is to teach the formal curriculum so as to equip them with the knowledge required in the finals . . . • I find myself explaining everything in great detail, so that they will understand what they see . . .
Assumptions about the learner	• They are so passive and dependent, I could not give them any sort of independent assignment . . . • Our task is to spoon-feed them . . . • . . . You have to make the connections for them . . . you cannot depend on their initiative to make decisions.
Teacher's responsibility	• . . . to transmit a lot of material in each learning period. • Where there is no control there is no learning . . .

assumptions about teaching and learning. This is conveyed by their statements in Table 15.2. Their conception of the relationship between school and community, adhered to an 'apprentice model'. According to this model the factory or public institution, is used as practicum for their students, as a place to practise what they have learned at school:

> Industry is best fitted to students of the mechanical stream . . . there they can learn how to be a mechanic, or a plumber . . .
> In the factory they have the best opportunity to apply all that they have learned at school.

An alternative model of the school of the relationship between school and community was implicitly introduced by some industry participants, as the 'system model'. Though not stated explicitly, it emerged from the meaning they associated with the concept of school in the context of community relationship. According to this model an industrial plant is a dynamic system, consisting of many interacting subsystems. As a system it also maintains an input–output relation with its environment or, in other words, is receptive and responsive to the changing needs and demands of the community. Careful not to give advice in curricular terms (an area beyond their proficiency) the industry participants claimed that a factory could serve as an example of a system, where 'system thinking' could be taught, and as such it would prepare the students for their future working life.

The idea of the factory as a system was vividly demonstrated by one of the industry representatives in the team, who was employed in the Negev ceramics factory. Holding a ceramic tile in his hand, explained:

> When you look at the product, it is just a ceramic tile, very simple . . . but just think how many processes are involved in its production: the basic materials; their transportation; weighing, grinding and modelling; checking or quality-controlling at each stage; then wrapping, parceling and storing; and finally marketing, shipping . . .

The confrontation between these two models became one of the major tasks of the facilitator. This is illustrated by the following excerpt, which was taken from a group discussion that followed a visit to the Negev ceramics factory.

Facilitator:	I suggest two opening questions: a) What can we learn from a plant such as Negev ceramics, a highly automated factory with very few workers? b) How could we use it as a learning medium?
Teacher:	I was struck by the scarcity of employed people. My prior image of a factory was of a row of workers along the production line.
Industry representative:	Today every worker is a sophisticated worker. As for the second question, I do not see the plant as a learning place, I see its task to trigger learning, mainly by visits (such as the one we have just experienced), for the student to see the process, to ask questions, and later decide what they would like to further investigate. Learning should be carried out by teachers within the school. And in any case, I wouldn't expose kids to conflicts among the workers . . .
Teacher of mechanics:	I can see the advantage of exposing the students, especially those from the lower streams, to the diversity and change of the factory. I would suggest to attach them each to a specific worker who would act as his guide.
Industry representative:	This arrangement would give a very limited experience to the student, of rather limited skills, instead of broadening his horizon.
Facilitator:	I see here two different orientations; the one, advocated by the teachers assumes that learning is achieved by following an expert and learning from him. The second one which is here introduced by our community partners, focuses on the plant, or the end product, as a whole. The assumption here is that this would trigger curiosity, and motivate the learner to follow his or her own inclination, or specific interest, and engage in a personal project type of learning. This second orientation naturally calls for a revolutionary change in the school curriculum, in this case in the technological studies, while the first orientation requires smaller changes and can be more easily applied.

Teacher:	I am for a compromise, a strategy that integrates the two together. Exposing the students to the end product, or the factory first, and then they could be guided each, by a specific worker.
Industry representative:	No worker has the time or the skills to teach kids, and judging from my experience, it takes a long time, even for engineers in the plant to learn from practice.
Teacher of electricity:	. . . It is the repetition of activities that I find so important for the mastering of skills. The theoretical principles I can teach in the classroom.
Community representative:	As I see it there would be less 'blue-collar' experts in the future, most tasks being replaced by machines. An employee would have to acquire very different skills. He would have to be capable of technical thinking rather than technical skills.
Teacher:	What do you mean by technical thinking?
Teacher of mathematics:	I can give you an example from my perspective, to cope with the final exams today, my students require more than *technical knowledge*. They are expected to be able to tackle problems they have never seen before. In other words, I have to teach them *mathematical thinking* . . . Now this discussion gave me an idea of how to approach statistics, a subject I have always wanted to introduce, especially for the biology students. I would start by taking the whole class to the factory and follow the process of quality control, the way samples of bottles are taken out to be checked for different parameters of quality. In this way I could introduce them to statistical thinking, to the basic principals in statistics as a most relevant subject . . . actualize the otherwise theoretical subject, by connecting it to concrete events.

This excerpt illustrates the teachers' discourse about school and about learning from industry, in other words about the relations between school and community. The ideas exchanged are not merely their espoused theories but rather their theories-in-use, extracted from their own teaching experience. The facilitator's major role in the process, is to trigger the dialectical process of reflection in the group. In this case, by shifting the discussion from the concrete to the abstract level, and emphasizing the tension between the two different models of school–community relationship, he promotes the teachers' reflection.

Reflection was categorized by various researchers in the literature into higher and lower levels (such as Carr and Kemmis (1986), van Manen (1977), Handal and Lauvas (1987), and others). The idea of levels of reflection implies that technical reflection at the level of action must somehow be transcended so that teachers can move to critical reflection (Zeichner, 1993).

Stimulating critical reflection, we see as essential for the process of teachers' conceptual change, and this is triggered by the facilitator by translating their familiar, routine way of teaching into a theoretical model or orientation, and confronting it with an alternative learning orientation. In this way he invited the participants to examine the rationale of their model, and to the extent it fits their ideas of teaching. In other words, he brings them to reflect critically upon their previous ways of teaching.

Naturally, some teachers were slower to grasp the differences between the two models, while others (i.e., the mathematics teacher) were quicker to articulate them into general criteria, such as 'technical knowledge' versus 'technical thinking'. Gradually they came to view the factory as a system, focusing their attention on the relationships between the subsystems, or different departments, as well as between the factory and its outside environment. This change of view is conveyed in the following excerpt, taken from the industrial-group meeting later in the year:

> Before the project I associated industry with technology only. Today I realize how much more complex it all is. This small bottle factory, for instance, is a dynamic system, the different departments are its sub-systems . . .

> Students can analyse the product; what it is made of, how it is marketed, etc., and through this type of learning they gain a wider outlook . . . This could help them in the future . . . facilitate their adjustment to their future jobs, to their future milieu . . .

> . . . It is always in progress here . . . what today is considered a technological achievement, in a few years time would be practically archaic, out of date.

These statements reflect a shift from positivistic to cybernetic orientation. Accordingly a factory is seen as a system consisting of various interacting sub-systems, a system adapted to the changing conditions and unforeseen problems. Yet in von Foerster's terms they indicate only a first-order cybernetics. A shift towards second-order cybernetics was provoked by moving to the second strategy of learning in the team, namely learning through their students' interaction with the community. Curious to try out some of these ideas, some teachers actually organized class visits to the factories. The facilitator, encouraging this step made sure that their students' feedback was illicited, recorded, transcribed and fed back into the group.

The following excerpt was taken from the students' discourse related to their experiences in the factory:

> It all looked so simple when presented in the classroom, but in actual life there are so many different aspects . . . It's to do with relationships, with people's different frameworks . . .

Table 15.3: *Teachers' statements at the end of the second year of the project, reflecting a more developmental approach*

Epistemological aspect Constructivism	• ... Teachers cannot be the centre of knowledge ... • Students can learn by a direct encounter with their environment; for example, their community or the factory.
Assumptions about the learner	• Students can observe, explain, evaluate and judge things ... here they can really learn by themselves ... • They discovered that they could use their initiative, that they can influence things ... It gave them a lot more confidence in their learning ...
Teacher's responsibility	• This is an opportunity to do really interesting things ... to indulge in small-group learning, where they learn by doing, through their own experience ... • ... Let's give the students the freedom to choose, to decide on their own course of learning.

I am not merely dependent on the quota alloted for me by the boss, it is very much up to me, the way I meet their requests, I respond to people ... It's sort of mutual. I sign my name, which for me is an indication that they trust my word.

Reflecting on this feedback, the teachers realized that their students were more capable to take responsibility, than they had assumed. Actually, through their students' highly interactive and complex ideas of their working place, they began to revise their prior assumptions about learning, and plan different ways of teaching:

We plan to open the curricular unit with a visit to the industrial plant. Only then, judging mainly by their reaction, by their level of involvement, we can know where their interests lie.

Let's not decide for them. Let them decide for themselves, otherwise we regress back to our conventional framework, where teachers make decisions for the students to submit.

In terms of their role conception, the participants of the industrial team have shifted to the developmental approach, as is conveyed by their statements on the second year of the project (see Table 15.3).

There remained an open question, to what extent this change of role conception actually implies a change of personal conception? To what extent does it imply a shift from first to second-order cybernetics? This brings us back to the process of conceptual change.

Conceptual Change: A Hypothetical Model

We hypothesized that conceptual change is a process that occurs in two interdependent contexts; a social and a practical one. The social context is a group where teachers can exchange their different ideas of teaching and engage in a dialectical process of reflection in the group. This is analogous to our collaborative teams' work.

The second context is the teacher's actual practice, where he or she can experiment with the new ideas and reflect on (or in) the experience. In other words, include in their observations themselves as observers too, and reconstruct his or her pedagogical knowledge. There is no necessary sequence between the two loci, the practical context can precede the social one, they are mutually dependent (Gorodetsky, Hoz and Keiny, 1993).

To test our hypothesis, we decided to focus on the locus of practice, where the new curriculum was implemented. We chose to follow up Batya, one of the participating teachers, who plunged into an experimental implementation of her new ideas in her own classroom.

Batya, a teacher for home economics, was a member of the community team. In her search for community collaborators, she formed a partnership with the staff of a modernly equipped day nursery, with the aim of developing a curriculum unit, titled: 'Child development'. Her target population was fourteen girls who consisted the lowest stream of the 11th grade, and were known as low motivated and underachieving students. Her practical team, consisted of the nursing staff, the regional coordinator and the pedagogical inspector of the nursery.

In one of the community group meetings, she describes how she negotiated the terms of this partnership:

> It was important for me to lay down some basic rules; for instance, the girls are here to learn and not as working aids . . . I expected the staff to be patient, and ready to answer their questions . . .

Practising the New Curriculum

After many weeks of careful planning, aided by her group facilitator she eventually began implementing her newly developed curriculum unit. Opening with a whole-class visit to the day nursery, with no formal introduction, she said to the girls: 'Look around, ask the nurses, try to figure the reasons . . .'

She allowed sufficient time for them to observe, wonder about, pick up a toddler, or play with a child, etc. Once assembled (in a small open-planned room at the centre of the nursery) again in a most informal way she encouraged the students to voice their impressions: 'What did you see? What do you want to know?'

Later she admitted her strong fears less the whole effort would fall flat, her serious doubts whether their interest, their curiosity could be aroused. To her relief they responded positively, and by the end of the session they managed to produce between them a list of some ten different topics, that stemmed from their own point of reference. For example:

- What happens if a child is hurt, who is to blame, what is to be done?
- Why do babies cry?
- What is required in order to become a nurse?
- Children's games in the playground.
- A lot of patience is needed for handling small kids.

(Note that the last two examples were not formulated as questions. Batya decided to stick to the original phrasing, instead of trying to teach the correct way. By doing so, she felt she gave more legitimacy to their ownership). Discussing the subject with her facilitator, she voiced her thoughts:

> The idea of shift of focus from 'home economics' to 'child development', formed the basis for my partnership with the day nursery. Yet only after we had started working over the curriculum, I realized the huge range of subjects that were reflected in the nursery. The girls had actually to cope with problems of education, dietary, management, psychology . . .

Having succeeded to arouse their genuine interest, their urge to know more, she was now faced with the methodological aspect. How to tackle their questions? How to proceed with the investigation?

This is where she switched to the social context, to the reflective process in the community team, presenting her 'practical problem' as a topic for discussion and exchange of ideas between all participants. Together they constructed a new 'inductive' teaching method, whereby students are guided to collect diverse kinds of data, and in this way extend their knowledge on the topic.

Back to her classroom, Batya encouraged them to collect more knowledge, each on her subject. For example, on the topic of why babies cry; to observe babies' behaviour, interview the staff, their own mothers, etc. Later, the girls initiated themselves an appointment with the local paediatrician, with the school psychologist for more expert knowledge. Theoretical knowledge was carefully introduced, first in the classroom, where different terms that had been accumulated, were looked up in the dictionaries (for example child development, accident, patience, etc.). Secondly, a visit to the local library was organized, where more material was found for their different subjects. This became also a major opportunity to expose them to books, and to teach them how to use a library.

Relating her teaching experience in the team, she said:

> . . . Their files gradually filled with field notes of their own experience (experiential knowledge) of their observations (observational knowledge) recorded interviews, etc. Spreading it all out on the desks, they realized what was missing: photos of the kids that would display their gestures, their behaviour, as well as the general setting of the nursery. The very next day they came with a pocket camera and took snapshots.

The general enthusiasm in the classroom managed to draw in even the most reluctant girls, and within a month they were all working on their personal projects. At this stage she handed out personal files, bearing the school badge. Apart from the practical aspect of storing all the collected material, there was another dimension to the file; it indicated a transfer of responsibility from teacher to student, with respect to knowledge. It implied that the pool of knowledge was the learner's creation; she was responsible to examine it, critique, and improve it or add the missing parts.

There remained one last essential problem which Batya, again, brought over to the community team: how to end the investigation, how to formulate an answer to the original question. This raised the whole issue of evaluation and in particular how to evaluate learning by inquiry, a topic that was elaborated in the team, at great length.

In her classroom, Batya chose to emphasize the diverse nature of the data collected, and to confront, for example, between theories about the welfare of babies, and between the nurses' or mothers' practical knowledge; or between observational data and reflective, or interpretive explanations. Her implicit message was that there is not one simple, correct answer.

The group discussions, on the other hand, led towards establishing a framework for the written assignment, the contents, and most important, the concluding chapter which they had titled: 'What have I learned or, how can I evaluate my learning?' Thus the issue of evaluation was simultaneously dealt with in both loci, the social context of the community team and the practical context of the classroom.

The last excerpts, taken from the team's discourse, convey Batya's attempts to evaluate the process of learning in her classroom, the process she had initiated and was responsible for:

> I cannot tell you how encouraged I am today by the progress in my classroom, especially since I had such small expectations from my under-achieving girls. Today, they are actually able to work independently, each on her personal project . . .
> Now I understand our main goal rather in terms of enhancing the students towards becoming independent learners . . .
> When asked to evaluate the project; there is the product (pointing to the final assignment) and the process, namely the learning process resulting in this written work. But to me, the so-called marginal products of the process are no less important. For instance, my girls actually learned to use the library, I see this as a most significant 'product' . . . the implications of which are infinite . . .

Batya's experimental implementation of her planned curriculum unit illuminates a few important points that can help us understand the process of conceptual change. First and foremost, in order to turn the nursery into a learning medium, she formed a partnership with the nursing staff. They were rather 'apprentice'-oriented and inclined to see the girls as working aids more than as active learners. Batya learned to negotiate her terms and manoeuvre delicately between conflicting interests. Her intuitive idea of a curriculum unit that focused on child development, had to be practised and reflected upon, before its enormous potentiality was revealed. She herself admits her surprise at the wide range of subjects unfolded from the curriculum. Naturally this pilot experimental setting was accompanied by doubts as to the feasibility of such a curriculum, and fears less it would not attract her fourteen low-achieving girls, who could turn the whole endeavour into one big joke . . .

One of these challenges she could handle alone: for example, negotiating norms of intervention with her nursery partners. Others had to be practised first and reflected upon, with the assistance of the community team facilitator. For example, after the opening visit to the nursery, in which the facilitator acted as observer, they were able to carry out a 'reflective dialogue' and deliberate at length on all the details, before finally eliciting the girls' personal topics from the discussion. Issues of a more theoretical nature, such as inductive learning, or evaluation, she had to thrash in her peer group.

Batya, I believe, was not aware of such classification. Relying on her practical knowledge, she intuitively made her decision, seeming to 'know' which of the two loci was more appropriate for a particular problem.

In this respect Batya displayed second-order learning. Aware of the two different types of learning, in the two different loci, she was able to make a decision when and where to use each. Metalearning is reflected through her awareness of her students, her attempt to promote higher levels of learning, responsibility and ownership. Moreover, by taking responsibility to her own interpretation and explanations to the ways she builds her system of knowledge, she also acts as a second-order cybernetician.

Discussion

Teachers' conceptual change, I believe, occurs in two interactive contexts; in the teacher's actual practice and in a social context such as a reflective team. School projects that aim to achieve conceptual change, have to ensure a framework that provides the two necessary loci. This double setting was built in the comprehensive-community-school project. The collaborative teams as medium for deliberations for exchange of ideas and for the dialectical process of reflection in the group served as social locus, while the experimental implementation of the curricula units, where participants reflected on their action, acted as the locus of practice.

To trace the teachers' conceptual change, I chose to focus on the evolution of their idea of the relationship between school and community. The CCS project, by definition, was based on the cybernetic paradigm, whereby school is not merely seen as part of the community, but maintains a dynamic, interactive learning relationship with it. Though introduced from the outside, the CCS project was intentionally presented as an abstract, general idea, aimed to trigger the participants 'to construct their own model of community school', according to their needs and within the constraints of the system.

We assumed that their joint motivation and degree of involvement are the main prerequisites for the project to succeed. It was their initiative to invite the community people to share in the process, and their internal motivation to come, after a long working day, and to devote many hours of their free time to the project.

Yet the teachers were anchored in the positivistic paradigm, adhering to the conventional idea of school as a place where theoretical knowledge is acquired (see Table 15.2). The participating teachers were unaware of the conceptual gap that existed between the conventional and proposed new way. Neither were they conscious of the radical changes entailed, in their epistemology, basic assumptions about learning and teaching, and the relationship between school and community.

The introduction of the system model (which is a cybernetic model) by the community partners, and the confrontation between the two different models within the team, became the turning point in the process of their conceptual change. The interaction within the collaborative teams on the basis of developing an integrative curriculum unit, led to a complete dismissal of the classical split between theoretical and practical knowledge. Their discourse indicates that they do not regard school as a place for theoretical learning, and the community's industrial plants or day nurseries, as sites for practice. Moreover, learning was finally understood, by both teachers and students, as a complex process of construction of subjective knowledge (von Glasersfeld, 1989). Accordingly their idea of knowledge became multifaceted, and multidimensional conveying different representations of reality. Their encounter with the factories led also to the realization of the interrelations and interconnectedness of the different components in our reality, and thereby to the impact of global changes (such as the common market) on local factories as well as community institutions (including schools) as well as upon the individual's welfare.

Thus teachers who like Batya actually implemented their curricular ideas, became second-order cyberneticians, with respect to taking responsibility for their newly generated knowledge. The 'child development' curriculum clearly reflected Batya's observations, explanations and interpretations to her way of building her system of knowing and acting. It stemmed from her basic egalitarian beliefs in the right of her low-stream girls to learn, or the accessibility of knowledge. It also induced her behaviour, not merely as a teacher, but also as a member of a collaborative team. With respect to school community relationship, she saw it as her responsibility, her role as a teacher, to educate her students to become active, responsible citizens involved in their community's future welfare.

References

BATESON, G. (1978) 'Steps to an Ecology of Mind', London, Granada.

CARR, W. and KEMMIS, S. (1986) *Becoming Critical: Education, Knowledge & Action Research*, London, The Falmer Press.

EBBUTT, D. and ELLIOTT, J. (1985) 'Why school teachers do research?', in EBBUTT, D. and ELLIOTT, J. (Eds) *Issues in Teaching for Understanding*, Cambridge, Institute of Education.

ELLIOTT, J. (1992) *Action Research for Educational Change* (Developing Teachers & Teaching Series), Open University Press.

FOERSTER, H. VON (1992) 'Ethics and second order cybernetics', *Cybernetics & Human Knowing*, 1, 1, pp. 9–19.

GLASERSFELD, E. VON (1989) 'Cognition, construction of knowledge and teaching', *Syntheses*, 80, 1, pp. 121–40.

GORODETSKY, M., HOZ, R. and KEINY, S. (1993) 'The relationship of teachers' collective conception and school renewal', A paper presented in the International Conference on Science Education in Developing Countries: From Theory to Practice, Jerusalem.

HANDAL, G. and LAUVAS, P. (1987) *Promoting Reflective Teaching: Supervision in Action*, Milton Keynes, Open University Press.

KEINY, S. (1985) 'Action research in the school: A case study', *Cambridge Journal of Education*, 15, pp. 155–61.

KEINY, S. (1993) 'School-based curriculum development as a process of teachers' professional development', *Educational Action Research*, 1, 1, pp. 65–93.

KEINY, S. and DREYFUS, A. (1989) 'Teachers' self-reflection as a prerequisite to their professional development', *Journal of Education for Teaching*, 15, 1, pp. 53–63.

SCHÖN, D.A. (1983) *The Reflective Practitioner*, London, Temple Smith.

STENHOUSE, L. (1975) *An Introduction to Curriculum Research and Development*, London, Heinemann, pp. 142–65.

VAN MANEN, M. (1977) 'Linking ways of knowing with ways of being practical', *Curriculum Inquiry*, 6, pp. 205–28.

ZEICHNER, K.M. (1993) 'Research on teacher thinking and different views of reflective practice, in teaching and teacher education', A paper presented at the 6th International Conference of International Study Association on Teacher Thinking. Goteborg, Sweden.

Chapter 16

Making Sense of the Curriculum: Experienced Teachers as Curriculum Makers and Implementers

Tapio Kosunen

Abstract

The aim of this study is to understand the interpretations of experienced and less experienced primary-school teachers concerning the written curriculum and to ascertain how the intended curriculum is related to their instructional planning and teaching practices. Of special interest is how the curriculum makers, i.e., experienced teachers who had been members of planning teams developing the curriculum, interpret the written curriculum. The methods used to determine the views of primary-school teachers were questionnaires (n = 85), planning simulations, thinking-aloud techniques, journal writing and in-depth interviews (n = 6).

According to the results of this study, the curriculum makers had internalized the core idea of the curriculum innovation. They used student-oriented teaching methods more often than other teachers did, were more often development-oriented and, in addition, individualized and differentiated their instruction more often than their colleagues did. The curriculum makers stressed the importance of using the written curriculum as the basis for their instructional planning. They preferred long-term planning (whole school year and/or term) before they did any short-term planning (week, day) and they also preferred to integrate their teaching and foster theme-based teaching.

The curriculum makers' role as an alternative to isolated teachers is discussed. It is argued that the real potential in curriculum making and curriculum development lies in making good use of the practical knowledge of experienced teachers: their sophisticated understanding of practice, their broad knowledge of instructional and management routines and their reflectivity.

Teachers as Curriculum Makers

Curriculum improvement in terms of a school-based curriculum is one of the main educational issues currently under public discussion in Finland. Traditionally, the national curriculum in Finland has been very centralized, although since 1985 communities have received much more power to decide the ways in which the local curriculum will be developed and implemented. The present curriculum reform towards school-based curricula took place in autumn 1994. Until then a number of pilot schools continued working to produce their own solutions for curriculum development, which could later be utilized and further developed in schools all over the country. The fundamentals of the national-curriculum work as a loose general framework for decision-making in schools as they develop their own curricula. It has been emphasized as an important goal of the curriculum project that it is essential in terms of curriculum improvement to increase freedom of choice in schools, to strengthen the self-evaluation of schools and to support schools in finding and developing their own strengths and uniqueness. The importance of a supportive, collegial school culture for improving the curriculum is stressed.

During recent years the economy in Finland has been very weak, and there has been a drastic cut in the resources available for schools. At the same time the schools have received more economic, administrative and pedagogical independence. Consequently, they have obtained more power and greater possibilities than ever, but less resources to organize and improve the instruction given on the premises. Accordingly, most committed sceptics have been ready to announce that the school-based curriculum is doomed to end in fiasco.

Several Finnish studies, the most recent which was by Atjonen (1993), have shown that most teachers do not use the written, i.e., intended curriculum in the way the innovators, curriculum planners and legislators have anticipated. Teachers do not seem to think and act intentionally and consciously according to the goals and objectives written in the curriculum. In fact, most teachers say that they do not read or use the curriculum. Instead of the written curriculum, teachers in general and primary-school teachers in particular seem to lean on learning materials. The same message is found in international studies on teacher planning: the 'objectives first' model is not used in teacher planning (McCutcheon, 1980; May, 1986; Clark and Peterson, 1986; Brown, 1988; Borko *et al.*, 1990).

From the viewpoint of the teacher, the curriculum has at least two aspects. Firstly, it is seen as a course of study, a kind of book of instructions or framework according to which the authorities oblige the teachers to plan their instruction and, in addition, to locate themselves in 'the curricular system'. If they want to put the policy into practice, however, teachers possess a great deal of pedagogical freedom to interpret the goals and objectives and to choose the contents, materials and methods they use. Secondly and even more importantly, the teacher considers the curriculum not as a text but as a process, an educative experience (Jackson, 1992), life lived in classrooms and school, and 'something experienced in situations' (Connelly and Clandinin, 1988; Clandinin and Connelly, 1992).

When curriculum improvement is discussed, it has perhaps not often been stressed that the innovators and the teachers do not necessarily construe the school practice in the same way. Too often teachers are seen as mere agents fulfilling someone else's intentions and as transmitters of external knowledge (Clandinin, 1986). The teacher should be seen more clearly as an integral part of the curriculum constructed and enacted in the classroom. As Brown, and McIntyre, (1993, pp. 15–16) stated, the major constraint on the acceptance of innovations by teachers is their perceived impracticality. To have some changes perceived as practical, plans for innovation would have to take into account what is already being done well in the classrooms.

The role and importance of the teacher are essential in making changes and improving the school, even to the extent that when reformers try to do something for the public good, often with disappointing results, teachers are usually seen as the principal impediment. The idea that an educational innovation can be put into practice by presenting teachers with a new list of objectives has often been implicit in curriculum innovations. The curriculum has been seen as an instrument of school reform and teachers as mediators between the curriculum and the intended outcome. Accordingly, Clandinin and Connelly (1992) claim that a 'conduit' metaphor has shaped the world of curriculum and teachers. Using this metaphor, teachers have been placed at the receiving end of the conduit. Clandinin and Connelly, however, suggest that a more appropriate metaphor for describing the teachers' curriculum world would be 'teachers as curriculum makers' (Clandinin and Connelly, 1992, p. 372).

Consequently, Clandinin and Connelly (1992) stress the need to examine the curriculum from the point of view of the teacher:

> Teachers and students live out a curriculum; teachers do not transmit, implement or teach a curriculum and objectives; nor are they and their students carried forward in their work and studies by a curriculum of textbooks and content, instructional methodologies, and intentions. An account of teachers' and students' lives over time is the curriculum, although intentionality, objectives, and curriculum materials play a part in it. (Clandinin and Connelly 1992, p. 365)

Improving the curriculum and the school in a way that provides effective education requires patience and time. As Olson (1992) put it, new ideas are 'shifts in orientation, new sets of unclear meanings, whose implications take time to emerge. What these meanings are we must learn from teachers who can tell us what they understand the new ideas to be and what significance they attach to them. We need to see how the intentions of teachers are connected to problems they are trying to solve,' (Olson, 1992, p. 4). It is not necessarily easy to change current practice. As Stenhouse (1975, p. 25) stated, 'new teaching strategies are extremely difficult to learn and to set oneself to learn, especially when they cut across old habits and assumptions and invalidate hard-won skills.'

Is it, however, really possible to improve the curriculum in such a way that the teachers will be activated to process the objectives and contents of the curriculum? How can we make sure that innovation in the curriculum really leads to changes in the practice of teaching? According to Stenhouse (1975), there can be no curriculum development without teacher development. At the moment there is an urgent need in Finland to activate teachers to produce school-based curricula. Nevertheless, the administrative emphasis of the curriculum has evidently been too strong during the past years (Malinen, 1992). This has happened at the cost of the curriculum as a means for the teacher to improve his or her own teaching and his or her school. Simultaneously, when using the systemic planning model or the bureaucratic model (Olson, 1992), the school administration seems too often to have ignored the needs of the teachers.

Efforts are being made to bring curriculum improvement closer to the teachers and schools. Malinen (1993) pointed out the need to make the current rational (Tylerian) model of curriculum planning more complete by including into it practical thinking about the curriculum. Otherwise, the pilot schools in the current-curriculum improvement may be the only ones that receive some advantage from it. The rest of the schools may just copy the curricular solutions the pilot schools have made in their plans and then forget these plans and solutions without any further processing.

Practical Arguments in Teachers' Curricular Thinking and Action

What do the teachers really think about the intended curriculum? Has no change taken place in the meaning-making of teachers concerning the curriculum even though many teachers have taken part in planning and making the local, intended curriculum? How do teachers use the written curriculum in their instructional planning?

To answer these questions, we have to take into account the studies made on teacher thinking and action and especially teacher planning, intentions and routines (Shavelson and Stern, 1981; Clark and Peterson, 1986; Clark and Yinger, 1987; Borko *et al.*, 1990); the second-generation studies on teacher planning, in which emphasis is placed on studying planning in context (Clark and Dunn, 1991); and perspectives in the professional development of teachers. Calderhead (1992) lists five of these perspectives:

- socialization into professional culture;
- development of knowledge and skills;
- the moral dimension of teaching;
- the personal dimension of teaching; and
- the reflective dimension of teaching.

Studies made on the development of knowledge and skills of the teachers have shown that experienced teachers (experts) have a much more sophisticated understanding of their practice than less experienced teachers (novices) do. They have larger, better-integrated schemata: stores of facts, principles, and experiences to draw upon as they engage in planning, interactive teaching, and reflection (Livingston and Borko, 1989; Leinhardt and Greeno, 1986; Hammrich *et al.*, 1990). Because experts have well-developed and easily accessible schemata for aspects of teaching such as instructional activities, content and students, they are able to plan quickly and efficiently (Livingston and Borko, 1989).

Educational researchers have consistently found differences between the planning of experienced teachers (experts) and student teachers (novices). According to Borko *et al.* (1990), these differences lie in the planning process and in the nature of the plans. Experienced teachers' plans are more detailed than the plans of novices; they include more information about instructional strategies and activities and more instructional and management routines. Experienced teachers plan more quickly and efficiently than novices do. At the same time, they are more selective in their use of information in deliberations. In addition, experienced teachers pay more attention to long-term planning and less attention to Tyler's means-ends model. (Borko *et al.*, 1990, pp. 42–3).

Morine-Dershimer (1991) has defined four of the most influential current approaches to research on teacher thinking:

- the schema theory approach;
- the reflection-in-action approach;
- the pedagogical content knowledge approach; and
- the practical argument approach.

'Which suggests that teachers' perceptions of the instructional situation, their principles of practice, and their sense of desirable outcomes all contribute to their pedagogical decisions and actions.' Several researchers have shown an interest in the practical argumentation of teachers and in conceptualizing their practical knowledge. According to Johnston (1992), even though several terms are used for knowledge that guides practice, in every case this knowledge is built on personal and professional experience, is not readily articulated by the teacher and is used in complex ways during the process of planning for and executing teaching activities, as well as in making sense of previously made decisions (Johnston, 1992, pp. 124–5).

The arguments and definitions of practical knowledge (Elbaz, 1983), and practical theories (Handal and Lauvås, 1987) or personal practical theories (Cornett *et al.*, 1990) offer an interesting starting point for studying teachers' curriculum knowledge and curricular action. Several authors have stressed the importance of teachers' personal practical knowledge and idiosyncratic principles, beliefs and theories in the interpretation of the curriculum (Munby, 1983; Day, 1990; Hannay and Seller, 1990; Cronin-Jones, 1991; Thompson, 1992).

The aim of this study will be an attempt to determine and understand the curriculum knowledge of primary-school teachers and to determine how the curriculum knowledge and curricular action which these teachers possess is related to their personal interpretations, principles, beliefs and theories (Handal and Lauvås, 1987; Cornett *et al.*, 1990). However, in this chapter the focus will be narrower. The emphasis is on curriculum makers' (i.e., experienced teachers who have been members of planning teams developing the curriculum) instructional planning and the ways in which teachers make sense of, and interpret, the curriculum and then use it for planning their own instruction. An attempt is made to answer the following questions:

1 How do curriculum makers' ways of utilizing the written curriculum in their instructional planning differ from other teachers' ways of using it?
2 In which ways do curriculum makers' curricular thinking and, accordingly, their teaching practices differ from other teachers' teaching practices and ways of thinking?

Methods

The data were collected during the spring of 1993 (see Table 16.1). Subjects in this study were all the primary-school teachers in the town of Joensuu, Finland (n = 134), each of whom received a questionnaire. Three experienced in-service primary-school teachers (eight to fifteen years of teaching experience) and three less experienced in-service teachers (three to four years of teaching experience) were each interviewed three different times (semi-structured theme interviews). The interviews took about four to five hours per teacher. The results are reported in more detail elsewhere (Kosunen, 1994).

Table 16.1: Timetable for data collection

Method	Time	Focus
a) Preliminary interview (n = 4)	12/92	designing a long-term planning model for drawing comparisons
b) Questionnaire (n = 134)	03/93–04/93	
c) First interview (n = 6)	01/93	long-term planning
d) Second interview (n = 6) Thinking aloud	03/93–05/93	short-term planning
e) Journal writing until the third interview (n = 6)		
f) Third interview (n = 6) using journal notes	03/93–05/93	reflection on planning and teaching

The six interviewed teachers compared their own long-term planning strategy to a planning model which had been constructed in the course of the preliminary interviews. The thinking-aloud technique was used when the teachers were engaged in planning a one-week teaching period. Reflective journal writing (Yinger and Clark, 1981) was used to stimulate teachers to reflect on their teaching (Table 16.1).

The questionnaire was answered by eighty-five primary-school teachers (63 per cent of the sample). Of the respondents, forty-nine were women (58 per cent) and thirty-six were men (42 per cent); 25 per cent had less than three years of teaching experience and 50 per cent had fifteen years or more years of experience. Most of the questions were organized in the form of attitude scales (Likert scale).

Findings

Teachers' responses to the inquiry indicated that the written curriculum is not the most important factor affecting the work of a primary-school teacher. The primary-school teachers consider the most important factors affecting their work to be: teacher–pupil relationship ($\bar{x} = 4.82$); teacher personality ($\bar{x} = 4.53$); varying teaching methods ($\bar{x} = 4.45$); and teacher cooperation and colleagueship ($\bar{x} = 4.41$). The teachers reported that for them the written curriculum plays a more important role in their teaching than the learning materials do. The written curriculum ($\bar{x} = 3.74$) was ranked in sixth place after teaching aids ($\bar{x} = 3.78$). Primary-school teachers integrate knowledge of the above-mentioned into their practical knowledge. The four first factors are parallel to the findings of a nationwide study made in Finland by Kuusisto (1989). In addition, the teachers reported the written curriculum to be a more important factor in their professional practice than any of the teaching materials.

Primary-school teachers seem to engage in both long-term and short-term planning. The most important sequences in planning mentioned by these teachers were: weekly planning (35 per cent); term planning (19 per cent); yearly planning (18 per cent); and daily planning (15 per cent). Nearly half of the teachers (49 per cent) in this study reported that most of their planning is mental and that they seldom put their plans on paper. As Borko *et al.* (1990) stated, a large portion of teachers' planning is mental, often spontaneous, occurring throughout the day, and rarely recorded on paper.

One of the interests here was to study potential differences between curriculum makers (twenty-three teachers) and those who had not taken part in developing the local curriculum (sixty-two teachers). In this study, teachers were defined as being experienced teachers if they had a minimum of eight years of teaching experience. Of the twenty-three curriculum makers, twenty were experienced teachers with eight to thirty-three years of teaching experience. Thus it was to be expected that there might be similarities in the findings for experienced teachers and curriculum makers. A total of fifty Likert-scaled attitude variables were factorized in nine factors and they were further analysed by discrimination analysis.

As Stenhouse (1975, pp. 167–68) has put it, 'curricular changes of real significance almost always involve changes in method and ways of working.' The discrimination analysis showed that the curriculum makers more often than other teachers used student-centred teaching methods in their instruction and also more often differentiated their instruction. It was no surprise that the curriculum makers knew better than other teachers the goals and contents of the curriculum. However, it could be confirmed on the basis of interview data that the curriculum makers had internalized the very idea of the curriculum innovation, i.e., the idea of considering the pupils as unique learners and individuals in the learning process. The process of curriculum development might have directed or strengthened their views and principles concerning teaching methods, the role of the teacher and the teacher–pupil relationship in the same student-oriented direction.

In addition, the curriculum makers were more often than other teachers goal-oriented and interested in developing the curriculum and the school, and they also expressed more often than other teachers that they regard developing and improving both the curriculum and the school as a natural part of a primary-school teacher's work (t = 2.67, p = .009).

Two-way analysis of variance was used to determine whether teaching experience and taking part in curriculum making had simultaneous main effects on the nine factor variables. No evidence of such simultaneous effects was found. Accordingly, the effects of teaching experience and curriculum making could be studied independently. When the attitudes of experienced teachers were compared to those of other teachers, statistically significant differences were found that paralleled the differences found when curriculum makers' attitudes were compared to those of other teachers. In addition, the experienced teachers tended more often than less experienced teachers to think that they did not have problems maintaining discipline in the classroom and that they received enough respect and appreciation from their pupils. However, this was not a statistically significant, merely a suggestive, difference (t = −1.72, p = .089).

On the other hand, the curriculum makers seemed to differ from other experienced teachers in some respects. These differences should, however, be interpreted with caution, because they were not statistically significant but are merely suggestive differences. The most interesting difference was that the curriculum makers seemed to foster collegiality and stress the importance of good school climate, peer support and collaboration more often than other teachers did (t = 1.82, p = .074). The curriculum makers had a tendency to think that they have an excellent working atmosphere in their staff room and that they can sense there a spirit of solidarity. They also expressed more often than their colleagues that they have good possibilities to exchange views and discuss with their colleagues and that they can get help, support and encouragement from their colleagues when they need it.

In addition, the curriculum makers tended to stress that they had good possibilities to plan their instruction independently and to fulfil themselves in their school (t = 1.89, p = .062). There also seemed to be a tendency for the curriculum makers to stress the importance of instructional planning (both mental and in writing) more often than other teachers and more often to find the (written) curriculum to be an important instrument in the work of primary-school teachers (t = −1.81, p = .074).

Women more often than men regarded both mental instructional planning and planning in writing to be important and more often found the written curriculum to be an important instrument in the work of primary-school teachers (t = −3.77, p = .000). In addition, women did not as often as men use workbooks in their teaching (t = −2.26, p = .026).

When the interviews of the three experienced teachers (curriculum makers) and the three less experienced teachers were analysed, some interesting findings were noted. Firstly, the curriculum makers (eight to fifteen years of teaching experience) stressed the importance of totality and wholeness in their instructional planning. They preferred producing a plan for the whole school year and/or term and then proceeded to plan smaller units, components of the totality (a unit, a week, a day). The curriculum makers stressed the importance of the written curriculum as a framework for helping them to obtain a relevant picture of the totality of the goals and contents for the grade they teach.

The less experienced teachers (three to four years of teaching experience) stressed short-term planning. They concentrated directly on weekly and daily/hourly plans without explicitly connecting their plan to the whole term or school year. Secondly, while the curriculum makers based their planning on the written curriculum and also utilized textbooks as means of sequencing their instruction, the less experienced teachers indicated that for them the textbook replaces the written curriculum. They sequenced their instruction according to the textbooks.

Thirdly, the curriculum makers tended to integrate their instruction. They seemed to prefer conducting theme-based instruction where different points of view were utilized from different school subjects to serve as instruction for the theme. On the contrary, less experienced teachers leaned on textbooks in planning their instruction; and accordingly, their instruction was very subject-centred. Fourthly, the findings based on the interview-data confirmed the previous finding that curriculum makers fostered student-oriented working methods and differentiated their teaching, while the less experienced teachers preferred teacher-centred working methods and very often concentrated on lecturing to the whole class. Fifthly, the notions based on interview-data confirmed that curriculum makers are eager to develop and improve the curriculum and the school ('progressive' attitude) while the less experienced teachers seemed not to be development-oriented. They might even oppose curriculum and school improvement ('conservative' attitude).

These results indicate that the curriculum makers may represent a teacher type opposite to an isolated type of teacher, when a teacher type is defined in terms of conservatism, individualism and presentism (see Lortie, 1975). Instead of resisting change (conservatism), the curriculum makers were innovation- and development-oriented; instead of unwillingness to cooperate with their colleagues (individualism), they tended to stress the importance of cooperation and collegial support; finally, instead of concentrating on short-term planning only (presentism), they stressed wholeness in their planning. They used the curriculum as a framework for their planning and planned their instruction long-range (year and/or term).

Discussion

According to an old joke, if you want to hide money in the staff room, you had better put it between the pages of the written curriculum and then you can be sure that no one will ever find it. If the curriculum makers reflected on their own practice when listening to this joke, they apparently would not recognize themselves in it. The reason for this is very simple: they would not have had any difficulties to find the hidden money, because they used the curriculum. They enacted the curriculum in the way that the designers of the national curriculum and they themselves as developers of the local curriculum had originally intended all teachers to do.

Consequently, compared to the aims of the latest curriculum reform and according to its criteria, the curriculum makers seem to represent a kind of ideal teachers and potential for change. We still do not know, however, which of these desirable features are a result of the process of curriculum development and which are part of the curriculum makers' practical knowledge that they already possessed before taking part in the curriculum-development project.

The findings of this study indicated, however, that the curriculum makers' views of the role of the curriculum in teachers' work seemed to differ in a very essential way from the views of those teachers who had not been members of any curriculum-development team. The curriculum makers knew and read the curriculum and used it in their work. They had more often than other teachers internalized the core idea of the curriculum innovation: the idea of considering students as unique learners and individuals in the learning process. Consequently, they more often than other teachers used student-centred teaching methods and differentiated their instruction to fit the individual needs of pupils. They were also more often than other teachers willing to develop the curriculum and the school. In these respects the views of the experienced teachers were similar to those of the curriculum makers.

When curriculum makers were compared to teachers who had not been members of curriculum-development teams, some additional suggestive differences were found. These suggestive differences were not found when the views of experienced teachers were compared to those of other teachers. The most important of these differences was that the curriculum makers tended more often than other teachers to foster collegiality, peer support and cooperation in their work.

In this study the curriculum makers did not fit the criteria for isolated teachers, i.e., if teacher isolation is related to conservatism, presentism and individualism as defined by Lortie (1975). The curriculum makers were development-oriented long-term planners. In addition, they tended to foster collegiality more often than their peers did. As Stenhouse (1975) put it, there is no curriculum development without teacher development. Consequently, perhaps as a result of the ongoing project on curriculum development, instead of teacher isolation we will have more reflective cooperation in schools as the experienced teachers more often engage in developing school-based curricula. Maybe they more often engage in reconstructing and developing their practical knowledge and practical theories by reflecting on their experiences. Accordingly, we may have more dynamic interaction between teachers' personal and collective practical theories and their teaching practices. Consequently, the school may be developed towards 'extended collegiality'. Handal (1991) uses this concept of 'a collective, critical and reflective practice concerning the total work of school which considers the practice, the code and the epistemology as problematic and continuously works to develop it' (Handal, 1991, p. 331). It remains to see whether the innovation of a school-based curriculum releases the capacity of teachers to develop professionally and to improve the curriculum and the school.

McCutcheon (1980) stated that primary-school teachers' planning was short-range and that long-range planning was perceived as partly being done by the textbooks. In this study the less experienced teachers only seemed to plan their instruction in the way McCutcheon described. They concentrated on weekly and daily/hourly plans without connecting their plan to the wholeness of the school year or the term. The less experienced teachers indicated that for them the textbook replaces the written curriculum and sequenced their instruction according to the textbooks. In this sense their unit-planning was perceived as being done completely, not only partly as McCutcheon suggested, by textbooks. Consequently, their instructional planning was very subject-centred and was split into the contents of different subjects in the way they were described in textbooks.

National curricula in the Nordic countries allow teachers considerable pedagogical freedom to decide how to organize their instruction. It is very desirable and is actually ideal to regard curriculum materials and packages as 'curriculum potential'. The teacher should not hand over his or her pedagogical freedom and the responsibility for choosing the contents of his or her teaching to textbooks and other teaching materials. If he or she retains his or her freedom and keeps the responsibility, the teacher construes his or her teaching very freely from the elements he or she considers to be most suitable for his or her own use in teaching. In this situation the meaning-making, beliefs and theories of the teacher are of special importance.

When teachers not only enact but also actively make and develop the curriculum, it is both desirable and obvious that the conduit-metaphor (Clandinin and Connelly, 1992) will lose its power. However, it is possible that especially those teachers who have based their work on textbooks and workbooks and teacher-centred teaching methods do not see any reason to change their teaching practices at all. Textbooks and teachers' guides sequence and rule instruction and the teacher remains at the receiving end of the conduit.

Malinen (1993) pointed out the need to make the current rational model of curriculum planning more complete by including into it practical thinking. However, all too many of the authorities and teachers in Finland seem not to have understood that teachers' professional development and curriculum development are closely connected. Consequently, teachers' possibilities to obtain in-service training is not considered to be as a central question in communes and schools, which are responsible for allocating resources. However, participation in curriculum development and teachers' professional development seem to be dialectically related. Taking part in improvement of the curriculum and of the school stimulates the teachers to think critically, not just reflecting on their own practice but rather broadening their individual perspectives of their own work from a narrow 'my classroom is my castle' perspective to seeing their work in the broader school context of the whole school.

In summary, it is important to note that there is not only one (negative), compact way in which teachers think and feel about the curriculum, but rather several different ways. When it comes to the attitudes of less experienced teachers about curriculum, perhaps not everything possible has been done to acquaint these young teachers with the totality of the intended curriculum and long-term instructional planning instead of technical, short-range planning based on textbooks and teachers' guides. Studies of experienced teachers and teacher expertise may tell us more about the different phases of teachers' professional development and support us in developing programmes of in-service training for teachers. Teachers as curriculum makers tell their own stories. It is in these stories that their assumptions, principles, beliefs and theories of learning, instruction and the work of a teacher are to be found. It is here that we can locate and trace teachers' knowledge of, and attitudes toward, the curriculum. We still need to know more about how teachers feel and think about the curriculum as part of their practical knowledge and how they construe their reality in the school context. We also need to know more about the practical theories on which they base their thoughts and actions. By giving teachers an active role as curriculum makers and by studying their instructional planning in the school context, we can learn more about the complicated process of how teachers think and act in terms of curriculum planning and use.

References

ATJONEN, P. (1993) 'The local curriculum as an object and instrument in the administrative and pedagogical development of the school system', University of Oulu. Acta Universitatis Ouluensis (Series E) *Scientiae rerum socialum*, 11.

BORKO, H., LIVINGSTON, C. and SHAVELSON, R.J. (1990) 'Teachers' thinking about instruction', *Remedial and Special Education* (RASE), 11, 6, pp. 40–9.

BROWN, D.S. (1988) 'Twelve middle-school teachers' planning', *The Elementary School Journal*, 89, 1, pp. 69–87.

BROWN, S. and McINTYRE, D. (1993) *Making Sense of Teaching*, Buckingham, Open University Press.

CALDERHEAD, J. (Ed) (1988) *Teachers' Professional Learning*, Basingstoke, The Falmer Press.

CALDERHEAD, J. (1992) 'The Professional Development of Teachers in Changing Europe', Keynote address at the 17th Conference of the Association for Teacher Education in Europe (ATEE), Lahti, Finland, 30 August–4 September.

CLANDININ, D.J. (1986) *Classroom Practice: Teacher Images in Action*, Philadelphia, The Falmer Press.

CLANDININ, D.J. and CONNELLY, F.M. (1992) 'Teacher as curriculum maker', in JACKSON, P.W. (Ed) *Handbook of Research on Curriculum*, A Project of American Educational Research Association, New York, MacMillan.

CLARK, C.M. and DUNN, S. (1991) 'Second-generation research on teachers' planning, intentions, and routines', in WAXMAN, H.C. and WALBERG, H.J. *Effective Teaching: Current Research*, Berkeley, McCutchan.

CLARK, C.M. and PETERSON, P.L. (1986) 'Teachers' thought processes', in WITTROCK, M.C. (Ed) *Handbook of Research on Teaching* (3rd ed.), New York, MacMillan.

CLARK, C.M. and YINGER, R. (1987) 'Teacher planning', in CALDERHEAD, J. (Ed) *Exploring Teachers' Thinking*, London, Cassell.

CONNELLY, F.M. and CLANDININ, D.J. (1988) *Teachers as Curriculum Planners: Narratives of Experience*, New York, Teachers College Press.

CORNETT, J., YEOTIS, C. and TERWILLIGER, L. (1990) 'Teacher personal practical theories and their influence upon teacher curricular and instructional actions: A case study of a secondary science teacher', *Science Education*, 75, 5, pp. 517–29.

CRONIN-JONES, L. (1991) 'Science teacher beliefs and their influence on curriculum implementation: Two case studies', *Journal of Research in Science Teaching*, 28, 3, pp. 235–50.

DAY, C. (1990) 'The development of teachers' personal practical knowledge through schoolbased curriculum development projects', in DAY, C., POPE, M. and DENICOLO, P. *Insight into Teachers' Thinking and Practice*, London, The Falmer Press.

ELBAZ, F. (1983) *Teacher Thinking: A Study of Practical Knowledge*, London, Croom Helm.

HAMMRICH, P.L., BONOZO, J. and BERLINER, D.C. (1990) *Schema Differences Among Expert and Novice Teachers in Reflection About Teaching*, Arizona State University (ED 344837).

HANDAL, G. (1991) 'Collective time — collective practice', *The Curriculum Journal*, 2, 3, pp. 317–33.

HANDAL, G. and LAUVAS, P. (1987) *Promoting Reflective Teaching: Supervision in Practice*, Milton Keynes, Open University Educational Enterprises.

HANNAY, L. and SELLER, W. (1990) 'The influence of teachers' thinking on curriculum development decisions', in DAY, C., POPE, M. and DENICOLO, P. *Insight into Teachers' Thinking and Practice*, London, The Falmer Press.

JACKSON, P.W. (1992) 'Conceptions of curriculum and curriculum specialists', in JACKSON, P.W. (Ed) *Handbook of Research on Curriculum: A Project of the American Educational Research Association*, New York, MacMillan.

JOHNSTON, S. (1992) 'Images: A way of understanding the practical knowledge of student teachers', *Teaching and Teacher Education*, 8, 2, pp. 123–36.

KOSUNEN, T. (1993) 'Does Anything in the Curriculum Make Sense to the Teacher?', Paper presented at the 6th Conference of The International Study Association on Teacher Thinking (ISATT) in Gothenburg, August 10–15.

KOSUNEN, T. (1994) 'Primary School Teachers as Curriculum Makers and Implementers: Utilization of Practical Knowledge and Practical Theories in Teacher Planning', Manuscript of a Doctocal Dissertation, University of Joensum.

KUUSISTO, J. (1989) 'A Survey of Teachers' Views about Learning Materials in the Comprehensive School', (Publication series A. Research reports 26). University of Jyväskylä, Institute for Educational Research.

LEINHARDT, G. and GREENO, J. (1986) 'The Cognitive Skill of Teaching', *Journal of Educational Psychology*, 78, 2, pp. 75–95.

LIVINGSTON, C. and BORKO, H. (1989) 'Expert-novice differences in teaching: A cognitive analysis and implications for teacher education', *Journal of Teacher Education*, 40, 4, pp. 36–42.

LORTIE, D.C. (1975) *Schoolteacher: A Sociological Study*, Chicago, The University of Chicago Press.

MALINEN, P. (1992) *Opetussuunnitelmat koulutyössä*, Helsinki, VAPK-kustannus.

MALINEN, P. (1993) 'Arviointia opetussuunnitelmien laadinnan nykytilanteesta', Paper presented at the National Congress of Education in Jyväskylä, Finland, 15–17 June.

MAY, W.T. (1986) 'Teaching students how to plan: The dominant model and alternatives', *Journal of Teacher Education*, 37, 6, pp. 6–12.

McCUTCHEON, G. (1980) 'How do elementary school teachers plan? The nature of planning and influences on it', *The Elementary School Journal*, 81, 1, pp. 4–23.

MORINE-DERSHIMER, G. (1991) 'Learning to think like a teacher', *Teaching and Teacher Education*, 7, 2, pp. 159–68.

MUNBY, H. (1983) 'A Qualitative Study of Teachers' Beliefs and Principles', Paper presented at the Annual Meeting of the American Educational Research Association (AERA) in Montreal, April 11–14.

OLSON, J. (1981) 'Teacher Influence in the Classroom: A Context for Understanding Curriculum Translation', *Instructional Science*, 10, pp. 259–75.

OLSON, J. (1992) *Understanding Teaching*, Philadelphia, Milton Keynes, Open University Press.

POPE, M. (1991) 'Anticipating Teacher Thinking', Keynote address at the 5th Conference of the International Study Association on Teachers' Thinking in Guildford, 23–27 September.

SHAVELSON, R.J. and STERN, P. (1981) 'Research on teachers' pedagogical thoughts, judgments, decisions, and behavior', *Review of Educational Research*, 51, pp. 455–98.

SHULMAN, L.-S. (1987) 'Knowledge and teaching: Foundations of the new reform', *Harvard Educational Review*, 57, 1, pp. 1–22.

STENHOUSE, L. (1975) *An Introduction to Curriculum Research and Development*, London, Heinemann.

THOMPSON, A. (1992) 'Teacher beliefs and conceptions: A synthesis of the research', in GROUWS, D.A. (Ed) *Handbook of Research on Mathematics Teaching and Learning: A Project of the National Council of Teachers of Mathematics*, New York, MacMillan.

YINGER, R.J. and CLARK, C.M. (1981) 'Reflective Journal Writing: Theory and Practice', (Occasional Paper No. 50), Michigan State University, Institute for Research on Teaching.

Chapter 17

Professional Isolation and Imposed Collaboration in Teachers' Work

Elisabeth Ahlstrand

Abstract

Professional isolation in teachers' work is considered to be an obstacle to teacher development and school improvement. Efforts are made in many countries and school systems to get teachers to interact and collaborate in their work. Teachers in the Swedish compulsory school have been given time by regulations for work in so-called teacher teams. In the study reported here four teacher teams have been observed for one year. Besides this, the teachers have been interviewed about their experiences of the work in the teams. The observations show that teacher teams are heavily influenced by the school administration through the team leaders. The team leaders introduce matters that mostly deal with administrative matters. Those matters represent the formal part of the work of the teams, here called the formal arena. In spite of this the teachers use the teams for their own interests, for example they introduce matters that deal with pupil welfare and their own work situation. This part of the work is here called the informal arena. The teachers report in the interviews that work with pupil welfare is very important to them even if these matters are not very common in the work of the teams.

Background

Teachers' work has been looked upon as work in isolation (Sarason, 1971; Lieberman and Miller, 1990). The isolation is said to be one of the reasons why teachers have had difficulties in handling new demands in their work. Many causes have been identified why the isolation started to grow and how it persists and resists efforts to reduce it. One factor which helps the isolation is the architecture of schools; another is the socialization of new teachers (Lortie, 1975).

Two effects of the professional isolation of teachers can be that they have few opportunities to learn from each other (Rosenholtz, 1985; Darling-Hammond, 1990) and they have feelings of uncertainty about whether they fulfil all the demands that teachers' work makes on them (Lortie, 1975; Rosenholz, 1989). This uncertainty can better be described as feelings of guilt, anxiety and frustration, if the teachers themselves articulate their feelings about teaching (Hargreaves and

Tucker, 1991). In the end professional isolation affects teaching and the welfare of pupils.

Many new demands are being made on teachers in many school systems, in particular that children from different cultures are taught in the same class as well as children with different socioeconomic backgrounds and abilities (Darling-Hammond, 1990). There are many reasons for this, democratic as well as economic. A teacher as a single person will seldom be able to handle all these tasks and he or she will need some help. Fullan and Hargreaves (1991, p. 14) describe the situation like this: 'It is a problem of teaching being a changing job, of having wider and more diverse expectations, which requires more consultation and contact between teachers, their colleagues and a range of other adults — contacts for which they often have insufficient training, time and support.' Not seldom does the pupil have to go to special teachers for different needs and he or she has to integrate the different teaching and knowledge they get from different teachers. This problem is also apparent in a school organization where the subjects are taught by different teachers.

Purpose of the Chapter

Mutual support and teacher collaboration are very often held to be important factors in breaking professional isolation among teachers, in making professional growth possible and also as a means for school improvement (Little, 1982; McLaughlin and Marsh, 1978). In the Swedish compulsory school teachers are urged to collaborate and the strongest argument for this reform is to integrate the teaching for the pupils, particularly for those pupils who have special needs.

The work of teachers can be seen as a social process. Teachers negotiate (consciously and unconsciously) with themselves and their colleagues about how they see their roles as teachers. In these negotiations there are many weighty components, for example the expectations of society, the organization of the school nationally and locally, the culture of the work etc. (Ball, 1981; Handal, 1991).

In this chapter teachers' collaboration in teacher teams is focused upon as well as the work of teachers and the cultural basis of that work. The collaboration will be described on the basis of an empirical study of teacher teams in the Swedish compulsory school.

The aim of the chapter is to throw light on and describe how teachers use the time for collaboration in the teacher teams. This will be done by looking at the content and meaning teachers give to the tasks that are put before the teacher teams, which initiatives they take and how the teachers themselves look upon the collaboration.

In describing which problems and aspects of their work teachers are willing to bring into collaboration and which they still want to keep private, we can get some information about how teachers look upon their work. Do they themselves consider the work as work in isolation or not? Is imposed collaboration a way of breaking the professional isolation of teachers? Discussing these matters could give some more clues to the understanding of the very complex phenomenon that teachers' work is.

The Swedish System

According to Swedish regulations all compulsory schools shall be divided into smaller, so-called 'work units' with about two to ten classes and their teachers in each unit. According to this system, the teachers in such a unit are called a 'teacher team'. The teacher teams have opportunities to meet during regular working hours to discuss and decide about common matters in their work. The sphere of activity of the teacher teams is set and regulated by the compulsory-school curriculum, which is established on a national level. According to the national policy, teacher teams have the responsibility for the planning of lessons, the welfare of the pupils, and the forms and content of democratic cooperation between pupils and staff.

The reform was introduced as an integrated part of a wider aim to give the local authority more responsibility. Teachers were supposed to play a greater part in the development of their schools, specially with regard to curriculum development and evaluation.

Imposed Collaboration

The collective work that teachers in the Swedish compulsory school carry out can be called imposed collaboration. Teachers themselves have not decided that collaboration could be a way of meeting more demanding situations with more duties and more heterogeneous classes to work with. In most cases when collaboration is suggested for teachers, the suggestion comes from the administration or from researchers (Little, 1990a).

One prerequisite among others for teachers when establishing collaboration, is to have regular, collective time which is not occupied by lessons (Little, 1990b). In the Swedish compulsory school teachers who teach the same work unit have this opportunity. They are supposed to meet and discuss, plan and evaluate central tasks in their professional work.

One central question is: What will happen when teachers, who are used to individual lesson planning and to solving their problems by themselves, meet demands to cooperate around central tasks in their professional work? Somehow, of course, teachers come to terms with this situation and take possession of the reform. But how will they make use of the collective work? How will they use the time together? What issues will be dealt with and what issues will not?

The Study

In this study four teacher teams in four different schools were followed during the course of one year. The teacher teams included in the study were in the upper level of compulsory school, grades 7–9, at 'ordinary' schools. The main sources of data were observations of teacher teams and interviews with teachers.

Observations

There were two observers, each of whom followed two teacher teams. Primarily they followed the regular meetings of the teams. Meeting times varied between forty and ninety minutes. During the observation period the numbers of meetings in a school varied from six to fourteen, and the total time for the meetings from six to nearly fifteen hours.

The observations from the meetings were written down verbatim, in short-hand notes. The person who spoke was also indicated. Every topic discussed was noted, as well as how long the topic was dealt with. Following each observed meeting, on the same day, the handwritten notes were typewritten. No tape recorder was used during the observations, in order to disturb the regular procedures of the meetings as little as possible. The purpose of the observations was to catch the meaning of what was said and the context in which it was said. To make observations in this way and to get a picture of the natural situation in schoolwork is documented by for example Hammersley (1980) and Hammersley and Atkinson (1983).

The approach used in this study was that the observer was an 'outsider', and not a participant in the process being observed (Patton, 1983). The observer was visible to the observed persons, answered questions, but took no initiatives to communicate. The observation was open, in the sense that the observed persons were aware that observations were being made, could see notes being taken, and were acquainted with the observer. They also knew the purpose of the observations.

In the analysis the notes of the observations were first used to identify the topics that the teacher teams actually dealt with. On closer study a pattern became apparent showing that when a topic was introduced, several small topics, here called side topics, that were connected to the original topic, would be introduced. (The process of the task-treating could be described as a tree, where the original topic is the trunk and the side topics are branches growing out from the trunk).

The next step was to identify who introduced the original topics and the side topics. In each of the teacher teams, one of the teachers is formally appointed by the school administration to lead the work of the teacher team. In the records it was indicated if it was this formal leader or if it was one of the other teachers who introduced the topic.

The original topics and side topics were then analysed according to a model with two dimensions. One dimension deals with the content of the topics, categorized as: administrative matters (A), instructional matters (I), pupil welfare (Pw) and teachers' own work situation (Tw). The other dimension describes the organizational level in the school that the topic relates to. Four categories are used even here: the level of an individual pupil (p), a group or class of pupils (g), the work unit (wu) and the whole school (s). The model can be seen in Figure 17.1.

Interviews

When the observations were finished three teachers from each of the four teacher teams were chosen at random to be interviewed. In the group of twelve teachers there were six women and six men and they represented different subject combinations and varied in length of teaching experience. The interviews were half-structured, dealing with:

- collaboration in general in the school;
- collaboration in the work unit and the teacher team;

Figure 17.1: Model for topic analysis with reference to content and organizational level

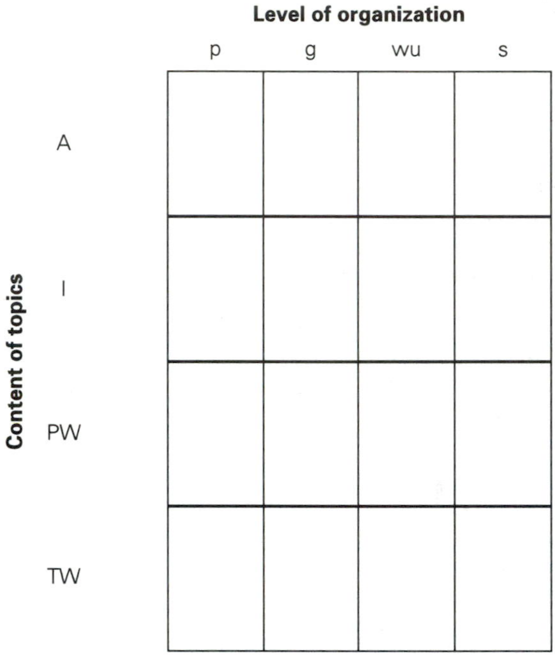

Level of organization

- how they looked upon the role of teacher as set out in the latest compulsory school curriculum; and
- how they managed in their work as teachers.

Under each area there were some questions which were used more as a guide than as a prescriptive scheme that had to be followed (Gordon, 1980; Spradley, 1979). The interviews took between one and one and a half hours each and they were all audio-taped. Afterwards they were all written down, word for word.

The interviews were analysed by means of a qualitative method (Ely *et al.*, 1991). There was an aim to describe and understand what the teachers themselves said about their work and what importance they put on the work with colleagues. The analysis was made on the basis of comparisons between answers from different teachers, and comparisons between answers to different questions from the same person. This was done to grasp the recognizable similarities and differences in order to identify categories or themes that described the values the teachers put on their work.

Some Results from the Observations

In the minutes, 214 original topics and 281 side topics have been identified. The original topics are those which are openly introduced to start with in the meetings, in writing or orally (the official agenda). These topics represent the formal aims and subjects during the meetings, a kind of formal arena. The side topics are introduced more or less spontaneously or *ad hoc* and represent a more informal arena of the work of the teacher teams (the unofficial agenda).

When the original topics and the side topics are compared, the following pattern can be seen:

- Administrative matters dominate both original topics (44 per cent) and side topics (38 per cent).
- Instructional matters are introduced equally often as original topics (26 per cent) and as side topics (28 per cent).
- Pupil welfare is not a very common content either in original topics (18 per cent) or in the side topics (11 per cent). Since the original topics can be looked upon as representing the formal aims of the work of the teacher team, the results show the teams more often treat pupil welfare in the formal arena rather than in the informal one.
- Topics that deal with the teachers' own work situations, appear rather rarely as original topics (11 per cent), but more commonly as side topics (23 per cent).

The team leader is supposed to take formal responsibility for the work unit and the most obvious expression of this is chairing the meetings of the teacher teams. The way teachers take the opportunity to introduce topics might reflect their views on this imposed collaboration. One way to describe the initiatives of the teachers in the teams, is to compare them to the initiatives of the team leaders.

Firstly frequencies of initiatives of team leaders and teachers are compared. The team leaders initiate nearly three times more original topics than the teachers do. The team leaders are willing to shoulder their responsibility and introduce the official agenda. Teachers and the team leaders, however, initiate an equal number of side topics. In the work both team leaders and teachers are active. Teachers are more disposed to contribute to the work when an original topic has already been introduced than initiate new ones. They introduce their interests more as side topics than as original topics, i.e., they use the unofficial agenda more than the official one.

Secondly the initiatives of team leaders and teachers are compared from two aspects, content and level of organization.

The Initiatives of Team Leaders

In Figure 17.2 the topics (both original and side topics) introduced by the team leaders are analysed according to the model described above.

Nearly half of the topics that the team leaders introduce have administrative content. Topics with content of pupil welfare are rare as well as those concerning teachers' work situations. More than half of the topics deal with the organizational level of the whole work unit. Topics dealing with individual pupils are a small proportion of the initiatives of team leaders. Matters that concern groups of pupils are also rare. No team leader introduces matters that concern teachers' work situations in relation to pupils. Topics that the team leaders introduce mostly come down from the school administration.

Figure 17.2: Content and level of organization of topics that team leaders introduce

Content of topics	Level of organization p (%)	g (%)	wu (%)	s (%)	S (%)
A (%)	1,6	4,5	28,5	12,2	46,8
I (%)	0,8	4,0	16,5	6,1	27,4
PW (%)	4,5	2,6	2,1	1,1	10,3
TW (%)		0,8	10,1	4,3	15,2
S(%)	6,9	11,9	57,2	23,7	≈100,0

Note: Percental distribution

The Initiatives of Teachers

In Figure 17.3 the analysis of the topics that the teachers introduce is presented.

According to Figure 17.3 teachers tend to introduce topics that mostly deal with administrative matters for the work unit, but the topics that teachers introduce are more evenly distributed over all the other categories, both for content and level of organization, than those introduced by team leaders. Topics concerning pupil welfare and the work situations of teachers are more commonly initiated by the teachers than by the team leaders. Teachers introduce a considerably greater number of topics dealing with individual pupils compared to the team leaders.[1]

The 'imposed/formal' cooperation is supposed to solve common concerns for the work unit, for example arranging projects with an interdisciplinary theme and managing pupil welfare. The cooperation in the teacher teams that have been studied seems to cover mostly administrative matters. The topics treated are more concerned with the administrative conditions for the instruction than with curriculum matters.

The study provides evidence for the assumption that teacher teams can be used for more informal cooperation. Despite the team leaders in their formal mandates directing the teams fairly strongly towards administrative matters, the

Figure 17.3: *Content and level of organization of topics that teachers introduce*

Level of organization

Content of topics	p (%)	g (%)	wu (%)	s (%)	S (%)
A (%)	6,9	3,8	12,3	9,8	32,8
I (%)	5,4	5,4	9,8	5,4	26,0
PW (%)	9,1	8,5	1,3	0,6	19,5
TW (%)	3,2	2,2	8,8	8,2	22,4
S(%)	24,6	19,9	32,2	24,0	≈100,0

Note: Percental distribution

teams, in the side topics, deal with other aspects of teachers' work. Besides, the teachers in their initiatives differ from the team leaders particularly concerning topics at the level of the individual pupil.

Although teacher teams can be looked upon as arenas for imposed/formal cooperation among teachers, they can also be used for a more informal cooperation that is not as strictly structured as the formal cooperation and where teachers take the opportunity to discuss matters that they care about. Teachers tend to introduce matters that concern their own work situations to a greater extent than the team leaders. They are also responsible for the introduction of the few topics dealing with pupil welfare. Besides the teachers in their initiatives differ from the team leaders particularly concerning topics at the level of the individual pupil.

In summary the teacher team is for teachers not only a formal arena but also an informal one, where they take the chance to talk about pupils from different viewpoints as well as about their own work situations.

Some Results from the Interviews

Relations with pupils are very important for teachers. It is getting more difficult to maintain good relations with all pupils when classes are heterogeneous as regards ability or social background. Under such circumstances expectations may vary more markedly among parents and teachers may feel at times that the school's standards have little to do with those of the parents. The teachers in the study say that their work is hard and they sometimes feel exposed and abandoned. New demands both from the work itself and the authorities create uncertainty. Teacher collaboration is not only one way to relieve the burdens and offset the uncertainty but also to enrich the work by giving inspiration.

The collaboration in the teacher teams, that is imposed, does not meet the expectations and needs of the teachers. The work is dominated by administrative matters that the team leaders bring to the teacher team from the school administration. It is a matter of fact on which all the teachers comment and with which they are not happy, as the experiences of two teachers illustrate.

> I think that the meetings are too much a forum for information and too little for discussions . . . I think we could do better if we had a common plan for our work concerning teaching and pupil welfare.

> You get so much information from the school administration. There is very little time to solve problems together. When you try to plan for thematic studies, you just have time to start in the teacher team. Then you divide the work between you, and you have to do the rest of it at your own desk.

Collaboration in teacher teams is justified because it gives an opportunity to *talk about* pupils. It is distressing to the teachers when their contacts with pupils do not function, when teaching does not work or when the pupils break the school rules. When there are problems in daily work and when teachers notice their inability to handle problems, the teacher team is useful. Two different teachers say:

> The purpose of meetings in teacher teams, is to become more acquainted with the pupils. I believe that you will become a better teacher if you care about the relations between pupil and teacher.

> In the teacher team you get an opportunity to talk about the pupils. You get a much better picture of which pupils have troubles and you ought to keep an eye on.

When the school and the teachers have lost control of a pupil and it is important to act immediately, the teacher team could become a base for that action. The teachers feel uncertainty about pupil welfare and express their lack of competence and need for advice and support. They consider matters that deal with pupil welfare and their own work situations as the most important matters to discuss. However, the frequencies of these topics are few in the work of the teacher teams, as the results from the observation study show. The teachers all agree on the importance of discussing pupil welfare in the teacher team, even if opportunities are limited.

The school situation of the pupils can be dramatically changed if they are under discussion in the teacher team. Decisions can be made about special help for any pupil within the work unit. The teacher team can also pass on responsibility for a pupil's future to others in the school (pupil welfare committee or the school administration). Even if the situation for teachers on the other hand, is not influenced by the decisions made in the teacher team in the long run, they do get relief in sharing problems about pupils.

For teachers, instruction and pupil welfare, however, are loosely connected. They rarely make plans together as to how their instruction might be changed for the pupils who are discussed in the teacher team. The information about pupils which the teachers get in the teacher team is useful for their own preparation or for their classroom practice. It does not produce more profound changes in their individual work because the teams rarely analyse the pupils' problems more generally in order to make up common plans for teaching that may facilitate the learning of pupils or support a more favourable social development for pupils in the school environment, plans that might differ from those that individual teachers make. The teachers also say that the teams rarely make decisions that really have any impact on the freedom of the teacher in the classroom.

In the study there are teachers who maintain that instruction and pupil welfare are two separate things, while other teachers insist that they are connected. Some teachers also are of the opinion, that a more common approach on the part of the teacher team, particularly about pupil welfare, would be beneficial both for these pupils and for the work of teachers. At least the teachers would feel more confident in what they actually do. In summary there are teachers who maintain that the time spent in the teacher teams could be used more effectively, not just to give relief but also to create a more conscious pupil welfare and work with long-term aims for pupils, for school improvement and for their own development as teachers.

If the collaboration in the teacher team is to have any chance of functioning well for the teachers, organization is very important. This is an opinion held in common by the interviewed teachers. Further they say that teachers belonging to the same teacher team, must teach the same classes and know all the pupils. It is an advantage if the teachers work with one work unit only. The teachers also say that further training to work in 'the new work organization' is not necessary. It is more essential, however, that the organization is arranged around the pupils and that the teachers meet regularly and have a reasonable period of time for the meetings.

Discussion

This study indicates that the work of teacher teams, where attendance is compulsory, can be divided into two arenas, one *formal* arena and one informal. The *formal* arena is used mainly for school administration and is dominated by discussions about conditions for instruction, especially school activities that break with the ordinary timetable, like excursions and interdisciplinary projects. Teachers do use the formal arena to introduce pupil-welfare problems, but to a limited extent. But when they have introduced a pupil problem in the formal arena all the teachers in the team at least know about it. Thus they can give special consideration to this pupil in their instruction and help each other to observe the pupil in breaks and lessons and how he or she behaves and copes with the school work. They can then share impressions in more informal situations like in the staff room or in the corridor.

Teachers use the *informal* arena to a greater extent than the formal one. They choose to introduce topics more as side (unofficial) topics than as original (official) topics and their initiatives deal more with their own situations than the original matters. Consequently one can say that the teachers are able to use the imposed collaboration for their own purposes. To what extent, however, is the imposed collaboration able to break the professional isolation of teachers?

In the interviews teachers say that the teacher team is able to break the isolation they have felt in their work. They have now got a forum to discuss their shortcomings and uncertainties, and they experience this as a great relief. This is important for them particularly in their relations to the pupils. One can even define the function of the teacher team like this: to bring a pupil into the arena, to show the difficulties he or she has and to collect the impressions the others have of the pupil. The point is to share what you are worried about and get relief and support. The pupil-welfare work, that teachers undertake in teacher teams, could for the pupils be described as a combination of care and control. For the teachers the work in the team is more about care for each other than for control. If the school as a workplace is to function as a place for teacher development, it should be based on relationships characterized by caring and helping. This is especially important for new teachers and may prevent them from withdrawing into isolation. 'It would make more sense to strive not for the creation of effective partnerships, but rather for the creation of caring and helping communities of learners', (Cole, 1991).

Teachers themselves consider that the teacher teams have broken an undesirable isolation, in the sense that they are no longer afraid to communicate about problems in their everyday work. Teacher teams have had an important impact on starting the process of getting to know each other, which in turn facilitates relations with the pupils. Teachers feel that personal relationships among the teachers are very important and even help to solve the pupils' problems. It can be concluded that turning the isolation into mutual support has been essential for the teachers. But can the collaboration in the teacher teams also bring the teachers to break their professional isolation, in the sense that the teacher teams even could be an arena for 'professional development, the implementation of change and the development of shared educational goals' (Hargreaves, 1990, p. 3)? Some teachers see this as a possibility which they also want to realize. Teacher teams could be a basis for developing more professional relations.

Note

1   C2-test shows differences (p <. 001) between team leaders and teachers in the distributions for content and level of organization.

References

BALL, S. (1981) *Beachside Comprehensive*, Cambridge, Cambridge University Press.
COLE, A. (1991) 'Relationships in the workplace: Doing what comes naturally?', *Teaching and Teacher Education*, 7, pp. 415–26.

DARLING-HAMMOND, L. (1990) 'Teacher professionalism: Why and how?', in LIEBERMAN, A. (Ed) *Schools as Collaborative Cultures: Creating the Future Now*, London, New York, Philadelphia, The Falmer Press.

ELY, M. *et al.* (1991) *Doing Qualitative Research: Circles Within Circles*, London, New York, Philadelphia, The Falmer Press.

FULLAN, M. and HARGREAVES, A. (1991) *What's Worth Fighting For? Working Together For Your School*, Ontario Institute for Studies in Education.

GORDON, R.L. (1980) *Interviewing: Strategy, Techniques and Tactics*, Homewood, IL, Dorsey Press.

HAMMERSLEY, M. (1980) 'Classroom ethnography', *Educational Anlysis*, 2, 2, pp. 47–74.

HAMMERSLEY, M. and ATKINSON, P. (1983) *Ethnograghy: Principles in Practice*, London, Tavistock.

HANDAL, G. (1991) 'Collective time — collective practice?', Paper presented at the Annual Meeting of the American Educational Research Association, Chicago.

HARGREAVES, A. (1990) 'Individualism and individuality: Reinterpreting the teacher culture', Paper presented at the Annual Meeting of the American Educational Research Association, Boston 1990.

HARGREAVES, A. and TUCKER, E. (1991) 'Teaching and guilt: Exploring the feeling of teaching', *Teaching and Teacher Education*, 7, pp. 491–505.

LIEBERMAN, A. and MILLER, L. (1990) 'The social realities of teaching', in LIEBERMAN, A. (Ed) *Schools as Collaborative Cultures: Creating the Future Now*, London, New York, Philadelphia, The Falmer Press.

LITTLE, J.W. (1982) 'Norms of Collegiality and Experimentation: Workplace Conditions of School Success', *American Educational Research Journal*, 19, pp. 325–40.

LITTLE, J.W. (1990a) 'The persistence of privacy: Autonomy and initiative in teachers' professional relations', *Teachers Collage Record*, 4, Summer.

LITTLE, J.W. (1990b) 'Teachers as colleagues', in LIEBERMAN, A. (Ed) *Schools as Collaborative Cultures: Creating the Future Now*, London, New York, Philadelphia, The Falmer Press.

LORTIE, D. (1975) *Schoolteacher*, Chicago, IL, University of Chicago Press.

McLAUGHLIN, M.W. and MARSH, D. (1978) 'Staff development and school change', *Teacher Collage Record*, 80, 1.

PATTON, M. (1983) *Qualitative Evaluation Methods*, London, Sage Publications.

ROSENHOLTZ, S. (1985) 'Political myths about education reform: Lessons from research on teaching', *Phi Delta Kappan*, January.

ROSENHOLTZ, S. (1989) *Teachers' Workplace: The Social Organization of Schools*, New York, London, Longman.

SARASON, S. (1971) *The Culture of School and the Problem of Change*, Boston, Allyn and Bacon.

SPRADLEY, J. (1979) *The Ethnographic Interview*, New York, Holt, Rinehart and Winston.

The Teacher-Innovator System

I Structuring Communications

A *Planning*

Goals and Standards		Contents		Procedures	
Directive	Negotiated	Directive	Negotiated	Directive	Negotiated
1	2	3	4	5	6

B *Implementation*

Instructional	Non-instructional
7	8

II Informational Communications

Level 1	Level 2	Level 3	Open	Opinion
9	10	11	12	13

III Feedback Communications

Positive	Neutral	Negative	Corrective	Repeat	Digression
14	15	16	17	18	19

The Stimulated Recall Analysis System (SRAS)

(Code) (Definition of Code)

T   **Text — evaluate material, exercise, topics; judge content of the lesson**

A   **Anticipation — anticipating student response**
A1   • hope students would follow instruction, respond, do the task, behave in an expected way.
A2   • not sure about students' ability to answer or understand question.
A3   • expect students are able to do the task, answer the question; expect a specific answer from an open-ended question; expect students' initiation of response.
A4   • speculate the progress and outcome of students' work.

Ch   **Checking — checking student progress**
Ch 1   • wait for students to finish a task.
Ch 2   • assess students' level of engagement / progress.
Ch 3   • aware of students being off-task.
Ch 4   • aware of students' problems in performing a given task; aware of their lack of understanding of the teacher's instruction; aware of varied patterns of work.
Ch 5   • pleased with students' progress.

S   **Silence — reflection on a lack of response**
S1   • surprised at the lack of response.
S2   • disappointed at the lack of response.
S3   • not sure how to help a student who does not respond to a question.
S4   • assess problems the responding student might encounter.
S5   • consider further hints following a question which receives no response.

R   **Receiving student response — reflection on and reaction to student response**
R1   • satisfied with the student response: an unexpected correct response, active student response, or initiation of a question from a student.
R2   • hesitate over an unexpected answer, unsatisfactory answer, not knowing what to do about it.

R3	• reject an unsatisfactory answer and look for the correct answer.
R4	• upset about students' undesirable reaction or discipline problems.
R5	• not sure what to do about the poor performance and how to help.
R6	• not identify a correct response as an indication of all students' general ability.
R7	• evaluate students' performance / response.
R8	• evaluate the teacher's way of providing feedback, accuracy of teacher feedback in relation to students' understanding.

(Code) (Definition of Code)

E   **Explanation — formulating/evaluating teacher explanation**
E1	• consider how to explain, what to explain.
E2	• not sure of the subject matter to be explained, and how to explain clearly.
E3	• bemused that students are not able to understand the teacher's explanation.
E4	• hope students are able to understand the teacher's explanation.
E5	• satisfied with the teacher's own explanation.
E6	• not satisfied with the teacher's own explanation.

P   **Planning–Evaluation–Decision**
P1	• make assumption about what students should know as a learning sequence.
P2	• aware of reasons behind the teacher's communications / teaching performance; concern to justify teaching steps.
P3	• frustrated, nervous, bemused at the loss of control.
P4	• evaluate the communication move just having taken place, assess students' feeling / response from their facial expression or knowledge about them.
P5	• consider the next teaching step.
P6	• consider the next teaching step and its pros and cons in the light of previous communication or students' progress or performance.
P7	• make decision about the next teaching step with reasoning.
P8	• realize a forgotten teaching step.
P9	• review a previous teaching step: confirm the decision was a good one; regret for having conducted it that way or made a mistake.
P10	• evaluation: pleased that the lesson was going smoothly; critical of the teacher's own performance and aware of general problems.
P11	• consider progress of lesson: timing and pacing.

Mcs   **Miscellaneous**
•	• can't remember; nothing.
Mc	• thoughts irrelevant to the immediate context.
N	• getting to know names of students.

Index